ALTERNATIVE DISPUTE RESOLUTION

SKILLS, SCIENCE, AND THE LAW

Other books by Irwin Law

Statutory Interpretation

Media Law

The Law of Trusts

Intellectual Property Law

Income Tax Law

The Law of Partnerships and Corporations

Constitutional Law

Immigration Law

Environmental Law

Young Offenders Law

International Trade Law

Computer Law

The Charter of Rights and Freedoms

Family Law

Legal Ethics & Professional Responsibility

The Law of Evidence 2/e

Copyright Law

Criminal Law 2/e

Remedies: The Law of Damages

The Law of Torts

Individual Employment Law

The Law of Equitable Remedies

CANADIAN LEGAL SKILLS

ALTERNATIVE DISPUTE RESOLUTION

SKILLS, SCIENCE, AND THE LAW

ANDREW J. PIRIE

Faculty of Law

University of Victoria

IRWIN LAW

A Quicklaw Company

ALTERNATIVE DISPUTE RESOLUTION
© Irwin Law Inc.

Published in 2000 by
Irwin Law
Suite 930, Box 235
One First Canadian Place
Toronto, Ontario
M5X 1C8

ISBN: 1-55221-006-5

Law
AKits
KE8615
P57
2000

Canadian Cataloguing in Publication Data

Pirie, A. J.
    Alternative Dispute Resolution

(Essentials of Canadian law)
ISBN 1-55221-006-5

1. Dispute resolution (Law) – Canada.   I. Title.   II. Series.

KE8615.P57 2000   347.71'09   C00-930142-9
KF9084.P57 2000

Printed and bound in Canada.

1   2   3   4   5   04   03   02   01   00

SUMMARY
TABLE OF CONTENTS

DETAILED
TABLE OF CONTENTS

FOREWORD

Over the past two decades, the field of alternative dispute resolution, or ADR, has grown tremendously in North America and around the world. Growth has occurred in terms of the diversity of innovative procedures developed to manage and resolve conflicts, the size and scope of issues addressed, and the number of practitioners engaged in this new profession.

ADR has its roots in efforts to find more effective means to resolve conflicts than traditional litigation, and in democratic social change movements. It encompasses collaborative approaches to reach agreements such as unassisted negotiations, and assisted problem solving such as mediation. It also includes voluntary third-party decision-making procedures such as arbitration. In addition ADR incorporates a wide range of other cooperative procedures to enhance the quality of information exchanged between contending parties, increase cooperation, promote efficient settlements, develop mutual gains outcomes, lower costs, and improve the quality and acceptability of outcomes. Some forms of ADR may also positively affect or transform the long-term relationships of contending parties.

ADR procedures have been utilized to address and resolve a wide range of issues, both legal and non-legal. Although potential applications seem unlimited, some areas where ADR has been most successfully applied include labour management and employment conflicts, family fights, criminal acts, business affairs, public disputes, environmental controversies, and intercultural differences.

For a number of years there has been a need for a comprehensive text on ADR beyond a compendium of writings on the topic or descriptions of specific procedures. This book is by far the best work written to date.

Alternative Dispute Resolution is extremely comprehensive. Professor Pirie presents an excellent overview of the principles and approaches involved in the field, a balanced assessment of the strengths and weaknesses of ADR, and analyzes the major issues and debates surrounding its use. The text addresses a number of broad philosophical issues related to disputing and resolution such as definitions and sources of conflicts, and explores a range of approaches to manage and address them. It examines differences in adversarial and non-adversarial thinking and how these influence both disputing processes and outcomes.

From a detailed examination of how to analyze the causes of conflicts, Professor Pirie moves readers through a highly enjoyable examination of a variety of procedures—negotiation, mediation, arbitration, and hybrid processes. His examination of processes is enhanced by a variety of brief illustrative cases that are highly engaging and that elucidate the issues or procedures under discussion. Of specific interest to many readers will be the in-depth case studies towards the end of the book that describe practical applications of ADR.

Alternative Dispute Resolution will be of interest to law faculty and students, practising lawyers, judges, ADR practitioners, and the lay public as one of the most accessible texts in the field. This book is both a valuable introductory text and an excellent reference for later practice. Andrew Pirie has made a significant contribution to the field and to our understanding of diverse alternatives for resolving conflicts.

Christopher W. Moore, Ph.D.
Managing Partner, CDR Associates and
author of *The Mediation Process*

ACKNOWLEDGMENTS

In 1983, as a young law professor, who had recently left the Toronto firm of Osler, Hoskin and Harcourt to pursue an academic career at the University of Victoria, I was fortunate enough to attend a conference in San Fransisco entitled "Beyond the Adversary Model: Teaching Mediation in American Law Schools." I was expecting some fairly standard fare and hoping the exposure to mediation would be an interesting addition to my practical experience as a litigation lawyer. In fact the conference was a life-changing event — one that many people delving into ADR can have.

This book on alternative dispute resolution is my effort at sharing the experiences I have had with ADR over the last twenty years from a practising lawyer's, law profeesor's, and mediator's perspectives.

However, in addition to my own experiences, many people, in one way or another, also have contributed to the book's final form and content. I would like to thank several ADR pioneers from the 1983 conference who inspired me to make ADR the focus of my teaching, research, and writing, particularly Gary Friedman, Jack Himmelstein, Len Riskin, and Carrie Menkel-Meadow. I also want to acknowledge how important Chris Moore, Susan Wildau, Bernie Mayer, and Mary Margaret Golten of CDR Associates were to my understanding of this field, particularily the mediation process.

I also am indebted to the many reflective ADR practitioners and academics in Canada and beyond with whom I have had rewarding exchanges of ideas and insights. I especially want to thank Marj Burdine, Jane Chart, Connie Edwards, Paul Emond, Neil Gold, Jerry McHale, Catherine Morris, Stephen Owen, Dean Peachy, Gordon Sloan, Dinah Stanley, and Bonita Thompson.

I was fortunate to have the assistance of several law students who helped with the collection and analysis of the materials that have gone into the book — Carole Aippersbach, Karyn Arter, Roshan Danesh, Allison Fieldberg, Misty Hillard, Wanda Kelley, Lex Reynolds.

The final production of this book also would not have been possible without the careful input of my assistant, Sheila Talbot, who kept order as the project built; the wonderful editing of Maraya Raduha; the constructive comments of an anonymous reviewer; and the trust and patience of Bill Kaplan to whom I now owe several blackened fish dinners.

Finally, I want to express my deep appreciation to my partner Debbie Harris who not only gave me unconditional support while I was writing the book but also showed me, time and time again, how good dispute resolvers work.

CHAPTER 1

THE MEANING OF ALTERNATIVE DISPUTE RESOLUTION

A. INTRODUCTION

Alternative dispute resolution might just as easily be referred to as alluring dispute resolution. Even the popular acronym ADR, which regularly replaces alternative dispute resolution in conversations would not need to be changed. Whether it is the ADR practitioner, the legal professional, the academic, the student, or even the critic, there continues to be a complicated fascination with what lies behind these three words. The allure may be what brought you to these pages in the first place, looking for something more about a modern phenomenon that is often referred to as the ADR movement. But the attraction to ADR and ADR's significance must depend on the answer to a single question: What is the meaning of alternative dispute resolution?

The answer to the question, which is the focus of this book, can be difficult to grasp. In a short period of time, alternative dispute resolution has become a field of study and an area of practice of enormous magnitude. In the legal profession alone, ADR has quickly gone from being viewed with some suspicion by many lawyers to being widely accepted as an integral part of the modern study and practice of law. Outside of law, diverse disciplines continue to contribute to the great variety of ideas and skills that collectively constitute ADR's body of knowledge, and myriad voices worldwide clamour for a say in educating about, or endorsing, ADR procedures and products. Alternative dispute resolution is also a subject matter that is experiencing rapid growth, with almost daily examples of new and far-reaching developments, initiatives, and experiments, not only locally but also globally. Many of these ADR efforts are said to be profound, educational, and transformative, or just more efficient when compared with existing disputing methods. Academic and popular literature on ADR proliferates and seems incapable of convenient collection except in select or partial bibliographies. Internet links can now be made to an increasing number of sites boasting access to ADR services or information. Describing what ADR is can be an imposing task.

What is the meaning of ADR? In its theories and practices ADR has become the accumulated answers to a widening web of questions. The questions go to the complex nature of disputes (and disputants) of every shape and form; to the many ways in which disputes are or can be facilitated, mediated, managed, resolved, negotiated, prevented, avoided, or otherwise processed; and to the practical skills that help disputes move along while avoiding the pitfalls that make matters worse. The study and practice of ADR covers a lot of ground.

To complicate matters, few of these ADR questions stand alone. A tug on one line of inquiry is inevitably felt elsewhere. Consider where the following questions might fit on an ADR web, how the answer to one question can depend on, or be affected by, several others, and how more ADR questions can easily be asked.

- What is a dispute?
- Is a conflict the same as a dispute?
- What causes disputes or conflicts?
- Can disputes be prevented or managed rather than resolved?
- Is there a difference between dispute resolution and dispute processing?
- Why are certain disputes so difficult to deal with and others so easy?
- Why do some disputes never get raised at all?
- What part does power play in dispute resolution?
- What is alternative dispute resolution or ADR?
- What is ADR an alternative to?
- Where did this expression come from?
- What are the methods or processes of alternative dispute resolution?
- Is one ADR method or process better than another?
- What are the practical skills needed to work in ADR?
- Are some individuals better at disputing than others?
- How can I become proficient in ADR?
- Is ADR a profession or part of the legal profession?
- Is there a place for the average person in the ADR field?
- Do ADR theories and practices work in different cultures?

- Is ADR an idea whose time has come or is there a dark side to the ADR movement?
- Who determines what is ADR and what is not?
- Why do we have ADR now?

The materials that follow help answer these and other questions about alternative dispute resolution. Although the book is directed primarily to the legal profession — lawyers, judges, legal academics, and law students — the content should be of interest to anyone first studying alternative dispute resolution or seeking to better understand or improve his or her work with disputes. I hope even the expert and seasoned ADR practitioner will learn something new. The materials guide you to current and practical information about ADR and its relevance to you, pointing not only to the promise of ADR but also to its peculiar and often political problems. The book's information will assist you in identifying important dispute resolution skills and in recognizing those ADR attributes that you might already possess. Above all, this book will enable you to become more informed about ADR and better equipped to make ADR decisions when the need arises.

Although the focus of the book is on the practical — the doing of ADR — the book tries to build a bridge between ADR practices and their theories. Wherever possible, practical examples and problems are used to illustrate how theories work in real-life situations. In chapter 9, for example, several case studies are used to illustrate how the ADR ideas and skills presented in the book can be applied to problems that people encounter in their day-to-day lives. However, the theoretical foundations and concepts that have been responsible for ADR developments cannot be overlooked. They help one make more sense out of actual ADR practices. This underlying knowledge base provides the essential frameworks for policy makers and practitioners alike to rely on when deciding how or whether to use ADR processes or techniques in various dispute settings. At the end of each chapter there are references to other ADR publications, which either expand on the materials presented here or offer other perspectives for more in-depth thought and success in working with ADR. While the emphasis of the book is on consensual approaches to dispute resolution, such as negotiation, mediation, and their hybrids, the widest ranges of ADR territory are also explored from both intellectually inquiring and practically useful viewpoints.

However, before going any further, a cautionary note is necessary. Behind the allure, as ADR enthusiasts know, lies a demanding field of study. The demands are due, in part, to the sheer scope of ADR's coverage. Few areas of human or organizational activity are insulated from disputes and disputing. For neighbours fighting over fences, divorcing parents arguing about child custody, businesses working out the terms of a contract, parties opposing the logging of a remaining watershed, governments disagreeing with Aboriginal peoples, organizations combating racism on the Web, nations almost going to war, or countries seeking truth and reconciliation, ADR, as a study of how we dispute or might dispute, can have something important to say.

Working with disputes involving such diverse subject matters and focuses can be challenging enough for the ADR student or practitioner, but ADR is further complicated by the simple truth: disputes and how we dispute often change the course of people's lives forever. The ways in which disputes are resolved can redefine relationships, redraw borders, redistribute wealth, reform laws, restrict movements, remove barriers, reshape thinking, reframe problems, and much more. Disputes, disputing processes, and dispute resolution ultimately make up much of our history. The study and practice of alternative dispute resolution cannot be undertaken lightly. There is almost always a great deal at stake even when the stakes in dispute may seem slim.

This opening caution is not merely to emphasize the obvious. To learn and to practice ADR well can require extraordinary efforts. Lawyers and others who have worked with people in conflict will know of the challenges involved. But the caution also extends to this book's opening question. What ADR is, what it is not, what it can be, and even what it is called are not free from controversy. Be prepared to discover there are disputes about the very meaning of alternative dispute resolution.

ADR can mean different things to different people. Some may suggest ADR is not an enormous concept but is simple common sense. If there is disagreement on what is common sense, others may portray ADR as mostly about saving time and money in dispute resolution — the achievement of economic efficiencies. Still others may say that ADR stands for a range of formal and informal processes that exist as alternatives to litigation. But some have called ADR "an umbrella term which encompasses litigation,"[1] even "the second coming of litigation."[2] Still others can cast ADR as a replacement for the diminished role of the family, the church, and the community in mediating disputes. ADR may be regarded as a road to peace and harmony. Some may view ADR as part of their profession while others may conclude

---

1   *Charting the Course: Report of the Canadian Forum on Dispute Resolution* (Ottawa: Department of Justice, 1995) at 12.

2   D. Small, "The Second Coming of Civil Litigation" (1996) 5 National 20.

that ADR, particularly mediation, is a new profession. Some want ADR to be BDR (better dispute resolution), or IDR (innovative dispute resolution), or, for convenience, appropriate dispute resolution. Some may prefer to substitute new paradigms of civil and criminal justice for the meaning of these three words. The relevance of ADR's theories and practices to just about everything we do and the potential of ADR to shape the future of any dispute, big or small, make the search for ADR's meaning not only an essential task but also a controversial one.

These definitional disputes, though complicating the study and practice of ADR, should be expected. What ADR means or is said to mean, after all, has critical consequences. What alternative dispute resolution means can determine whether a particular disputing practice and the actors who support that practice are favoured or ignored. Whether public and private dispute resolving resources are allocated or not, to what extent, and to which disputing subject matter or program, can be affected by the meaning of ADR. What ADR is understood to mean can have huge reform implications for existing disputing systems, whether they are formal systems of justice such as the courts or more informal and culturally unique traditions of resolving problems. For specific disputes, differences in ADR definitions may alter what is understood to be in conflict, change the course that a dispute takes, and modify or even determine the outcome of a discord. In the end, what are accepted as alternative dispute resolution's ideas and practices have the potential to profoundly influence the changes, the reforms, the histories, and the lives that emerge from the world of disputes and disputing. With different understandings of ADR, important disputing outcomes are not written in stone but are waiting to be shaped, in real and practical ways, by the shape of ADR.

Sorting out this preliminary dispute around the meaning of ADR — which meanings are kept, which ones are dropped — is a critical task and one that you could expect to be intriguing in a field devoted to dispute resolution. The task is complicated because there are no long-standing, official, or authoritative guides to ADR's meaning. While legal subjects such as contract law, tax law, and evidence have fairly well-defined boundaries from years of experience, ADR is much less confined. More akin to constitutional law, economics, politics, technology, globalization, or other complex concepts, ADR is open to interpretation but without well-defined or agreed-upon interpretative aids to understanding.

Accordingly, a first important step in studying ADR, in understanding its significance, and in identifying ADR skills, is to consider whether there is a coherent framework within which to locate the meaning of ADR; or it may be that ADR's sheer omnipresence makes the search for a consistent or contained explanation of ADR theory and practice a futile task. The answer to the question — what is the meaning of ADR? — can be explored by considering how you interpret the history of ADR, how you see ADR in context, and how you recognize the multidisciplinary nature of ADR.

B. THE HISTORY OF ADR

The meaning of ADR is found, to a great extent, in its history. As the name suggests, ADR began as a study of alternatives. In fact, the actual expression "alternative dispute resolution" emerged out of popular dissatisfaction with the administration of justice in the United States during the 1970s. Early ADR proponents cited a need to avoid the undue cost and delay of court adjudication and to increase access to justice while drawing attention to the transformative benefits of empowering disputing parties and communities to resolve their own problems. ADR looked beyond the adversarial arena of the courtroom and the dominant image of the lawyer as "a knight in shining armour whose courtroom lance strikes down all obstacles."[3] To a substantial degree, informal methods of dispute resolution became the first focus of ADR, especially negotiation, mediation, and other forms of consensual decision making, learning from disputing processes in other societies and from experiences in areas such as labour-management relations, international affairs, and religion.

If informalism or "informal justice" made up the large body of ADR, the heart of the movement clearly was mediation, the antithesis to court adjudication. Folberg and Taylor define mediation as "the process by which the participants, together with the assistance of a neutral

---

3   W. Burger, former chief justice of the United States Supreme Court, in "Isn't There a Better Way?" (1982) 68 A.B.A. J. 274 at 275, from the annual report on the state of the judiciary to the American Bar Association. Chief Justice Burger's plea to the legal profession to consider their traditional role as "healers of human conflict" and utilize more fully the negotiation and arbitration processes followed on the heels of various initiatives in the United States examining alternatives to court adjudication. Of particular note for the legal profession was the 1976 Pound Conference where Professor Frank Sander saw, in the future, not simply a courthouse but a dispute resolution centre or a multi-door courthouse where disputants would be screened and channelled to a variety of dispute resolution processes such as mediation, arbitration, fact-finding, malpractice screening panel, superior court, or an ombudsman. See F.E.A. Sander, "Varieties of Dispute Processing," 70 F.R.D. 111 (1976).

person or persons, systematically isolate disputed issues in order to develop options, consider alternatives, and reach a consensual settlement that will accommodate their needs."[4] Others simply say mediation is assisted negotiations. Lon Fuller in an early description of mediation's forms and functions said:

> The central quality of mediation is its capacity to reorient the parties toward each other, not by imposing rules on them, but by helping them to achieve a new and shared perception of their relationship, a perception that will redirect their attitudes and disposition toward one another.[5]

Not surprisingly, the perspective that ADR was a necessary response to failings in the existing justice system, more the norm than an alternative,[6] and better to boot, drew initial hostility and criticism. Several of these first critics came from a legal profession and judiciary that felt its court-centred procedures and economic structures were under attack from ADR and its many non-lawyer supporters.[7] Specific concerns often were directed at mediation, a process that was new and unfamiliar to most lawyers.[8]

The ADR movement was not stopped by these legal critics, but it was changed. With more lawyers taking leadership roles in the ADR movement, the anti-court sentiments were, in true mediation style, reframed. An example of this attempt to capture the essence of ADR is contained in the 1989 Canadian Bar Association Task Force Report on Alternative Dispute Resolution. The report urges lawyers, and presumably others working with disputes, to see their primary function as problem solving. Rather than separating ADR procedures from traditional court proce-

---

4   J. Folberg & A. Taylor, *Mediation: A Comprehensive Guide to Resolving Conflicts Without Litigation* (San Francisco: Jossey-Bass Inc., 1984) at 7.

5   L.L. Fuller, "Mediation — Its Forms and Functions" (1971 44 S. Cal. L. Rev. 305) at 325.

6   Professor Carrie Menkel-Meadow makes the obvious point that 90 to 95 percent of litigation is settled outside of court and that it is a "misnomer" to label processes such as mediation, negotiation, and arbitration as alternatives: "They are the norm in dispute resolution." See C. Menkel-Meadow, "Dispute Resolution: The Periphery Becomes the Core" (1986) 69 Judicature 300.

7   For example, see Chief Justice A. McEachern, "Chief Justice Puts Boots to ADR," *Lawyers Weekly* (26 October 1989), and A. Pirie, "The Lawyer as Mediator: Professional Responsibility Problems or Profession Problems?" (1985) 63 Can. Bar Rev. 378.

8   L.L. Riskin describes the tension between mediation and the lawyer's "standard philosophical map" in "Mediation and Lawyers" (1982) 43 Ohio St. L.J. 29.

dures, the problem solver needs to evaluate the entire continuum of dispute resolution techniques, skills, and resources and then choose the most appropriate steps to take. Rather than standing in opposition to the courts, ADR is an expression of the legal profession's continuing commitment to fair, effective, and accessible dispute resolution, whether that involves utilizing the traditional legal system or not. As the CBA Report states, "alternative dispute resolution will not be viewed as superior or inferior to, or indeed even separate from, court adjudication."[9]

Locating ADR within a problem-solving framework was not just a Canadian perspective. Within North America, problem solving was being viewed as "the overriding function of the lawyer, the general mission of lawyering,"[10] and the 1992 MacCrate Report on narrowing the gap between law schools and the profession confirmed the central role of problem solving to the lawyer's calling and to the role of lawyers in society.[11] For legal problem solvers, ADR mainly meant there were many ways that lawyers could "help others (their clients and communities) choose the appropriate methods to resolve a dispute or consummate a transaction and to be able to participate effectively in such a process once it is chosen."[12]

The preferred initials remain ADR although suggested replacements to avoid pitting or the appearance of pitting ADR against the courts include better dispute resolution (BDR), enhanced dispute resolution (EDR), innovative dispute resolution (IDR), judicially assisted dispute resolution (JADR) where judges help, or, for consistency, appropriate (not alluring) dispute resolution. Whatever the adjective, the emphasis is no longer primarily on alternatives to the court. A widely representative 1995 Canadian Forum on Dispute Resolution stated that alternative dispute resolution "should be considered an umbrella term which encompasses litigation, focusing on the appropriate method for resolving any given dispute."[13] The 1996 Report of the

---

9   Canadian Bar Association Task Force on Alternative Dispute Resolution, *Alternative Dispute Resolution: A Canadian Perspective* (Ottawa: Canadian Bar Association, 1989) at 4 [emphasis added].

10   L.L. Riskin & J.E. Westbrook, *Dispute Resolution and Lawyers* (St. Paul, Minn.: West Publishing Co., 1987) at 52.

11   See American Bar Association Section of Legal Education and Admissions to the Bar, *Legal Education and Professional Development — An Educational Continuum. Report of the Task Force on Law Schools and the Profession: Narrowing the Gap* (Chicago: American Bar Association, 1992).

12   Above note 10. For a more complete history on the rise of legal problem solving, see the bibliography in (1998) 34 Cal. W. L. Rev. 537.

13   Above note 1.

Canadian Bar Association Task Force on Systems of Civil Justice,[14] affirming a problem-solving orientation for lawyers, defined alternative dispute resolution as involving "a range of processes for resolving disputes"[15] excluding only a trial or hearing. The report specifically called for dispute resolution techniques to be promoted "not as alternatives to the civil justice system but as integral components of it."[16]

The historical evolution of ADR raises more than the cute distinction between ADR and BDR and the simple conclusion that the modern meaning of ADR includes court-connected and other formal justice processes. The history of ADR presents several ambiguities that complicate our understanding of what ADR is and what it can be.

The first ambiguity concerns the goals of ADR. How ADR is defined is determined to a large extent by what one is trying to achieve. Over time, there have been numerous expressions of the purpose of ADR. Goldberg, Sander, and Rogers list the sometimes competing justifications of the alternatives movement:

- To lower court caseloads and expenses,
- To reduce the parties' expenses and time,
- To provide speedy settlement of those disputes that were disruptive of the community or the lives of the parties' families,
- To improve public satisfaction with the justice system,
- To encourage resolutions that were suited to the parties' needs,
- To increase voluntary compliance with resolutions,
- To restore the influence of neighborhood and community values and the cohesiveness of communities,
- To provide accessible forums to people with disputes, and
- To teach the public to try more effective processes than violence or litigation for settling disputes.[17]

Other references, more or less ambitious or abstract, see ADR seeking to reorient the practice of law towards a higher quality problem-solving approach; to achieve extralegal justice by emphasizing the parties' needs and interests rather than their legal rights; to promote and maximize human interactions that are creative, enfranchising, enrich-

---

14   Canadian Bar Association Task Force on Systems of Civil Justice, *Report of the Task Force on Systems of Civil Justice* (Ottawa: Canadian Bar Association, 1996).
15   *Ibid.* at 26.
16   *Ibid.* at 18.
17   S.B. Goldberg, F.E.A. Sander, & N.H. Rogers, *Dispute Resolution, Negotiation, Mediation and Other Processes* (New York: Aspen Law and Business, 1999) at 8.

ing, and empowering rather than alienating and conflict provoking; and to integrate social justice and peace into the fabric of society.

Specific ADR programs identify more specific goals. Court-annexed programs strive, among other things, to decrease the court's docket, to speed the pace of cases to resolution, to increase litigant satisfaction with the court system, and to lower recidivism. Neighbourhood justice centres express interest in improving communication between parties; clarifying viewpoints, interests, and positions; and strengthening communities. Business people pledge allegiance to ADR because of its cost effectiveness compared with litigation and the ability to preserve continuing relationships. Governments want to reduce deficits by lowering the public cost of disputing.

In an attempt to add order to this diversity of goals, Bush clusters over fifty statements of sub-objectives for ADR into six "quality statement" goals:

1. **Individual Satisfaction**

   ADR leaves disputing parties feeling that their individual desires, as defined by themselves, have been satisfied, in terms of the experience and the outcome of the process; or

2. **Individual Autonomy**

   ADR strengthens the capacity and increases the opportunity for disputing parties to resolve their own problems without being dependent on external institutions, public or private; or

3. **Social Control**

   ADR facilitates or strengthens control of public and private institutions, and the interests they represent, over exploitable groups and over possible sources of social change or unrest; or

4. **Social Justice**

   ADR ameliorates, neutralizes, or at least does not exacerbate existing inequalities in the societal distribution of material wealth and power; or

5. **Social Solidarity**

   ADR provides common values, referents, or "texts" for individuals and groups in a pluralistic society, and thereby increases social solidarity among these individuals and groups; or

6. **Personal Transformation**

   ADR provides opportunities for and encourages individual disputants to experience personal change and growth, particularly in terms of becoming less self-centred and more responsive to others.[18]

---

18   R.A.B. Bush, "Defining Quality in Dispute Resolution: Taxonomies and Anti-Taxonomies of Quality Arguments" (1989) 66 Denv. U. L. Rev. 335, 347.

Others compartmentalize various expressions of ADR intent into two general categories of ADR goals: efficiency claims for ADR (cheaper, faster, more competitive) versus qualitative-justice claims (better).[19] Or, put differently, there are production (more with less) goals and quality (encompassing valued aspects of a process apart from time, cost, and institutional convenience) goals.[20]

The ambiguity around ADR's goals does not arise merely because different constituencies have pursued ADR for widely different reasons and that cheaper and faster is not necessarily the same thing as better. The ambiguity arises for three reasons. First, it is not always clear what goal is being pursued. Often the purposes of a particular ADR initiative or program can be vague or unstated. Second, the ambiguity also arises because ADR's efficiency goals may be incompatible with its qualitative-justice goals. For example, an ADR measure designed to reduce court delay may create barriers to quality justice if the speedier disposition of the case removes traditional procedural safeguards. Finally, there are concerns that market goals, particularly the reduction of litigation costs and delays, may be coming to dominate our thinking about what is ADR. Qualitative-justice goals that initially inspired the ADR movement may be ignored or marginalized when defining ADR because such goals are not commonly associated with the win-lose philosophy of adjudicative processes and are not valued by an economic efficiency model of dispute resolution.

So how we understand and define ADR is influenced by what we determine are, or can be, ADR's goals. Different goals will change not only our understanding and definition but also the ways in which ADR is practised. The history of ADR clouds the picture of what ADR is or should be.

ADR's history raises another related ambiguity that also concerns ADR's purposes but which involves a level of analysis that is openly political. There are critiques of ADR that suggest there is a darker side to the movement.

Contrary to claims that ADR's goal is better dispute resolution with its emphasis on informalism, efficiency, empowering disputants, harmony through consensus, and the like, some argue that the primary business of informal dispute resolution institutions in an advanced capitalist society is social control.[21] ADR, it is said, allows for the

---

19 C. Menkel-Meadow, "Pursuing Settlement in an Adversary Culture: A Tale of Innovation Co-opted or the Law of ADR" (1991) 19 Fla. St. U. L. Rev. 1, 6.

20 M. Galanter, "Compared to What? Assessing the Quality of Dispute Processing" (1989) 66 Denv. U. L. Rev. xi, xii.

21 R.L. Abel, ed., *The Politics of Informal Justice* (New York: Academic Press, 1982) at 5.

expansion of state control but disguises its coercion by relying on the language of the helping professions, and the buzzwords of inclusiveness, consensus, and community. ADR casts a broader social net than that of the traditional justice systems. ADR's quality attributes "are not merely masks for state power but are expressions of . . . the changing styles of social control."[22]

Other critics locate ADR within broader geographical and historical antecedents. They argue that reform movements, including ADR as a contemporary reaction against formal institutions, have never sought to replace the legalistic paradigm. Delegalization reforms, on the contrary, have ended up complementing existing adjudicative processes. ADR, rather than fundamentally challenging formalism, is linked to the reconstruction of judicial power and authority. In effect, ADR is "short form formalism"[23] or "shadow justice,"[24] potentially to be fully absorbed and co-opted by the powers of the established justice system.

This leads to a concern that ADR is a regressive reaction to the progressive legal rights victories of the 1960s and 1970s. Under ADR, it is argued, conflict is individualized, informalized, and privatized. Social change is thus inhibited because "individual demands are satisfied in order to forestall their aggregation."[25] Or, put another way, when the parties settle or are encouraged as a matter of general policy to settle, the job of the courts "to explicate and give force to the values embodied in authoritative texts such as the Constitution and statutes: to interpret those values and to bring reality into accord with them . . . is not discharged."[26]

The ADR-inspired shift in emphasis from legal rights to individual interests and needs also attracted criticism.

> ADR advances a non-rights based conception of the juridical subject.
> . . . Eschewing rights, ADR proponents deploy the discourse of interests and needs. They reconceptualize the person from a carrier of

---

22   C.B. Harrington & S. Engle Merry, "Ideological Production: The Making of Community Mediation" (1988) 22 L. & Soc'y Rev. 709, 713. Laura Nader also sees the "harmony ideology" of ADR as an "insidious exercise of power through indirect controlling process," and "mind colonization." See L. Nader, "Controlling Processes in the Practice of Law: Hierarchy and Pacification in the Movement to Re-Form Dispute Ideology" (1993) 9 Ohio St. J. on Disp. Resol. 1.
23   Above note 20 at xiv.
24   C.B. Harrington, *Shadow Justice: The Ideology and Institutionalization of Alternatives to Court* (Westport, Conn.: Greenwood Press, 1985) at 16.
25   Above note 21 at 4.
26   See O. Fiss, "Against Settlement" (1984) 93 Yale L.J. 1073.

rights to a subject with needs and problems, and in the process hope to move the legal field from a terrain of authoritative decision making where force is deployed to an arena of distributive bargaining and therapeutic negotiation.[27]

For the least powerful individuals or groups, perhaps due to gender, economics, race, culture, differing abilities, or other characteristics, a movement that placed great emphasis on interests as opposed to legal rights raised concerns about both individual harm and the perpetration of systemic inequalities.[28]

Richard Abel summarizes the political ambiguity that imbues the history of ADR:

> Yet if the goals of informal justice are contradictory, and if it is incapable of realizing them because of contradictions inherent in advanced capitalism, informalism should not simplistically be repudiated as merely an evil to be resisted, or be dismissed as a marginal phenomenon that can safely be ignored. It is advocated by reformers and embraced by disputants precisely because it expresses values that deservedly elicit broad allegiance: the preference for harmony over conflict, for mechanisms that offer equal access to the many rather than unequal privilege to the few, that operate quickly and cheaply, that permit all citizens to participate in decision making rather than limiting authority to "professionals," that are familiar rather than esoteric, and that strive for and achieve substantive justice rather than frustrating it in the name of form.[29]

The history of ADR, of course, is not over. ADR has moved beyond its country of origin and now attracts worldwide attention. Technological changes have resulted in the creation of virtual magistrates, cyberspace settlements, and other on-line experiments. ADR continues to evolve. However, the history of ADR does demonstrate that the meaning of ADR will depend on how closely and in what manner ADR is

---

27 For analysis of this change in emphasis, see S. Silbey & A. Sarat, "Dispute Processing in Law and Legal Scholarship: From Institutional Critique to the Reconstruction of the Juridical Subject" (1989) 66 Denv. U. L. Rev. 437 at 479.

28 For example, see R. Engler, "And Justice for All — Including the Unrepresented Poor: Revisiting the Roles of the Judges, Mediators and Clerks (1999) 67 Fordham L. Rev. 1987; P.E. Bryan, "Killing Us Softly: Divorce Mediation and the Politics of Power" (1992) 40 Buff. L. Rev. 441; and M.J. Bailey, "Unpacking the 'Rationale Alternative': A Critical Review of Family Mediation Movement Claims" (1989) 8 Can. J. Fam. L. 61.

29 Above note 21 at 310.

connected to the courts, on which goals dominate ADR policy, and on how the critiques of ADR are addressed.

C. ADR IN CONTEXT

In most societies, at any given time, many people are engaged in real-life controversies. As you read these words, a divorcing couple just down the street will be unable to agree on the amount and duration of support payments, on who gets the kids or the silver. Lawyers will have conflicting opinions for many reasons on their respective clients' responsibilities for the motor vehicle accident. The chair of a mining company will be denying insider trading allegations. A concerned community group will be reluctantly opposing the siting of a youth detention facility in their neighbourhood. Protesters and supporters will be completely at odds outside an abortion clinic. Trees will be spiked in an old growth forest. Shots will be fired across the bow of a fishing vessel, into a protesting crowd, or at a foe. Children will fight in a schoolyard. There will be disagreements on where to sleep, on what to wear, and on who did what to whom. There will be allegations and denials of abuse, harassment, assault, and discrimination at home and in the workplace. Daily and regularly, disputes will happen between people, within communities, and around the world.

Although disputes may be common and even expected occurrences, the details of these disputes and what happens next in any dispute can vary considerably. Where did the dispute occur? Who was involved? What was the dispute about? When did it start? Why is it happening in just this way? The answers to these and other questions will be important to every ADR student or practitioner concerned with a particular dispute's resolution. But the answers will not be uniform from one situation to the other. The custody fight in Canada will not have the same face as the one in Kansas or Kenya, even if all the disputants agree to focus on the best interests of the children or on allegations of spousal abuse. The Kansas couple may be willing to settle amicably and quickly because both parents want stability in their children's future. The Canadians may go to greater lengths because the questions — how will they settle and why? — are influenced by a certain lawyer's opinion or because sharing time with the kids feels too unsettling to one parent or the other. The Kenyans may follow the wishes of a village headman, or one of them may give up entirely to start afresh without the kids in another part of the country. Similarly, two neighbours quarrelling over noise might easily conclude their dispute with a handshake while the same disturbance for other neighbours, next door or not, might yield completely different results with the police called and charges laid. Even for the repeat player — say the worker who regularly files grievances against the company — the details, or many of them, will not be uniform from one dispute to the next.

The study and use of ADR obviously cannot be disassociated from this real-world mosaic in which disputes arise. The context that gives a dispute its shape and content and which ultimately influences the course a dispute takes must be well understood. Alternative dispute resolution and its practice, in part then, must mean appreciating the full where, who, what, when, and why of disputes. Consider some comments on each of these contextual reference points.

We know that disputes can happen in any place. There are no dispute-free zones. In fact, some locations are more prone to conflict than others. Sometimes places that look peaceful are, just below the surface, riddled with unrest. Although geographical borders and property lines can prevent some disputes from arising, such as controversy over land and resource ownership, immigration, citizenship, sovereignty, and the like, disputes and the disputing parties frequently cross over or disregard these boundaries. Often the physical boundaries themselves come into dispute. In the new frontiers of outerspace and cyberspace, many new disputes are already surfacing. Disputes appear to know few, if any, physical confines. The disputing venue, be it the hallowed halls of academe or the banking boardrooms, will add considerable flavour and complexity to the process of dispute resolution.

Wherever disputes occur, they can involve individuals, organizations, or nations. There may be two parties to a dispute or many parties. Sometimes we even dispute with ourselves. Morton Deutsch[30] calls disputes that originate in one person, group, or nation, *intrapersonal*, *intragroup*, or *intranational* disputes. Disputes between two or more persons, groups, or nations are called *interpersonal*, *intergroup*, or *international* disputes. It is also not unusual to have disputes between an individual and an organization, between an organization and a government, between a government and an individual, or any other permutation of these parties. Identifying who is in dispute is an important, but at times difficult, task. Like a silent partner, the most influential party to a dispute may be pulling the strings behind the scenes.

---

30   M. Deutsch, *The Resolution of Conflict: Constructive and Destructive Processes* (New Haven and London: Yale University Press, 1973).

What we dispute about seems unrestricted. There are numerous disputes about who owes what to whom; about the environment and what is sustainable; about gun control and noise abatement; about freedom of speech and the right to remain silent; about free trade; about the family; about taxes; about turf; about the right to life and the right to die; about equality in a free and democratic society; about self-government and nationalism; and so forth. Some subjects are more disposed to disputes than others. Family disputes over children and money and motor vehicle accident cases around responsibility and money regularly occupy a large percentage of a court's time. Constitutional discords may be less frequent but often last longer. And for any particular subject matter, there will be countless possibilities for a further focus. Was the money a loan or a gift? Who should be believed? How fast was he going? Has there been a breach of trust or an abuse of power? Do statistics show fewer guns mean fewer deaths? Are guns intrinsically bad? Should wealth be taxed? Is the property line here or there? What rules govern the separation of a province from a country? Asking what a dispute is about is an essential line of inquiry but correctly identifying all the issues is not always easy, even for the disputants.

Whenever disputes happen, they also always have a history. The history will be short when two cars collide and the drivers or their insurers disagree about who caused the accident or how much money should be paid. The history will be longer if the automobile accident is the result of one driver's drinking problem or if the accident raises the policy issue over whether or not to adopt a no-fault compensation scheme. In other cases, neighbours may have been feuding for years about an overhanging tree on a shared property line. In some situations, the history of the problem will span generations. Consider the claims of Indigenous peoples worldwide who want justice and fair compensation for colonization and other atrocities. Any dispute makes more sense when its particular history is taken into consideration.

But the venue of the dispute, who the unique parties to a dispute are, what the specific subject of the dispute is, and how long the problem has been brewing do not provide the complete contextual picture or the full "why" of the dispute. Disputes also arise against a contemporary backdrop of social, political, and economic conditions. Like a play, the drama of the dispute unfolds in a complex set of attitudes, beliefs, opinions, values, structures, and relationships that influences how the players — the disputants, other individuals, and society in general — create and experience the dispute, perceive its importance, and understand what should or can be done about it.

This influence can be easily recognizable. For example, recent gender equality disputes, whether occurring in the workplace (is this a case for equal pay for work of equal value?), around legislation (do tax laws requiring the inclusion of support payments in income violate section 15 of the *Canadian Charter of Rights and Freedoms?*),[31] or in a university (has the university professor sexually harassed the student?), encounter conditions different than would have been present for disputes with a similar subject (is a woman a person?)[32] raised earlier in the century. The recognition of women's rights and contemporary understandings of inequality mean that several barriers to raising and satisfactorily resolving some disputes about equality have been eliminated and in certain quarters new social attitudes and outlooks prevail. Two legal disputes concerning the notion of the Good Samaritan provide another illustration of the impact of context on how disputes are perceived, acted upon, and resolved. In 1913, when a shipping company and the parents of a drowning victim were unable to resolve the parents' claim for damages, a Canadian court decided there was no legal duty on the part of a ship's captain to take any steps whatsoever to rescue a seaman who had fallen into the water as a result of the seaman's own negligence. The judge's decision, for which there was no binding legal precedent, probably reflects various societal values — the individualism of nineteenth-century tort law, the capitalist notion of self-interest over benevolence, and the economic protection of a growing Great Lakes shipping industry. Sixty years later, the Supreme Court of Canada ruled this ratio was no longer "good law" in adjudicating essentially the same dispute involving the owner of a cabin cruiser called the *Ogopogo* and the estate of a guest who had accidentally fallen overboard and drowned.[33] The issue may have been identical — was there a duty to rescue? — but the times had changed what society expected from a good neighbour in Canada who this time was not a particularly competent seaman in charge of a cabin cruiser that likely came with liability insurance.

---

31 *Thibaudeau* v. *R.*, [1995] 2 S.C.R. 627 and the subsequent reform of federal laws respecting support payments for divorcing couples.

32 *Edwards* v. *Canada (A.G.)*, [1930] A.C. 124 (P.C. (Fed.)).

33 See *Horsley* v. *MacLaren* [1972] S.C.R. 441, which decided *Vanvalkenburg* v. *Northern Navigation Co.* (1914), 19 D.L.R. 649 (Ont. S.C.A.D.) was no longer good law. Section 2 of the *Quebec Charter of Human Rights and Freedoms* requires that "every person must come to the aid of anyone whose life is in peril, either personally or calling for aid . . . unless it involves danger to himself or a third person, or he has another valid reason."

The broader social context in which disputes play out, although recognizable, will not always be consistent from one setting or person to another. Consider, for example, those North American notions of business negotiations which emphasize speed, face-to-face meetings, sticking to clear agendas, and long, legally binding contracts as the best way to resolve commercial controversies. Such Western mores may be foreign concepts in Japan, China, and Asian countries where cultural, religious, or other contextual conditions demand approaches to negotiations which respect different traditions on dispute resolution such as relationship building, proper pacing of the talks and tasks, the power of ceremony, and cultural superiority. The modern negotiations of treaties with First Nations also reveal clear cultural divides around myriad dispute resolution issues such as attitudes about land, the content of self-government, and how justice can be done.

In many disputes, formal laws and legal rights are an important part of a dispute's context. Laws essentially institutionalize accepted social attitudes, create legal rights, and contribute to a general social ordering. This ordering can prevent some disputes from arising (the requirement of publicly traded companies to make financial disclosures to investors; the general rule that matrimonial property is to be divided equally on separation or divorce). The law also may prescribe a right or a remedy if certain standards are not met (damages for negligent acts causing injury; an injunction to prevent certain types of debtors from removing assets from the jurisdiction). However, there is not always agreement on what the law means or how it should be applied. This contextual confusion can be particularly problematic for disputants when competing values are in conflict (e.g., should a right to freedom of expression override a law that interferes with a person's right to privacy?) or when it is not certain what the legal outcome would be (e.g., will a judge find the facts necessary to hold the businessperson responsible for a breach of her fiduciary duty to the company shareholders?). The law, whether clear or not, often casts a long shadow over the disputing process.

A part of the contextual equation not to be forgotten will be the disputes themselves. Disputes are not only dependent on context; they often are instrumental in changing or reinforcing the broader social, economic, or political landscape.

An example of the reciprocal relationship between context and disputes might be found in discrimination disputes in the workplace. An employee claims that she was fired because of her race or religion. An intern says he was inappropriately touched by the CEO. An associate in a law firm suggests that women do not make partners as often as men because of their gender. A worker finds the office environment hostile because of the bad jokes. Over time, these disputes and others like them have led to changes in employment standards, hiring and advancement policies, working conditions, general attitudes about equality in the workplace, and how these types of workplace disputes might best be addressed. However, these contextual changes can then bring up concerns, complaints, and then disputes about reverse discrimination, harassment, equal pay for work of equal value, political correctness, radical feminism, immigration policies, and fairness in dispute resolution procedures. These new disputes thus operate to re-affect context and to reverse changes in the ways in which discrimination in the workplace is understood, responded to, and structured. The disputes themselves and the disputing process thus become forces that operate to change attitudes, values, structures, powers, and other contextual matters. This new context, in turn, has an impact on future disputing around workplace equality.

Thus disputes, the disputing process, and dispute resolution depend on the full context. Neither the dispute nor the course it takes could exist separately from these real-world details. It is the combination of the many contextual influences and reference points — the where, who, what, when, and why — that shapes the nature of a dispute, that influences how or even whether a dispute is brought forward, that affects the course the dispute takes, and that ultimately determines the dispute's outcome. Serious attention must be paid to the contextual equation that gives a dispute its unique form and the reciprocal impact of disputes on the framing or reframing of this contextual equation.

The practical importance of context to disputing can be illustrated by a story.

> Consider the story of two men quarreling in a library. One wants the window open and the other wants it closed. They bicker back and forth about how much to leave it open: a crack, halfway, three quarters of the way. No solution satisfies them both.[34]

What will happen next in this story? It is likely there will be a peaceful resolution to this dispute. But not necessarily. It depends on the answers to a number of contextual questions. For example, will one man avoid the dispute? Why? Do the men know each other? Is one of the men older, or stronger? Does their relationship, age, power, or gender matter? How have these men disputed in the past? In what country

---

34   From R. Fisher & W. Ury, *Getting to Yes: Negotiating Agreement without Giving In* (Boston: Houghton Mifflin Company, 1981) at 41.

is the library located? Are there laws or regulations about windows being open, or being broken? Is there a social norm about what to do? Are there laws about fighting in public? Will these men respect the law? Are the men from the same town, of the same nationality? What will they do if they can't agree? How much time do they have? Do they have access to any dispute resolution resources? What is it that is important to them in this dispute? What do they know about ADR? Will a wise librarian enter the fray and help them see a solution?

The answer to these and other questions begin to make up the context of the library dispute. This context is essential to understanding what happens or what could happen next in the library and in helping the quarrelling men to resolve their differences. The same reasoning holds true when the men in the library are neighbours locked in a feud over a pet's defecation habits, siblings dissatisfied with their mother's will, or relatives battling for the custody of a child. Without context, the dispute may be misunderstood or misinterpreted. Any attempted resolution may miss the mark. A third party who might intervene in the above disputes (another library user, a neighbour, a family lawyer) could do more harm than good if, for example, they do not realize one of the protagonists has a problem with controlling anger, with limited resources, or with always wanting to win.

Consider a real case. In *Sawan* v. *Tearoe*,[35] the Supreme Court of Canada was faced with a dispute between a child's birth mother, Cecilia Sawan, a member of the Woodland Cree Indian Band in Alberta, Canada, and the petitioners for an adoption order, James and Faye Tearoe, devout Christians living in Victoria, British Columbia. The Supreme Court of Canada refused to hear an appeal from the decision of the British Columbia Court of Appeal granting the Tearoes' petition for adoption and changing the child's name from Jordan Michael Sawan to David James Tearoe.

The facts of this dispute between Sawan and the Tearoes begin to disclose the dispute's context. When she was eighteen years of age and unmarried, the child's mother, Cecilia Sawan, had given her two-month-old child up for adoption to the Tearoes. Six days later she changed her mind and withdrew her consent. Although the Tearoes were told by both the mother and the Ministry of Family and Social Services within seven or eight days of picking up the child that the mother wanted the child back, the Tearoes did not return the child.

---

35 *Sawan* v. *Tearoe* (1993), 84 B.C.L.R. (2d) 223 (C.A.), leave to appeal to the S.C.C. dismissed without reasons [1994] 1 S.C.R. vi.

The law in Alberta at the time required any revocation of consent to adoption be in writing and be sent within ten days of the consent first being given. Although Sawan stated she had sent a written notice, it appeared from the evidence at trial that no such notice was ever received by the Ministry. Court proceedings were commenced in British Columbia by the Tearoes for adoption and by Sawan for return of the child. The key question for the Court of Appeal was whether it would be in the best interests of the child to revoke Cecilia Sawan's consent to adoption.

The following excerpt from the Court of Appeal decision illustrates more contextual features of this adoption dispute:

> Cecilia Sawan, now 20 years of age, is unmarried and is attending school. There is evidence that she has had some problems in her life, including alcohol abuse. There is also evidence that she has sought help for this problem.
>
> Ms. Sawan's mother is native; her father, non-native. Ms. Sawan stated that she wishes to raise her son in her native culture. Recently, she has gained status as a member of the Woodland Cree Indian Band. She has not lived on the reserve for approximately six years. There is evidence that she has an extended family living on the reserve and off the reserve. There is little, if any, evidence of any contact by her with members of her family. Ms. Sawan testified that she planned to return to the Band but was uncertain as to when. The Woodland Band members speak Cree. She concedes she would have difficulties living on the reserve because she does not know the language. However, her evidence is that there are facilities to assist her in learning Cree.
>
> Ms. Sawan's future plans are not settled. She wants to complete her education. At present, she is financially supported by social assistance and the Band. Ms. Sawan testified that she has a fiancé, who is not a native Indian, and that they plan to marry in July, 1994. Ms Sawan anticipates that her fiancé, who works in the oil fields in Northern Alberta, will live on the reserve with her and her child. Ms Sawan's fiancé was not called as a witness. . . .
>
> At the time of the trial the child was eighteen months old. It can be readily concluded from all the evidence presented that he is a healthy, happy, well cared for child. He is one-quarter native Indian. As just noted, his mother has placed his name on the list to become a member of the Woodland Cree Native Indian Band.
>
> From the time of the child's birth to February 6th, 1992, the child had been in his mother's care, in total, for twenty-two days. The child has been with the appellants continuously since February 6th, 1992. . . .

This test of the best interest of the child is most clearly enunciated in the often-cited passage from the case of *K.(K.) v. L.(G.)*[36] . . . This case was referred to by Madam Justice Prowse when she quoted from Mr. Justice McIntyre, who said this (at p. 101):

> "I would therefore hold that in the case at bar the dominant consideration to which all other considerations must remain subordinate must be the welfare of the child. This is not to say that the question of custody will be determined by weighing the economic circumstances of the contending parties. The matter will not be determined solely on the basis of the physical comfort and material advantages that may be available in the home of one contender or the other. The welfare of the child must be decided on a consideration of these and all other relevant factors, including the general psychological, spiritual and emotional welfare of the child. *It must be the aim of the Court, when resolving disputes between rival claimants for the custody of a child, to choose the course which will best provide for the healthy growth, development and education of the child so that he will be equipped to face the problems of life as a mature adult. Parental claims must not be lightly set aside, and they are entitled to serious consideration in reaching any conclusion. Where it is clear that the welfare of the child requires it, however, they must be set aside.*" (My emphasis)

Earlier, Madam Justice Wilson, in *R.(N.A.) v. W.(J.L.)* [37] . . . , discussed the best interest test when dealing with an adoption which involved inter-racial considerations. After commenting that the child should not become "a battleground" she stated (at pp. 187–88):

> "In my view, when the test to be met is the best interests of the child, the significance of cultural background and heritage as opposed to bonding abates over time. The closer the bond that develops with the prospective adoptive parents the less important the racial element becomes."

This child was with his mother, in total, for twenty-two days. The child had been with the Tearoes for over 16 months when this matter went to trial. On the evidence, the trial judge's conclusion that the child was with his mother for a "considerable period of time" is plainly in error.

---

36   (*Sub nom. King v. Low*), [1985] 1 S.C.R. 87.
37   *Racine v. Woods*, [1983] 2 S.C.R. 173.

The trial judge's conclusion that "the connection between the mother and the child has not been irretrievably broken" is not supported by the evidence. There is no evidence from which to conclude either that a bond between the mother and the child had ever been established in the period during which the child was with her, or that if any such bond had been established it was likely still remaining at the time of trial. Indeed, the evidence establishes beyond doubt that the only mother and father this child knows are Faye and James Tearoe.

The welfare of the child is the paramount concern. This child presently lives in a loving, stable, comfortable environment, with a family that has looked after all his needs for virtually all his life. By all accounts the child is thriving. To end that relationship would destroy the family bonds that have been established between the child and the adoptive parents.

Although she offered no specific plans for the future, it is quite possible that Ms. Sawan could also provide a loving environment in which the child could thrive if he were returned to her. But in the absence of any evidence from which it could reasonably be inferred that there ever was or now remains any bond between natural mother and child, or that such a bond could now successfully be established, it is impossible to conclude that the best interests of the child require the consent to adoption to be set aside.

Furthermore, common sense dictates that to disrupt the child from his present environment, and to put him through the uncertainty associated with an attempt to establish a bond with his natural mother, would cause him considerable trauma. In the absence of evidence from which it could reasonably be inferred that such trauma would be both minimal and fleeting in nature, it is impossible to conclude that the best interests of the child would now be met by setting aside the consent to adoption.

The trial judge stated the Tearoes are "competent, caring, loving, proposed adoptive parents" and that a close relationship had developed. To return this child as requested by the respondent, is to place him in an uncertain future that would take away from him the continuity and stability which he now has. As in the R.(N.A.) case, the cultural background and heritage must give way in the circumstances of this case. A difficult choice must be made. The child's best interests must come first. The respondent has not discharged the onus which s. 8(7) places on her. It is not in the best interests of this child to revoke Ms. Sawan's consent to adoption.[38]

---

38   *Sawan v. Tearoe*, above note 35 at 227, 228, 232–34 (cited to B.C.L.R.).

As an ADR case study, there is a lot to learn from *Sawan* v. *Tearoe* about the influence of context on disputes and the course they take. In hindsight, the disputing moves and non-moves of the parties as well as the court decision itself are more understandable upon examining the real-life context in which Sawan, the Tearoes, and their lawyers found themselves. This context would include the economics of the parties; the culture, religion, and geography that separated them; the outlooks on the family that were advanced and accepted; the relative power of the parties; and the personal and colonial histories at play. Talking about context makes the course of the dispute and the adoption of David James seem almost predictable.[39]

But if this dispute were starting over again, an ADR inquiry in context might mean a change. An alternative dispute resolution perspective might ask in this specific context with its unique combination of characters, locations, points of contention, timing, and disparities, whether dispute resolution mechanisms other than the courts might be more economical, effective, or acceptable, or whether something else might work better for the Tearoes, Ms. Sawan, and her child. If an ADR advocate had been a lawyer for the parties, she might have changed the course of history. If a consensus-based approach to the problem had been taken, a mediator might have encouraged or prompted the parties to craft a creative solution such as an open adoption or continued contact with the birth mother. ADR in context might suggest that judges, lawyers, social workers, parents, and interested observers need to know a good deal about the where, who, what, when, and why of transracial adoption disputes to understand fully what is occurring between

---

39 The court reasoning does not refer to a significant body of work adding contextual sophistication to "best interests of the child" determinations in transracial adoptions. For example, see C. Metteer, "Pigs in Heaven: A Parable of Native American Adoption under the Indian Child Welfare Act (1996) 28 Ariz. St. L J. 589. For a reversal of reasoning but the same result, see *D.H. v. H.M.*) (1998), 156 D.L.R. (4th) 548 (B.C.C.A.). The British Columbia Court of Appeal granted custody of a child of Aboriginal descent to the child's maternal biological grandfather who was of Aboriginal background as opposed to the mother's adoptive parents who were non-Aboriginal. The Court of Appeal decided that the trial judge had placed undue emphasis on economic matters and underemphasized the ties of blood and culture in awarding custody to the adoptive grandparents. The Court of Appeal referred to "a very considerable history of unsuccessful outcomes" of cross-cultural adoption involving Aboriginal children and recent legislative initiatives stressing the importance of preserving the cultural identity of Aboriginal children when considering the best interests of the child. On appeal, the Supreme Court of Canada was not impressed and restored the custody order in favour of the adoptive grandparents. See *H.(D.) v. M.(H.)*, [1999] 1 S.C.R. 328.

Sawan and the Tearoes, to assess what the course of this dispute could or should be, and, more important, to be able to intervene in such demanding disputes. Thus ADR in context can show there is much more to disputes and disputing than often meets the initial eye.

D. THE MULTIDISCIPLINARY NATURE OF ADR

The following two excerpts are illustrations of neighbour disputes that escalated to distressing proportions:

> No one can say for sure how these two men first came into conflict, but it appears to have begun with a disagreement over their common property line.
>
> During the years that followed, police officers in the county's Fifth Precinct were summoned by one family or the other and presented with a series of accusations: litter thrown in the yards, water sprayed in the windows, mysterious telephone calls, musical instruments too loud on one side, radios blasting on the other.
>
> Then, according to the police, the "harassment," as each side called it, took a different turn.
>
> The Galluccios accused Peters of assaulting Galluccio with a belt buckle, knocking his glasses off. They contended that Mrs. Conforto attacked Mrs. Galluccio with a rake, that animal feces were smeared on their cars and the vehicles vandalized.
>
> The Peters, through their lawyer, accused the family next door of setting fire to Mrs. Conforto's car and charged that Galluccio had threatened Joanne Peters with a knife and had assaulted Peters with the lid of a garbage can.
>
> On July 5, according to authorities, Joanne Peters, after an argument with her neighbors, tossed eggs at their house. Galluccio retaliated by spraying water at Miss Peters, who was inside her house by a window, according to authorities. It was then that James Peters went to get his rifle.[40]

What appears to have been a simmering dispute between neighbours over a cat ended in the fatal shooting Saturday of a 28-year-old woman, police said.

---

40   M. Norman, "A suburban tragedy" *New York Times* (11 October 1984) 21.

The gruesome scene unfolded as a group of children played in a nearby park.

One woman heard what she thought were firecrackers and assumed that people at a birthday party nearby were setting off fireworks.

The dead woman and a neighbour fought constantly over [a] cat urinating and defecating in the yard and the sandbox, she said.

She also said the neighbour resented the amount of time his wife spent with the other woman.

"They were always bickering at each other," said the woman.

Police have charged [a] 77-year-old with second-degree murder.[41]

Disputes can and often do result in personal tragedies. Although many disputes are resolved quickly and amicably, others are not so lucky. The feuding ex-spouses can engage in legal battles that deplete the very assets they are fighting over and ruin the relationship their young children need somewhat intact. The reputation of a politician accused of fraud can be difficult to repair when the court proceedings drag on for a decade. Even a plaintiff who wins at trial may lose it all when a vindictive defendant obstructs the enforcement of a court-ordered judgment. The consequences of disputing can leave long-lasting scars on the disputants and others around them.

Although the modern emergence of ADR was, in part, directed to reducing or eliminating destructive consequences of disputing, understanding just what is needed to accomplish such a goal (and perhaps other ADR goals) is another story. What would our neighbours need to know or be able to do to avoid these turns of events? What knowledge and skills would an ADR practitioner need to possess to really understand these types of disputes, to foresee how they might take a more constructive course, or to be able to intervene and assist the parties to do things better?

When these questions are posed for the great array of disputing scenarios, particularly for cases where tragedies lie waiting, the questions and their answers surely point to the conclusion that ADR must be a field of much multidisciplinary study and practice. Understanding how any dispute happens, what explains disputing behaviour, and what is necessary to constructively assist the resolution process will not be the exclusive preserve of one profession. The knowledge and skills relevant to ADR will be found in sources such as the sociology of disputing, the psychology of human behaviour, communication theories, history,

---

41   "Argument over cat ends in shooting; woman left dead" *The [Toronto] Globe and Mail* (10 August 1998).

anthropology, social work, economics, and the law. Depending on the context, being aware of theories of organizational behaviour, management styles, and leadership qualities may be as critical as drafting skills to a lawyer when working with two firms attempting to iron out wrinkles in a joint venture agreement. Being able to classify how parties approach and respond to conflict, perhaps relying on the Myers-Briggs Type Indicator test or a Thomas Kilmann Conflict Mode analysis, or using Neuro-Linguistic Programming may be invaluable techniques to negotiators when dealing with a contentious multi-party matter. Having the skills to clearly advise on the law and predict the likely result if the case goes to trial could help a mediator break a negotiation impasse. Listening effectively, both actively and passively, and accurately interpreting non-verbal communication might make a real difference with two neighbours who can see no way out of their troubles.

It should not be surprising that the study of ADR requires a multidisciplinary focus for several reasons. First, the study of disputes and dispute resolution has been of long-standing interest to the law and social science community. Whether it was an anthropological analysis of disputes and disputing behaviour to understand law and legal institutions, a criminological construction of a different ideology of crime and punishment to facilitate a change in justice policy, or a sociological search for science in law by attention to the empirical reality of dispute processing, the particular social relationship we call a dispute extended the study of law well beyond traditional legal scholarship. It was only natural that the many disciplines long interested in disputes and conflict resolution now contribute to, and compete for, a say in what constitutes ADR.

Second, having a multidisciplinary point of view is not a unique concept even within traditional types of disciplines or enterprises. For example, businesses commonly recognize that effective management requires economic, accounting, psychological, and public relations skills. Running a business may depend on the bottom line but many sources of education and understanding contribute to the successful venture. Governments often need more than public opinion to make the best decisions. Input from different disciplines, often with competing ideological bents, will vie for political attention and be used in setting policy, enacting legislation, and generally good governing. In law, there are increasing examples where legal developments depend on input from non-legal sources. For example, the Supreme Court of Canada was asked recently to decide if the government of the province of Quebec could effect the secession of Quebec from Canada unilaterally. This was a momentous question for the Court. The judicial decision reflects the process of combining "legal and constitutional questions of the utmost subtlety and complexity with political questions of great sensitivity" and the Court's obvious reliance on history and political theory.[42] Charter of Rights decisions, criminal cases, and human rights matters also regularly invoke references to non-legal resources. In many cases, experts from outside the law make important contributions to the lawyering process. Legal education at its best shows off the multidisciplinary make-up of law.

Finally, the multidisciplinary nature of ADR is in accord with the contextual complexities that accompany the arrival of most disputes. Getting a grasp on the full where, who, what, when, and why of a dispute and trying to understand what might happen next surely can best be appreciated from a wide multidisciplinary point of view. Each of many different disciplines will have something to contribute, and the combination of these inputs gives ADR more substance. The careful analysis and delineation of the important issues in dispute, which is part of thinking like a lawyer, could be effectively paired with a social worker's or psychologist's communication skills of reframing and paraphrasing to present the issues to the disputants in the most effective manner. Being aware of the anger arousal cycle and when people in conflict are less able to participate meaningfully in productive discussions because of high emotions could influence the timing of constructive interventions into disputes by an experienced business negotiator. The big ADR picture only becomes clear when all the pieces can be put together. Not understanding and practising ADR as a truly multidisciplinary concept means that only parts of the whole are ever articulated, accentuated, or acted upon.

The multidisciplinary nature of ADR holds both promise and problems. Understanding ADR as a multidisciplinary field of study that can focus on disputes of every conceivable type opens up rewarding possibilities for cross-disciplinary education and exchanges. Such initiatives might make a difference to disputing neighbours, spouses entrenched in their positions, or others who find themselves, as disputants or not, in the midst of a controversy. Any of the goals to which ADR aspires might be more easily achieved when the ADR practitioner knows and is able to do as much as possible — more than a single centre, degree, or discipline could provide. Partnerships between and among the many actors who already work with disputes and their resolution could yield results greater than would be realizable through individual action. But ADR's multidisciplinary character also means that many voices can

---

42   See *Reference re Secession of Quebec*, [1998] 2 S.C.R. 217.

compete for a say in the leadership of the movement, what directions it should take, what are its defining moments, what are its goals, and who can be on board. Differences are likely to exist in how ADR is understood and practised when there are many contributors to the meaning of this modern expression.

E. ADR IN THEORY AND PRACTICE

What then is ADR? While difficult to define, complex and ambiguous, is there a framework for ADR that lends coherence to its diversity? Or is ADR's beauty in the eye of each beholder?

At one level, ADR can remain amorphous, distinguished mainly by the many and varied initiatives that claim ADR status. These eclectic endeavours and their goals can be narrow or broad. ADR, for example, can be the development of cost-effective dispute resolution rules for mobile home disputes.[43] ADR also can be the institutionalization of enormous experiments in land use and resource management mediation, not just to save money but to encourage more participatory democracy in public policy decision making.[44] For the legal profession, ADR may be a label for a renewed examination of systems of justice with only the trial process itself excluded from inquiry. Although formal court-connected processes may occupy some ADR space, ADR can be viewed by lawyers as moving attention away from the courts where a judge imposes a decision to a range of processes where the parties themselves have an increasingly greater say in the shape of the process used and in any eventual resolution.

This type of understanding for ADR has several benefits. With such a focus, lawyers and others can begin to identify in a concrete manner the knowledge and skills required to be a competent practitioner in ADR processes such as negotiation, mediation, arbitration, and hybrids

---

43   For this example see *Residential Tenancy Act*, R.S.B.C. 1996, c. 406, ss. 65–77.

44   The now defunct Commission on Resources and Environment (CORE) in British Columbia was an example of the mega-mediation project. CORE's mandate, set out in the *Commissioner on Resources and Environment Act*, 1992, S.B.C., c. 34, was to develop a province-wide strategy for land use and related resource and environmental management. To develop plans for Vancouver Island, Chilcotin, East Kootenay, and West Kootenay Boundary, comprising over 10 million hectares of land and home to a long history of land-use conflicts, CORE relied heavily on a "shared decision-making" model, meaning that all public interests as well as the provincial government, with the assistance of professional mediators, would work for a limited time in an effort to reach a consensus.

such as mediation-arbitration (where a mediator unable to get agreement then acts as an arbitrator), mini-trial (where the parties can combine negotiation and mediation in a non-binding adjudicative process), and neutral case evaluation (where the parties get a non-binding opinion from a neutral third party). Attention can be paid to finding the best processes and practices to suit particular disputes and parties.

The downside to this approach is that inquiry and critique can be dampened because, after all, almost anything can be ADR. Without more structure, ADR is a wide-open smorgasbord of what is good in disputing, or what are best practices in dispute resolution. Although individual ADR offerings can be scrutinized, criticized, and taken or not, ADR itself is mostly a mantra for common sense. ADR means alternative, or perhaps better or appropriate, dispute resolution.

At another level, however, ADR can be well understood if its theories and practices can be located within a framework for analysis which is able to accommodate three general conclusions arising from the preceding pages. First, the modern history of ADR reveals not only the pursuit of complex and conflicting goals but also a highly political analysis and critique of it's purposes. These issues cannot be ignored. Second, ADR cannot be studied or applied out of context. The where, who, what, when, and why of disputes are obviously essential contributors to any informed examination of disputing and dispute resolution. The full context can be complicated. Third, ADR has been and must continue to be shaped by multidisciplinary influences.

One framework that can encompass these conclusions is the concept of ideology.[45] An ideology can be understood as a cluster of beliefs, values, and images through which meanings and values are attached to people and practices in such a way that the power relations in society are established and maintained. More simply, ideology tells us what is natural, normal, and essential in all our lives. So, for example, a dominant ideology of the family can be the pairing of a heterosexual couple, the marriage of a husband and wife, prescribed roles in and outside the home, and so on. Less dominant family images (or more dominant depending on context) might include partners with varied sexual orientations, same-sex couples, community-based childcare, all partners or parents working outside the home, home-schooling, no children, many children, shared power, and so on. In the same way, there are

---

45   For a window on the concept of ideology, see M. Cormack, *Ideology* (Ann Arbor: University of Michigan Press, 1992).

dominant and less dominant ideologies of matters such as success, economics, politics, and freedoms.

Surely then, ADR essentially is an ideological expression. Its meaning seeks to inform our thought processes about what is natural, normal, and essential about disputing behaviour and disputing institutions, about what are good disputing practices and what are not, about what is common sense in dispute resolution and what is not, about how the world is and how the world must be vis-à-vis disputes, and about how the web of ADR questions are posed and answered.

As ideology, ADR is open to full understanding and informed practical use, with ample room for the politics and contradictions of ADR. There are opportunities to accept or question the meanings of such concepts as consensus, mediation, personal transformation, and efficiency, when juxtaposed with the severe reality of many disputes that are part of serious and systemic economic, political, and social inequalities. ADR as ideology would, as a matter of course, seek to understand the impact of dispute resolution initiatives and processes on existing power structures. ADR as ideology would not ignore or fail to understand the accumulating activities that come under its umbrella, but these activities would be seen as part of a larger project promoting certain disputing behaviours and institutions and, at the same time, marginalizing others. ADR as ideology would seek to understand the significance and impact of its history, would want to see the full disputing context, and would recognize its obviously multidisciplinary nature.

But the interesting question is — what is this ideology? On the one hand, do the beliefs, values, and images that make up ADR mirror what was there before? Does the ideal in disputing still involve judges, courts, lawyers, and other professionals as the dominant actors, still mostly individuals fighting it out to determine who is right, who is the winner, and who is the loser, so that any real change may be hard to come by, particularly for the least powerful in society? Have global economics and economic interests taken over ADR to force inefficient dispute resolution systems, including the courts, to be competitive in a world market? Is ADR displacing the state in dispute resolution and substituting a private, market-driven model for those who can afford it? Does the harmony promised by ADR mean preservation of the status quo with ADR a coercive mechanism of pacification? Or does the truth and reality of ADR mean alternative images of disputing that more accurately mirror people's diverse experiences, that overcome barriers to bringing disputes forward, that reduce dependence on professionals, that empower those who traditionally have been excluded from having their important struggles aired, and that take a more holistic view of the dispute?

The correct answer is — it depends. The ideology of ADR depends on whether some goals overshadow others, whether and to what degree the context of disputes matters, and which disciplines contribute and how to ADR's expression. What ADR is depends on what is constructed and presented as natural, normal, and essential about disputing and on who does the constructing and presenting. Although the answer is not always clear, thinking of ADR as ideology can bring a sharper, more critical focus to what is being done, or could be done, about mobile home disputes, land-use problems, adoption controversies, neighbourhood fights, Good Samaritan miscues, equality demands, and the panoply of disputes that can arise in a modern society. ADR as ideology is the larger disputing picture. The reflective ADR practitioner, lawyer, judge in court, government official, business executive, student first studying the field, disputants themselves, and interested observers will be able to see which parts of the ADR terrain are being examined and whether some sections are being hidden from view. By locating ADR within an ideological framework, both ADR proponent and critic have a means to assess what particular ADR initiatives might mean in theory and in practice.

FURTHER READINGS

AUERBACH, J.S., *Justice without Law? Resolving Disputes without Lawyers* (New York: Oxford University Press, 1983)

AXELROD, R.M., *The Evolution of Cooperation* (New York: Basic Books, 1984)

BROWN, H.J., & A.L. MARRIOTT, *ADR Principles and Practice* (London: Sweet & Maxwell, 1993)

BUNKER, B., & J. RUBIN, eds., *Conflict, Cooperation and Justice: Essays Inspired by the Work of Morton Deutsch* (San Francisco: Jossey Bass, 1995)

BURTON, J.W., *Conflict: Resolution and Prevention* (New York: St. Martin's Press, 1990)

CHORNENKI, G.A., & C.E. Hart, *Bypass Court: A Dispute Resolution Handbook* (Toronto: Butterworths, 1996)

COLLINS, R., *Conflict Sociology: Toward an Explanatory Science* (New York: Academic Press, 1975)

DE BONO, E., *Conflicts: A Better Way to Resolve Them* (Middlesex: Penguin, 1985)

EDELMAN, L.B., & M.C. SUCHMAN, "When the "Haves" Hold Court: Speculations on the Organizational Internalization of Law" (1999), 33 Law & Soc. Rev. 941

LEESON, S.M., & B.M. JOHNSTON, *Ending It; Dispute Resolution in America* (Cincinnati: Anderson Publishing, 1988)

MCLAREN, R.H., & J. SANDERSON, *Innovative Dispute Resolution: The Alternative* (Toronto, Carswell, 1994)

SANDOLE, J.D., & H. VAN DER MERWE, eds., *Conflict Resolution Theory and Practice: Integration and Application* (New York: St. Martin's Press, 1993)

SCHELLING, T.C., *The Strategy of Conflict* (Cambridge: Harvard University Press, 1960)

STITT, A.J., & R. JACKMAN, eds., *Alternative Dispute Resolution Practice Manual* (Toronto: CCH Canadian Limited, 1996)

TILLETT, G., *Resolving Conflict: A Practical Approach* (Sydney: Sydney University Press, 1991)

WOOLF, H.K., *Access to Justice: Final Report to the Lord Chancellor on the Civil Justice System in England and Wales* (London: HMSO, 1996)

CHAPTER 2

KEY CONCEPTS IN ADR

A. INTRODUCTION

For almost everyone, the study of ADR will involve exposure to new ideas and skill sets. This should be expected given the historical, contextual, and multidisciplinary complexities of ADR described in chapter 1. Whatever ADR means, it is not unusual for those who work with or study ADR to acknowledge that this subject matter takes them, to a greater or lesser degree, into unfamiliar territory.

For some people, the new ideas and skills of alternative dispute resolution may fit easily with long-standing beliefs that existing systems of justice are flawed and in need of repair, and that changes are necessary in how we go about disputing in our society. However, the fit may be less comfortable for others. ADR may suggest a radical departure from disputing traditions or cultural norms. It may appear to question or ignore conventional wisdom about the role of the courts, the significance of due process, the importance of legal rights, the exercise of power, the struggle for equality, and the utility of commonly accepted concepts associated with the resolution of disputes. Some ADR ideas and skills may seem incongruent with personal dispute resolution practices and habits that are familiar and time-tested. The discomfort with ADR may be particularly painful for individuals and organizations with well-established stakes, both personal and economic, in the status quo of dispute resolution. Of course, the reaction to the new ideas and skills of ADR will depend on the meaning that is attributed to this expression.

Whatever the initial reaction to ADR, an understanding of key concepts as outlined below in sections B to E will help in several ways. First, these key concepts are a way to unpack and see more clearly the essential elements that are used to give ADR its meaning in theory and practice. Second, they illustrate there are different ways of thinking about and practising dispute resolution that may either open up or foreclose dispute resolution opportunities. In other words, they provide interesting approaches to how disputes can be analyzed, reacted to, and resolved. Finally, these concepts can point to the knowledge and skills that are necessary for practical proficiency in ADR work.

B. THE TERMS AND TERMINOLOGIES OF ADR

Understanding and working in ADR increasingly is requiring access to a new vocabulary. This type of prerequisite is a common experience in various occupations. In law, for example, lawyers and law students have always been accustomed to using terms and terminologies unique to that discipline. While *mens rea*, consideration, the reasonable person, fee-simple, divisions of power, what is justifiable in a free and democratic society, and other words may have limited use and even much mystery in everyday discourse, these expressions make up the working language and foundations of criminal law, contract law, torts, property law, constitutional law, and other legal subjects.

Like law, ADR has a language that is becoming more and more its own. There are terms and terminologies that provide the grounding on which the study and practice of ADR are being built. Words such as interest-based bargaining, transformative, mediation-arbitration (med-arb), reframing, and dispute itself are a part of the ADR vocabulary. Those who speak about ADR are expected to be familiar with this language. Arbitrators have to ask about awards while mediators mention trust, uncovering underlying interests, and caucusing. In negotiation there are high opening demands, boulewareism, and BATNAs. Restorative justice and sentencing circles are on the agenda of the criminal justice system. Some suggest NLP (Neuro-Linguistic Programming) and music therapy can help. Others offer advice on the conflict continuum, an elicitive approach to culture, conflict management education (CME), or the work of Deutsch, Menkel-Meadow, Fisher, and Black.

But the terms and terminologies of ADR are unique from those of other professions or followings in two important ways. First, there are many sources for the language that makes up alternative dispute resolution theory and practice. As discussed in chapter 1, many disciplines contribute to the knowledge necessary for a complete understanding of ADR. The number of sources may vary depending on how widely or narrowly ADR is viewed but there is really no serious debate that ADR is not a multidisciplinary field. This multi-sourced lexicon can create special challenges to mastering the language of ADR. Sorting out where the ADR expression comes from or should come from so that it can be understood is taxing enough work but deciding on the right meaning of a word or expression can be particularly problematic when the various contributors provide conflicting definitions, understandings, or ideologies. The relationship between conflict and dispute, discussed below, is one example. Some say that conflict and dispute are more conceptually and practically similar than distinct while others propose the terms are significantly different. The meaning of culture is another case in point where the same word can have different definitions depending on whom you ask. How much of any one discipline's own language belongs in ADR also can be difficult to determine. The feminist critique of mediation suggests a working knowledge of equality theories should be part of a mediator's repertoire. The expression of strong emotions in disputing points to the need for dispute resolvers to be familiar with active listening, the anger arousal cycle, and more but a line is often drawn between therapy and the activities of ADR practitioners. Second, unlike law, as ADR's popularity grows, a wide range of individuals, organizations, and governments increasingly want to learn, use, or be certified in, the language of ADR. This deepening desire for accessibility to disputing developments is not surprising. ADR is a growth industry in a multidisciplinary field. There are opportunities for advancement, success, satisfaction, stability, and adventure in this growth. Certainly the attraction of ADR can depend on its ambiguous meaning. If ADR was mostly focused on court-connected reforms, the movement might have caught the attention of only a few lawyers and litigants. But with ADR goals of economic efficiencies in dispute resolution, personal empowerment and transformation, and a reshaping of entire justice systems, the interest increases. And, because no one is completely insulated from disputes, everyone has probably engaged in some form of dispute resolution, whether on their own behalf or for someone else. All these factors add up to a huge potential demand for acquiring ADR expertise — a demand far exceeding the usual limits imposed on entry into other professions or callings with a specialized language. Because of this demand, the road to linguistic proficiency in ADR passes some unusual crossroads around consistency and standardization in what is ADR talk, how to set or pass the threshold to be understood and accepted in this new language, who could or should control entry, and professionalization generally.

Given these caveats about becoming fluent in the language of ADR, the following sections discuss several important terms and terminologies that are part of the ADR vocabulary. These specific sections are followed by a general glossary of ADR terms.

1) Conflicts and Disputes

The word conflict from the Latin word *fligere*, meaning to strike, can easily conjure up an image of a fight or a struggle. The word pulls our attention to events we know about at home or away, that we read about in the newspaper or hear on radio, that we encounter on the Internet or see face to face. The essential ingredient of these events and what distinguishes them from others is the fight, the disagreement, the back-against-the-wall, the violence, the pushes and pulls, the line in the sand, the struggle, or the competition. Such a confrontational mindset is evident in some modern definitions of conflict:

> Conflict is an expressed struggle between at least two interdependent parties who perceive incompatible goals, scarce reward or resources, and interference from the other party in achieving their goals.[1]
>
> Conflicts involve struggles between two or more people over values, or competition for status, power or scarce resources.[2]

Others say it more simply. Conflict exists whenever incompatible activities occur.[3]

Is a dispute different from a conflict? The definitions of conflict sound suspiciously similar to how a dispute could be defined. There is a suggestion that a dispute occurs "when conflict becomes particularized concerning a specific issue or set of issues."[4] Or that conflict is natural whereas dispute is a cultural phenomenon that originates through some kind of domination or oppression. Analyzing a conflict

1   M. Duryea, *Conflict and Culture: A Literature Review and Bibliography* (Victoria, BC: UVic Institute for Dispute Resolution, 1992) at 5.
2   L. Coser, *Continuities in the Study of Social Conflict* (New York: Free Press, 1967) at 20.
3   M. Deutsch, *The Resolution of Conflict: Constructive and Destructive Processes* (New Haven, CT: Yale University Press, 1973) at 10.
4   Above note 1.

over time or in terms of the relationships between the objective state of affairs and the parties' perspectives — is it, as Deutsch describes: veridical (existing objectively and perceived accurately), contingent (existence dependent upon contingencies not recognized by conflicting parties), displaced (a manifest conflict expresses an underlying conflict in a symbolic or idiomatic form), misattributed (the real conflict, parties, and issues are not properly identified either intentionally or unintentionally), latent (the conflict should be occurring but it is not yet experienced), and false (a conflict for which there is no objective basis)?[5] — can provide different typologies of conflict and valuable insights into what the conflict is about and why it is, or is not, proceeding in a particular manner. Constructing disputes as not natural can focus attention on the reasons for this categorization and on the essential elements that give a dispute a form different from that of a conflict. But conflict and dispute resemble synonyms more than words with any meaningful theoretical or practical distinctions. The difference in terminology seems to be a product of different disciplinary interests in the subject, with sociology, anthropology, and law favouring dispute, and psychology, social psychology, and economics preferring conflict, rather than any important or practical differences *inter se*.

Whether it is conflict or dispute, ADR is a modern response to the incompatibilities, interferences, and divergencies behind these terms. In a conflict-free world, there would be no need for alternative or more mainstream dispute resolution. But given the capacity for conflict, ADR attempts to understand the contextual complexities and consequences surrounding conflict or dispute and then to establish what are or should be the normal and essential responses when conflict occurs.

But, interestingly, the concept of conflict/dispute as a configuration that depicts a confrontation or fight is surely not a universal mindset. In some non-Western societies there is no easy translation for conflict. In certain communities conflict *per se* is not part of the vocabulary but rather is replaced by several different words, each associated with a specific fact situation or event. In this latter case, conflict has meaning only in context. Although some individuals may associate conflict with fighting and struggling, winning and losing, being damaging and dysfunctional, other people may take conflict in stride, see positive opportunities in conflict situations, avoid it easily, or delegate the resolution of conflict to others, generally not equating conflict with confrontation. For some people, the face of conflict may change regularly. Conflict may be quite heated, pitting one party against another at one point

---

5   Above note 3 at 12–15.

in time but become more conciliatory, characterized by open and honest dealings, at another point in the conflict's course. How a conflict or dispute is understood can vary considerably from one place to another, from one culture to another, and certainly from one person to another.

If broad-based consensus on the meaning of conflict or dispute does not exist, there are important implications for ADR. The diverse meanings attached to conflict suggest that ADR practices and processes should not be naturally uniform or necessarily transferable across different contexts. What are perceived as legitimate and appropriate ADR principles and activities will depend, in part, on how conflict is defined. A face-to-face or mandatory meeting in mediation to share decisions may be an acceptable process for some people who see conflict as an opportunity to take responsibility or to get things off their chest. Others may regard this direct and demanding process as intrusive and counter-productive, not part of good ADR, if conflict for them requires withdrawal, separation, submission to authority, or respect for elder advice. For proper ADR in the latter case, something would have to take the place of mediation or alternatively, the underlying meaning of conflict, which informs one's disputing perspective, would have to be adjusted. ADR practitioners and policy makers will face special challenges when conflicts involve people, organizations, or countries with competing or contradictory cultural views of what are acceptable and unacceptable understandings of conflict. Deciding what is normal and essential about dispute resolution requires extraordinary qualities if there can be no agreement about what is normal and essential in disputing. In fact, Donald Black suggests that the meaning of conflict (and perhaps, by implication, ADR) is only attainable through the establishment of a separate field of sociology. Black believes that

> [c]onflict . . . is ubiquitous. It is not merely crime and punishment. It is not merely disobedience, disagreement, or a demand for damages. It is not merely the topics covered in fields of social sciences such as criminology, the sociology of law, the anthropology of dispute settlement, conflict resolution, and mental health. It is vastly more. . . . The clash of right and wrong pervades the social universe and dominates history. Even so, conflict is commonly unseen and unrecognized, shrouded in darkness. It is often mistaken for something else, misclassified and misunderstood by experts who know little about it. Why? Conflict is not yet established as a separate field of sociology. Although pervasive, it is not recognized as a subject matter in its own right. . . . [I]f studied at all, it is typically by experts unschooled in its behavior and unfamiliar with the larger family to which it belongs.[6]

---

6   D. Black, *The Social Structure of Right and Wrong* (San Diego, CA: Academic Press, 1998) at xiii–xiv.

The concept of conflict offers another insight for alternative dispute resolution. Although the meaning of conflict may vary, the presence of conflict seems common and universal. However defined, conflict is an eternal feature of human existence. Scientists also confirm competitions and compromises in the natural worlds. There seems never to have been an era, a place, or a person immune from conflict. Whether it takes the form of a struggle, a journey, or other conceptualization, occurs within a single individual, between two or more persons, or involves entire countries, conflict has been and will continue to be an ever-present force in the history of the world.

ADR should not attempt to deny or deplore the existence of conflict. Conflict has value. Deutsch points out:

> It prevents stagnation, it stimulates interest and curiosity, it is the medium through which problems can be aired and solutions arrived at, it is the root of personal and social change. Conflict is often part of the process of testing and assessing oneself and, as such, may be highly enjoyable as one experiences the pleasure of the full and active use of one's capacities. In addition, conflict demarcates groups from one another and thus helps establish group and personal identities; external conflict often fosters internal cohesiveness.[7]

Coser adds to these benefits:[8]

> [C]onflict within a group frequently helps to revitalize existent norms; or it contributes to the emergence of new norms. In this sense, social conflict is a mechanism for adjustment of norms adequate to new conditions. A flexible society benefits from conflict because such behavior, by helping to create and modify norms, assures its continuance under changed conditions. Such a mechanism for readjustment of norms is hardly available to rigid systems: by suppressing conflict, the latter smother a useful warning signal, thereby maximizing the danger of catastrophic breakdown.
>
> Internal conflict can also serve as a means for ascertaining the relative strength of antagonistic interests within the structure, and in this way constitute a mechanism for the maintenance or continual readjustment of the balance of power. Since the outbreak of a conflict indicates a rejection of a previous accommodation between parties, once the respective power of the contenders has been ascertained through conflict, a new equilibrium can be established and the relationship can proceed on this new basis.

---

7   Above note 3 at 8–9.
8   L. Coser, *The Functions of Social Conflict* (Glencoe, IL: Free Press, 1956) at 154–55.

If conflict signals a need or desire for change, whether for good or bad, ADR draws our attention to the process and associated problems of that change. How does a conflict, wherever situated, get articulated? Are there barriers that prevent some conflicts from being raised, thereby blocking necessary change? Is the real conflict about whether change is necessary? Will the conflict and any change be constructive or destructive? What knowledge and skills on the part of disputants, their lawyers, and others contribute to progressive or regressive dispute processing? Is the personal, social, or political change signified by the conflict desirable? Avoiding the naivety of a conflict-free world, ADR benefits from recognizing the symbiotic and positive relationship between conflict and the process of social change as well as ADR's role in strengthening or weakening that relationship. Seeing conflict as anything less than it truly is, particularly as negative and undesirable, is limiting.

2) Dispute Prevention, Dispute Management, Dispute Resolution and Dispute Processing

In ADR, it is worth noting the distinctions between concepts of dispute prevention, dispute management, dispute resolution, and dispute processing. Some of these distinctions are fine and mostly indicate that disputes (or conflicts) are capable of being analyzed and acted upon at different times and for different purposes. However, some of the differences in these terms are more illustrative of a stark divide between the theoretical and practical ways that disputes can or should be analyzed and acted upon.

Dispute prevention involves analysis and planning initiatives that persons or organizations take to structure their activities to avoid or minimize the risk of disputes arising in the first place. Dispute prevention might take the following forms:

- *Legal audit* — a review of an organization's activities by a lawyer or other person to identify sources of potential or actual disputes and to restructure current activities to reduce or eliminate the risk of those disputes arising.

- *Negotiated rule making* — a wide variety of processes in which a rule maker, such as a government department, regulatory agency, or other body with rule-making power, incorporates input from those persons interested in, or affected by, a proposed rule or regulation into the substance of the new rule.

- *Partnering* — within a contractual relationship, partnering establishes a formal, mutually developed strategy of problem solving as the parties carry out the terms of the contract. The partnering process usually establishes a working relationship based on (1) commitment, (2) equity, (3) trust, (4) development of mutual goals and objectives, (5) implementation, (6) evaluation, and (7) timely responsiveness. The goal is a more harmonious contractual relationship.

Dispute management points to practices and strategies that are applied to disputes once they have arisen, often with a view to avoiding litigation or reducing the costs of any litigation. Dispute management would involve processes such as:

- *Convening* — when a dispute arises, the parties have agreed to meet to select, with the help of a neutral adviser, the dispute resolution process that will best suit the dispute at hand. Convening allows the parties flexibility to tailor their dispute resolution process to the particular circumstances.

- *Risk management analysis* — like a legal audit after a dispute has arisen, an analysis is undertaken to identify the cost and benefits associated with handling the dispute in different ways as well as potential cost savings. The analysis can also include complicated calculations of likely outcomes in various disputing scenarios.

- *Discovery control* — a process to organize the pre-trial or pre-settlement procedures that can occur in litigation with a view to keeping control over the expenses, time, and other costs that can arise when the parties resort to the courts to resolve disputes.

Dispute resolution is, at times, used interchangeably with ADR. Dispute resolution discourse tends to emphasize, not surprisingly, the resolution of disputes although, most often, better resolution than before. Both theoretical and practical discussions of dispute resolution tend to focus on discrete, often "new," dispute resolution mechanisms and their advantages and disadvantages. The central question becomes "what dispute resolution process or combination of processes is effective for resolving different types of disputes?" This question is often answered by placing dispute processing techniques into separate clusters, by cataloguing the essential elements of the techniques in each cluster, and then by matching a dispute to a dispute processing technique. Although dispute resolution thinking has expanded the traditional scope of issues and disputing processes that lawyers and others consider relevant, the term dispute resolution embraces an ideal of effective resolution: "that given the right match of dispute and dispute processing technique, harmony can be restored and problems can have resolutions that satisfy the disputants and are therefore likely to be final. . . . This emphasis on resolution suggests a preference for an image of social life in which harmony prevails; conflicts are idiosyncratic; and mediation, arbitration, adjudication and other dispute processing techniques work to resolve problems."[9] Dispute resolution can cast a linear shadow on disputes and dispute processing. There is a beginning, the dispute, and eventually an end, the resolution. Alternative dispute resolution, as the modern version of what is good, fast, inexpensive, or otherwise desirable in dispute resolution, can imply moving along and not off this line.

Dispute processing would inform ADR in sharply different ways. The sociology of disputing and dispute processing emphasizes greater indeterminacy, variability, and open-endedness than dispute resolution says is possible or desirable. The more mechanical matching process of dispute resolution is replaced by a focus on significant political and normative issues facing ADR such as the place of disputes and disputing in advancing desirable political changes, the difficulty of separating public and private spheres of disputing, and the problems associated with privileging an individualistic, voluntarist vision of social ordering. Dispute processing does not ignore the new formalism of dispute resolution but instead opens the field of inquiry to possibilities neglected by more essentialist understandings of ADR.

For example, consider how the following five propositions suggested by existing sociological work on dispute processing demonstrate the divide between concepts of processing and resolution:[10]

1. "The sources of disputes are as important as the disputes themselves."

   The source of the dispute is important to understand why so many grievances are never articulated as disputes. The problem is less one of resolving disputes than of designing processes that facilitate the emergence of disputes that are rarely articulated (e.g., sexual harassment). There is a need to overcome barriers to disputing.

2. "Disputes, even after they emerge and are articulated, are indeterminate. They do not exist in fixed form prior to the application of particular dispute processing techniques; they are instead constituted and transformed as they are processed."

---

9   A. Sarat, "The New Formalism in Disputing and Dispute Processing" (1987) 21 L. & Soc'y Rev. 695 at 698.

10   *Ibid.* at 708–11.

This viewpoint raises doubts about the search for a "match" between a fixed dispute and a fixed array of disputing processing techniques.

3.   "Dispute processing techniques are internally inconsistent and adaptive. They are transformed by and adapt to the problems that are brought to them."

Neither disputes nor dispute processing means the same thing in different places or at different times. Efforts to define the essential attributes of mediation or other dispute processing mechanism may be futile.

4.   "The boundaries between and differences among dispute processing techniques are shifting and often blurred."

Although the indeterminacy may be uncomfortable, neither disputes nor dispute processing exists as entities with positive content separate from the contexts and discursive practices through which they are constructed. The emphasis should be on more contingent concepts of dispute processing.

5.   "Disputes are more often processed than resolved, and in that processing, mediation, and arbitration as well as other so-called informal dispute processing techniques serve as important vehicles for maintaining the political status quo."

Where dispute resolution suggests finality, sociological research recognizes the open-textured nature of disputing. Dispute resolution's emphasis on finality is particularly troubling when considering whether or how dispute processing techniques serve social control purposes and inhibit political opposition by individualizing and privatizing grievances.

The gap between ideas of processing disputes and resolving disputes needs to be bridged. As the divide widens, there is a risk that ADR structures and procedures will come more and more to resemble, ironically, the more rigid and mechanical systems that they were designed to fix or replace.

3)   Destructive and Constructive Conflict[11]

Bitter enemies in the beginning now shake hands. Spouses who could not live together sign a comprehensive separation agreement. Business people and union leaders who traded harsh accusations on the picket line settle their differences. The survivor of childhood sexual abuse

---

11   These concepts come from Morton Deutsch, above note 3.

touches her father's hand for the first time in twenty years in a brief handshake as the mediated agreement is signed. Feuding neighbours suspend their hostilities.

The course that a conflict takes often involves both destructive and constructive features. On the one hand, talks have broken down or been suspended, the dispute has escalated, the parties are being unreasonable, dirty tricks are being used, violence flares, and so on. On the other hand, progress is being made, lines of communication have been opened, trust has been restored, the talks have been productive, peace appears within reach.

These and other expressions are used to describe conflict when it is either destructive or constructive. In studying and practising alternative dispute resolution, it is useful to be able to distinguish between destructive and constructive conflict. What are the typical features of destructive and constructive conflicts? What factors contribute to more constructive dispute resolution practices? Can ADR promote constructive rather than destructive conflict?

Destructive conflict is characterized by its tendency to expand and escalate. Expansion can occur in the number and size of the immediate issues; the number of parties; the number and size of principles and precedents seen to be at stake; the costs; the exemption from norms of acceptable behaviour; the intensity of negative attitudes towards the other side. Conflicts escalate as there is increasing reliance on a strategy of power; greater use of threats, coercion, and deception; and shifts away from conciliation, mutual understanding, and goodwill.

As a result of this expansion and escalation, destructive conflict often becomes independent of its beginning causes. What caused the conflict in the first instance either is forgotten or becomes insignificant compared with new developments.

The tendency of the conflict to expand and escalate may be due, in part, to perceptions by the participants that their goals are negatively correlated. In other words, what one party wins, another must lose. The conflict and its resolution therefore become a competitive process. As the conflict expands and escalates, destructive effects tend to be produced, such as:

- Communication between the parties becomes unreliable and impoverished.
- A solution appears possible only if it is imposed by one side or the other by means of a superior force, deception, or cleverness.
- Suspicious, hostile attitudes develop that accentuate differences and minimize similarities.
- Misjudgment and misperception increase.

- Justification is given (for cognitive and social consistency) for behaviour that would otherwise be considered outrageous.

Constructive conflict, on the other hand, would be similar to the processes involved in creative thinking. Accordingly, the presence of elements such as the following could lead to constructive conflict: (1) sufficient motivation or commitment to solve the problem; (2) the establishment of conditions that allow the problem to be reformulated or viewed from different perspectives if customary processes fail to solve the problem; and (3) the availability of diverse ideas than can lead to new and creative solutions.

For the emergence of constructive conflict, participants would not view their goals as negatively correlated. Participants would see their goals being achieved if, and only if, others attained their goals. The conflict would be viewed as a common problem in which the conflicting parties have the joint interest of reaching a mutually satisfactory solution. This cooperative process would lead to

- open and honest communication of relevant information among the participants;
- the recognition of the legitimacy of the other's interests and the necessity to look for a solution that is responsive to the needs of each side; and
- a trusting, friendly attitude that increases sensitivity to similarities and common ground.

Ultimately, the distinctions between destructive and constructive conflicts are found in both process — the course the conflict takes — and outcome — the level of participant satisfaction-dissatisfaction or perception of gains and losses.

The concepts of destructive and constructive conflict are important in the study of ADR. If conflict can advance desirable changes in society, both of an individual and systemic nature, these changes seem more likely to occur with constructive conflict and less likely to occur with destructive conflict. A challenge for ADR is to identify what disputants, lawyers, or others need to know or be able to do to foster constructive conflict characteristics and practices. ADR's emphasis on collaborative approaches to problem solving, keeping cases out of court, interest-based bargaining, and broader transformative goals has been a clear illustration of a preference for constructive conflict. Interestingly, Morton Deutsch concluded that whether conflict would be destructive or constructive rested on a simple concept: "The characteristic processes and effects elicited by a given type of social relationship tend also to elicit that type of social relationship." In other words, "cooperation breeds cooperation while competition breeds competition."[12] Thus,

> a conflict orientation that highlights mutual interests, seeks the enhancement of mutual power, and defines the conflict as a mutual problem is more likely to take a constructive course than an orientation that emphasizes antagonistic interests, seeks to maximize power differences, and defines the conflict in win-lose terms. Similarly, a trusting, friendly orientation to the other, with a positive interest in the other's welfare and readiness to respond helpfully to the other's needs and requests, is less likely to lead to a destructive conflict than a suspicious, hostile attitude, with a readiness to exploit the other's needs and weaknesses and a negative responsiveness to the other's requests. A perceived similarity in beliefs and values, a sense of common bonds and interests between oneself and the other, is more likely to produce a constructive conflict than a sense of opposed beliefs and values. Full, open, honest communication free of malevolent distortion, which is persuasive rather than coercive in form and intent, is less likely to lead to destructive conflict than blocked, misleading, or autistic communication.[13]

4) A General Glossary of ADR Terms

Although correctly categorizing a conflict as destructive or committing to convening are examples of competent ADR talk, a brief description or definition of several additional ADR words in common use is included here. Many of these words — dealt with in detail later in this book — focus on a process side of ADR: the types of dispute resolution processes, details about these processes, and other related matters. Understanding these words should help both comprehension of, and participation in, ADR-related discussions. The words also begin to say something about the ideology of ADR.

Adjudication: Any dispute resolution process in which a neutral third party hears each party's evidence and arguments and renders a decision that is binding on them. This decision is usually based on objective standards. The term adjudication includes arbitration and litigation.

Advisory opinion: A dispute resolution process where a mutually acceptable neutral third party, after reviewing each party's case, offers

---

12   *Ibid.* at 367.
13   *Ibid.* at 368.

an objective assessment of each side's strengths as well as an opinion regarding the outcome of the case should it proceed to trial. The advisory opinion is designed to encourage settlement.

Arbitration: A dispute resolution process where, in an informal hearing, a mutually acceptable neutral third party hears evidence and oral arguments and renders a decision based on the merits thereof. The process can be either voluntary, where the parties choose to submit their dispute to arbitration, or compulsory, where a contract, court, or statute requires the submission. The decision reached by the arbitrator can be either **binding** or **non-binding**. Where the arbitration is mandated by the court, or where court approval is required in the appointment of the arbitrator, the process is referred to as **court-annexed**; in other cases it is referred to as **private** arbitration.

Avoidance: A form of dispute resolution in which an aggrieved party forgoes his or her rights and seeks no remedy, thus putting an end to the dispute.

Circle sentencing: A reconfiguration of what usually takes place in the sentencing of an accused person convicted of a crime. Although the usual format is itself changing, normally the responsibility for imposing a penalty rests with a judge or jury in a formal justice system after hearing legal submissions. Circle sentencing involves changes in how and what submissions are made. The submissions are made by a circle of people with certain connections to the case. It can be thought that circle sentencing should generally be used in cases involving Aboriginal people since the process is said to be modelled on Aboriginal practices. The actual connection between circle sentencing and Aboriginal justice can vary considerably from one place to another.

Conciliation: A form of dispute resolution wherein a neutral third party serves as an intermediary or messenger between disputing parties who are unwilling to meet. This term is often used interchangeably with mediation. The process can also be court-connected.

Confidential listening: A dispute resolution process wherein both parties give confidential settlement positions to a mutually acceptable neutral third party for consideration. After reviewing these positions, the third party advises the disputants whether a negotiable range of settlement exists. Should the parties so desire, it can be decided in advance that the midpoint of a certain range that is revealed will be the point of settlement.

Conflict management: An approach to conflict whereby parties can develop protocols or arrangements for preventing disputes from occurring and pre-determining the range of appropriate responses to conflict should one arise.

Consensual processes (also consensus making or consensual resolution): All dispute resolution processes in which the disputing parties must reach agreement for the issues to be resolved. Consensual processes include negotiation, mediation, conciliation, and therapeutic intervention and are distinct from processes such as litigation and arbitration in which a third party can impose a solution without the parties' agreement.

Court-annexed mediation: This form of mediation exists where mediation services are incorporated into the court process and may either be ordered by the court or voluntarily agreed to by the parties. The parties maintain their rights to proceed to trial if mediation fails. Any settlement that is reached may become a judgment of the court. The term is often used interchangeably with court-annexed conciliation.

Court-connected ADR processes: Any process wherein parties to a court proceeding submit part or all of their dispute to an ADR proceeding prior, during, or after a trial has begun. Court-connected ADR processes come in many forms.

Diversion: Diversion is the practice of removing certain types of criminal cases from the ordinary criminal justice system, and utilizing alternate mechanisms of prosecution and sentencing. Many forms of diversion utilize mediation and negotiation.

Early neutral evaluation: A non-binding process, typically required under the relevant rules of court, wherein the parties and their counsel meet shortly after the initiation of a court proceeding and confidentially present the factual and legal bases of their cases to each other and a third-party lawyer experienced in the substantive area. The third party identifies issues, assesses the strengths of the cases, structures a plan for the progress of the case, and if requested by the parties, may encourage settlement.

Hybrid processes: Hybrid ADR processes combine various elements of negotiation, adjudication, and mediation to form a unique method of dispute resolution. Examples are mediation-arbitration, ombudsman, the mini-trial, summary jury trial, rent-a-judge, and neutral expert fact-finding.

Institutionalization: The process through which ADR principles and processes are integrated into the central systems of society — including the justice, corporate, and government systems. Examples include the incorporation of ADR processes into Rules of Court, legislation that mentions or mandates ADR, and corporate management practices.

Interest-based bargaining: An approach to negotiation that is characterized by a focus on underlying interests rather than positions. An interest is a need, desire, concern, want, or fear that motivates behaviour in negotiation. A position is a desired outcome in the negotiation. Behind every position taken in negotiation will be stated or underlying interests. Focusing on interests can open up opportunities for creative solutions.

Judicial dispute resolution: An expression, sometimes called judicially assisted dispute resolution (JADR) that refers to in-court methods of resolving differences where judges play key roles. Examples of JDR include judge-assisted mediations, pre-trial and settlement conferences, mini-trials, and case flow management projects.

Mandatory court-annexed arbitration: A process whereby parties to litigation are required to present their cases before a court-appointed arbitrator, usually a retired judge or senior lawyer, in an informal meeting. The arbitrator renders a non-binding decision that will be entered as a judgment of the court if not disputed by any party. If the award is not accepted, the parties retain their rights to proceed to a traditional trial without reference to the arbitrator's decision, although a party rejecting that decision and requiring a trial will typically be subject to cost penalty if a more favourable decision is not obtained.

Mediation: A process in which a neutral third party, who has no decision-making power, uses various procedures, techniques, and skills to assist disputing parties to resolve their dispute by a mutually acceptable agreement. The process can involve legal counsel. As in arbitration, the process can be court-annexed. In addition, the process can be either closed, where all discussions are confidential and the mediator cannot be a compellable witness in any future proceeding, or open, where the mediator can be a compellable witness or where she or he must file a report with the court or other body that ordered the mediation. A variation on mediation is therapeutic intervention, where not only is the dispute solved, but the parties' relationship is repaired and their conflict-solving abilities are improved.

Negotiation: Any discussions or dealings wherein parties with opposing interests seek to establish areas of agreement, settlement, or compromise so as to manage and ultimately resolve their dispute. This does not include methods of resolution that entail arbitration or any judicial process. Negotiations can be principled. This occurs when the parties, rather than focusing on their "positions," deal with the underlying issues, seek to appreciate the needs of the other party, and try to achieve an agreement based on objective standards.

Ombudsperson: An independent person who deals with citizens' complaints against perceived administrative, governmental, or organizational injustice. This person has the power to investigate and publicize the complaint as well as mediate, make recommendations, and, in some limited instances, award compensation.

Pre-trial conference: An informal dialogue between a judge and counsel, or the parties themselves, directed to encouraging settlement, focusing the issues for trial, obtaining agreements as to evidence, refining the cases to be presented at trial, and providing a non-binding assessment of the dispute by a judge. The issues that a particular conference focuses on vary between systems and judges. The parties to the dispute can be encouraged or mandated to attend these meetings.

Preventative dispute resolution: Any actions taken by parties either to assist in preventing disputes from arising or to manage disputes to avoid unnecessary costs and delays.

Private courts: Retired judges and senior lawyers can provide, for a fee, a range of dispute resolution services outside of the publicly funded court system. The services can include full adjudicative hearings as well as mediation or other ADR procedures. Early private courts were referred to as **rent-a-judge** schemes.

Restorative justice: Restorative justice would create a new goal or principle for the criminal justice system. Instead of pursuing a punishment-oriented agenda on crime, restorative justice would emphasize reconciliation for both the perpetrators and victims of crime. Healing would be added to the pre-existing goal of rehabilitation within the criminal justice system. Restorative justice can be related to ideas of reconciliation and can be thought to have some genesis in Aboriginal justice systems or the values of various faith communities.

Summary judgment: A formal pre-trial procedure by which parties to litigation may apply to a judge to obtain a full or partial judgment. This is usually done in cases where there are few facts in dispute and the area of disagreement is a question of law or where the discord pertains to the application of law to the facts.

Summary jury trial: A pre-trial procedure in which disputing parties' cases are presented to a mock jury, the members of which are chosen by the court from the jury list. The mock jury hears the evidence and arguments and then returns a verdict. Although the verdict is not binding, the members of the jury are not informed of this until after the verdict has been rendered. The procedure generally takes place late in the litigation process, when negotiations have come to a halt, and is meant to indicate to the parties the likely decision of a real jury so as to assist them in reaching a settlement without having to go to trial. Counsel may review the case with the jury after the verdict.

Transformative justice: An approach to justice that calls for the restoration or repair of relationships in both civil and criminal matters to be the guiding goal.

C. ADVERSARIAL AND NON-ADVERSARIAL THINKING

The distinction between adversarial and non-adversarial thinking is an important one to make in developing an understanding of ADR's meaning and in identifying ADR skills.

Before examining the adversarial/non-adversarial mindset, one must recognize that the line between these two ways of thinking does not necessarily represent, as one might think, a fine distinction between traditional systems of dispute resolution, such as the courts, and alternative dispute resolution, such as mediation. There does not exist a consensus that ADR inculcates a truly non-adversarial approach to dispute resolution, particularly if ADR is broadly defined or if it is practised adversarially. In addition, the North American legal system, in which over 90 percent of all cases are settled out of court, is not in all cases truly adversarial. However, the line between adversarial and non-adversarial approaches to dispute resolution is important to draw because these different ways of thinking can influence how ADR is understood and practised.

1) The Adversarial Mindset

An adversary can be defined as an opponent, an antagonist, or an enemy. Applying this definition to a dispute setting, having an adversarial mindset implies perceiving other parties as enemies who have opposing positions that must be overcome. Thinking adversarially about a dispute can mean conceiving of the dispute as a battle that must be won through triumph over the other parties involved.

Thinking adversarially brings to mind the traditional system of litigation that exists in North America. In fact, adversarialism is so prevalent in our system of settling disputes in court that it is called an "adversary system." The following quote from a judge in a court case highlights key features of this system, which can reflect and reinforce a highly adversarial approach to dispute resolution.

> Our mode of trial procedure is based upon the adversary system in which the contestants seek to establish through relevant supporting evidence, before an impartial trier of facts, those events or happenings which form the bases of their allegations. This procedure assumes that litigants, assisted by their counsel, will fully and diligently present all of the material facts which have evidentiary value in support of their perspective positions and that these disputed facts will receive from a trial judge a dispassionate and impartial consideration in order to arrive at the truth of the matters in controversy. A trial is not intended to be a scientific exploration with the presiding judge assuming the role of research director; it is a forum established for the purpose of providing justice for the litigants.[14]

Lawyers play key roles in the adversary system of justice. It is useful to consider the lawyer's mindset about disputing. How exactly do lawyers think?

Law schools generally receive credit for teaching the lawyer's thought processes although learning to think like a lawyer continues in bar admission programs, continuing legal education courses, and law practice itself. Even with their educational mandate, law schools, like the lawyers they educate, have not been immune from criticism. There have been stinging critiques of what is, and is not, taught in law school and of how these legal subjects should be taught. As a result there have been many subject matter and pedagogical reforms that influence how today's lawyers think.

Despite curricular changes, there appears to be one common, dominant, and enduring feature of Western legal education. In a lawyer's education, what fundamentally informs the process of learning "to think like a lawyer" is, in fact, the adversary system. Whether it is through mooting programs; through specific courses such as advocacy, evidence, civil procedure, and the like; through the inherent message in learning the law by studying previously decided court cases (the case method);

---

14 *Phillips v. Ford Motor Co.* (1971), 18 D.L.R. (3d) 641 at 661 (Ont. C.A.).

or through the typical law school exam, the adversary system is the omnipresent influence on the way lawyers are trained to think about disputes. This influence is both structural and cultural.

Structurally, "thinking like a lawyer" in an adversary system means accepting that party autonomy and partisan representation are the twin pillars of legal disputing, both inside and outside court.

Party autonomy means that the parties to a dispute are independent and have the responsibility for defining the problem and putting forward their case. In practice, parties often delegate this responsibility in large measure to their lawyers. This structure emphasizes and often exacerbates the separation and distance between the parties. The judge's role is limited to deciding issues that have been presented to her or him.

Partisan representation means that lawyers act as advocates for one party or the other in the dispute. There can be no conflicts of interest. The lawyer's ethical duty, according to modern Codes of Professional Conduct, is "fearlessly to raise every issue, advance every argument, and ask every question however distasteful, which the lawyer thinks will help the client's case" and "to endeavour to obtain for a client the benefit of any and every remedy and defence which is authorized by law."[15]

Culturally, "thinking like a lawyer" in an adversary system means accepting as common sense that disputes and their resolution occur in an adversarial context. There is more to this idea than stating the obvious or following the adversary system's structure to its logical conclusion. Accepting without question that disputants are adversaries and opponents, in competition, and are trying to win or outmanoeuvre the other side is part of legal culture with its origins in Anglo-Saxon law. Lord Brougham's classic formulation in 1820 reflects a long-standing way of thinking within the legal profession.

> An advocate, by the sacred duty which he owes his client, knows in the discharge of that office but one person in the world, that client and none other. To save that client by all expedient means, to protect that client at all hazards and costs, to all others, and among others to himself, is the highest and most unquestioned of his duties; and he must not regard the alarm, the suffering, the torment, the destruction which he may bring upon any other. Nay, separating even the duties

---

15   See Canadian Bar Association, *Code of Professional Conduct*, c. ix, "The Lawyer as Advocate." Lawyers also have ethical duties to promote the interests of the state, serve the cause of justice, maintain the authority and dignity of the courts, be candid and courteous in relations with other lawyers, and demonstrate personal integrity. The duty to a client cannot be exercised in such a way as to violate these other responsibilities.

of a patriot from those of an advocate, and casting them, if need be, to the wind, he must go on reckless on the consequences, if his fate it should unhappily be to involve his country in confusion for his client's protection.[16]

For lawyers and the disputants themselves, there are benefits associated with the use of an adversarial system and the deployment of an adversarial mindset in resolving disputes. The main advantages usually attributed to the adversary system are as follows:

- **The adversary system increases the accuracy of fact-finding.** The adversary system promotes more accurate factual discovery about past events. The interested parties have the opportunity to present full evidence and arguments to a trier of fact who withholds judgment until all the proof has been elicited.
- **The adversary system best protects individual rights.** The adversarial approach to settling disputes facilitates the ability of every individual to assert, and have protected, their individual rights and freedoms.
- **The adversary system removes power differentials.** The use of partisan representation ensures that power differentials between the disputants will be removed because the parties have skilled representatives who can best argue their case for them.
- **The adversary system is cathartic.** The adversary system satisfies the psychology of the disputants by legitimizing a courtroom duel as a substitute for more direct forms of hostility. Reflecting its ancestry in blood feud, trial by battle or ordeal, the modern adversary system is now civilized and satisfying.
- **The adversary system is an integral part of the rule of law in a democratic society.** The adversary system is consistent with, and reinforces, prevailing social and political ideologies of Western society. The system best reflects notions of individualism that stress the autonomy and rights of every individual to be free and to protect their rights and interests to the fullest extent and to have decisions made according to the "rule of law."

The strength of these benefits depends on a critical assumption — that these advantages are generally realizable in the day-to-day operation of an adversary system. This assumption is increasingly coming under attack.

---

16   For the historical context of Lord Brougham's statement as counsel for Queen Caroline in her trial before the House of Lords, see D.L. Rhode, "An Adversarial Exchange on Adversarial Ethics: Text, Subtext and Context" (1991) 41 J. Legal Educ. 29.

Complaints about unacceptable delays in getting disputes to court, high legal costs, procedural and substantive complexities in the justice system, bias in laws and judicial decision making and other access to justice issues suggest the adversary system is flawed. Indeed, as discussed, interest in alternative dispute resolution was in large part a response to concerns about the effective functioning of the traditional adversary system.

However, it is not clear if the adversary system *per se* is to blame. The Canadian Bar Association Task Force Report on Systems of Civil Justice[17] discovered that "many Canadians feel that they cannot exercise their rights effectively because using the civil justice system takes too long, is too expensive, or is too difficult to understand." Nevertheless, the Task Force concluded that "the adversarial approach is central to the civil justice system, and should remain a key feature in the future" with the caveat that "a preoccupation with gaining advantage through an adversarial approach too often has the result of displacing substantive communication, common sense and a problem-solving orientation, all of which assist in resolving disputes."[18]

Other critiques, however, directly challenge the worth of the adversary system and its adversarial way of thinking about dispute resolution. At the philosophical or moral level, there is the argument that an adversarial mindset and system of dispute resolution encourage certain beliefs and attitudes that not only obstruct the fair and effective resolution of disputes but which also are socially undesirable. Competitive aggression is encouraged over reciprocity and empathy; hostility trumps trust; selfishness supplants generosity; antipathy replaces care. At the extreme, there are tragic examples where the adversarial way of thinking about dispute resolution nurtures disrespect, disregard, violence, and even death.

The adversarial way of thinking about disputes also has attracted criticism from a procedural perspective. For the adversary system to function, disputes must fit or be made to fit into this system. At times this match between dispute and disputing system is made whether or not the context in which the dispute arose, the needs of the disputants, or other factors suggest that the relationship between the particular dispute and the adversary system will be an unhappy one.

To make this match, typically lawyers representing the disputants will transform what their clients have told them about a dispute into the proper shape — a shape that other lawyers and judges immediately

---

17   Canadian Bar Association Task Force on Systems of Civil Justice, *Report of the Task Force on Systems of Civil Justice* (Ottawa: Canadian Bar Association, 1996).
18   *Ibid.* at 18.

will recognize. The reconstructed dispute most likely will resemble, in format and language, the highly structured proofs and arguments that are required by the rules and procedures for the adversary system's ultimate decision maker: the judge in court. Although the process of dispute transformation may vary, a lawyer typically will (a) analyze the facts, (b) identify the legal issues, (c) find the relevant case or statute law, (d) analyze the law and apply it to the facts, (e) consider how a court might decide the legal issues and in whose favour, and (f) advise the client on their legal rights. The order might vary from one lawyer to another. What a client then decides or is advised to do with respect to a dispute is inexorably influenced by how the lawyer has constructed the case to be in accord with the structure and culture of the adversary system. The family case that might be settled tomorrow goes to trial and gets a different result because of what the lawyer and client said about the other spouse in the petition for divorce.

Carrie Menkel-Meadow describes this process of the transformation of disputes by the adversarial system:

> [T]he grievant tells a story of felt or perceived wrong to a third party (the lawyer) and the lawyer transforms the dispute by imposing "categories" on "events and relationships" which re-define the subject matter of a dispute in ways "which make it amenable to conventional management procedures." This process of "narrowing" disputes occurs at various stages in lawyer-client interactions.[19]

While the adversarial way of thinking about disputes and the ensuing benefits cannot and should not be completely discounted, the adversarial mindset can present numerous obstacles for effective dispute resolution. Thinking adversarially about disputes can

- increase contentiousness and aggravate conflicts to dangerous extremes;
- drive parties further apart and harm continuing relationships;
- narrow the focus of disputes with complicated contextual features and even miss what is really at issue;
- lead to polarized, prolonged, and expensive problem solving;
- routinize demands;
- be a disincentive to airing disputes;
- lead to a reliance on outside professionals;

---

19   C. Menkel-Meadow, "The Transformation of Disputes by Lawyers: What the Dispute Paradigm Does and Does Not Tell Us" [1985] Mo. J. Disp. Resol. 25 at 31. See also W.F. Felstiner, R.L. Abel, & A. Sarat, "The Emergence and Transformation of Disputes: Naming, Blaming, Claiming" (1980–81) 15 L. & Soc'y Rev. 631.

- ignore possible solutions;
- make resources outside the law appear irrelevant to dispute resolution; and
- promote destructive conflict.

The relationship between ADR and adversarial thinking will be interesting to follow. On the one hand, the enthusiastic embrace of ADR by the legal profession has in some ways tempered the harsh tones that are often heard emanating from an adversary system. As more and more lawyers, judges, law students, and the many others associated with dispute resolution become mediators, learn negotiation and consensus-building skills, implement new and improved cost- and time-saving measures for disputing, consider how people can avoid destructive conflicts, and hope for societal transformations in disputing practices, the impact on a preoccupation with the adversarial approach is felt. On the other hand, as those parts of ADR that are the antithesis of adversarial thinking come face to face with the strengths of the adversary system, it is not always the adversarial nature that will yield. In a highly competitive, adversarial North American society, the eventual thinking about ADR or dispute resolution may be more adversarial than not. Jerold Auerbach notes:

> It is chimerical to believe that mediation or arbitration can now accomplish what law seems powerless to achieve. The American deification of individual rights requires an accessible legal system for their protection. Understandably, diminished faith in its capacities will encourage the yearning for alternatives. But the rhetoric of "community" and "justice" should not be permitted to conceal the deterioration of community life and the unraveling of substantive notions of justice that has accompanied its demise. There is every reason why the values that historically are associated with informal justice should remain compelling: especially the preference for trust, harmony, and reciprocity within a communal setting. These are not, however, the values that American society encourages or sustains; in their absence there is no effective alternative to legal institutions.
>
> The quest for community may indeed be "timeless and universal." In this century, however, the communitarian search for justice without law has deteriorated beyond recognition into a stunted offshoot of the legal system. The historical progression is clear: from community justice without formal legal institutions to the rule of law, all too often without justice. But injustice without law is an even worse possibility, which misguided enthusiasm for alternative dispute settlement now seems likely to encourage. Our legal culture too

accurately expresses the individualistic and materialistic values that most Americans deeply cherish to inspire optimism about the imminent restoration of communitarian purpose. For law to be less conspicuous Americans would have to moderate their expansive freedom to compete, to acquire, and to possess, while simultaneously elevating shared responsibilities above individual rights. That is an unlikely prospect unless Americans become, in effect, un-American. Until then, the pursuit of justice without law does incalculable harm to the prospect of equal justice.[20]

2) The Non-adversarial Mindset

Although the meaning of adversarial thinking is relatively easy to understand, the concept of the non-adversarial mindset is more difficult to explain. There does not exist a single definition of what it means to behave in a non-adversarial manner nor is there any consensus about whether it is even possible to neatly differentiate between adversarial and non-adversarial thinking in dispute resolution. However, there are indicators that suggest adversarial thinking is not always present in dispute resolution, and there may be significant advantages in thinking about dispute resolution from a non-adversarial point of view.

One way to distinguish non-adversarial thinking from adversarial thinking is to recognize that differing values underpin each approach. If the adversarial mindset predominantly reflects values of *individualism*, non-adversarial thinking about dispute resolution would emphasize *communitarian* values. In a conflict situation, the protection and preservation of one's individual rights would not be of sole or perhaps even primary importance to a non-adversarial thinker. A more contextualized approach to individual rights would be taken that infuses dispute resolution with what it means to be fully human. Carrie Menkel-Meadow describes what this approach would look like for lawyers:

> [L]awyers need to learn to experience "the other" from the values that the other holds, not those of the lawyer — this is the challenge of most lawyer-client relations and lawyer-opposing side relations. While I and others have called this an "ethic of care" in other contexts, what I mean is a willingness to truly apprehend the reality of the other (be it client or administrative bureaucrat or opposing counsel); not just to understand instrumentally how to move, persuade or

---

20   J.S. Auerbach, *Justice without Law?* (New York: Oxford University Press, 1983) at 145–46.

affect that person, but to understand what meaning the interaction had for that person in a caring and existential sense.[21]

and further:

> An ethic of care in law could mean a number of concrete things. It might mean involving all the parties to a dispute, rather than only formally plaintiffs, defendants and interveners. It would invoke client participation in decision-making. It might alter some of the professional ethics prescriptions under which lawyers currently operate that preclude them from "caring" for the other side or other side's lawyer. It might alter behaviors within the conventional adversary system to include more trust and altruism and less unnecessary aggressive behavior.[22]

Non-adversarial thinking would not mean simply bridling zealous advocacy, quantitatively reducing the degree of aggression, or avoiding a preoccupation with gaining advantage through an adversarial approach. Non-adversarial thinking would mean morally responsive advocates who would go beyond the duty to their clients and abstract notions of justice to arrive at a more contextually oriented outcome. The adversary system would shift to "a more cooperative, less war-like system."[23]

In a related way, the non-adversarial mindset in dispute resolution also can be thought of in terms of the behaviour that this type of thinking generates. Whereas competing and winning may be identifiable traits in an adversarial approach to dispute resolution, problem-solving behaviours will chiefly characterize a non-adversarial approach to disputing. The behaviours of problem solving will be many and varied. But, essentially, the notion of problem solving encourages disputants and their lawyers to view the dispute as a mutual problem and to take a collaborative approach to the process of resolution. Rather than a clash

---

21   C. Menkel-Meadow, "Narrowing the Gap by Narrowing the Field: What's Missing from the MacCrate Report — Of Skills, Legal Science and Being a Human Being" (1994) 69 Wash. L. Rev. 593 at 616–17.

22   C. Menkel-Meadow, "Exploring a Research Agenda of the Feminization of the Legal Profession: Theories of Gender and Social Change (1989) 14 L. & Soc. Inquiry 289 at 316.

23   C. Menkel-Meadow, "Portia in a Different Voice: Speculations on a Woman's Lawyering Process" (1985) 1 Berkeley Women's L.J. 39 at 54. For an excellent discussion of whether the "ethic of care" might be female gender-specific, found in different cultural or minority groups within society, or part of the debilitating effects of sexist socialization, see C. Hotel & J. Brockman, "The Conciliatory-Adversarial Continuum in Law Practice" (1994) 12 Can. J. Fam. L. 11.

of conflicting demands, an exchange of threats and counterthreats, a contest of wills and resources, lawyers and disputants as problem solvers would find themselves working to find solutions that would be mutually satisfactory or win-win.

Engaging in dispute resolution in a manner that emphasizes communitarian values and that demonstrates problem-solving behaviour does not mean abandoning fairness, effectiveness, or efficiency in dispute resolution. Nor does it mean that lawyers will not be representatives who speak for their clients. In fact, taking a non-adversarial approach to dispute resolution can avoid the very problems of unfairness, ineffectiveness, and inefficiency that have plagued the adversary system. What is being worked on is a mutual problem — a problem being viewed from all sides to arrive at a win-win solution.

Consider how a non-adversarial mindset might work in a practical example of a dispute between a homeowner and a contractor. The homeowner is upset and dissatisfied with the quality and timeliness of the contractor's renovations. Much more money than expected is being demanded, and the work is not completed. The parties have hired lawyers.

Thinking adversarially, it would not be unusual for a lawyer to see the details of this dispute as involving, for instance, issues about breach of contract and questions of available remedies. Whether the contractor had breached the contract and, if so, what could be done, would depend on legal sub-issues such as the existence of conditions or warranties, express or implied; the application of the parol evidence rule (can a written contract be altered by unwritten agreements); the availability of specific performance; the assessment of quantum of damages. The lawyer also would consider procedural legal issues such as which court has jurisdiction, what is the appropriate venue, would any judgment be enforceable and the like. If the homeowner and contractor go to court, these issues would be reflected in "the pleadings," the written documents that form the basis of the court case. Even if the homeowner and contractor resolve their differences without going to court, which would be normal, hard bargaining would still be done in the shadow of the law created by the lawyers and the adversary system.

Non-adversarial thinking would not make this dispute go away, change the facts, or reduce the intensity of the feelings being experienced by the disputants. But non-adversarial thinking would move this dispute in different directions. The complete contextual picture of this dispute and its potential solutions would not be blurred by any unnecessary reliance on legal categories. Although non-adversarial thinking would not ignore legal rights and the relevance of courts to make authoritative pronouncements about these rights, consider how an ethic of care and a focus on mutual problem solving might be important to these further facts about the homeowner and contractor dispute and its resolution.

- The disputants live in a small town and see each other regularly on social occasions.
- The homeowner is a young, sole-support parent, living on a very modest income. The contractor is nearing retirement age and is a wealthy and experienced businessperson.
- The disputants had a "public" shouting match in front of several community members which "really embarrassed" the contractor.
- The homeowner is a relatively unassertive person when it comes to standing up for her rights; the contractor is a real competitor and lives to "win."
- Reputation is very important to the contractor; the homeowner feels the contractor tried to take advantage of her because she is a woman.
- The contractor is president of the local homebuilders' association whose members have been lobbying government to "toughen" the laws respecting delinquent debtors.
- The homeowner is a member of a visible minority and recently arrived in the country; the contractor is a long-time resident of European descent.

Thinking non-adversarially about these facts and the problem might mean that the continuing relationship between the homeowner and contractor and their respective reputations would be as important as, if not more important than, the money. Power disparities, if they existed, would not be exploited by disputants who viewed themselves as part of the same community. Differences in age, gender, social status, and cultural heritage would be respected and understood in a disputing process that was dominated by non-adversarial thinking. With adversarial thinking, it could be different.

The influence of non-adversarial thinking on ADR will depend on the evolving and interrelated meanings of both expressions. Can ADR, with its non-court roots, continue to accommodate a type of thinking that could be costly? Is the ethic of care the way to go? The fit between the two will likely depend on the size of the incongruities. For example, the legal profession in North America has gone from mediation opponent to mediation advocate in a decade or so. The general acceptance of ADR by lawyers has depended on the ease with which alternative dispute resolution is understood and practised by the legal community and the manner in which ADR affects or seeks to affect significant legal change. Despite major ADR advances, at the moment the ethic of care has clearly not displaced the more traditional adversarial mindset within the legal profession. Even when lawyers are encouraged by other lawyers to see problem solving as their primary role, a shift away from adversarialism may not be regarded as part of the ADR package. Lawyers and other persons or professionals working with disputes and disputants likely will fully embrace non-adversarial thinking as a concomitant component of ADR only when an ethic of care is congruent with their or their profession's disputing outlook.

D. THE ANALYSIS OF CONFLICTS AND DISPUTES

In medicine, the road to wellness often begins with an accurate diagnosis of the patient's problem. If the complaint or condition is inaccurately or incompletely diagnosed, any treatment is likely to be ineffective. A misdiagnosis may make matters much worse. The same can be said about alternative dispute resolution. Good dispute resolvers or "healers of human conflict"[24] need to know a great deal about the disputing condition before attempting a diagnosis or calling upon the range of available resources that might be best suited for that particular problem. The study of ADR has drawn attention to several diagnostic or analytical tools that can reveal critical information and insights about the dispute and what to do about it. Rather than being surprised at a disputant's intransigence, annoyed when an offer to settle is soundly rejected, frustrated that hours of bargaining have produced no results, or disappointed when an unsatisfactory agreement is reached on the courthouse steps, the careful analysis of disputes can lead to healthier results.

1) The Cause of Conflict

A conflict exists "whenever incompatible activities occur . . . An action that is incompatible with another action prevents, obstructs, interferes, injures, or in some way makes the latter less likely or less effective."[25]

---

24   W. Burger, former chief justice of the United States Supreme Court, in "Isn't There a Better Way?" (1982) 68 A.B.A. J. 274, referred to the legal profession's historical and traditional obligation of being "healers of human conflict" when dealing with disputes.

25   Above note 3 at 10.

Although conflict may be easy to recognize, it is not always clear what is causing the problem. What is it that is incompatible? Why are reasonable offers rejected? What blocked the agreement? Why are the parents fighting over the custody of the children? Why are lawyers unable to settle a certain personal injury case? Why are the owners and the players in a professional sport disagreeing? Why are protesters defying a court injunction and blockading a logging road? Why are constitutional talks so difficult? Why does a truce seem impossible? What is actually at the centre of the conflict?

The cause of conflict is an important concept for alternative dispute resolution. If the root cause of the conflict is misunderstood, or even missed, by either the parties or their lawyers, it is unlikely the conflict will be easily, satisfactorily, or constructively resolved. By focusing on the cause, not the symptoms of conflict, ADR may assist the parties, their lawyers or others to

- better understand what is really underlying the conflict;
- bring forward all the issues that are at stake;
- identify effective interventions;
- craft solutions suited to the real problem;
- promote constructive conflicts; and
- recognize that some conflicts are difficult to resolve by the parties themselves.

Christopher Moore identifies five kinds of conflict.[26] These categories are not necessarily exhaustive. However, they do provide a helpful framework for unravelling the contextual complexity of a given conflict in a manner different from traditional legal analysis.

1. Data

- Data refer to facts, information, knowledge.
- Data conflicts are caused by
  - lack of data or incomplete data;
  - misinformation or inaccurate information;
  - different views on what is relevant;
  - different assessments of data; or
  - different legal analyses.

---

26   C.W. Moore, *The Mediation Process: Practical Strategies for Resolving Conflict*, 2d ed. (San Francisco: Jossey-Bass, 1996) at 60–61.

Example: The lawyer for the plaintiff, a young girl seriously injured in a motor vehicle accident, and the lawyer for the defendant, the driver of the car that struck the child, cannot agree on quantum of damages, although the defendant admits liability. Each lawyer has exactly the same data — medical records, actuarial reports, and case law. However, the plaintiff's lawyer is assessing damages much higher than the defendant's lawyer. The data conflict exists because the plaintiff's lawyer is interpreting recent case law to stand for the proposition that damages for the lost earning capacity of female plaintiffs with no earning history have been inappropriately undervalued due to gender bias. The defendant's lawyer reads the same judicial comments about gender bias as not binding or *obiter dictum*.

If the problem is identified as a data conflict, possible interventions might include

- reaching agreement on what data is important;
- agreeing on a process to collect data;
- developing common criteria to assess data;
- using third-party experts to break deadlocks over data;
- presenting data in a different manner;
- deciding how data will be used; and
- considering alternative options for resolving data disputes.

In the above example, once the disputants' lawyers recognize that their dispute about damages depends on different interpretations of judicial pronouncements about gender bias in damage awards, the lawyers will need to determine, or get help in determining, whether, and to what extent, these judicial comments are binding or, perhaps, should be binding. Trying to reach agreement on the meaning of, and weight to be given to, specific data — especially when the data may be unclear — is an approach to dispute resolution that is different from merely trying to persuade the other party that her or his offer of settlement is too high or too low. The former task is focused on what is really causing the dispute: a data conflict.

2. Interests

- Interests refer to a person's needs, desires, concerns, hopes, or fears. These interests can motivate behaviour.
- Interests may be substantive (economic needs resulting from injuries suffered in a motor vehicle accident; concerns about the availability of another job in a wrongful dismissal case; a fear about your home's security after a break and enter); procedural (a hope to have one's day in court; a fear of going to court); or psychological (a concern for your child's safety in a custody dispute;

a desire for self-respect in a divorce situation; a need for control in a business merger; an emotional need attached to a substantive or procedural interest).

- Interest conflicts are caused by actual or perceived interference in having one's interests satisfied.

Example: Separated spouses cannot agree on the amount of support to be paid. The wife suggests $1,500 per month. The husband refuses to pay more than $500. No previously decided cases on spousal support provide a clear solution and support guidelines are not determinative. What lies behind the proposed support payments are the spouses' interests. The husband is afraid of reducing the standard of living he enjoyed prior to separation (substantive and psychological needs), while his wife wants financial support to obtain the training necessary to pursue a new career and to re-establish her independence (perhaps substantive, psychological, and procedural needs).

If the problem is identified as an interest conflict, possible interventions might include

- focusing on the interests that need to be met in any resolution;
- developing creative solutions that meet the needs of all parties;
- searching for ways to expand options to satisfy more interests;
- weighing the strengths of various interests;
- assessing the legitimacy of the interests; and
- considering whether interests can be changed.

In the above example, the dispute needs to be understood as involving more than offers to settle that are far apart with little likelihood of reaching agreement on a middle ground amount without protracted proceedings. If the interests or needs behind the offers are identified, a solution could be sought that provides the wife with a level of support necessary to pursue a new career and re-establish her independence *and* that does not inappropriately reduce the husband's standard of living. Developing a common goal statement for the disputants based on their interests may result in a consideration of options for resolving the problem that were more difficult to see when the dispute was viewed in a different light. Clearly articulating the conflicting interests in difficult cases does not necessarily mean the search for a solution is simple. For example, without any change in how the husband perceives or experiences economic fear, it may be that no dollar figure above $500 by itself would be acceptable to the husband. Creative financing schemes, assessments of trading off interests (how much is early settlement and peace of mind worth financially), or careful calculations of what a protracted court case would cost may be negotiation activities that are critical to the interests at stake. Identifying the interests or needs that underpin what is important to the parties in any resolution of a dispute does again direct attention to the cause of the dispute, not to a symptom.

3. Relationships

- Relationships involve continuing or past social interactions that vary in duration, physical proximity, purpose, and emotional involvement.
- Relationship conflicts are caused by
  - repetitive negative behaviour;
  - violence or abuse;
  - poor communication or miscommunication;
  - misperceptions or stereotypes; or
  - assumptions about behaviours.

Example: Neighbours are unable to discuss, let alone agree on, what to do about conflicting uses of their property. One neighbour operates a home office requiring quiet study and precise preparation of design documents. The other neighbour runs a licensed family day care. The noise from the day care regularly disturbs the home office work. Angry words have been exchanged, by-law enforcement officers called, and threats made of a lawsuit for nuisance. There are talks of other actions.

If the problem is identified as a relationship conflict, possible interventions might include

- improving the quality and quantity of communication;
- blocking negative repetitive behaviour;
- developing solutions that address both past and future behaviour;
- separating relationship conflicts from other sources of conflict where possible; and
- identifying the relationship needs that are part of the dispute.

In the above example, although there are clearly "interest" and perhaps "data" disputes between the neighbours around the respective and apparently legal uses of their property, there is also a related relationship dispute that is blocking the neighbours from resolving, or even addressing, their needs about property use. This dispute also will likely erode other neighbourly functions. If a continuing relationship is important to the neighbours or if they want to deal with the property-use dispute, the relationship dispute needs to be identified and resolved. What the solution will involve (e.g., apologies, agreements on when and how to communicate, affirmations of the value of good neighbours, undertaking not to involve the authorities, and so on) is important. But a key is analyzing the situation as involving more than a data dispute (does the noise level at the day care exceed municipal by-law or other community standards?), a limited interest dispute (the economic and self-esteem needs of both neighbours to carry on their respective businesses), or an unwieldy legal file. A relationship dispute is part of the picture.

4. Values

- Values are attitudes, beliefs, or principles that determine, influence, or justify one's behaviour, choices, and judgments.
- Clusters of values can make up an ideological viewpoint.
- Value conflicts are caused by
  - claims that one value should dominate;
  - claims or other actions that suggest a certain value is superior or inferior;
  - claims that a value should be applied generally even by those holding different values; or
  - competing ideologies or different ways of life.

Example: The landlord refuses to rent an apartment to a same-sex couple, stating that the apartment is only suitable for one tenant. The next day the landlord rents the apartment to a heterosexual couple. The same-sex couple files a human rights complaint. The landlord, in fact, is homophobic and completely devalues the same-sex couple's sexual preference.

If the problem is identified as a value conflict, possible interventions might include

- allowing the parties to agree to disagree;
- recognizing value conflicts are difficult to resolve by consensus;
- looking for interests or goals that are common to the conflicting values;
- separating value conflicts from other sources of conflict when possible;
- identifying non-consensual dispute resolution forums; and
- considering whether values can be changed.

In the above example, recognizing that the landlord's homophobic attitude is the cause of the problem (as opposed to a data dispute over apartment suitability) assists in the dispute resolution process. The analysis may help to focus attention on what evidence is necessary in an adjudicative hearing, anticipate and respond to "false" causes being raised by the landlord, or bring about a transformation in the landlord's way of being. It may be that the landlord won't or can't change his values. If the resolution of this value dispute is an important part of any settlement package, attempting negotiation or mediation might be futile. While the parties may have a common interest in a positive landlord-tenant relationship, they have conflicting values about the relevance of sexual preference in that relationship and generally within society.

5. Structures

- Structures refer to institutions, organizations, systems, practices, or other physical or psychological forms of ordering of human affairs.
- Structural conflicts can arise due to
  - unequal control, ownership, or distribution of resources;
  - unequal power or authority;
  - limited resources;
  - inequalities arising from various political, social, and economic orders;
  - physical, environmental, or time constraints; or
  - other structural deficiencies.

Example: Law students demand representation on a law school committee that oversees promotion and tenure decisions for faculty members. This demand is vigorously opposed by a number of professors who fear students will bring improper motives to the evaluation process particularly for the more "radical" faculty. Concerns also are raised that students are not qualified to make the necessary assessments of a professor's work and that the university constitution does not permit student membership on this committee. The students, who are supported by some faculty members, want a strong say in the evaluation of their professors.

If the problem is identified as a structural conflict, possible interventions might include

- recognizing structural conflicts are difficult to resolve by consensus;
- identifying forums suited to structural change;
- separating structural conflicts from other sources of conflict when possible;
- attempting to modify or change structures responsible for conflict; and
- utilizing interest-based bargaining.

In the above example, data disputes (can the students do the job?) and interest conflicts (is academic freedom challenged? does a strong student voice matter?) about student participation are evident. However, there is also a structural dispute about the form of decision making or the sharing of decision-making power. The matter, if not resolved, would proceed to a Faculty Council meeting where more faculty than student members would vote on the question after debate and discussion. The majority would win, subject to any appeals to the University Senate. Alternatively, a mediated attempt could be made to carefully identify whether everyone's common interests in encouraging the highest quality of faculty endeavours and maintaining positive student faculty relations could be the basis for some types of meaningful student participation in promotion and tenure decisions, with appropriate safeguards in the evaluation process.

There may be other ways of describing the causes of conflict but often these other sources will fit into Moore's five broad categories. Consider the spouse who is pushing the custody case to the limit in terms of money and time for emotional reasons. The dispute over custody of the children may involve data matters (how much can each spouse pay?) and interest concerns (a desire for a university education, a worry about good parenting). Any agreement will need to cover these points. However, if it is the spouse's anger or jealousy that is really moving the dispute along, this is a relationship or a hidden interest dispute that needs to be resolved just as importantly as, and perhaps before, the issues around parenting responsibilities. What about the client going to court on principle? The economic concerns around quantum of damages in the personal injury case may pose only a small data dispute for experienced lawyers. The principle preventing settlement may be the plaintiff's desire to make a statement about the arrogance and the unsavoury tactics of the insurance company. The real cause of the dispute is more about competing values or interests around respect or even structural deficiencies in a fault-based tort system. However the cause of the conflict is described, getting to the root of the problem can cause constructive changes in how the dispute proceeds.

Locating the cause of conflict, even with an analytical framework, can be difficult for a number of reasons. First, conflict is rarely one-dimensional. Conflicts often will have several causes. A complaint of discrimination to a human rights commission may involve conflicting factual accounts (data); demands for and refusals to provide certain remedies (substantive interests); a need for privacy by one party, publicity for the other (psychological interests); evidence of racism (relationship or values); and concerns that industry practices permit wide-spread discrimination (structures). Conflicts also can escalate from a single, and perhaps easily identifiable, beginning cause into multi-issue matters that may not be as clear. For example, an apparently straightforward data dispute over who is responsible for damages to a carpet between a landlord and tenant becomes more complex, and more difficult to settle, when the landlord publicly accuses the tenant of dishonesty and stupidity, which results in the tenant suing the landlord for libel.

Second, some sources of conflict may be hidden, intentionally or unintentionally. For example, the manifest problem for the divorcing couple (who gets the silverware) with its seemingly simple solution (equal economic division) is not being resolved. The underlying psychological interest or value problem (a desire to punish a spouse for infidelity and deceit during the relationship) may not surface, preventing the resolution of "easy" substantive economic interests.

Third, as with traditional legal analysis, who defines the problem is critical. Demanding damages, including punitive damages, in a wrongful dismissal lawsuit is only one way to describe a dispute between a dismissed employee and his or her former employer. This lawyer-framing of the problem may capture important economic interests of the parties but it may miss other causes of the dispute emanating from the employment history. The lawsuit with its Statement of Claim may itself add another layer to the cause of the dispute when, for example, the employer is deeply offended by the lawsuit's language describing the callousness of the dismissal process. Often the parties themselves are most likely to know what is at issue although this is not always true. However, dispute processing mechanisms that provide for party involvement and assessment may be helpful in getting an accurate description of what is causing the conflict and pointing out what needs to be done.

Uncovering the cause of the conflict can point to creative solutions, new ways of bridging distant positions, or other constructive interventions. But, of course, even with this type of ADR analysis, some cases may still need to be decided in court. The insurance company is convinced the plaintiff intentionally set fire to the business premises. The plaintiff cannot admit to arson and needs the money. Resolving the data dispute (who set the fire? can arson be proven on the balance of probabilities?) may not be done consensually even if some sort of compromise makes economic sense. Intertwined with the data conflict and more significant than economic interests may be conflicts around the insurance company's interest in avoiding a bad precedent, both parties' reputational concerns, and the insurance company's perception of strongly conflicting values. Their respective interests in a day in court can be better understood by breaking down the other causes of the conflict.

Another example might be constitutional cases. Although constitutional disputes involving the construction of, or challenges to, fundamental structures in society do get resolved consensually, many of these structural disputes may be most amenable to courtroom adjudication especially when a public precedent to guide future cases is desired. For example, in computing income for tax purposes, suppose a single-parent mother is required to include child support payments she receives from her ex-partner. The ex-partner is entitled to deduct these payments from his taxable income. The single-parent mother believes that this inclusion/deduction tax structure contained in income tax legislation violates her section 15 equality rights under the *Canadian Charter of Rights and Freedoms*. The government cannot agree. The single-parent mother sues the government to strike down the offending legislation. There is a dispute over whether a systemic inequality exists in tax legislation that violates constitutionally protected rights. Although an individual disputant is taking action, the dispute and how it is resolved have broader implications. Resolving such a fundamental disagreement when the dispute is also part of the larger complaint of systemic oppression of women probably requires resort to dispute resolution forums designed to deal with these problems and provide effective responses such as striking out or amending the offending legislation.[27]

2) Conflict Behaviour

How conflict is understood and caused help to explain the course of a conflict and how it might be resolved. However, even using these concepts, there are times when conflict seems to have a life of its own. What people do in disputing can seem strange, uneven, and unpredictable. One neighbour may call the police or take the law into his own hands to stop a neighbour's noise. Another nearby resident might ignore the offending behaviour or even wear earplugs! Still another resident might talk to the noisy neighbour to determine if the activity producing the noise can be carried on in a way that doesn't interfere with other residents' reasonable enjoyment of their property. What is it that explains a person's behaviour in conflict settings?

Human behaviour is complex. There is usually no simple explanation of what causes or influences a person to act in one way or another and no way of guaranteeing that different people will react identically to the same or similar situations. Conflict adds a complicating layer to behaviour. The varying social, political, and economic contexts in which conflicts occur, discussed in chapter 1, make accurate predictions or even reasonable assumptions about disputant moves and counter-

---

27   Resort to the courts was taken in *Thibaudeau v. R.*, [1995] 2 S.C.R. 627.

moves uncertain at best. Yet people in conflict do make moves, take actions, start lawsuits, avoid lawyers, bang tables, raise voices, talk quietly, accept offers, shake hands, and so on. Identifying the cause of the conflict can help. The disputant who has pressing economic needs may be expected to react positively to a fair settlement offer. An apology for past indiscretions may be exactly what is needed to jump-start the talks on child custody. An unsettled but pressing equality issue around a mother's rights is likely to go to the highest court to effect a systemic change in government policy.

However, several interrelated theories also have been developed that shed more light on these and other conflict behaviours. Six theories are briefly presented here: motivational or drive, psychoanalytic, cognitive, conflict style, social exchange, and personality typing. The following descriptions summarize several ideas that are relevant to the ADR field and that might be helpful to ADR practitioners and students. The various behavioural concepts are an illustration of the multidisciplinary reach of ADR. A better understanding of conflict behaviour can

- assist in assessing just how the parties view the conflict;
- aid in explaining your own and others' actions;
- help in deciding what dispute resolution process to follow;
- point to steps or actions necessary to change undesirable behaviour; and
- suggest satisfying solutions.

Motivational or drive theories seek to explain behaviour in terms of psychological or physiological motives. They attempt to show how intrapersonal states and mental activities result in certain behaviour in social settings. A key premise of these theories is that basic human drives exist that determine our behaviour, often subconsciously. People engage in or avoid certain activities to satisfy these internal motives. A conflict arises when there is a perception that these desired activities or drives conflict with another's desired activities. For example, the manager's desire to be promoted on merit appears blocked by his supervisor who wants a harder-working employee. The resulting disputing behaviour, which may focus on one matter or another, can best be understood and responded to by appreciating that these conflicting motives exist. Such an appreciation may provide a different perspective on the problem, enable one of the parties to excuse objectionable behaviour, or be the springboard for a review of evaluation procedures.

Psychoanalytic theorists such as Freud, Adler, Sullivan, Rapaport, and Erikson describe a need to satisfy basic instincts or impulses, such as the need for self-preservation, love, social support and the controversial instinct towards aggression. If these internal drives go unfulfilled or are suppressed by conflict, substitute activities or rechannelling will occur. Maslow, a behavioural psychologist, saw behaviour being motivated by a hierarchy of needs. Basic or deficiency needs such as the need for food, warmth, shelter, safety, and security must largely be met first. Once these basic needs are met, a person seeks to satisfy growth or self-actualization needs such as the need for self-respect, personal worth, and the need to know and understand. It is only when basic and self-actualization needs are met that a person then seeks to satisfy aesthetic needs such as an appreciation of beauty or art. For example, the business partners cannot agree on office art. One partner has no worries about the financial obligations involved. The original painting will be inspirational. The other partner likes the art but has a family to support. Buying the painting will create an economic burden that could threaten his family relationships. The psychological needs and their respective strengths need to be addressed to deal with the conflict as effectively as possible.

Cognitive models of human behaviour suggest that behaviour is determined or directed by a thought process such as an ideological orientation or a plan. For example, field theorists see behaviour predicated upon the attainment of important goals. The path to achieve these goals is influenced by the climate of the person's environment or their "social field." Morton Deutsch identified a crucial element of climate as the type of interdependence established between the persons involved. Deutsch argues that perceptions of promotive interdependence (people stress mutual interests, exhibit trusting and friendly attitudes, perceive one's gains will promote the other's gains while losses will promote losses, and communicate more openly and honestly) will encourage cooperative climates. Perceptions of contrient interdependence (people focus on antagonistic interests, constrain each other, exhibit suspicious and hostile attitudes, perceive one's gain will be the other's loss, and communicate in a misleading and restrained manner) will create competitive climates.[28] For example, the president of the Law Society wants to abolish articling in order to establish new mentoring rules that would make it impossible for as many law graduates to work as lawyers despite being called to the bar. Some lawyers support this goal; others oppose it. The negotiations around this matter can better be understood both by appreciating that conflicting goals exist and by analyzing the nature of the climate that exists between supporters and opponents.

---

28   Above note 3 at 20–22.

Conflict style theorists focus on styles of conflict interaction. Thomas and Killman identified five types of conflict behaviour using the Thomas-Killman Conflict Mode Instrument. Their classifications are based on two variables: a person's assertiveness — defined as behaviours intended to satisfy one's own concerns; and a person's cooperativeness — defined as behaviours intended to satisfy the other's concerns. The following chart indicates the general types of conflict styles that emerge when assertive and cooperative behaviour collide.

Figure 2.1   Conflict Styles

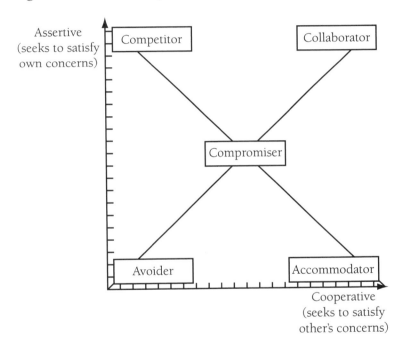

For example, the defendant's lawyer could seek instructions to offer more in response to a concession granted by the plaintiff's lawyer. However the defendant's lawyer is a competitor. He is a person who wants his client to pay as little as possible or to win in the negotiation. The concession granted by the other lawyer is seen as a sign of weakness not as an opportunity to reciprocate. An understanding of different conflict styles can help to explain and respond to these conflict behaviours.

Social exchange theory and economic analysis also provide important perspectives on what motivates people in conflict settings. These theories in general assume that the guiding force behind conflict behaviour is self-interest and that people prefer behaviour that promises rewards and avoid behaviours for which costs are greater than benefits. The resources to be exchanged determine the rewards and the costs. These resources, which are essentially the outcomes of the dispute, can include monetary or physical objects as well as less tangible items such as information, approval, respect, or relationship. Whatever the resources, disputants will seek outcomes to a conflict that are based on their perception or assessment of the potential rewards and costs associated with different actions. For example, the company refuses to admit their product is dangerous because the profits from continued global sales will far exceed the costs of defending any challenges to the right to sell or associated with paying successful damage claims. The costs and benefits figures need to be closer together before any consensual settlement of the dispute is possible for disputants moved mainly by economics.

Personality typing, based on the work of Carl Jung, Katharine Briggs, Isabel Myers, David Keirsey, and others, is an attempt to create models or general archetypes of personality. Understanding and appreciating differences in personality types can assist individuals to better understand themselves and their development, aid in facilitating communications and relationships with others, and provide insights into people's approaches to perception and decision making. For example, the Myers-Briggs Type Indicator (MBTI) divides personality into four independent scales: energizing (how we deal with the outside world); attending (how we take in and assess data or what a person pays attention to); deciding (how a person decides); and living (how we prefer to live). Within each scale are two opposite and equally good preferences.

1. Energizing

Extroversion (E)
— influence of outside world of people, actions, or things
— speak without thinking, people of action

Introversion (I)
— influence of internal world of ideas, emotions, or impressions
— quiet reflection

2. Attending

Sensing (S)
— preference for using senses to notice what is important
— reliance on experience and facts
— practical, orderly

| Intuition (N) | – preference for using imagination to envision what is possible |
| | – creative, imaginative, look for the big picture |

3. Deciding

Thinking (T)	– decide in a logical, objective way
	– organized and structured
	– impersonal
Feeling (F)	– decide in a personal, value-oriented way
	– know what is "right"
	– value harmony, good at persuasion

4. Living

Judging (J)	– preference for being planned and structured
	– have matters settled and decided
	– take action quickly
Perceiving (P)	– preference for being spontaneous and open
	– matters can be unstructured and flexible

There are sixteen ways to combine the preferences (i.e., ISTJ, ISTP, ISFJ, ISFP, and so on) resulting in sixteen MBTI types. Different combinations of scales and preferences define particular and unique personality archetypes. For example, in a conflict setting, Interactive Thinkers (Analysts) will make decisions with their heads more than their hearts, value intelligence and competence, and are idea-oriented. Intuitive Thinkers can tend to ignore facts and details. Intuitive Feelers (Empathists) prefer decisions made by the heart, for they are "people people," caring and passionate. Truth and personal authenticity are important. Intuitive Feelers tend to make decisions on a personal basis, which can be contrary to logic. It is not difficult to see how dispute resolution can often run into difficulties and how personality clashes and conflicts can occur.

For the student or practitioner of ADR, theories about conflict behaviour can be used to help unravel the seemingly odd or incoherent responses and counter-responses that can emanate from disputants. Consider the following real-life scenarios:

• A dissatisfied purchaser's refusal (apparently unreasonable) to accept an offer of a monetary settlement for damages caused by the misrepresentation of a product's qualities may be motivated by a desire to punish the seller for the purchaser's humiliation in the industry at being deceived. Money, unless it is enough to be punitive, will not satisfy the purchaser. Careful questioning, a more thorough analysis, or a hunch may disclose what is blocking resolution and accounting for the purchaser's actions. A settlement package from the seller that includes an apology, a promise to change selling practices, and even an offer of special treatment for the purchaser for future business might meet the purchaser's need to feel her outrage has been recognized.

- A mechanic may be unwilling to admit that he did not complete a proper inspection of the vehicle's braking system and therefore to take responsibility for the accident for fear of the irreparable harm to his reputation in the community. Stressing the public nature of a litigated outcome may cause the mechanic to consider how secrecy of settlement terms might be the key to any agreement.
- An employee who is reluctant to complain to supervisors about incidents of racial harassment may need a supportive advocate to bring the issues forward.
- The party in the disputed custody case who is resorting to every procedure and tactic to intimidate the opposite party may not be open to any productive consensual settlement discussions. Court adjudication may be the best, and only, appropriate process.
- A plaintiff may reject a generous settlement offer from the defendant because, from her perspective, the extra costs of going to court including the uncertainty of recovering more money than offered do not exceed the benefits of having her day in court and forcing the defendant to explain his actions.
- Settlement negotiations may stall because a person injured in an automobile accident who feels she should be treated with compassion (given her injuries and the 100 percent liability of the other driver) is offended by the cold rationality of the insurance company's adjuster as he outlines the way in which the company has carefully calculated the without prejudice settlement offer.

While theories can help us understand why people behave in certain ways and perhaps predict responses in particular conflict contexts, there are clear limits to their use. First, effectively analyzing a conflict from a behavioural perspective requires, for practical purposes, an in-depth understanding of, and an ability to work with, these theoretical models. A little knowledge not only can be a dangerous thing but also can lead one in the wrong direction in a dispute or provide incomplete results. For example, a lawyer who is adamantly and, in your opinion, unreasonably refusing to settle a case may be mostly exhibiting a long-learned competitive conflict style as opposed to your more reasonable and recently acquired collaborative approach. This behavioural analysis may help both in understanding and not reacting to his competitive tactics but also in pointing to an early application for summary judgment or a pre-trial conference as the best process response to the lawyer's behaviour. On the other hand, the lawyer's intransigence may be an example of contrient interdependence brought on unknowingly by an unintended action on your or your client's part. Moving quickly to summary judgment might be viewed as another example of hostility and make matters much worse. Or, the lawyer and his client may have evaluated the case differently than you and estimate that the benefits of resisting settlement exceed the costs. Unearthing the differences in how the case and potential outcomes are viewed through a negotiation process or other form of communication may be a wiser move than asking a judge for a decision, given your opponent's economic approach to the dispute. In short, working practically and accurately with theories about conflict behaviour requires considerable skill.

Second, it is questionable whether largely European-based accounts of conflict behaviour are transferable across culturally diverse communities. Attempts to predict or explain behaviour in conflict settings with a cultural twist are challenging (culture and conflict are canvassed more completely in chapter 7). The diversity of definitions for conflict which exist for peoples throughout the world also means that how one responds to conflict will be diverse. Relying on a particular model of interpreting conflict behaviour can be unreliable. The emphasis that ADR proponents have placed on interest-based bargaining is an example. Thinking that good mediation or negotiation involves, as a matter of best practice, the parties disclosing and then efficiently satisfying their underlying needs may require allegiance to foreign and unworkable beliefs and values for many communities and individuals.

Third, care must be taken not to give behavioural theories more credit than is due. While these theoretical tools can offer practical and insightful perspectives into conflict behaviour that would not otherwise be possible, the course and content of conflict, as discussed in chapter 1, can be uncertain, shaped inevitably by the panoply of contextual conditions surrounding the dispute — its where, who, what, when, and why. The disputants and their motives, personalities, thinking, and needs are a part of the equation. But it is unrealistic to expect that theories of conflict behaviour, however useful, would fully remove all the uncertainty that comes with the ADR field.

E. THE MAIN METHODS OF DISPUTE PROCESSING

Disputes move along in different ways. A well-known businessperson regularly takes or threatens to take the media to court alleging libel. Union representatives appear before a labour relations board opposing a company's application to restrict picketing. A divorcing couple meet with a mediator to discuss their future parenting responsibilities. Aboriginal, provincial, and federal government negotiators talk about treaties. One neighbour ignores another's noise. Countries go to war.

When a dispute emerges, the course that it will take may be clear. No one expects neighbours to resort to violence over a disputed property line. Discussions between the neighbours or calling in a surveyor or municipal officer would be the norm. On the other hand, a call-to-arms on a regular basis will be quite predictable as ethnic groups struggle to draw dividing lines between regions where the boundaries have been in dispute for several centuries. An allegation of serious medical malpractice will not be resolved in informal meetings between doctor and patient. Litigation including a trial would likely be necessary. In other situations, custom, contract, or legislation can dictate how a dispute is to proceed.

But this type of certainty does not always prevail in dispute resolution. The course that a dispute takes is often unpredictable, even surprising. While the full context in which the dispute arises must influence and ultimately determine the nature of a dispute and how it is brought forward, the study of ADR has focused much attention on the various methods that can be used to process disputes. The purposes of becoming familiar with these methods of dispute processing are

- to understand how complex disputes shape and are shaped by these mechanisms;
- to assess whether or how a particular method will contribute to constructive or destructive conflict resolution;
- to learn what knowledge and skills are necessary to participate effectively in a particular process;
- to help dispel the myth that the courts are the dominant method of dispute processing; and
- to assist disputants or others in choosing one of these methods.

There are several ways of looking at and understanding the methods of dispute processing.

1) Primary and Hybrid Processes

Some writers conceptualize dispute processing as being made up of primary and hybrid processes.[29] The primary processes are labelled as adjudication, mediation, and negotiation.

The most common and familiar process is seen as bargaining or negotiation in which the parties themselves control the process and the solution. The other primary processes involve a third party. In mediation, the mediator has no power to impose a solution but assists the disputants to arrive at a mutually satisfactory solution. If a third party has the power to impose a decision on the disputants, the process is adjudication when performed by a judge in court or arbitration when the decision is made by a private adjudicator called an arbitrator.

Hybrid dispute resolution processes or processes that combine elements of the primary disputing methods are often seen as a product of ADR. Some examples of hybrid processes are outlined below:

Advisory opinion: A non-binding, objective assessment of the relative strengths of the opposing positions in a dispute and the probable outcome of the case if it were to proceed to trial, rendered by a neutral third party, provided to stimulate settlement.

Confidential listening: A process wherein a neutral third party reviews the confidential settlement positions of all parties and advises the parties whether a negotiable range exists. The parties may agree beforehand to settle at the midpoint in a certain range revealed by the process.

Early neutral evaluation: Typically institutionalized in Rules of Court, this non-binding process provides litigants with an opportunity to have an early evaluation of their case by a neutral third party, often a lawyer experienced in the substantive area of the dispute. The parties or their counsel can confidentially present their side of the case to the neutral who is then in a position to give the parties an assessment of how the case might be settled.

Med-Arb: The process commences as a mediation of a dispute by a neutral third party, but if the mediation does not successfully resolve the dispute, the third party assumes the role of arbitrator and imposes a typically binding decision upon the parties.

---

29 For example, see S.B. Goldberg, F.E.A. Sander, & N.H. Rogers, *Dispute Resolution: Negotiation, Mediation and Other Processes*, 3d ed. (New York: Aspen Law & Business, 1999) at 3–6.

Mini-trial: This informal and inherently flexible process, often used in commercial disputes between corporate entities, combines mediation, negotiation, and non-binding arbitration. The exact structure is determined by agreement between the parties, but involves, after a limited preparation period, the summary presentation by counsel of each party's best case to a panel consisting of the opposing decision makers (who may have had no personal involvement in the dispute) and often a neutral third party. The third party may render an advisory opinion at the conclusion of this "information exchange." The principals then attempt to negotiate a settlement with the assistance of the third party acting as mediator. If no settlement is reached, the parties may proceed to trial. This process is distinguishable from a summary trial.

Neutral case evaluation: Any process within litigation in which the parties or their counsel present their cases to a court-appointed, neutral third party, typically a senior lawyer with expertise in the substantive area of the dispute, who renders an advisory opinion on the issues presented.

Ombudsman: An independent officer of a government or other large institution who investigates complaints of administrative injustice and attempts to mediate disputes between aggrieved members of the public and the government or institution. The traditional use of the word has been limited to government and public bodies such as universities, but the concept has been adopted in private and professional organizations.

Private judging: A process agreed to by the parties whereby the dispute is presented to a neutral third party, typically an experienced lawyer or retired judge, hired by the parties, who renders a binding decision. The third party may be drawn from a "private court." The process assumes the form of a private trial, governed by the rules of the private court, rules specifically drafted by the parties or relevant arbitration legislation. The judge may serve as a mediator initially.

2) Major Methods of Dispute Processing

Other authors describe five major categories of dispute processing,[30] stressing the presence or absence of a third party or the role of planning and prevention:

---

30   For example, see L.L. Riskin & J.E. Westbrook, *Dispute Resolution and Lawyers* (St. Paul, MN: West Publishing Co., 1987) at 2–6.

- *Adjudicative processes*, including court and administrative proceedings, arbitration, and private tribunals.
- *Consensual processes*, including ombudsperson, fact-finding, negotiation, mediation, and conciliation.
- *Mixed processes*, including mediation-arbitration, mini-trial, summary jury trial, and unstructured settlement negotiations.
- *Litigation management and planning*, including lawyer practices to plan for and control the course of litigation such as case review, discovery control, and risk analysis.
- *Prevention*, including strategies to plan transactions, to avoid disputes, partnering principles, and consensus building.

The latter two categories can expand thinking about the methods of dispute processing. Litigation management and planning demonstrates that what happens next in litigation is very much dependent on a number of decisions. ADR techniques can be considered and resorted to even as a case proceeds to trial. There may be several simultaneous tracks on which the dispute is moving along. Budget decisions can become integral parts of dispute processing under this category. The prevention of disputes opens up ADR to an even wider range of possibilities. Relationship-building processes, both before and after businesses agree to work on a project, become part of an ADR inquiry. The practice of writing ADR clauses into contracts also counts as prevention. Rather than waiting for the inevitability of disputes in certain contexts, the idea of dispute prevention can be analogous to the practice of preventative medicine.

3) Dispute Resolution Continuum

ADR's magnitude is illustrated by those writers who locate the various methods of dispute processing on a dispute resolution continuum as illustrated in Figure 2.2.[31]

Three observations can be made about the continuum manner of organizing the various methods of dispute processing. First, the techniques that can be used to resolve disputes are not finite. All the ADR wheels have not been invented yet. Although the continuum contains a number of well-known and comfortable locations, new and innovative techniques can be developed to respond to old problems (e.g., where will the waste facility be sited?) and to emerging conflicts (e.g., the dissemination of hate literature on the Internet). Interest in dispute reso-

---

31   For example, see Moore, above note 26 at 7.

Figure 2.2   Dispute Resolution Continuum

Private decision making by parties	Private third-party decision making	Legal (public) authoritative third-party decision making	Extralegal coerced decision making

conflict avoidance	Informal discussion, negotiation, and problem solving	Mediation	Adminis-trative decision	Arbitration	Judicial	Legislative	Non-violent	Violent

———————— Increased coercion and likelihood of win-lose outcome ⟶

lution systems design (what can two new technology companies do that find themselves in dispute over ownership of a critical idea or product so as not to jeopardize needed investment?) for both public and private settings will add new points of call to this continuum of disputing processes. Second, ADR should not ignore the potential significance of any particular point on the continuum. ADR emerged, in part, out of a concern that too much emphasis was being placed on court adjudication to the detriment of more widely used procedures such as negotiation. Though the mediation and negotiation processes capture headlines, the importance of understanding the full range of disputing methods cannot be overlooked. Avoiding disputes is a very common response and often a wise move. Similarly, the use and efficiency of peaceful protests or civil disobedience as a means to effect change need to be well understood. Third, the continuum suggests that the various methods of dispute processing can be characterized, and hence located on the continuum, according to who is the decision maker in the dispute resolution process and the degree to which the resolution of the dispute may be coercive or win-lose. These disputing characteristics can be important factors in deciding which method to use.

There may be different ways of categorizing and differentiating methods of dispute processing, but several common themes emerge from the above classifications. First, the array of disputing procedures, however organized, reinforces the conclusion reached by the research. The courts are not the norm in dispute processing. Only a small percentage of civil actions actually proceed to trial, probably between 3 to 5 percent. Family disputes and personal injury claims often make up the largest number of these cases. The balance of legal cases are settled out of court. In addition, lawyers and the disputants themselves regularly resolve disputes without commencing litigation while many more disputes never reach a lawyer's office, let alone a courthouse. Those methods of dispute processing often thought of as alternatives are, in fact, the norm in dispute resolution.

Second, having a working understanding of the processes by which disputes are resolved points to the skills that will be needed to participate effectively in these processes. Some skills will be generic. For example, a lawyer will need to be a good listener whether acting as an advocate before an administrative tribunal or a mediator in a family dispute. However, many skills will be unique to the process within a specific context. A mediator will not use the decision-making and associated reasoning skills required of an arbitrator, while an arbitrator is unlikely to need the same rapport and trust-building skills often used by mediators who do not have the authority to impose a decision. The chapters that follow on negotiation, mediation, and arbitration highlight in more detail skills required for proficiency in these major disputing processes.

Third, a thorough understanding of the various methods of dispute processing and how they function obviously will be helpful when the disputants, their lawyers, legislators, or others have to make choices about whether or not to use them. Using or considering the full range of dispute processing techniques may not always be possible. For example, a procedure may be too costly or time-consuming, not be in existence, or be otherwise inappropriate. However, a working understanding of how disputes can get resolved is essential to any informed decision.

4) Matching the Process to the Problem

Making choices about using one method of dispute processing or another raises the issue of whether it is possible to match a specific dispute resolution method with a particular type of dispute. This issue is extraordinarily complex. The contextual complexity and general uncertainty surrounding most disputes and their processing suggest natural matches between disputes and processes are not only impossible but impractical. However, there have been suggestions that a taxonomy of disputing characteristics will point to one process or another.[32] For example:

---

32 See S.B. Goldberg, E.D. Green, & F.E.A. Sander, *Dispute Resolution* (Boston: Little Brown and Company, 1985); and E.A. Sander & S. Goldberg, "Fitting the Forum to the Fuss: A User-Friendly Guide to Selecting an ADR Procedure" (1994) 10 *Negotiation. J.* 49.

- **The relationship between the disputants**

  When there is an ongoing relationship, it is important that the parties work out their own solutions to ensure any agreement is acceptable and long-lasting, and the relationship is preserved. Accordingly, negotiation or even mediation would be preferable.

- **The nature of the dispute**

  Some disputes are "test" cases and require a definitive precedent to be set by a court. "Polycentric" problems or disputes with no clear governing guidelines and broad implications may be best handled by the disputants themselves rather than opting for an externally imposed solution.

- **The amount at stake**

  Although disputes involving small amounts of money may seem suitable for pared-down procedures (small claims court, economical litigation projects, less-costly dispute resolution mechanisms), cases where large sums of money are in issue should be adjudicated with the full panoply of due process protection. However, some small cases are complex; a big case may be simple. The novelty or complexities of the issues at stake, as opposed to the dollar amount, may be the better indicator of whether a dispute resolution forum is needed to provide full opportunities for the presentation of evidence and argument.

- **Speed and cost**

  The resolution of all disputes should be speedy and cost effective, but some disputes, because of the amount involved or the consequences of delay, will require a dispute resolution process that is faster and cheaper than full court adjudication.

- **Power relationships between the parties**

  Where differences in bargaining strength exist between the disputants, an adjudicatory or other dispute resolution forum that can eliminate or reduce the inequalities in power would be preferable.

Choosing the most appropriate dispute resolution method also can be seen as a process of weighing the advantages and disadvantages of different techniques. Consider how Figure 2.3, listing the advantages and disadvantages associated with various dispute resolution methods, would help disputants or their lawyers decide which method to use.[33]

---

33 Adapted from Riskin & Westbrook, above note 30 at 420.

Figure 2.3   Advantages/Disadvantages Associated with Dispute Resolution Mechanisms

	Advantages	Disadvantages
1. Court Adjudication	• public norms applied • precedent • deterrence • uniformity • independence • binding/closure • enforceability • already institutionalized • publicly funded	• expensive • requires lawyers and relinquishes control to them • mystifying • lacks special substantive expertise • involves delays • time-consuming • issues redefined or narrowed • limited range of remedies • no compromise • polarizes, and is disruptive
2. Arbitration	• privacy • parties control forum • enforceability • expedience • expertise • tailors remedy to situation • choice of applicable norm	• no public norms • no precedent • no uniformity • lack of quality • becoming encumbered by increasing "legalization"
3. Mediation-Negotiation	• privacy • parties control process • reflects concerns and priorities of disputants • preserves continuing relations • flexible • finds integrative solutions • addresses underlying problem • process educates disputants • high rate of compliance	• lacks ability to compel participation • not binding • weak closure • no power to induce settlements • no due process safeguards • reflects imbalance in skills (negotiation) • lacks enforceability • outcome need not be principled
4. Administrative Decision Making	• defines problems systematically • devices aggregate solution • flexibility in obtaining relevant information • accommodates multiple criteria	• no control by parties • not independent • not individualized

	Advantages	Disadvantages
5. Ombudsperson	• not disruptive to ongoing relations • flexible • self-starting • easy access	• lacks enforceability • no control by parties
6. Internal Tribunal	• privacy • responsive to concerns of disputants • enforceability	• not independent • no due process safeguards • not based on public norms • may reflect imbalance within organization

Matching disputes to appropriate dispute resolution processes also can depend on the meaning attached to ADR. How ADR, its ideology, and its goals are understood will influence how different disputing methods are assessed. A narrow view of ADR may exclude some methods from consideration. Certain methods of dispute processing may be highly regarded only if they achieve a specific goal. For example, if a government wants to reduce the public costs of maintaining courts, preference could be given to low-cost, private, and consensual methods of dispute resolution or mandatory, court-annexed mediation. These same general methods would certainly be chosen if the transformative or quality goals of ADR were dominant, although the processes themselves would likely be longer, more costly, and involved where more than money was driving ADR policy.

Each of the above approaches for matching a dispute to a process has practical merit. A lawyer and her client will evaluate the pros and cons of sitting down to negotiate with the other side or hiring a neutral third party to help mediate a resolution. Disputants in real life will consider whether a specific ADR process such as med-arb or the mini-trial might be advantageous to them in achieving desirable outcomes. Public and private institutions will carefully review the advantages and disadvantages before making mediation mandatory or promoting consensual methods of dispute resolution. However, in the many situations where disputants and their lawyers can make choices about whether or not to go down a particular dispute resolution path, these approaches may be incomplete and even misleading. The process of searching for a match between a fixed dispute and a set array of dispute processing techniques is, in practice, more indeterminate.

Consider the parents who want a divorce but cannot agree on who gets the kids. One divorcing couple may enthusiastically embrace mediation to deal with custody. Another couple may reject mediation in favour of their lawyers negotiating the issue. Still another couple may battle for the children all the way to court and beyond. These different decisions about disputing methods surely depend on subjective assessments of the context surrounding the dispute and the dispute resolution method. These assessments can be uncertain.

One of the divorcing spouses may value the speed and lower costs associated with mediation while the other spouse may view these attributes as negative if he is content with the status quo and the mediation process threatens this condition. On the other hand, the informality, slow pace, and non-binding nature of mediation might well suit a spouse who wants to prolong the battle or avoid some of the rigours of the formal justice system. Similarly, the public nature of the courtroom may be an advantage for a disputant who hopes the adjudication of her abuse complaint is a deterrent to others. Another disputant with a similar complaint may see this publicity as re-victimizing her, whatever the deterrent effect might be. It is simply difficult to say, out of context, whether an attribute of a particular dispute or dispute resolution method or a consequence associated with its use will be viewed as positive or negative by disputants, their lawyers, or others. Some disputants even regard the high costs and lengthy delays of litigation as a plus if these features pressure the other side to settle for less or deter a claim from being made in the first case.

Understanding that a dispute is not static but changes over time also imperils the idea of a fixed match between a particular dispute and an appropriate method. The dispute might initially emerge as a disagreement over what is in the best interests of the child but be changed by the actions of the disputants or their lawyers into a profound contest of wills. What had initially seemed ripe for mediation might now need the authoritative hand of a judge in court. The neighbours who could at first glance seem capable of talking reasonably about a pet's unwanted behaviour may without much effort require the intervention of sensible lawyers to help them respond to charges of threatening behaviour. The idea that disputes are constituted and transformed as they are processed suggests more open-ended practices in evaluating and choosing dispute processing techniques.

Finally, the inconsistencies and variabilities in the dispute processing techniques themselves also argue against the notion that certain disputes can be methodically matched to a particular process. Many different activities are labelled as mediation but with varying degrees of allegiance to the mediation ideal. For example, tightly scheduled mediations in case-reducing mandatory settlement conferences before judges in courthouses will be substantially different processes than the mediations of the same cases conducted in local community justice centres, even though both are called mediation. Considering that mediation can be facilitative, evaluative, transformative, bureaucratic, open or closed, activist or accountable, less professionalized or pragmatic,[34] choosing mediation will depend more on the different ways mediation is practised in different contexts and by different mediators than on channelling fixed ideas of disputes into processes with essential and fixed attributes most suited to such disputes. The same can be said for the negotiation process. What happens next in negotiation can depend on who the negotiators are and the approach they take to the negotiation discussions. Even the formalized procedures of court adjudication and the carefully constructed rules for commercial arbitration do not always lead to fully predictable results: who the judge is, where the court is located, the availability of a jury, the lawyer's experience, the existence or non-existence of legal precedents, and other factors can mean litigation is sometimes preferable but sometimes not.

Of course, choices will be made about the methods of dispute processing. A disputant and her lawyer will decide to go to court, or to pursue a negotiated settlement. A government will legislate mandatory mediation for all child custody disputes or not. ADR developments have focused considerable and important attention on the choices. Understanding that these various dispute processing methods "are objects as well as agents of transformation" brings a more contextual and "real life" perspective to these choices than does the notion that an ideal fit between dispute and process exists in most cases.

FURTHER READINGS

BURTON, J., ed., *Conflict: Human Needs* Theory (London: Sage, 1990)

MENKEL-MEADOW, C., "The Sciences of the Restatement of the Law Governing Lawyering: Lawyering as Only Adversary Practice" (1997) 10 Geo. J. Legal Ethics 631

MERRY, S., & S. SILBEY, "What Do Plaintiffs Want? Reexamining the Concept of Dispute" (1984) 9 Just. Sys. J. 151

MURRAY, J., A. RAU, & E. SHERMAN, *Processes of Dispute Resolution: The Role of Lawyers*, 2d ed. (Westbury, NY: Foundation Press, 1996)

---

34   See chapter 4 and the fuller discussion on mediation for an explanation of these terms.

OGLEY, R.C., *Conflict under the Microscope* (Vermont: Avebury, Gower, Aldershot, 1991)

RUBIN, J.S., PRUITT, D.G., & S.H. KIM, eds., *Social Conflict: Escalation, Stalemate, and Settlement*, 2d ed. (New York: McGraw-Hill, 1994)

UNGER, R.M. *What Should Legal Analysis Become?* (London: Verso, 1996)

YARN, D.H., ed., *Dictionary of Conflict Resolution* (San Francisco: Jossey-Bass Inc., 1999)

CHAPTER 3

NEGOTIATION:
WE CAN WORK IT OUT

A. INTRODUCTION

Consider the following passage from P.G. Wodehouse's *Aunts Aren't Gentlemen* (1974):

> "How much do I want, sir?"
>
> "Yes. Give it a name. We won't haggle."
>
> He pursed his lips.
>
> "I'm afraid," he said, having unpursed them, "I couldn't do it as cheap as I'd like, sir . . . I'd have to make it twenty pounds."
>
> I was relieved. I had been expecting something higher. He, too, seemed to feel that he had erred on the side of moderation, for he immediately added:
>
> "Or, rather, thirty."
>
> "Thirty!"
>
> "Thirty, sir."
>
> "Let's haggle" I said.
>
> But when I suggested twenty-five, a nicer looking sort of number than thirty, he shook his grey head regretfully, and he haggled better than me, so that eventually we settled on thirty-five. It wasn't one of my better haggling days."

Negotiation is a common and familiar dispute resolution process. A sample of the various definitions of negotiation illustrate the prevalence of this process in all people's lives, the obvious importance of good "haggling," and the relationship between negotiation and ADR:

"To discuss a matter with a view to some settlement or compromise"
(*Oxford English Dictionary*)

"Whenever people exchange ideas with the intention of changing relationships, whenever they confer for agreement"
(Nierenberg, *Fundamentals of Negotiating*, 1968)

"Any form of verbal communication, direct or indirect, whereby parties to a conflict of interest discuss, without resort to arbitration or other judicial processes, the form of any joint action which they might take to manage a dispute between them"
(Morley & Stephenson, *The Social Psychology of Bargaining*, 1977)

"One kind of problem-solving process — one in which people attempt to reach a joint decision on matters of common concern in situations where they are in disagreement and conflict"
(Gulliver, *Disputes and Negotiations: A Cross-Cultural Perspective*, 1981)

"A basic means of getting what you want from others. It is back-and-forth communication designed to reach an agreement when you and the other side have some interests that are shared and others that are opposed"
(Fishery & Ury, *Getting to Yes*, 1981)

"Concerned with situations in which two or more parties recognize that differences of interest and values exist . . . and in which they want (or in which one or more are compelled) to seek a compromise agreement"
(Raiffa, *The Art and Science of Negotiation*, 1982)

"Communication for the purpose of persuasion"
(Goldberg, Sander, & Rogers, *Dispute Resolution*, 1999)

Essentially, negotiation allows two or more parties to accomplish by agreement what no single party could do, or would want to do, alone. In the language of ADR, negotiation is a consensual dispute resolution process.

Practising lawyers spend a good deal of their professional time negotiating. Legal negotiations take place in contexts such as the sale or lease of property, the design of a partnership agreement or company structure, the break-up of a family, the settlement of a personal injury claim, plea bargaining in a criminal case, or the development of government regulations or policies. Some lawyers negotiate international agreements and treaties. A few lawyers negotiate the creation of new constitutional accords. Apart from negotiating on behalf of clients, lawyers also will negotiate with their staff, associates, and partners in practice over a wide range of office management matters. Negotiation is not some marginal or peripheral aspect of what lawyers do. It is the central core, the primary means of resolving legal disputes. Statistics show that over 95 percent of all civil cases commenced are resolved without trial, primarily by negotiation. Any lawyer would be hard-pressed to dispute the wisdom in the comments of former Chief Justice Warren Burger of the United States Supreme Court when he said that "of all the skills needed for the practising lawyer, skill in negotiation must rank very high."[1]

But these sentiments surely apply to everyone if we all negotiate whenever we want something from somebody. For business people, politicians, public officials, the wide range of professional persons, service providers, representatives of non-governmental organizations, community workers, and people in their day-to-day activities, negotiation also is central to what they do.

Moving from an intellectual understanding that negotiation is vital to almost every endeavour to being an effective negotiator in practice is not always an easy task. Negotiation is a big and complicated subject. Like ADR, many disciplines, including law, have studied the negotiation process and have made significant contributions to our understanding of what it is and how it is practised. However, prior to the modern emergence of ADR, education or training in negotiation was irregular and spotty. Even though negotiation was a core experience for many professionals and other individuals, there was no regular and thorough examination of its workings. As a result, just because most people are everyday negotiators does not mean that everyone is good at it. Practice, without more, may not make perfect. For example, in the legal profession, the extensive use of negotiation as a dispute resolution process to resolve 95 percent of the cases can obscure the facts that these settlements may not always be reached in a timely way or that clients and lawyers are not satisfied with the results. In addition, cases not settled by negotiation that go to trial may be a result of deficiencies in negotiation skills and not the unsuitability of the case for consensual resolution.[2]

Accordingly, even though there is considerable experience in negotiating, negotiations do not always proceed smoothly. Problems can arise. Negotiations can break down. For example, consider how a negotiation would be affected if the negotiator

---

1   W. Burger, former chief justice of the United States Supreme Court, in "Isn't There a Better Way?" (1982) 68 A.B.A. J. 274 at 275.

2   These results are suggested in a survey of trial lawyers in British Columbia. See A.J. Pirie, "A.D.R. in Practice: Making an Informed Choice" in Annual Meeting Papers of the Canadian Bar Association (Vancouver, British Columbia, 1989) at F. 3.01.

- is not fully prepared;
- is confused about how to start or end a negotiation;
- doesn't know what, if any, information to disclose;
- is too trusting of the other negotiator;
- makes too many concessions in the negotiation;
- makes agreements without clear client instructions;
- is exploited;
- gets angry or reacts very emotionally in the negotiation;
- seems to just "argue" and get nowhere;
- doesn't know how to break off or end negotiations;
- provides misleading information or "lies" to the other negotiator;
- makes too high or too low an opening offer;
- finds own ego is preventing agreement from being reached;
- fails to accurately record any agreement;
- fails to listen or listens poorly;
- underestimates the other side or overestimates their own case; or
- misuses power.

Sometimes success or failure in negotiations depends on the answers to certain questions. How would a good negotiator answer the following questions?

- How much do you need to know about the subject matter under negotiation?
- What do you need to know about the other negotiators? About yourself?
- Are there clear negotiating conventions or protocols?
- How much information should you, or must you, disclose?
- Who should make the first offer?
- Where should the negotiations take place?
- When should they start?
- Should you use an agenda?
- What if their agenda conflicts with yours?
- How do you respond if the other side makes a concession, uses a dirty trick, says "take it or leave it," asks an unexpected question, or makes a threat?
- Is trust important in a negotiation?
- Can you exaggerate, bluff, or even lie in a negotiation?
- What should you do if there is a negotiation impasse or deadlock?
- When do you adjourn negotiations?
- Are there cases when negotiation is not useful, appropriate, or safe?
- Would the answers to negotiation questions change if the negotiation involved noisy neighbours, the purchase and sale of a used car, a multimillion dollar lawsuit involving failed technology in a satel-

lite communication system, the development of a new constitutional accord between various levels of governments in a country, or a "jurisdictional" dispute between rival motorcycle clubs in a large urban centre?

• What makes a good negotiator?

This chapter on negotiation and its suggested readings are designed to offer answers to these and other questions, to demonstrate where negotiation fits in the ADR field, particularly in relation to mediation, and to help you to become a more informed, skilful, and efficient negotiator whatever the subject matter of the negotiation. Although negotiation, like ADR, has theoretical and practice complexities, the essence of negotiation can be distilled by understanding the language of negotiation; inquiring into what makes up strategic negotiation practices; identifying helpful (and unhelpful) negotiation techniques; thinking of negotiation as a staged process; knowing when (and when not) to negotiate; and assessing the impact of power on the negotiation process.

B. THE LANGUAGE OF NEGOTIATION

Whether you are preparing for, or participating in, a negotiation, you need to be fluent in the language of negotiation. This fluency applies both to the substantive side of negotiation — what the negotiation is about — and to the process of negotiation — how the negotiation takes place. As you develop this fluency, you need to be particularly familiar with how the language of negotiation intersects with the language of ADR.

The substantive side of negotiation refers to the context within which the negotiation arises. The significant influence of context on disputes and dispute resolution was discussed in chapter 1. The same holds true for the impact of context on negotiations. Real-world details shape and influence how negotiations proceed and what agreements are reached. To be effective, negotiators must be as familiar as possible with these details and the ways in which this context affects the actual negotiation process and its outcome.

The negotiating context will involve, at a minimum, the subject matter under discussion. Whether the negotiation involves determining the amount of compensation or other redress for personal injuries, assessing the tax implications of a signing bonus in professional sport, unravelling the shifting standards to be applied in a medical malpractice case, or fixing the purchase price of a used car, effective negotiation in any of these circumstances requires the negotiators to be familiar with the knowledge base that makes up the negotiation's subject matter. A good negotiator must be able to talk about fractured femurs, the impact of the *Income Tax Act* on deferred income, the risk at a certain point in time of HIV infection during artificial insemination, or the depreciated value of a used automobile in order to help fashion an effective agreement. Absent this substantive information, a negotiator would be at a serious disadvantage vis-à-vis another negotiator who was fully informed. Depending on the subject matter of the negotiation, the acquisition of the necessary knowledge base can be an easy or a daunting task.

The negotiating substance also includes details about negotiating venue, the parties themselves and their representatives, and any background to the substantive issues in dispute. A negotiator may be quite at ease with complicated commercial lease provisions. However, where the negotiation takes place (is it China or Canada?); who is involved (is it Microsoft or a small family flower shop; a bottom-line oriented CEO or a lawyer who believes in getting to yes?); and whether there is a history to the problem (is the leasing part of a long-standing and politically charged issue between a city and a pro sport franchise or the first meetings in a new business relationship?) will add considerable substantive complexity to the actual negotiation. Many opportunities may be missed if these ins and outs are not clear.

The context within which the negotiation is taking place also includes relevant social, political, and economic conditions. These conditions are connected to the negotiation's subject matter but add increasing levels of sophistication to any analysis of, or participation in, a particular negotiation. For example, the policy of a medical insurer to strongly resist settling all but the most blatant of medical malpractice cases may be as critical contextual information for a claimant's negotiator as is a thorough understanding of the likely quantum of damages in the case. Is this insurance practice an interest capable of being included in the negotiations or a value incapable of change without structural improvements to how insurers think? The cultural significance of a Sun Dance ceremony for Aboriginal peoples is as important, if not more important, to effective negotiations as is an understanding of property and criminal law when attempting to negotiate how or when the Aboriginal Sun Dancers will leave private property. An agreement reached peacefully through some type of mediation might require more time, if more time is politically possible, to respect the culture. A provincial government's negotiation of compensation for the cancellation of a large hydroelectric completion project will involve assessments of potential political fallout and any adverse impact on continued capital investment in the province as much as complicated calculations of a company's lost profits due to the cancellation. Familiarity with drafting complex contractual conditions may be of secondary importance in an industry where handshakes on principles are the norm in any negotiated agreement. In some societies, building relationships between negotiators may be as essential a part of successful negotiations as is determining delivery dates or warranty terms for the product being sold. Gender may mean that listening and compromise are valued more in negotiation than argumentation and grudgingly granting concessions. More might be gained by being nice.

Because negotiations take place in these diverse contextual settings, developing the requisite substantive or contextual fluency for all situations is probably impossible. As a result, negotiators often specialize. For example, a lawyer may finely tune her or his practice in negotiation around wrongful dismissal disputes, intellectual property matters, labour discords, personal injury cases, or other settings. Business people may limit their negotiations to a particular industry. Negotiating outside of these areas can be analogous to visiting a new country and trying to speak the language. One may get by with a few key words here and there but proficiency and efficiency in communicating are not often attainable without a lengthy stay.

In addition to the substantive side of negotiation, effective negotiators also must be able to speak the language of process. There are certain negotiation process terms that can be viewed as generic to many negotiation processes. These terms represent a breakdown of the overall negotiation process into its essential procedural components. Effective negotiation involves acquiring the knowledge and skills that lie behind each of these terms and then being able to apply this knowledge and these skills in a particular negotiation context. Each of the following negotiation terms is described in more detail in later pages as well as other negotiation words or expressions falling under these headings.

Strategy: An orientation or approach to negotiation that is an overall plan for achieving your goals in a negotiation. A negotiation strategy influences a person's negotiating behaviour.

Tactic: A specific negotiation behaviour or technique. A series of tactics make up your negotiation strategy and represent the primary way in which the negotiating strategy is implemented.

Issues: The substantive questions or matters that the parties disagree about and for which an agreement is being sought.

Position: A proposal for a solution or agreement on an identified issue, which a party holds or puts forward.

Options: A range of alternative or possible solutions.

Interests: The needs, desires, concerns, fears, and hopes that must be satisfied if a negotiated agreement is to be satisfactory to a party.

Type: The general category of the negotiation. Negotiations can be about disputes (what has already occurred) or about transactions or rules (what will happen in the future).

At times the negotiating process can become more than a vehicle for handling the substantive side of the negotiation. The process of negotiation itself can become a contested negotiation issue or part of a desired solution. For example, one party may want to delay proceedings with the expectation that the delay will be helpful in achieving a more advantageous resolution. Slowing the negotiation process down may be seen as just as important a substantive outcome as any agreement on the merits. Another party may adopt a negotiating strategy or tactic that offends the opposite party. Instead of proceeding to negotiate solutions to the substantive issues, the negotiators may find it necessary to negotiate agreements on how to respond to, or eliminate, the offensive behaviour. In other words, the parties may need to negotiate agreements on how to negotiate. Negotiation substance and process often can be interdependent, more intertwined than separate concepts.

Being conversant with the substantive side and process attributes of a negotiation is important for effective negotiations. Negotiating without a full appreciation of context or a careful understanding of process can result in incomplete and probably unproductive discussions. But fluency in the substantive and procedural language of negotiation does not guarantee a predictable negotiation conversation. The negotiation process will vary widely from one case to another because differing and unique contexts will always be at play, and the choices and uses of negotiation procedures will not be uniform over space and time. Even negotiations involving the same subject matter, such as wrongful dismissal cases, or recurring negotiations between the same parties, such as collective bargaining sessions, will be bound to exhibit differences of one degree or another. The uncertainty, variability, or indeterminacy associated with negotiation is consistent with the general ideas of dispute processing discussed in chapter 2. In resolving a dispute or planning a transaction by negotiation, the search must be for the substantive and procedural knowledge and skills necessary for effective negotiation. Fluency in the substantive and procedural language of negotiation will help in acquiring the needed knowledge and skills.

C. STRATEGIC NEGOTIATIONS

If a negotiation strategy is an overall plan for achieving your goals in a negotiation, three questions arise. First, are there different negotiation strategies? Second, if so, what determines which strategy to use in a specific situation? Third, are some strategies better than others?

The literature on negotiation is voluminous.[3] Some negotiation materials are specifically directed to a particular industry or subject matter. Other negotiation writings are more generic in their application. In this literature, discussions of strategic approaches to negotiation include references to terms such as:

- competitive negotiation
- compromise negotiation
- cooperative negotiation
- distributive bargaining
- integrative bargaining
- interest-based bargaining
- positional bargaining
- principled negotiation
- value-claiming negotiation
- value-creating negotiation

There are also expressions of negotiation strategy such as hard bargaining and soft bargaining, win-lose and win-win results of negotiation.

Effective negotiators need to know the meaning of these negotiation expressions. These words, all of which are discussed below, are part of a good negotiator's vocabulary. But, more important, effective negotiators need to be able to implement or use a particular negotiation strategy. As a first step in doing this, negotiators need to remind themselves that a negotiation strategy is essentially an overall plan for achieving your goals in a negotiation. Accordingly, a negotiation strategy must be defined by, finely tuned to, and designed to achieve a negotiator's goals.

What are the goals in a negotiation? Given the diverse settings in which negotiation takes place, goals can be as varied as the context of the negotiation itself. There may be substantive goals — to reach an acceptable agreement; to receive fair compensation; to make as much as possible; to buy the property; to eliminate the competition; to get a job back; to reduce the noise. There may be procedural goals — to

---

3   Consider, as a start, the texts in Further Readings at the conclusion of this chapter.

avoid court; to settle quickly; to settle slowly; to save money; to keep things quiet. There also may be personal or psychological goals — to feel satisfied or empowered; to see justice done; to be vindicated; to be safe; to be fair; to maintain a relationship; to out-manoeuvre the other negotiator. Some negotiation goals obviously relate directly to an anticipated substantive agreement while other goals are linked closely to the process of negotiation itself. But goals are outcomes anticipated from the negotiation. Because negotiation and mediation (assisted negotiation) have been a significant focus of ADR, the various overarching goals of alternative dispute resolution described in chapter 1 also may be the desired goals of a negotiator in a specific setting, such as wanting "ownership" of any negotiated agreement, feeling empowered, or reaching agreement quickly and inexpensively. These general ADR goals also may be the motivations and desired outcomes of governments or institutions that mandate or encourage the use of negotiation for resolving a dispute or planning a transaction.

In most cases, negotiators will have packages of substantive, procedural, and psychological goals that are being pursued in a particular negotiation. These goals will usually have a direct correlation to what caused the conflict to emerge in the first instance. The wrongfully dismissed employee may want not only twelve months' salary in lieu of notice (a substantive goal) but also assurances from the employer that no future statements will be made or actions taken that could harm the employee's reputation in the industry (a psychological/procedural goal). The sexually harassed university student will want the offending behaviour to stop. However, she also may hope to avoid undue publicity to protect her privacy and, just as important, demand promises and protections so that other students will not experience the same misconduct. A defence lawyer may plea bargain with the Crown prosecutor if a negotiated agreement to plead guilty, perhaps to a lesser charge, would minimize the time that the client spends in jail and would get the case over with the least publicity. Even the seemingly singular goal (a disgruntled customer wants her money back) may reveal with careful scrutiny other goals (a desire to be treated respectfully, a fast and cheap solution) that are integral to a successful negotiation.

Whether there are multiple negotiation goals or apparently only one, a negotiated agreement will be possible only if these goals are achieved unless, of course, the goals are modified or abandoned by the parties. The degree and nature of any change in negotiation goals will depend on their strength — how important it is to the negotiator that this goal is met. In some cases, goals in a negotiation may be presented, explicitly or not, as non-negotiable. For example, unless the spouse apologizes for having the affair, the opposite spouse adamantly states there will be no negotiated agreement in the divorce case. In other cases, there will be a certain amount of interplay and exchange between and among negotiation goals. A sexual abuse survivor may be willing to voluntarily accept less monetary compensation than a court would award if the case is settled quickly or if the retelling of past tragedies in court can be avoided. Another claimant may give up negotiation demands that her lawyer or perhaps a judge in a pre-trial conference labels as unrealistic. Mounting legal costs, the stress and strain of a lawsuit, the impact of negotiating tactics employed by the other side, new information, the passage of time, or other events may affect, either positively or negatively, how important it is for a negotiator to get something in a negotiation.

Whether the negotiation goal is substantive, procedural, or psychological, a highly specific goal such as a closing date in a real estate transaction or a less tangible goal such as being treated fairly by the insurance company, or a fixed or shifting package of such goals, it is these goals or expected negotiation outcomes that drive the negotiation forward. Thinking strategically about negotiation is essentially thinking about adopting or mandating an approach to the negotiation and utilizing negotiation behaviours that are most likely to help achieve these outcomes and about avoiding approaches to negotiation that will not be helpful or that will be counter-productive. You also need to consider how your chosen strategy will affect the other negotiators who are also pursuing their own negotiation goals.

Despite the enormous variability that will exist in negotiation goals and the range of references about strategies in the negotiation literature, there are three widely recognized and broadly defined North American orientations towards negotiation that merit attention: competitive or adversarial negotiation, problem-solving or principled negotiation, and compromise negotiation.

Each of these negotiation strategies, because of its nature and characteristics, implies that its adoption and use may result in the achievement of certain general goals in a negotiation. These strategies also have obvious implications for assessing whether a negotiator's more specific goals are likely to be achieved.

Riskin and Westbrook[4] describe adversarial negotiation and problem-solving negotiation:

---

4   L.L. Riskin & J.E. Westbrook, *Dispute Resolution and Lawyers* (St. Paul, MN: West Publishing Co., 1987) at 116.

The adversarial orientation usually is grounded upon the assumption that there is a limited resource — such as money, golf balls, or lima beans — and the parties must decide whether and how to divide it. In such a situation, the parties' interests conflict; what one gains, the other must lose. An adversarial orientation naturally fosters strategies designed to maximize the client's position with respect to the resource in question. And the typical techniques include those designed to uncover as much as possible about the other side's situation and simultaneously mislead the other side as to your own situation. Until recently, the adversarial orientation has been the basis for most of the writing about negotiation by lawyers, as well as most of the popular writing about negotiation.

The problem-solving orientation is quite different. It seeks to meet the underlying needs of all parties to the dispute or transaction, and, accordingly, tends to produce strategies designed to promote the disclosure and relevance of these underlying needs. The recommended techniques include those intended to increase the number of issues for bargaining or to "expand the pie" before dividing it.

There are references to compromise bargaining as a separate negotiation strategy. Sometimes referred to as soft-bargaining or give-and-take bargaining, compromise bargainers believe trade-offs are necessary to get an agreement. There is an expectation that trade-offs from one side will result in reciprocal and roughly equal concessions from the other side. In this type of bargaining, the negotiators anticipate meeting somewhere in the middle. A competitive bargainer often can offer false concessions to give the appearance that compromises are being made. Success in compromise negotiation depends on the negotiator feeling that he or she has been reasonable, which means accommodating the other party to a certain extent, and that the negotiation has involved roughly equivalent concessions on both sides. Provided the final result is in the range of what is deemed acceptable, compromise negotiators are satisfied.

Problem-solving negotiation is sometimes used interchangeably with principled negotiation or, alternatively, interest-based bargaining. Popularized by Fisher and Ury in *Getting to Yes*,[5] principled negotiation has five key characteristics.

---

5   R. Fisher & W. Ury, *Getting to Yes: Negotiating Agreement without Giving In* (Boston: Houghton Mifflin Company, 1981).

1. **Separate the people from the problem.**

   Human beings are involved in negotiations. The interpersonal relationships between negotiators can often become entangled with the
   discussion of substantive issues in a negotiation. Positional bargaining (framing a negotiation as a contest of wills over positions), misperceptions, strong emotions, and miscommunications can create
   "people problems." These people problems, both yours and the other
   side's, must be dealt with directly and regularly in the negotiation.
   However, do not try to solve them with substantive concessions.

2. **Focus on interests not positions.**

   In a dispute, each party has certain needs, desires, concerns, fears,
   and hopes that motivate them to make, to accept, or to reject offers
   or counter-offers. However, behind offers or opposed positions
   often lie shared and compatible interests, as well as conflicting ones.
   Identifying these important interests and insisting that they be reconciled in any agreement can lead to more creative and mutually
   satisfying solutions.

3. **Invent options for mutual gain.**

   By avoiding obstacles to creative thinking in a negotiation (premature judgment, searching for a single answer, assuming a fixed pie,
   it's their problem), there are opportunities to broaden the options
   on the negotiating table and consider how shared and different
   interests can lead to mutual gains.

4. **Insist on objective criteria.**

   Avoid trying to settle differences of interest on the basis of will-
   power. Never yield to pressure but rather negotiate using objective
   criteria that are independent of the will of any negotiator. Objective
   criteria are what the negotiators decide are fair standards (the blue
   book value of a car in a claim against an insurance company) or fair
   procedures (the advice of a judge given in a pre-trial conference on
   who is at fault).

5. **Know your best alternative to a negotiated agreement (BATNA).**

   Rather than using a "bottom line" in a negotiation, develop your best
   alternative to a negotiated agreement. Your BATNA is the standard
   against which any proposed, and perhaps unexpected, offer can be
   measured. Your BATNA can protect you from accepting terms that
   are too unfavourable and from rejecting a good agreement.

The distinction between adversarial and problem-solving negotiation is not that experienced negotiators ignore their own interests or those of their clients and focus solely or unthinkingly on demands or positions. Behind every position or demand in a negotiation will be basic needs or concerns that the proposed solution seeks to satisfy. For example, in a personal injury case, the insurance company's settlement offer will probably reflect, among other things, an amount that is economically affordable to the company and consistent with amounts paid in similar cases so as not to set an undesired precedent. In negotiations for the sale of a business, the demand by the purchaser's negotiator for a non-competition clause in the purchase and sale agreement will provide the purchaser with needed income security by limiting the rights of the seller to carry on a similar business within a specific geographic location for a period of time. In adversarial negotiations, the focus may be more on the development of proposed solutions or offers and counter-offers with less explicit attention being paid to the important needs or concerns that underlie these positions.

The same reasoning holds true for compromise negotiators. Compromises or concessions are not made in the abstract or without thought. When a negotiator offers to drop demands for a five-year guarantee, hoping for a corresponding price reduction, or suggests splitting the difference between the two outstanding offers, there is an implicit, if not explicit, understanding that the proposal will satisfy the needs of the negotiator or those of the client. Concession granting is much more a technique for effectively moving parties to a resolution than an abandonment by any of the negotiators of what is really important to them in the negotiations. Indeed, one of the important interests of compromise negotiation is to go through a process of making these concessions in a fair and reasonable way. A well-done compromise negotiation process actually meets important psychological needs of the negotiator — to be fair and be seen to be fair through a process of give and take and to expect reciprocal behaviour.

However, a more important distinction between adversarial, compromise, and problem-solving negotiation is one of goals. Underpinning each of these negotiating strategies are some fundamentally different goals. Consistent with adversarial thinking discussed in chapter 2, a primary goal in adversarial negotiation is to obtain the largest possible share of what is at stake in the negotiation. The bottom line is that the adversarial negotiator wants to win. Because the negotiation is viewed as a zero-sum game — what one party gains the other must give — success, or maximizing individual gain, in a negotiation means that the other party must lose. This emphasis on distributing a fixed quantity of resources between the parties to a negotiation has been called distributive bargaining. What one side wins, the other side must, as a matter of course, lose.

Although the goal of compromise negotiation is not exactly lose-lose, meeting somewhere in the middle is. The strategy of the compromise negotiator is to induce, directly or indirectly, the other party to cooperate and to make reciprocal concessions until a solution is reached. Rather than resorting to the tactics of the competitive or adversarial negotiator, the compromise negotiator makes moves to establish a trusting, cooperative atmosphere to reach a fair resolution, which means each party has given up something to reach a compromise.

Problem-solving negotiation has a different goal; it seeks to meet the needs of all parties to the negotiation. Problem-solving negotiators want a win-win result. This goal is sought to be achieved by explicitly recognizing the underlying interests or needs of *all parties* to the dispute or transaction and then by creatively developing options or solutions that meet these needs. Rather than seeing the negotiation as necessarily involving a fixed quantity of resources or a process of give and take, problem-solving negotiators try to "expand the pie" by integrating the parties' needs into a larger basket of solutions than might have seemed possible without disclosure of underlying interests. This approach to negotiation can be called integrative bargaining or interest-based bargaining. The parties collaborate or work together in a cooperative way to further the interests or aims of all. Flowing from this primary problem-solving goal may be others — faster, cheaper, empowering, or perhaps several of the various goals of ADR articulated in chapter 1.

Fisher and Ury provide a simple example of the distinction between adversarial and problem-solving negotiation strategies with their library dispute:[6]

> Consider the story of two men quarreling in a library. One wants the window open and the other wants it closed. They bicker back and forth about how much to leave it open: a crack, halfway, three quarters of the way. No solution satisfies them both.
>
> Enter the librarian. She asks one why he wants the window open: "To get some fresh air." She asks the other why he wants it closed: "To avoid the draft." After thinking a minute, she opens wide a window in the next room, bringing in fresh air without a draft.

---

6   *Ibid.* at 41.

In the library, the initial negotiation is adversarial. The focus is on positions — what each person wants. The parties are engaged in positional bargaining, each one trying to persuade the other that their position or proposed solution is best. But the positions are incompatible. If one side wins, say the window is open, the other side loses. If the window is open halfway, a compromiser's position, both parties may be dissatisfied. The librarian changes the negotiation to problem solving. She identifies the underlying interests — why the proposed solutions are important. She then proceeds to "expand the pie" by identifying a creative solution that satisfies one party's need to avoid a draft, the other party's need for fresh air, and their common need for a comfortable reading environment.

Consider another practical example that illustrates the distinction between adversarial and problem-solving negotiation.

The apparent controversy is over the cost of automobile repairs performed for Stork Delivery Inc. by City Auto Services Ltd. There is no issue about the quality of the work. The dispute is about the extent of the repairs given the age and condition of the Stork delivery vehicle. The owner of Stork is demanding a large refund. Lawyers for Stork and City Auto, trying to avoid an expensive, time-consuming, and uncertain day in court, have been negotiating politely, but adversarially. The lowest refund acceptable to Stork still is being rejected by the owner of City Auto until an important event. The owner of City Auto discloses that he is worried about losing the respect of his employees by agreeing to pay the requested refund, even though the amount is economically fair, reasonable in all the circumstances, and makes good business sense. This new fact represents disclosure of an important psychological or procedural interest on the part of City Auto's owner. The solution pie is expanded when the owner of Stork agrees to write a letter to City Auto employees commending them on their work, acknowledging the dispute arose out of a mutual misunderstanding, noting the compromise settlement was fair to both businesses, and stating she would recommend City Auto services to other businesses in her industry. The deal is clinched. Although resources are distributed eventually in this negotiation (a refund is paid), recognizing and responding to the integrative aspects of the dispute (a concern about losing face; an appreciation for the quality of the work) allows for a mutually satisfactory solution. Problem solving opens up opportunities for value-creating negotiating, which leads to more satisfactory distributions or value-claiming negotiation.

While adversarial, compromise, and problem-solving approaches to negotiation are widely recognized as negotiation strategies, these orientations to a negotiation undoubtedly do not exhaustively describe all the overall plans that can be adopted for achieving one's negotiation goals. Given the incredible diversity of negotiating settings and scenarios, it would be presumptuous to assume that only three general approaches to negotiation are possible. Also, as discussed in chapter 7, "ADR and Culture," the theory and practice of problem-solving negotiation have deep roots in Westernized notions of negotiation and may have little meaning in non-Western cultures. However, these three negotiation strategies do provide guidance. They illustrate that different approaches to negotiation and to the achievement of negotiation goals are possible. They point to the importance of outcomes in negotiation and the significance of choosing a plan to achieve those outcomes. They show the need for a positive correlation between a negotiation plan and the steps that are actually taken in the negotiation. Finally, the descriptions of these strategies point to the knowledge, skills, and attributes that a negotiator would need to successfully implement one of these strategies. For example, listening carefully or asking the right type of question (open, closed, yes/no, leading) would be skills needed by any type of negotiator. Credibly presenting an unrealistically low opening offer to the plaintiff's lawyer and then grudgingly granting small concessions (to convince them there is little room to move even though the client will authorize substantially more money to be paid) would represent skills used by an adversarial negotiator. The principled negotiator, on the other hand, would need, *inter alia*, to be able to uncover the underlying interests important to both sides respecting the economic issues in the negotiation before discussing any possible solutions.

1) Choosing a Negotiation Strategy

Choosing and using a particular negotiation strategy is not always a conscious and deliberate decision. In many cases, the plan for a negotiation may be more ad hoc or limited to following practices that have worked well for a negotiator in previous situations. A negotiator may be attempting to achieve well-defined goals such as stopping a planned development project or settling a business dispute quickly but with little thought given to a strategic plan to achieve these goals. For a variety of reasons, full attention may not be given to a process of selecting an overall negotiation plan that is most likely to result in the achievement of desirable goals. However, as more and more negotiators develop comprehensive understandings of the orientations that can be taken to a negotiation and how these different orientations can help or hinder the achievement of goals in a negotiation, the careful choice of a negotiation strategy will become a more common and integral part of the decision to negotiate.

The choice of which negotiating strategy will be most effective in any given case will depend on how a number of variables are assessed. A particularly important consideration will be the degree to which the goals being pursued in the negotiation match the goals commonly associated with the chosen negotiation strategy. For example, in a residential real estate transaction, a purchaser's goal of paying as low a purchase price as possible, even a price that is unfair to the seller, may be incongruent with choosing a primarily problem-solving orientation to bargaining with the seller over purchase price. The purchaser's win-lose approach does not match the problem-solving search for a mutually satisfactory solution. Conversely, an employer who wants a dismissed manager's severance package to be mutually fair, to ameliorate the manager's financial stress during re-entry into the marketplace and to enhance the employer's progressive reputation would find an adversarial negotiation strategy and its distributive, zero-sum outlook incompatible with these goals.

Apart from ensuring that there is an acceptable degree of goal consistency between the proposed negotiation strategy and what the particular negotiator hopes to achieve in the negotiation, several other factors can have a bearing on the effectiveness of a negotiation strategy:

- The probable strategy of the other parties to the negotiation

  From past dealings, demands made, documents exchanged, or other sources, a negotiator may be able to discover the general objectives of the other parties to the negotiation. This information may suggest what orientation or strategy will most likely be followed by the other side. Knowing the probable strategies of the other parties to the negotiation can assist in determining your own negotiation strategy. Will you be able to successfully implement a problem-solving approach against a tough adversarial negotiator? Are you prepared for the type of negotiation process that will occur if both parties adopt adversarial strategies or if only one side takes a problem-solving orientation? Will a cooperative negotiation orientation, either principled or compromise, be seen as weak or be exploited by an experienced competitive negotiator? Will two principled negotiators resolve matters quickly and fairly? Being aware of the probable approach to the negotiation that will be taken by the other side also can help you plan specific moves or tactics in the negotiation and be prepared to respond to likely behaviours coming from the other party.

- Integrative or distributive issues

If the issues to be negotiated are viewed as distributional or zero sum — one for me is minus one for you — some would argue that a problem-solving strategy that seeks to discover creative and integrative solutions neglects the harsh reality and hard bargaining that accompany the ultimate distribution of limited resources.[7] An automobile accident between strangers often is portrayed as a classical distributive problem — benefits or compensation to one party come only at a significant cost to the other party. Attempts to convert an essentially distributive problem into an integrative one through a careful articulation of *all matters* that are important to the parties in the automobile accident may ignore the fact that the most demanding aspect of nearly every negotiation is the distributional one. Eventually, one negotiator seeks more at the expense of the other. On the other hand, understanding that the distributional gap between financial offers and counter-offers is due to interests such as economic fears, timing concerns, or future relationship worries can perhaps lead to cooperative considerations of alternative solution packages for bridging this gap. The insurance company may agree to pay more if the deal is kept confidential. An apology might be worth a lot.

- The necessary knowledge and style

The successful implementation of a negotiation plan requires knowledge and skills, and a particular style, complementary to the chosen strategy. What is required is a full conceptual understanding of what the specific negotiation orientation entails and the personal and professional abilities to use the appropriate techniques and skills associated with that orientation. As discussed in chapter 2, some people's styles of conflict interaction, personality type, or other behavioural attributes may be incompatible with one or other of the negotiation strategies even if their goals suggest one negotiation orientation is an obvious choice.

For example, some people are too nice to be adversarial negotiators. Their personal attitudes, beliefs, and values do not allow them to think only of their own needs or the needs of their client. Similarly, other negotiators may be unable to think or act collaboratively because of the highly competitive ways in which they respond to conflict situations. As the number of parties to a negotiation increases, including lawyers or other representatives, the potential for yawning

---

7   J. White, "The Pros and Cons of 'Getting to Yes'" (1984) 34 J. Legal Educ. 115.

gaps between personal conflict styles and the requisite skills needed to implement a desirable negotiation strategy will increase.

- Perceived advantages and disadvantages

The decision to use a negotiation strategy will probably involve a weighing of the strategy's advantages and disadvantages compared with the benefits and costs associated with another strategy. Although adversarial negotiation may help to maximize gain and avoid a risk of being exploited, there are risks of this strategy creating misunderstanding, encouraging retaliatory or similar aggressive behaviour, causing a premature breakdown or negotiation impasse, harming continuing relationships, or resulting in similar obstacles associated with adversarial thinking.

Compromise negotiators can reach fair and favourable outcomes and avoid fewer impasses or breakdowns in the bargaining process but their cooperative moves may be interpreted as signs of weakness. This assessment, although inaccurate, may actually increase the level of demands and expectations coming from the opposite side. In addition, compromise negotiators may be seriously disadvantaged by making far too many concessions unilaterally, hoping to encourage the other side to reciprocate. Before they recognize the risk, compromisers have given away far too much.

Problem-solving negotiation may yield higher joint benefits, maintain positive long-term relationships, and generally avoid the risks of a more aggressive approach. However, there is again a risk that the problem-solving negotiator's collaborative overtures may be perceived as weak or the principled negotiator may be surprised or taken aback if the other side does not act in a similar manner. This surprise can become unproductive when the problem solver realizes not everyone values their principled approach and has difficulty separating the people from the problem. Problem-solving negotiators may also unnecessarily abandon goals of maximizing gains.

- Cultural considerations

Although the impact of culture on dispute resolution practices is more fully dealt with in chapter 7, cultural considerations will play a role in choosing a negotiation strategy. Like the concept of conflict, the expressions "adversarial negotiation," "compromise negotiation," or "problem-solving negotiation" may have little meaning or, at least, no easy translation in certain cultural contexts. In different countries or regions or within specific communities, there may exist more culturally determined definitions of what are useful and acceptable negotiation approaches. Culture may also prescribe very clear goals for the negotiation of disputes such as maintaining social harmony, respecting or being submissive to accepted class structures, avoiding confrontations with authority figures, emphasizing healing within the community or maintaining a struggle for social justice. These goals, if accepted, may make the choice between more adversarial, more compromise, or more problem-solving approaches to negotiation an obvious one. In choosing a negotiation strategy, care must be taken to assess whether any specific negotiation strategy can be successfully shipped off to another country or culture or whether it will be difficult to adapt a particular strategy to the cultural conditions.

- The changes in negotiation strategy

Choosing a negotiation strategy does not always mean making a stark and static choice between warring conceptions of the bargaining process. It is true that some negotiators may be highly competitive throughout a negotiation process. Adversarial negotiators may commonly rely on intimidation, threats, blaming behaviour, and their own superiority to get all that they want out of negotiations. These negotiators may regularly make extreme demands and few, or small, concessions as they seek to win in the negotiation. Other bargainers may regularly exhibit classic problem-solving or compromise characteristics in their negotiations such as moving to establish common ground, emphasizing shared values, and being trustworthy, fair, objective, and reasonable.

However, it should not be uncommon for strategies to change during the course of negotiations. If circumstances dictate a change in a negotiator's goals, if an impasse arises, if new information surfaces, or if there are other developments that affect the perceived efficacy of a negotiation plan, good negotiators will reassess their strategy and make necessary changes. For example, an adversarial negotiator, trying to pay as little support as possible to his ex-spouse and attempting to maximize time with the children, may be forced to alter approaches if his goal of maintaining a positive working relationship with his ex-spouse is being jeopardized, contrary to expectations, by his overly competitive approach. A principled negotiator, who has observed the mounting impact on the client of the dirty tricks and tactics, changes to a winner-take-all approach on the client's instructions.

Most commentators also agree that although adversarial and problem-solving processes are antagonistic, both are present in virtually every negotiation. According to Lax and Sebenius, "no matter how much creative problem solving enlarges the pie, it still must be divided; value that has been created must be claimed."[8] As a result, there is an essential tension in many negotiations between collaborative attempts to create value and competitive moves to claim it. For example, in a libel case against a newspaper, a proposed negotiated agreement may include innovative terms around the type and timing of an apology, measures to prevent future libels while ensuring respect for investigative reporting, payment to a charity in lieu of damages, and reimbursement of legal costs. Although the agreement may "expand the solution pie" and generally reconcile the shared and competing interests of the parties, at some point the true distributive aspects of the problem need to be addressed. In this libel case, it is likely that the amount of money paid to the charity and for legal costs will need to be decided in a more competitive, less interest-based manner because attempts to finalize the amount using objective criteria (what is fair? what would a court award?) will only provide a range of what the money payment could be. The plaintiff is likely to want as large a payment as possible while the defendant will usually hope to pay as little as possible. The negotiations to determine how much money should be paid will be, necessarily, of a zero-sum nature.

D. NEGOTIATING TECHNIQUES

If a negotiating strategy is an overall plan for achieving desired goals in any negotiation, negotiating techniques represent how a chosen strategy is primarily implemented. Negotiating techniques are the specific behaviours or collections of behaviours that are intended to help negotiators achieve their goals. Karass calls negotiating techniques "the fine-tuning mechanisms by which goals are reached."[9] Negotiating techniques include the reactions or responses that are made to the other negotiator's behaviour, again with a view to successful achievement of desired goals.

Negotiating techniques are often presented as a catalogue of tactics. The following list provides examples of ten commonly employed negotiating tactics. For each tactic there is a brief description of what a negotiator would need to do to employ the tactic, followed by reasons

---

8   D.A. Lax & J.K. Sebenius, *The Manager as Negotiator* (New York: The Free Press, 1976) at 30.

9   C.L. Karass, *The Negotiating Game* (New York: Thomas Y. Crowell Co., 1970) at 183.

why such tactics might be used, risks associated with their use, and possible responses to such negotiating behaviour. Comments on several other negotiating techniques follow. This list of tactics is not exhaustive because negotiating behaviours are essentially infinite in their possibilities. The examples given are illustrations of common tactics that can be used to implement a particular strategy or attain negotiating goals. The descriptions should also aid in deciding when such tactics should be used.

1. **Agenda**: In preparing for the negotiation or during the actual negotiations, the negotiator creates a list of the issues or topics to be addressed and the order in which they will be covered. This tactic can be used

   • to ensure an important matter is on the table or to attempt to keep certain issues from being discussed;
   • to establish order for the issues to be negotiated;
   • to take some control over the negotiations; or
   • to focus attention and provide a sense of progress in negotiations.

   Risks include creating disputes about the issues and the order for discussion if there are conflicting agendas.

   Responses include

   • presenting or negotiating an alternative agenda; or
   • assessing the agenda to determine what is important for a successful negotiation.

2. **Boulwareism** (take it or leave it): The negotiator may present an offer based on thorough "homework" that is "fair," takes account of any concession she might make, and is, or is presented as, not negotiable. This tactic can be used

   • to save time;
   • to avoid haggling;
   • to give them control or power;
   • to put pressure on the other side; or
   • as a bluff.

   Risks include

   • causing resentment, which may prevent the other side from seriously considering the offer;

- losing credibility; the other side will not believe the statement and will assume the negotiator will give more. If there is no movement, an impasse will frequently be reached; or
- encouraging the other side, which gets nothing in the process, to sabotage the outcome.

Responses include

- confronting the tactic. Let the negotiator know you are unwilling to accept the tactic; or
- giving the negotiator the opportunity to move from the position, allowing for face-saving. For example: "You've obviously given this a lot of thought. It would make it easier for me to look at this if you could tell me how you calculated this." Use questions and active listening until the underlying problem is on the table.

3. **Brer Rabbit**: The negotiator asserts plausible, though actually unimportant, demands on the assumption the other party will want to thwart them and thus give the negotiator what is really wanted. This tactic is related to false demands where a negotiator disguises false demands as real demands that are later yielded in the negotiations for some gain. This tactic can be used

- to disguise the negotiator's real motives;
- to provide something on which the negotiator can yield at no real cost to himself;
- to put the other side off balance; or
- to offset demands made by the other side.

Risks include

- triggering more demands from the other side;
- diverting both negotiators' attention from their real concerns and ways of meeting them;
- creating bad will and mistrust as the other perceives the manipulation being attempted;
- wasting time; or
- bringing the negotiations to a halt.

Responses include

- expressing disbelief;
- ignoring or deferring discussion of the demand; or
- probing the basis of the demand. Ask "why?" "What would happen if . . ." "Please explain . . ."

4. **Brinkmanship**: The negotiator delays until the outside limit of the established deadline for any meeting, stalls until the end of the meeting to reach the major issues, or creates new, earlier deadlines. This tactic can be used

- to generate pressure and anxiety, and induce a fear in the other side that no deal will be made unless concessions are offered;
- to increase the perceived control of the person using it;
- to assess how sure the other side is; or
- to increase the other side's investment in the negotiation, in emotional, time, or financial terms, inducing them to believe some settlement is necessary having come this far.

Risks include

- miscalculating: the other side may simply refuse to operate on this basis;
- increasing the costs resulting from the delay;
- causing the time pressure and resulting emotionality to impede the development of the most advantageous outcome; or
- creating anger and resentment that may negatively influence future negotiations or implementation of settlement terms.

Responses include

- ignoring the alleged deadline, assuming the other side will extend it;
- withdrawing from the negotiation;
- dividing the negotiation into phases, and resetting times with desirable deadlines;
- demanding or requesting an extension, and explicitly rejecting the limit set by the other side; or
- seeking the factual basis of the deadline, offering alternative means of meeting the other's concerns underlying it, and, at the same time, informing the other of the reasons the deadline is unacceptable.

5. **Concessions**: The negotiator makes early concessions to the other side. Typically, concessions are made in respect of positions. This tactic can be used

- if one concession will produce another from the other side; or
- if making a concession will demonstrate good faith that will be reciprocated, facilitating the discussions.

Risks include

- having the tactic interpreted as a sign of weakness to be exploited; or
- inflating the other side's expectations and demands.

Responses include

- expressing appreciation and continuing to talk about the issues;
- responding with a less significant concession; or
- using it as a wedge to obtain a greater concession.

6. **Good Cop, Bad Cop**: One negotiator conveys the impression that he is being reasonable and fair while his co-negotiator (who may be the client who has to give instructions to settle) is the one who is standing firm or being unreasonable. This tactic can be used

- to give the impression that a change in position is unlikely;
- to avoid breakdowns by having only the good negotiator in the face-to-face negotiations; or
- to respond to concerns of unfairness.

Risks include

- being too transparent and ineffective; or
- being unable to respond to a principled negotiator.

Responses include

- naming the tactic and calling for a more principled approach; or
- identifying why the bad negotiator is unable to agree with the good negotiator.

7. **Questions**: In a negotiation, a negotiator can ask open-ended questions (why do you say my client is liable?), closed or yes-no questions (are there any witnesses to the accident?), clarifying or leading questions (there is no case support for that head of damage, is there?). Questions might also be classified as probing, hypothetical, and rhetorical. This tactic can be used

- to gather information;
- to point out weaknesses in the other side's case; or
- to stress the strengths of your case.

Risks include

- asking the wrong questions; or
- allowing the other side to bolster their position with their answers.

Responses include

- not answering or answering selectively; or
- asking your own questions.

8. **Split the Difference**: When the parties are near agreement on a particular issue, one negotiator can propose a final settlement at the mid-point between two outstanding positions — settle for $74,000 when the plaintiff's and defendant's last offers are $78,000 and $70,000 respectively. This tactic can be used

- to help negotiators move from entrenched positions or as a means of breaking a deadlock;
- to save face when a change in positions is needed to reach agreement; or
- when the difference between outstanding offers is small enough.

Risks include

- compromising too much; or
- using the tactic when too large a gap exists between positions.

Responses include

- accepting or rejecting the proposal;
- focusing on objective criteria to narrow the gap; or
- using other creative problem-solving techniques.

9. **Trial Balloon**: The negotiator floats an idea or position to determine if it will receive support or not. The idea or position, even if well thought out and a desired solution, is presented as preliminary thinking or open to change or outright rejection. This tactic can be used

- to test the strength of a proposal without attracting an unduly critical response if it is not acceptable; or
- to hide a negotiator's support for a solution.

Risks include causing an adverse reaction even if the idea or position is presented as tentative and preliminary.

Responses include

- rejecting the idea or position; or
- exploring changes that might make the solution acceptable.

10. **Unrealistic Demand**: The negotiator makes an offer, sets out a position, or requests something in the negotiation that is much above or below what the negotiator reasonably expects to give or receive in the negotiation. This tactic can be used

- to throw the other off balance, sow the seeds of doubt about the relative strengths of the parties (particularly if the other is ill-prepared), and create anxiety about whether a settlement is possible (to induce concessions); or

- to uncover the other side's position before revealing its own.

Risks include

- losing trust and credibility; this kind of game-playing can be perceived as inconsistent with good faith and a serious barrier to reaching a settlement; or
- precipitating a breakdown of the negotiation; the other party refuses to play the game on this basis.

Responses include

- responding with laughter, ridicule, disbelief;
- repeating the extreme statement to the other side, which is then compelled to explain or justify it;
- demanding the factual and legal basis for the statement; or
- moving the discussion away from the *position* inherent in the offer/demand to an exploration of issues and interests: "Before we look at figures, I'm interested to know how you see. . ."

Edwards and White describe other negotiating techniques[10] that are designed to change an opponent's settling point or used to enable one to resist changes in one's own bottom line. Several other techniques are as follows:

- **anger, feigned and real** — an exhibition of anger, real or not, is used to communicate a message in negotiations such as the negotiator is serious, unhappy with a position being taken, or otherwise wanting changes in the negotiation process.
- **inscrutability** — a disguising of one's true reactions through silence or being "poker-faced."
- **first offer, large demand** — a defence to convention or demands requiring a negotiator to make an opening offer. The unrealistic opening offer can get negotiations under way and avoid losses that could occur if a realistic opening offer is much lower than the other negotiator expects to pay.
- **whipsaw** — the other side in the negotiation is made to believe there is a competitor in existence and the results of any negotiated agreement will be assessed against what could be obtained through such a competitor.

---

10   H.T. Edwards & J.J. White, *The Lawyer as a Negotiator* (St. Paul, MN: West Publishing Co. 1977) at 112–41.

- **expose the jugular** — a technique whereby a negotiator decides to display his or her weakness vis-à-vis the other negotiator and seeks a fair settlement offer by relying on the goodwill and compassion of the opposing side.
- **negotiator without authority** — the negotiator has no final authority to conclude an agreement and consequently can seek to alter the terms of a proposed settlement when the negotiator with authority has reviewed them.
- **draftsperson** — a negotiator can take responsibility to draft the document incorporating the terms of a negotiated agreement. In this manner a negotiator can take initial control of the way in which the agreement is worded and perhaps add important wording that will not be objected to by the opposite party.
- **threat** — any communication indicating an action or actions will be taken on the happening of some condition precedent (e.g., if we are unable to agree today, my client will ask the court to rule on the question; if payment is not made, further shipments will be stopped).
- **place of negotiations** — decisions made about the venue for negotiations.

1) Choosing and Using Negotiating Techniques

In choosing and using particular negotiating techniques, four factors need to be kept in mind. First, the negotiating techniques need to fit the negotiating strategy being employed whether the technique is planned or in immediate response to another negotiator's action. A feigned threat to walk away from the negotiating table may be used in an effort to move the other negotiator off an unrealistic negotiating position or to pressure the other side to accept your offer. The plaintiff's lawyer may make a high opening demand and offer increasingly small concessions to make the defendant's lawyer believe that settlement is impossible at a substantially lower figure. The seller of a business may tell the prospective buyer that a third party has submitted an attractive offer to persuade the buyer to increase her offer even though no third party offer exists.

These types of tactics — feigned withdrawal, high opening demand, concession making, fabrication — may be effective in furthering the achievement of the negotiator's goals. However, these behaviours are more consistent with an adversarial negotiation strategy and its goal of winning than with a problem-solving approach.

This is not to suggest that a problem-solving negotiator may not encounter the same circumstances that resulted in the above behaviours from the adversarial negotiator. But the problem-solving tactics should be different. Faced with an unrealistic negotiating position or offer, the problem-solving negotiator might ask a question — how did you arrive at that figure? — or suggest an adjournment to review recent case law. Both behaviours, the question or the suggested adjournment, are made in an effort to encourage reliance on more objective criteria in decision making and to allow the other negotiator to withdraw the unacceptable offer without losing face. The problem-solving negotiator does not need to rely on deceit or lies to move the other negotiator off his position. Focusing on the other party's needs may help generate non-economic terms in the agreement that make up for a lower-than-desired price. Or, the problem-solving negotiator may adjust her position on price if a careful review of the BATNA shows the buyer's offer, if final, should not be rejected. Simply put, some negotiation tactics do not suit or help the problem-solving negotiator.

Second, similar to the process of choosing an overall negotiation strategy, the choice and use of negotiating tactics will depend on a consideration of a number of practical variables in addition to the tactic's compatibility with the chosen strategy. One consideration is whether the negotiator has the requisite knowledge and skills to use the tactic? For example, can the negotiator be effective in speaking to the media, drafting an agenda, or asking the right questions? Will a recess or caucus be called at an appropriate time and in an appropriate way? Will a take-it-or-leave-it offer, feigned withdrawal, or threat be convincing? The competency of the negotiator is crucial to the effective use of negotiating techniques.

Related to competency, the consequences of using a particular negotiation tactic also need to be understood. Negotiators need to have considered carefully what the likely reaction to a tactic will be. An anonymous media leak may expose the other negotiator's objectionable behaviour to public scrutiny and criticism with the hoped-for result that this behaviour is not repeated. But negotiations are not always predictable and are often indeterminate. Even a well-intentioned and well-executed media leak may produce results that impair the negotiation process. The other negotiator might suspect or even discover who made the leak and regard that tactic as a serious breach of trust. Negotiations could be stalled or made much more complicated until trust is restored. Accordingly, negotiators need to understand that the course a negotiation takes is not pre-set but determined by what the negotiators say and do. What worked well in one negotiation may well backfire in another. Carefully considering the consequences of one's negotiating behaviour in context can lead to more constructive results.

In some situations, certain negotiation techniques may produce disastrous results for cultural reasons. Sitting with crossed legs and arms to emphasize rejection, raising your voice to pressure or make a point, or getting physically close to ensure the message is clear may be effective negotiating behaviours in a corporate boardroom in North America. Yet exactly the same tactics can derail or at least disrupt negotiations in non-Western settings where the behaviour, rather than producing positive results, is seen as highly insulting and disrespectful.

Negotiators, particularly adversarial negotiators, also must remember that some negotiating behaviour may work in the short term but be counter-productive in the long term. The unrealistic opening demands, refusals to make concessions, threats and bluffs may force the other side to concede this time but the reputation of being an unreasonable and unfair negotiator may make future negotiations with the same or other parties much more difficult and less productive. In addition, sometimes the consequence of employing an adversarial negotiation tactic is that any negotiated agreement can be challenged legally. Under contract law there are a number of circumstances in which a court can examine the pre-contractual deliberations to determine if a negotiated contract should be set aside. For example, if a negotiator makes a material misrepresentation (the business has been profitable for the last five years) that induces a buyer to enter into a contract of purchase and sale, the contract may be voided when the buyer uncovers the truth (the business has lost money for the last three years).

A third factor to consider when choosing and using negotiation techniques is the issue of ethics. Negotiation ethics may prohibit certain behaviour, and personal sanctions can be the penalty for their violation. For example, codes of professional conduct for lawyers prohibit a lawyer from threatening to lay a criminal charge or make a complaint to a regulatory authority for the collateral purpose of enforcing the payment of a civil claim. The lawyer cannot threaten to report the CEO to the authorities if the shareholder's claim of insider trading is not dealt with fairly, quickly, and quietly. This prohibition is more than a reminder that extortion is a criminal offence because probably a lawyer could do some threatening without necessarily committing a crime. Although such a threat (either pay the full damage claim or we'll have to report your illegal immigration status to the authorities) might carry great weight in a negotiation, this tactic is deemed unethical.

Honesty in negotiation is a more complex matter. Dishonest behaviour, misleading statements or omissions, and lying are not all that unusual in negotiations. In some cases, say where a police officer is negotiating with a hostage taker, lying to secure the safe release of the hostages would be perfectly justified. In many other cases, say when you are determining the quality or age of a silk rug at a bazaar or the qualities of a used car at a curbside lot, openness and honesty cannot always be presumed. However, when the negotiators are members of a professional body, dishonesty is unprofessional and unethical and the negotiators will be disciplined for violating this ethical standard. For example, lawyers' ethical codes are usually clear that lawyers have a duty and responsibility to adhere to time-honoured virtues of probity, integrity, honesty, and dignity, to avoid sharp practice, and generally serve the cause of justice. In some jurisdictions, the language is clearer. Lawyers can be ethically prohibited from making material misrepresentations of fact in a negotiation. Lawyers caught lying in a negotiation can have a hard time defending their behaviour. However, the lines between lying, misleading, bluffing, and puffing can be blurry and paradoxical, particularly in an adversarial context where the lawyer has an ethical obligation to do the best for his client while at the same time upholding the dignity of the court and the right image for a respected profession. Whether there is a lie or not may depend on the tense of a verb or the interpretation of a word.

White offers several examples of negotiation behaviour that demonstrate the difficulty in making the distinction:[11]

- The lawyer misrepresents his true opinion about the meaning of a case or statute in attempting to persuade the opposing party to drop a cash demand.
- The lawyer distorts through puffery the value or strength of the case (this case is worth $250,000; it's a winner if we go to trial) to extract a higher settlement.
- The lawyer makes a false demand (my client must have a non-competition clause in the agreement) to trade it for a significant concession.
- A lawyer misrepresents his authority to settle when he, obviously at some risks, tells the other side his client will not settle for less than $1 million when the client has given permission to accept an offer of $750,000.

Despite these difficulties, professional conduct codes seek to provide direction and guidance on acceptable negotiation behaviour. For example, consider the case of the lawyer representing a real estate developer.[12] The dispute was whether a claim by a concrete forming

---

11   J. White, "Machiavelli and the Bar: Ethical Limitations on Lying in Negotiation" [1980] Am. B. Found. Res. J. 926 at 931–35.

12   The Law Society of British Columbia, (1998) Discipline Case Digest No. 2.

contractor had been paid. The lawyer for the real estate developer took the position that the consulting engineer on the project had already approved the work and material at issue and that payment had been made. The contractor's position was that the claim was distinct from, and not covered by, the earlier ruling of the engineer.

In negotiations, the lawyer for the real estate developer stated that he had spoken to the consulting engineer and created the impression that the engineer agreed with his position. In fact, the lawyer had not spoken with the engineer.

The parties caucused. The contractor and his lawyer called the consulting engineer who denied the conversation with the developer's lawyer. When the negotiation resumed, the developer's lawyer, when questioned about the discussion with the engineer, initially gave further untrue details. However, when confronted with the true facts, the lawyer admitted he had been untruthful, apologized orally, and wrote a letter of apology.

The discipline hearing panel found this instance less serious than other cases in which lawyers have lied. "The potential advantage . . . in making the false statement was illusory since it did not influence the opposing party to settle the claim . . . there was no potential harm to others." However, the panel noted that "any lie told by a lawyer diminishes the stature of the legal profession in the eyes of the public and other members of the profession and therefore must be strongly denigrated and discouraged." The lawyer was publicly reprimanded and ordered to pay a $10,000 fine and the costs of the hearing.

A final consideration to bear in mind when choosing a negotiation technique is whether in general some techniques are more effective than others at implementing your strategy. In other words, what do successful negotiators do? Much like the meaning of ADR, the question and its answer depend on perspective. Given the variety of goals that can be pursued in negotiation, the best result will be achieved by trying to match one's negotiating behaviour to desirable goals and appropriate strategies. However, some research does suggest that for certain goals there are generally effective and also ineffective negotiator traits.[13] Figures 3.1 and 3.2 show the traits or behaviours used by both effective and ineffective negotiators, given some general goals and using either cooperative or competitive negotiation strategies. Exhibiting the effective behaviours or traits should be helpful in achieving the objectives noted.

---

13   G.R. Williams, *Legal Negotiation and Settlement* (St. Paul, MN: West Publishing Co., 1983).

Figure 3.1   Effective Legal Negotiators

Cooperative (but not soft)	Aggressive (but within limits)
Objectives in Negotiating	
1. Conduct self ethically	1. Maximize settlement for client
2. Maximize settlement for client	2. Obtain profitable fee for self
3. Get a fair settlement	3. Outdo or outmanoeuvre opponent
4. Meet client's needs	4. Conduct self ethically
5. Satisfaction in using legal skills	5. Satisfaction in using legal skills

"Cooperative" Traits	"Aggressive" Traits
1. Trustworthy, ethical, fair	1. Dominating, forceful, attacking
2. Courteous, personable, tactful, sincere	2. Clever
3. Fair-minded	3. Unrealistic opening position
4. Realistic opening position	4. Gets to know opponent, is uninterested in needs of other party
5. Accurately evaluates the case	5. Careful about timing and sequence of actions, rigid, uncooperative
6. Does not use threats	6. Uses threats
7. Willing to share information	7. Reveals information gradually
8. Skilfully probes opponent's position	8. Willing to stretch the facts

Traits Shared by Both Types
1. Prepared
2. Honest, ethical
3. Adheres to customs and courtesies of the Bar
4. Perceptive, skilful in reading cues
5. Realistic, reasonable, analytical, rational
6. Convincing
7. Effective trial attorney
8. Self-controlled

Figure 3.2 Ineffective Legal Negotiators

Cooperative (and soft)	Aggressive (beyond reasonable limits)
Objectives in Negotiating	
1. Conduct self ethically	1. Maximize settlement for client
2. Maximize settlement for client	2. Outdo or outmanoeuvre opposing attorney
3. Meet client's needs	3. Obtain profitable fee for self
4. Maintain good relations with opposing attorney	
5. Get a fair settlement	
"Cooperative" Traits	"Aggressive" Traits
1. Trustworthy, ethical, fair, honest	1. Irritating
2. Trustful	2. Makes unreasonable opening demands, bluffs, uses take-it-or-leave-it, withholds information, attacks, argumentative, quarrelsome, demanding, aggressive
3. Courteous, personable, sociable, friendly	3. Headstrong, rigid, egotistical
4. Obliging, gentle, adaptable, patient, forgiving	4. Arrogant, uninterested in needs of others, intolerant, hostile
5. Intelligent	
6. Dignified	
7. Self-controlled	
8. Unskilful in reading cues	

E. THE STAGES OF NEGOTIATION

Although negotiation strategies and techniques play important roles in the achievement of negotiation goals, another concept critical to effective negotiations is the idea of negotiation as a staged process. Rather than thinking of negotiation as unstructured or made up of ad hoc moves, the negotiation process can be viewed as consisting of a number of sequenced stages or steps. Within each stage, micro-steps or stage-suitable tactics take place. The thesis is that following and competently completing these steps is likely to assist in reaching a satisfactory agreement or other negotiation goals.

Several models of negotiation as a staged process have been formulated. Three examples follow.

Williams[14] describes legal negotiation as a repetitive process that follows reasonably predictable patterns over time. He separates the negotiation process into four stages with each stage involving a checklist of steps that are taken in that stage:

I. Stage One: Orientation and Positioning

1. Orientation
   a. Opposing attorneys begin dealing with each other.
   b. Relationships are defined and established.

2. Positioning
   a. Negotiators talk primarily about the strengths or merits of their side of the case (often in very general terms).
   b. Negotiators work to establish their opening positions. Possible positions include:
      (i) *Maximalist position* — asking more (sometimes much more) than you expect to obtain.
      (ii) *Equitable position* — taking a position you feel is fair to both sides.
      (iii) *Integrative position* — presenting or seeking to discover alternative solutions to the problem as a means of putting together the most attractive package for all concerned.
   c. Each side creates the illusion of being inalterably committed to the opening position.
   d. Time span of this phase is usually measured in months or years.

II. Stage Two: Argumentation

1. Each side seeks to present its case in the strategically most favourable light.

2. Each side seeks to discover the *real* position of the other, while trying to avoid disclosing its own real position:
   a. Issues become more clearly defined.
   b. Strengths and weaknesses of each side become more apparent.

---

14   *Ibid* at 70–72.

3. Each side seeks to discover and reduce the real position of the other.

4. Each side's expectations about what can be obtained in the case undergo substantial changes.

5. Concessions are made by one or both sides.

III. Stage Three: Emergence and Crisis

1. Negotiators come under pressure of approaching deadlines.

2. Each side realizes that one or both of them must make major concessions, present new alternatives, or admit deadlock and resort to trial.

3. Each side seeks and gives clues about areas in which concessions might be given.

4. New alternatives are proposed; concessions are made.

5. Crisis is reached:
   a. Neither side wants to give any more.
   b. Both sides are wary of being exploited or taken advantage of.
   c. Both sides have given up more than they would like.
   d. Both sides know they must stop somewhere.
   e. The deadline is upon them; one of the parties must accept the other's final offer or there is a breakdown and impasse.
   f. The client worries whether to accept the attorney's recommendation to settle.

IV. Stage Four: Agreement or Final Breakdown

1. If the parties agree to a settlement, Stage Four includes:
   a. working out the final details of the agreement;
   b. justifying and reinforcing each other and the clients about the desirability of the agreement; and
   c. formalizing the agreement.

2. If the negotiations break down and are not revived, the case goes to trial.

Williams' model may encompass adversarial, problem-solving, and compromise negotiations. The four stages demonstrate how lawyers can move from their initial meeting and positioning through an argumentation or dialogue stage to a point where time or other pressures mean that there will either be a negotiated agreement or, in Williams' model, resort to trial.

Problem-solving negotiators often break down the negotiation process into component parts that reflect an emphasis on principled or interest-based bargaining. Within each stage are a number of tasks or moves that need to be taken.[15]

Stage I: Preparation

- Be mindful of existing levels of agreement.
- Determine what you need to know (and already may know) about the other.
- Anticipate the other's approach.
- Consider whom you might talk to about the negotiation.
- Ask whether any third parties need to be involved.
- Establish the relative importance of relationship and outcome.
- Decide where and when to meet.

Stage II: Introduction and Establishment of Expectations

- Establish the need to negotiate.
- Discuss whatever ground rules may be needed.
- Set a positive, future-focused tone.
- Express areas in which there is already substantial agreement.
- Meet the other's communication style.
- Get commitment to proceed.

Stage III: Discussion and Definition of the Issue(s)

- Give an unpositional statement of the issue(s) as you see it.
- Invite a similar response and listen carefully.
- Verbally recognize interests as they arise.
- Try to limit questions to those that clarify information.
- Fractionalize (break) the issue into more manageable parts.
- Summarize what both have said, emphasizing common issues.
- Frame the issue(s).

Stage IV: Identifying and Revealing Interests

- Ask probing and clarifying questions.
- Test hypotheses about the other's interests.
- Give affirmation and acknowledgment to the other's interests.
- Make your interests known.
- Remain unpositional.
- Formulate a neutral goal statement (how can we achieve all our interests as agreed?).

---

15   From the Continuing Legal Education Society of British Columbia, "Negotiation," materials prepared for a training workshop on Advanced Negotiation Skills, 12–13 December 1990.

Stage V: Generating Options and Solutions

- Summarize areas of present agreement.
- Consider suggesting an "easy fix."
- Keep in mind areas of interest that must be met.
- Consider brainstorming and other forms of "listing."
- List objective criteria against which options can be measured.
- Seek solutions to maximize mutual gain and meet joint goals.
- List and evaluate options and select fair, agreeable solutions.
- Reality-test solutions by raising hypotheticals.

The five-stage problem-solving model of negotiation highlights a principled orientation and an emphasis on interest-based bargaining. In Stage III, the issues or questions to be negotiated are presented in a non-positional way. Stage IV is devoted to probing for and revealing interests while keeping possible solutions off the table (focus on interests, not positions). It is only in the last stage that options and solutions are pursued in order to achieve a win-win solution.

There are also descriptions of the "principal" stages of negotiation: preparation for negotiation, the negotiation itself, and documenting any agreement, and the steps that adversarial and problem-solving negotiators might take within each stage.[16]

I. PREPARATION FOR NEGOTIATION

(*denotes steps or actions that would not always be taken by positional bargainers)

A. Analysis

1. Complete fact investigation, subject to obtaining further facts during the negotiation.
2. Identify and prioritize the issues to be negotiated that are important to your client.
3. Predict the legal and non-legal issues that you think will be important to the other party or parties to the negotiation.
4. Finalize the legal research on all legal issues. You should be fully familiar with the law (cases, statutes, regulations) relating to these issues.
5. Gather information about the parties (e.g., backgrounds, authority, experience, reputation) involved in the negotiation, including other lawyers. This information will help you in formulating your

---

16 A.J. Pirie, "The Principal Stages of Negotiation" in N. Gold, K. Mackie, & W. Twining, *Learning Lawyers' Skills* (London: Butterworths, 1989) at 199–202.

approach to the negotiation and in predicting actions taken by other parties.

6. For each issue, summarize the relevant facts.

7. Identify any deficiencies in information. Determine whether the negotiation can go ahead without this information or whether the information can be obtained in the negotiation or through some other course of action.

8. * Identify the interests or needs of your client which must be met if a negotiated solution is to be acceptable. Remember, interests are different from positions.

9. * Predict the interests that the other party or parties to the negotiation would like to have met.

10. * Identify alternative solutions that will satisfy your client's interests and resolve the issues.

11. * Identify alternative solutions that other parties might find acceptable.

12. Determine whether common interests exist, whether any alternative solution might be acceptable to all parties, and what differences exist among issues, interests, and solutions.

13. Classify the negotiation as generally integrative (win-win) or distributive (win-lose).

14. Determine what other courses of action (e.g. legal proceedings, investigation) need to be taken in addition to the negotiation.

B. Planning for Negotiation

1. Institute other proceedings, including further information gathering, to be carried on before and during the negotiation.

2. Predict the approach and tactics that will be used by other parties to the negotiation.

3. As a result of 2 and your analysis, choose an appropriate negotiating strategy and tactics. Remember that a focus on adversarial tactics can encourage positional bargaining.

4. Develop objectives criteria (such as custom, market values, social values, precedent) for resolving conflicting interests.

5. Develop, with your client, the best alternative to a negotiated agreement (BATNA) for your client and other parties.

6. Select an appropriate time and location for the negotiation session(s).

7. Draft an agenda to structure the negotiation. You will want to organize information and issues in a sequence where information is best presented and issues are best solved.

8. Clarify instructions from your client respecting the scope of your authority (disclosure of information, settlement).

II. THE NEGOTIATION

A. Preliminaries

1. Initiate contact with the other negotiator.
2. Establish effective communication with the other negotiator.
3. Obtain further information (questioning, exchange of documents, listening, and observing) respecting issues, interests, solutions, strategies, or tactics.
4. Re-assess your analysis stage in light of any new information.
5. Obtain agreement on the time and location for the negotiation.
6. Advise your client.

B. Discussion

Problem Solving	Positional
1. Agree on any necessary procedures to be followed.	1. Agree on any necessary procedures to be followed.
2. The parties define and clarify the issues to be discussed.	2. Identify the issues and/or let other party identify them.
3. Differences in information (data, perception) are discussed. Further information obtained (questioning, exchange of documents, listening, and observing).	3. Obtain further information (questioning, exchange of documents, listening, and observing).
4. Establish the sequence for discussing the issues.	4. Put forward agenda.
5. Identify and clarify the interests or needs of all parties. You should understand the needs of the other party as well as your own.	5. Parties present maximum positions to achieve goals.
6. Jointly generate alternative solutions that will satisfy the combined needs (develop options for mutual gain).	6. Discuss persuasively the reasons and arguments that support your position.
7. Use appropriate negotiating tactics that are not inconsistent with a problem solving approach.	7. Present counter-proposals.
8. Assess the alternative solutions based on the interests of each party.	8. Use negotiating tactics (e.g. threats, bluffs, anger/aggression) to support or enhance your position, to discredit opposite position.

Problem Solving	Positional
9. Eliminate unacceptable or unworkable alternatives and review most acceptable alternative.	9. Identify and narrow the bargaining range.
10. Generate proposals based on your assessment and review.	10. Search for trade-offs, concessions, and compromises.
11. Deal with deadlocks if they arise (summarize, move to different issue, make a disclosure).	11. Adjourn the negotiation, if necessary, to obtain further information, to discuss matters with client, or to obtain instructions.
12. Adjourn the negotiation, if necessary, to obtain further information, to discuss matters with client, or to obtain instructions.	
13. If negotiating with a positional bargainer, a) continue to focus on your client's interests; encourage the other negotiator to do the same; b) don't argue; incorporate problem-solving techniques; c) separate the people from the problem; d) insist on objective criteria and not unprincipled pressure; e) bring in a third party (mediator, expert, the parties themselves) where appropriate; or f) consider changing your approach or ending negotiations if risks are high.	

C. Agreement or Final Breakdown

1. If possible, reach agreement on an appropriate solution, subject to client approval unless clear instructions to settle.
2. Advise your client, obtain instructions, and confirm in writing the agreement with all other negotiators.
3. If no agreement is possible and the negotiation has reached an impasse, adjourn the negotiation, advise your client, and obtain

instructions as to alternative course(s) of action to be followed to a negotiated agreement.

III. DOCUMENTING THE AGREEMENT

1. Formalize the agreement where necessary and confirm in writing with all parties.
2. Write your client a reporting letter confirming instructions and terms of the agreement.
3. Carry out all relevant practice operations (registration, filing, and so on) to implement agreement.

There are several benefits to thinking of negotiation as a staged process. First, the stages and the steps to be taken in each stage can act as a checklist of what needs to be done in the negotiation and in what order such steps have to be taken. Omissions can be avoided.

Second, the description of the stages of negotiation will provide an indication of the practical knowledge and skills that are necessary to effectively complete each stage. For example, separating the people from the problem may require active listening skills (I can see the progress of the talks has been frustrating); questioning skills (are there any precedents for awarding damages for lost opportunity costs in these circumstances?); listening skills (there are no cases in point but my client is absolutely adamant that losing a chance to go to the Olympics is worth a lot!); and relationship-building skills (let's see if we can work on a plan together to satisfy your client's concern and my client's need for a fair agreement). A negotiator can begin to identify her or his particular strengths and weaknesses.

Finally, thinking of negotiation as a staged process helps to better understand and to evaluate the events taking place within the dynamics of an ongoing negotiation. The rejection of a competitive negotiator's immediate and forceful "take-it-or-leave-it" offer may signal a negotiation breakdown but, depending on the circumstances, is more likely being made at a stage in the negotiation where an appropriate response (e.g., how did you arrive at that figure?) can lead to further productive discussions. One negotiator's persistent insistence that negotiations are over may be better understood, depending on the circumstances, as more of a persuasive technique accompanying an offer, perhaps a feigned withdrawal, than as a true signal that the end of negotiations has been reached. The concept of negotiation stages is a surprisingly powerful tool that can assist inexperienced and experienced negotiators alike, help avoid the use of unnecessary or even harmful tactics, and avoid precipitating unnecessarily a final breakdown in the negotiations.

Thinking of negotiation as a staged process does not mean that negotiations are linear, step-by-step, mechanical processes that closely follow one of the above models or a variation of them. In fact, many negotiations may be, or certainly appear to be, quite unstructured.

However, the concept of negotiation stages does suggest that moving from the decision to negotiate a transaction or dispute through to a final agreement necessarily involves the completion of a number of tasks by each of the negotiators. For example, whatever the negotiation context, negotiation preparation will be needed. Of course, the degree and nature of the preparation will vary from context to context. A police officer negotiating with a spouse who is threatening violence will have less time to get ready for the specific crisis situation at hand than the union and management negotiators who have been anxiously waiting and planning for the expiration of the existing collective agreement for many months. Also, at some point in every negotiation, the negotiators will need to communicate, verbally or non-verbally, in writing, or by some other medium such as phone, fax, e-mail, or other technology. While not occurring in every negotiation, presenting and accepting or rejecting an offer, counter-offering, creating a negotiation agenda, researching the applicable law, developing a negotiating mandate, and assessing options to a negotiated agreement are examples of actions commonly completed in negotiations. Thinking carefully in each case about what are the necessary negotiation tasks and how best to sequence them can improve negotiating effectiveness. Stages of negotiation are a way to organize the tasks that need to be completed.

One may hope that the decision to negotiate will lead speedily and inexpensively to a satisfactory agreement. But at every stage in the negotiation process, there can be movements back and forth between what have been identified as essential negotiation tasks or steps. The decision to adopt a certain negotiation strategy, to make an offer, to set a deadline, to create an agenda, or even to pursue negotiations in the first place may be reassessed depending upon what has transpired in the negotiation. The stages of negotiation can provide a general road map through the negotiation terrain, but they should not obscure the real-life complexity and uncertainty of many negotiations. Appreciating that necessary negotiation tasks may need to be revisited or redone as the negotiation unfolds will more accurately represent the dynamic nature of negotiation processes. Rather than seeing negotiation as a linear process, the stages of negotiation and the tasks making up these stages are more mutually interdependent, linked at every point in the negotiation. And when negotiations involve multi-parties and multi-issues, or when negotiators at the bargaining table are themselves engaged in negotiations with their respective constituencies on how best to proceed through the main negotiation, a rigid or linear map of the negotiation process does not reflect reality and can lead negotiators in the wrong direction.

F. KNOWING WHEN (AND WHEN NOT) TO NEGOTIATE

Being fluent in the language of negotiation, knowledgeable of different negotiation strategies, aware of the range of negotiating tactics, and cognizant of the stages of negotiation are essential prerequisites for effective negotiation. Having, or not having, these negotiation capacities and related skills obviously will be a factor in deciding whether or not to engage in negotiations. However, there are other factors that also will be relevant in choosing the negotiation process to resolve a dispute or plan a transaction in the first place.

The decision to negotiate almost always will involve a weighing, in some manner, of the advantages and disadvantages of negotiation compared with the benefits and costs associated with other methods of dispute processing. The test will be whether a negotiator's desired substantive, procedural and personal goals are more likely to be achieved through negotiation than through some other dispute resolution process. Or, put simply, will negotiation produce something better than, or as good as, the results you can obtain without negotiating?

As discussed in chapter 2, it is highly problematic to assume that negotiation will invariably be useful for particular types of disputes or transactions or to know for certain what the results of the negotiation will be. Although negotiation is extremely common, the decision to negotiate must be made in context. Whether negotiating will help to achieve desired goals depends on how negotiation goals are framed and on how the negotiation process is evaluated in light of these goals.

For example, one spouse in a custody dispute may see a negotiated agreement helping to preserve a necessary future working relationship between the parents. The other spouse may want a court to authoritatively adjudicate on the custody issue and may not be willing to assume that a face-to-face negotiation process is necessary or even desirable to ensure that the parents can deal with their future parenting responsibilities. The utility of negotiation in preserving future relationships can depend on how each parent constructs his or her future relationship goal. For one parent, maintaining a workable future relationship vis-à-vis the children may depend on keeping a semblance of what the relationship was like before separation. For the other parent, a less intimate and more businesslike relationship is all that is required. Negotiating a custody agreement may be absolutely critical in the former case, much less so in the latter.

Even when the parties have the same goals, choosing to negotiate will depend on context not formula. In many situations, negotiation will be seen as a preferable process because it will clearly lead to a faster and less expensive resolution. Saving time and money is surely a major reason for the negotiated resolution of most personal injury cases rather than using the courts with their associated delays and higher costs. However, negotiating may not always be faster and cheaper. The complexity of the subject matter, such as exists in treaty negotiations with Aboriginal peoples, or the behaviours/abilities of the negotiators may mean that other methods of dispute resolution will be more efficient in terms of time and cost.

The same contextual indeterminacy can exist when assessing other attributes of the negotiation process. If privacy or confidentiality can be maintained in the negotiation process, does that factor help a negotiator reach her or his goals? Is privacy a negotiation goal in itself? The dispute between two songwriters over who is entitled to the substantial royalties and fame from a popular tune may be best resolved in the corporate boardroom of the advertising agency that purchased the rights to the song. These negotiation confines can allow for full and frank discussions as well as keep the inner workings of the industry from public view. On the other hand, the publicity of a lawsuit against a popular artist may count as valuable airtime in the larger picture. Privacy might help the parties settle but the private compromises that would have to be made may be far outweighed by the media coverage of a two-week court engagement with the possibility of winning fully at trial. The flexibility in the negotiation process, particularly if it is principled, for parties to be creative in decision making might be a big plus for a complicated commercial case. This same plus might be viewed as dangerous or problematic to a single parent who is being supported by a tenants' advocacy group in making a discrimination complaint against a large corporate landlord. Even if the landlord exposed its jugular in negotiation and invited the tenant to craft an accord, any "win-win" agreement might not be good enough if the case is seen as a "test" case with good prospects of success in court. Deciding to negotiate depends, in part, on a careful consideration of negotiation's attributes in the context of the particular dispute.

G. POWER AND POWER IMBALANCES IN NEGOTIATION

In negotiation, by definition, the parties seek to reach a voluntary agreement that is mutually satisfactory, as opposed to having a solution imposed on them either by one of the parties or by a judge or arbitrator. However, it would be wrong to assume that the negotiation playing field is always level and that impositions of one sort or another are absent from negotiated agreements. In practice, there almost always will be differences or imbalances in power in bargaining situations. Being able to assess the impact of this power asymmetry on the negotiation process and on any negotiated outcome is an important part of knowing whether and how to begin or to continue negotiations.

But what exactly is power? Consider the following definitions of power and what they suggest about the use of power in a negotiation:[17]

"The simple definition of human power, the ability to get what we want"
(Boulding, *Three Faces of Power* at 17)

"Power is 'the ability or capacity of O to produce consciously or unconsciously intended effects on the behaviour or emotions of another person P.'"
(Winter, *The Power Motive* at 5)

"If I have negotiating power, I have the ability to affect favorably someone else's decision."
(Fisher, "Negotiating Power" at 78)

"One can conceive of power — 'influence' and 'control' are serviceable synonyms — as the capacity of one actor to do something affecting another actor, which changes the probable pattern of specified future events"
(Lukes, *Power: A Radical View* at 13)

---

17   For an entry into the world of power, see B. Barnes, *The Nature of Power* (Oxford: Polity Press, 1988); M. Blalock, *Power and Conflict: Toward a General Theory* (Newbury Park, CA: Sage Publications, 1989); K.E. Boulding, *Three Faces of Power* (Newbury Park, CA: Sage Publications, 1989); S.R. Clegg, *Frameworks of Power* (Newbury Park, CA: Sage Publications, 1989); R. Fisher, "Negotiating Power: Getting and Using Influence" (1983), 27 Am. Behav. Sci. 149 at 150; H.M. Lips, *Women, Men and the Psychology of Power* (Englewood Cliffs, NJ: Prentice-Hall Inc., 1981); S. Lukes, *Power: A Radical View* (London: MacMillan, 1974); D. Neumann, "How Mediation Can Effectively Address the Male-Female Power Imbalance in Divorce" (1992) 19 Mediation Q. 227; K. Ng, *The Social Psychology of Power* (London: Academic Press, Inc., 1980); and D.G. Winter, *The Power Motive* (New York: The Free Press, 1973).

From these definitions, two essential elements of power emerge. First, the concept of power appears to pivot around a capacity to create or suppress change. Second, and related to the idea of change, power can be viewed as a behavioural force that influences how people think, act, and interact. For the negotiation process and its focus on persuasion, joint action, settlement, or compromise, the importance of power is obvious. Whether one is employing a negotiating strategy to achieve desired goals, using specific negotiating behaviours, or following one stage or another of the negotiation process, power will always be at play. In other words, if influencing behaviour and controlling change are essential to the definition of power, these ingredients are also at the heart of the process of negotiation — human interaction in order to reach agreement. Indeed, if conflict is at the root of personal, social and political change and ADR is a modern response to the concept of conflict, power will be inextricably linked not only to the negotiation process but also to the ADR field generally. As Coser states, "conflicts, as distinct from other forms of interaction, always involve power" and "whatever the goals of conflicting parties, power is necessary for their accomplishment."[18]

Thinking about power as influencing behavior and controlling change in a negotiation does not necessarily mean that power will always be coercive. Certainly, the exercise of power can be highly coercive. For example, a manufacturer of a defective birth control device may use superior financial resources to increase the costs of a lawsuit against it (by delays, lengthy discoveries, pre-trial motions), to place economic pressures on the other side to accept a lower settlement offer in negotiations, and to deter others from suing. The company might also instruct its lawyers to vigorously explore a complainant's history of sexual relations to challenge her allegation that the intrauterine device caused the injuries. This line of inquiry is designed to promote, or will have the effect of promoting, settlements.

However, power can be facilitative, "a deliberative or purposive influence . . . that can be 'for' as well as 'against'."[19] So, a university facing a complaint of systemic discrimination in hiring practices provides resources in a negotiated settlement for the establishment of a permanent equity issues office on campus as part of an agreement to withdraw the complaint.

---

18   L.A. Coser, *The Functions of Social Conflict* (London: Routledge and Kegan Paul Ltd., 1968) at 134.
19   M. Deutsch, *The Resolution of Conflict: Constructive and Destructive Processes* (New Haven, CT: Yale University Press, 1973) at 86–87.

However, for the skilled negotiator there is more to power's make-up than merely knowing that it can be coercive or facilitative. It is also important to understand where this power comes from and what practical forms power can take in order that any differences or imbalances in bargaining power can be appropriately addressed.

Social psychologists suggest there are three general but interrelated sources of power: power from oneself, power from relationships, and power from social structures.

1) Power from Oneself

The individual person is often identified as being a source of power. The ability to influence or control behaviour or events depends on the traits or characteristics of the person exerting the influence or the person being influenced. Accordingly, power is found in genetic or historical characteristics such as physical appearance or strength, class, race, intelligence, gender, knowledge, age, wealth, credibility, and other individual traits. In a negotiation, a senior lawyer who suggests to a younger counsel that "my many days spent in the courtroom tell me that your client would be well served if you reviewed your assessment of the potential damages a jury might award in this case" is using the power of her experience and expertise to persuade the other lawyer to re-evaluate and perhaps change his negotiating position on damages.

2) Power from Relationships

Power also can be viewed as arising from a relationship, not a person. In other words, a person cannot be an influencer if there is no one to influence. The exertion of power requires a relationship with some degree of mutuality or goal interdependence such as parent-child, teacher-student, wife-husband, employer-employee, lawyer-client, buyer-seller, relatives, friends, and so on. A threat by a large forest company to slap a lawsuit on a group of environmentalists unless they stop their efforts to encourage a boycott of the company's products is an example of the use of power based on the disparity in economic resources between the company and the individuals. The wealth and property that an individual or organization holds in relation to another is the source of power, not the wealth or property by itself.

3) Power from Social Structures

Increasingly, power is seen as coming from social structures or institutions. Power is not located in personal characteristics or relationships *per se* but in the ideas, values and beliefs that structure or order individual lives, relationships among people, or society in general. Thus, for example, being a member of a prestigious law firm, being associated with a renowned university, belonging to a popular political party, or being involved with a respected conservation agency can be empowering because these structures are regarded as dominant ones generally as well as being at the top of the hierarchy in the professions, education, politics, or popular causes. Similarly, alliance with, or conformity to, dominant ideas of the family, economic order, equality, the rule of law, religion, or even dispute resolution can grant privileges and the ability to influence which do not accrue in the same way to "outsiders" or those who do not adhere to established orders. From a structural perspective, power derives only from personal characteristics or relationships if these personal traits or relationships are themselves a component of a privileged or hierarchical structure. So, in a patriarchal society, a husband in a divorce case will have real abilities to influence the negotiation process and any negotiated outcomes concerning the divorce because there is a systemic privileging of his gender, which, in turn, grants authority to what he might say and how he might say it. The white male university professor may rely on power from several structural sources to influence negotiations around a complaint by a female graduate student alleging sexual harassment.

Power from the above sources may be readily identified, easily used, and highly predictable in some negotiations. For example, the wealthy businessperson threatens to bring protracted legal proceedings if a small, independent newspaper does not publish a full apology for an alleged libel. The husband tells his ex-wife that she only "deserves" minimal support payments. Or lawyers rely on previously decided cases to determine how much to compensate a young girl who has been disabled by a serious personal injury.

However, in many cases power will not be localized in one spot or another, to be appropriated and employed like a commodity or piece of wealth. Power will be a more dynamic force, indeterminate, dependent on context, not only causing change but changing itself. For example, the enormous economic clout wielded by a respected and long-established electric power company might seem to dwarf the bargaining power of a small group of Aboriginal people opposing a hydroelectric development project on their traditional territory. This apparent power imbalance changes when the genocidal nature of the proposed project is given widespread publicity, and a major contract to purchase power from the company is cancelled due to the company's failure to follow environmental impact assessment procedures.

4) The Exercise of Power

Whether power derives from personal characteristics, attributes of a relationship, social structures, or a combination thereof, there are at least eight ways that power can be exercised in a negotiation setting.

1. **Reward power** — A person can deliver positive incentives or consequences or remove negative consequences.

   Example: The plaintiff in a personal injury case offers to discontinue the lawsuit if the defendant agrees to pay $100,000 in damages.

2. **Coercive power** — A person can deliver negative consequences or remove positive consequences.

   Example: The politician threatens to sue for defamation if the newspaper does not publish a full apology.

3. **Normative power** — There are obligations, real or perceived, to accept influences as a result of social norms governing the situation.

   Example: In a sexual harassment dispute, a white male professor may be believed over a female student if there are differing factual accounts about the harassing behaviour.

4. **Ecological power** — A person can exert control over, or change, another's social or physical environment to induce desired behaviour or prevent undesired behaviour.

   Example: Building a fence between neighbours' properties may eliminate unsightly views or prevent trespasses by children or pets.

5. **Legitimate power** — There is an acceptance or perception that a person ought to have power because of position or responsibilities.

   Example: In a mandatory, pre-trial settlement conference, the parties and their lawyers accept the non-binding opinion of a judge as to what would be a fair settlement.

6. **Referent power** — There is a desire to identify with, be similar to, or be liked by, some person or group.

   Example: One neighbour agrees not to play music after 10:00 P.M. because this solution was suggested by a close and admired friend.

7. **Expert power** — There is a belief that a person has a special knowledge or skill and is trustworthy.

   Example: A young lawyer agrees to settle a case for an amount that a senior counsel suggests a jury would award in the circumstances.

8. **Informational power** — There is a belief that a person has useful knowledge not available elsewhere.

Example: An accused agrees to plead guilty because there is a reliable eye-witness to the assault.

Given the dynamic nature of power and how it can be exercised, it is rare for power to be distributed evenly among, or used proportionately by, all parties to a negotiation. When power differentials arise, they can negatively affect negotiation in two ways. First, as conflict is characterized by less and less mutual influence among disputants, the conflict becomes more and more destructive. The consequences are familiar and all too common.

The constructive use of power is impaired. Any objectivity in information or experience is rejected because each disputant views the other as trying to use informational or expert power for purely personal purposes. Trust is gone. The utility in legitimate or referent power is undermined by increasing levels of hostility and distrust. Reward power can be used as an aggressive negotiating tactic (an unrealistically low offer), perceived as a bribe or point to an unacceptable degree of dependency. With a deterioration in these positive power bases, the parties can begin to rely more and more on the use of coercive power which can further complicate the conflict.

Second, any solution arrived at when power imbalances are abused, whether in an adjudicative setting or a consensual process, may not be fair or is unlikely to be mutually satisfying and lasting. Agreements that are reached as a result of undue or improper influences may also be legally challenged at a later date.

Accordingly, before beginning negotiations and during the course of negotiation, it is important to assess the impact of bargaining power on the negotiation process. This assessment can involve asking questions such as:

- Do I have bargaining power? Where does it come from? How will I use it?
- What about the other parties to the negotiation? What is the source of their bargaining power? How is it likely to be used or how is it being used?
- Is there an obvious power difference or imbalance? Can any imbalance be corrected?
- Will a power imbalance result in destructive patterns in the negotiation or lead to an unfair or unworkable agreement?

The answer to these types of questions will influence the decision to negotiate and whether to continue with negotiations or pursue a better alternative. An assessment of your own and the other parties' bargaining power will also be a factor in choosing and using negotiating strategies and in determining what negotiating tactics might be most helpful. A careful analysis of bargaining power will likely allow you to avoid the negative consequences that can result from serious imbalances in bargaining power.

If power imbalances in negotiation are common, what can be done to correct these imbalances? As discussed in chapter 2, hiring a lawyer and having access to remedies in the formal justice system are often touted as ways to level the playing field. ADR proponents also suggest cataloguing strategies for productively balancing power, often by expanding all parties' sources of power rather than expanding one party's power at the expense of another. Some strategies require the presence of a skilled mediator to assist the negotiations. Suggested techniques include the following:

- Ensure equal time to speak.
- Slow down the pace of a meeting.
- Share information.
- Emphasize mutuality or respect.
- Point out the power dynamics at work in the moment it occurs.
- Meet separately with parties to explore their sense of the balance of power.
- Model communication and listening skills that demonstrate respect.
- Design processes that address issues of power imbalance.

The catalogue approach raises several concerns. First, will some power imbalances be difficult to detect, particularly if the power disparities are viewed as normal? The husband may continue "to bully" his wife in a divorce mediation in subtle ways that avoid attention but that reflect his enormous privilege in a patriarchal society. Second, if the power imbalance is so acute, will equal power ever be possible? Consider, for example, the power imbalance in disputes involving physical or psychological abuse. Can any ADR process provide the survivor with the necessary power to counterbalance what may have been a long history of abuse? Finally, is the assumption correct that the parties or others can artificially alter power structures in disputing by adding or subtracting a pinch of power here or there? Giving a person more time to speak because of inferior language skills may simply reinforce perceptions of who has strength. If the power imbalance is the cause of the conflict (e.g. I want to control the kids; gays and lesbians are not entitled to social benefits), it is not clear how any listed technique, by itself, would persuade the more powerful party to share control through a negotiated agreement. When power imbalances cannot be adequately addressed, consensual methods of dispute resolution, including negotiation, may not be the best processes to pursue.

FURTHER READINGS

BAZERMAN, M., & M. NEALE, *Negotiating Rationally* (New York: The Free Press, 1991)

BRESLIN, J.W., & J.Z. RUBIN, eds., *Negotiation Theory and Practice* (Cambridge: Program on Negotiation Books, 1991)

DRUCKMAN, D., ed. *Negotiation: Social-Psychological Perspectives* (Beverly Hills: Sage, 1977)

FISHER, R., & S. BROWN, *Getting Together: Building Relationships as We Negotiate* (New York: Penguin Books, 1989)

FISHER, R., W. URY, & B. PATTON, *Getting to Yes: Negotiating Agreement without Giving In*, 2d ed. (New York: Penguin Books, 1991)

GULLIVER, P.H., *Disputes & Negotiations: A Cross-Cultural Perspective* (New York: Academic Press, 1981)

————, "Negotiations as a Mode of Dispute Settlement: Towards a General Model" (1973) 7 L. & Soc'y Rev. 669–91

LAX, D.A., & J.K. SEBENIUS, *The Manager as Negotiator* (New York: The Free Press, 1976)

LEWICKI R.J., et al., *Essentials of Negotiation* (Chicago: Richard D. Irwin, 1996)

MORLEY, I., & S. GEOFFREY, *The Social Psychology of Bargaining* (London: George Allen & Unwin Publishers Ltd., 1977)

RAIFFA, H., *The Art and Science of Negotiation* (Cambridge: Harvard University Press, 1982)

RUBIN, J.Z., & B.R. BROWN, *The Social Psychology of Bargaining and Negotiation* (New York: Academic Press Inc., 1975)

SCHELLING, T.C., *The Strategy of Conflict* (Cambridge: Harvard University Press, 1980)

URY, W., *Getting Past No: Negotiating with Difficult People* (New York: Bantam, 1991)

——, *Getting Past No: Negotiating Your Way from Confrontation to Cooperation* (New York: Bantam Books, 1993)

WILLIAMS, G.R., *Legal Negotiation and Settlement* (St. Paul, MN: West Publishing Co., 1983)

——, "Negotiation as a Healing Process [1996] J. Disp. Resol. 1

ZARTMAN, W., ed., *The Negotiation Process: Theories and Applications* (Beverly Hills: Sage Publications, 1978)

MEDIATION: THE SCIENCE AND THE SKILLS

A. INTRODUCTION

> Mediation, in a relatively brief span of time, has evolved from a bold, innovative challenge to conventional methods of decision making and dispute resolution to a more professionalized and institutionalized practice.[1]

Menkel-Meadow's words provide an important preface to any study of mediation as an integral part of alternative dispute resolution. Her comments suggest some rather profound and rapid changes in the status of mediation within the developing ADR field. The nature and extent of mediation's modern evolution is a key part of getting the full ADR picture and is essential background to understanding modern day mediation practice. It is also critical in identifying the practical knowledge and skills that good mediators must have and be able to use.

---

1   C. Menkel-Meadow, "The Many Ways of Mediation: The Transformation of Traditions, Ideologies, Paradigms, and Practices" (1995) 11 Negotiation J. 217.

B. THE MODERN EVOLUTION OF MEDIATION

As discussed in chapter 1, mediation led the way as the concept of ADR emerged in the United States and Canada in the 1970s and 1980s. As a consensual dispute resolution process in which a neutral third party called a mediator helped participants to make decisions and reach agreements, mediation struck a responsive chord with those persons dissatisfied with the formal administration of justice and the high costs, long delays, and win-lose (at times lose-lose) results associated with going to court. Mediation became the alternative of choice in the ADR movement as ADR supporters cited studies of mediation-like dispute processing in other communities and societies,[2] the long-time application and successes of mediation in labour relations disputes and international affairs, and commentators on the forms and functions of mediation.[3]

The rise of mediation was predicated on a simple assertion — it worked. The mediation process was a natural remedy for the ills of existing disputing systems. In contrast to the clogged and costly courts, mediation would be faster and cheaper. Instead of the adversarial attitudes and the win-lose results that characterized legal proceedings, mediation would bring the parties together to address the real issues in dispute. Rather than imposing a decision on them, mediation would empower the parties to make their own decisions. Mutual respect among the disputants would be fostered in mediation, and mediated agreements reached would be honoured and enduring win-win results. Continuing relationships could be preserved and harmony restored if mediation were used. The parties who went through mediation would even learn from their experience how to better handle future problems. In the early days of ADR, for some lawyers and others who were dissatisfied with the heavy costs and general unpleasantness that often accompanied traditional dispute resolution practices, mediation, with its offers to ease or eliminate these disputing burdens, was both enticing and intriguing.

While claiming mediation was not a panacea for every dispute, mediation proponents nevertheless increasingly touted it as a serious contender for resolving disputes of every form. Mediation was not to be limited to those types of disputes where maintaining close and con-

---

2   L. Nader & H.F. Todd Jr., eds., *The Disputing Process — Law in Ten Societies* (New York: Columbia University Press, 1978).

3   L.L. Fuller, "Mediation — Its Forms and Functions" (1971) 44 S. Cal. L. Rev. 305.

tinuing relationships was an essential requirement of any dispute resolution process. Therefore, mediation quickly moved beyond family fights, divorce and custody cases, and neighbourhood and community quarrels to victim-offender reconciliation in criminal cases, commercial conflicts, medical malpractice and automobile accident cases, environmental clashes and development discords, public policy decision making, sexual harassment and sexual abuse issues, human rights matters, hostage taking, and even to warring nations. Mediation, it was said, could be useful when interconnections and common interests among the disputants did not exist. With some exceptions, all that mediation needed was a dispute.

As discussed in chapter 1, the dynamic and rapid development of mediation provoked some early resistance and dismissals, particularly from the legal profession.[4] This legal opposition was understandable. Unlike negotiation, mediation was not a well-known process to most lawyers and judges. Mediation methods also appeared to stand in stark contrast to the legal profession's preferred disputing process — court adjudication. The adversarial thinking of many lawyers and several long-standing ethical principles, such as not acting for clients with conflicts of interest, seemed at odds with what was expected from a mediator, particularly if the mediator was also a lawyer. The proliferation of many non-lawyer mediators also threatened to further erode, if not outright challenge, both the economics and status associated with the privilege of "practising law," for which the legal profession had been granted a statutory monopoly. Practising law, it had been assumed, included many of the negotiation, problem-solving, and other dispute resolution activities that non-lawyer mediators now were performing. Were non-lawyer mediators engaged in the unauthorized practice of law? It was not surprising that mediation proponents caused a considerable stir in the legal community.

However, the difference a day makes is perhaps best illustrated in the following two quotes, the first from an address by the Chief Justice of British Columbia Supreme Court in 1989 "putting the boots to ADR," the second from a brochure promoting a 1994 ADR conference sponsored by the Canadian Bar Association.

> ADR is often supported by well-intentioned people who, for a variety
> of reasons, are anxious to reorganize society and procedures of courts
> with naive, theoretical concepts of humanity and efficiency . . . soci-

---

4   For an early chronicle, see A.J. Pirie, "The Lawyer as Mediator: Professional Responsibility Problems or Profession Problems?" (1985) 63 Can. Bar Rev. 378.

ety's decent people need the no-nonsense, straightforward procedures of courtroom litigation to fight unreasonable claims and not the "soft" procedures ADR offers.[5]

This symposium is for practitioners, judges, educators and government officials who have already heard all the arguments and are ready and eager to use these new forms of dispute resolution in appropriate circumstances.[6]

The sentiments in the latter quote accurately describe the present position of mediation. From a bold challenger of powerful legal institutions and ways of thinking, mediation has become a champion of dispute resolution, endorsed and accepted by the very structures and interests that it challenged in the first instance. Judges are becoming mediators in the courtroom, in case management initiatives, and in mandatory settlement conferences. Court-annexed mediation programs are expanding, and in increasing instances these programs are made mandatory for all or most civil cases. Lawyers and many other professionals are taking training courses in mediation and being accredited as mediators. Classes in mediation are springing up in the law schools. As a method of dispute resolution, mediation will probably continue to expand in disputing areas where it is presently used and will be applied increasingly to new disputing terrain.

The modern evolution of mediation deserves comment because it raises several questions. How did an essentially anti-establishment process come to be accepted by the establishment? What do these developments suggest about mediation's modern meaning for the mediation student, practitioner or participant? What shape will mediation take in the future and who will control this dispute resolution process? And what significance does mediation's evolution have for the ADR field?

Much like the meaning of ADR in chapter 1, at one level the acceptance of mediation can be presented as natural and unproblematic, just common sense. In a relatively brief span of time, many people have had an opportunity to become familiar with the mediation process and its attributes. Mediation has been detailed worldwide in an ever-increasing number of scholarly and popular books and articles. The media has focused attention on the use and success of mediation in high profile disputes such as baseball strikes, armed stand-offs and the like. A pleth-

---

5   Chief Justice A. McEachern, quoted in "Chief Justice Puts Boots to ADR," *Lawyers Weekly* (26 October 1989).

6   Canadian Bar Association, Conference on Alternative Dispute Resolution in Action in Canada (Vancouver, British Columbia, 11–12 March 1994).

ora of mediators have been trained both inside and outside the legal academy. This mass of mediators, willing to supply mediation services, also has nourished the demand for this type of dispute resolution process from individual, organizational, and governmental consumers who are more and more knowledgeable about just what mediation is. Juxtaposed against continuing criticisms of traditional justice mechanisms, it was only natural that mediation practice would expand.

However, education and economics do not fully explain the modern popularity of mediation, particularly within the legal profession. The full explanation probably comes from understanding the malleability of the mediation process and its goals and from understanding the way that mediation theory and practice fit with the ambiguity of ADR's ideology, described in chapter 1.

There is probably no single way to define mediation, but different definitions of mediation do reveal a process of decision making that harbours a healthy respect for liberal notions of party autonomy and individual self-determination:

> The process by which the participants, together with the assistance of a neutral person or persons, systematically isolate dispute issues in order to develop options, consider alternatives, and reach a consensual settlement that will accommodate their needs.[7]

> The intervention into a dispute or negotiation by an acceptable, impartial and neutral third party who has no authoritative decision-making power to assist disputing parties in voluntarily reaching their own mutually acceptable settlement of issues in dispute.[8]

> A process whereby a third party from a position of apparent neutrality assists disputants towards an outcome agreed between them.[9]

Typically, the essential elements of mediation that distinguish it from other dispute resolution processes are the use of a neutral third party with no authority to impose a decision, and an emphasis on the parties themselves reaching mutually satisfactory resolutions.

However, despite some definitional common ground, mediation processes from one context to another often bear little resemblance to

---

7   J. Folberg & A. Taylor, *Mediation: A Comprehensive Guide to Resolving Conflict without Litigation* (San Francisco: Jossey-Bass, 1988) at 7.

8   C. Moore, *The Mediation Process: Practical Strategies for Resolving Conflict*, 2d ed. (San Francisco: Jossey-Bass, 1996) at 14.

9   H. Astor & C. Chinkin, *Dispute Resolution in Australia* (Sydney: Butterworths, 1992) at 61.

one another. A fly-on-the-wall observing a mediation of a dispute in a community justice centre between neighbours over noise would see a different process than the fly-on-the-wall watching a labour mediator shuttle back and forth between union and management. The labour mediator, who may be well known to the parties, probably has a fair idea of what compromises are needed to reach agreement and may be actively pushing the parties to that middle ground. He might even be required to submit a report to the parties or to government setting out the terms of an agreement that he thinks are fair. On the other hand, the volunteer community justice centre mediator or co-mediators, who probably have just met the disputants, may be far less interventionist, preferring to ask gentle questions, reflect feelings, and consciously avoid suggestions of, or divert requests for, solutions. In a similar way, the tightly time-constrained mediations conducted by judges in mandatory settlement conferences would not resemble mediations between victims and offenders in serious criminal cases. In the time bureaucratically available for the settlement conference mediation, the judge as mediator could only hear an abridged version of the facts from the parties before possibly hinting at how she would decide the case if it went to court and then urging the parties to amicably agree on some middle ground if the case seemed a grey one. This can sometimes be referred to as muscle or compromise mediation. In the victim-offender reconciliation program, intense meetings between victim and offender or complicated individual meetings with the mediator could take place over several months with the mediator being much more focused on what is really at stake for the parties and for victim-offender programs in general. For related reasons, the formalized mediation of liability or quantum of damage issues in automobile accident cases would be dramatically different from the amazingly moving mediation sessions and resulting resolutions that could occur between father and adult daughter and other family members around issues of incest and childhood sexual abuse. The mediation of a commercial controversy over, for example, the ownership of rare stamps, and the mediation in a hostage-taking incident would be far apart in common process features. The mediation process, in actual practice, can be remarkably unique.

The diversity of mediation processes — where they take place, how long they take, who is present, what the mediator and parties say and do, and what happens next — is probably not surprising. Given the enormous variability in disputing contexts described in chapter 1, it would be unrealistic to expect mediations of these disparate disputes to look alike. Because of context, including the mediator's training and orientation, actual mediation processes will differ considerably with respect to how strongly and in what shape the essential attributes of mediation are present. At some point, say where a mediator directly and explicitly imposes a solution, the process should not be called mediation. The absence of a neutral third party also would disqualify a dispute resolution process from being named mediation. But the slow-moving informality of a mediation process in a community justice centre can be replaced easily by the speedy formality followed by a judge mediating a dispute in a courtroom during a settlement conference without jeopardizing the fact that both processes of dispute resolution can be mediation. Any judge lacking, or perhaps just not exercising, jurisdiction to actually order a result (perhaps a judge in her chambers hearing from the opposing lawyers) can be a mediator in name just as easily as a person from one of the helping professions with interpersonal skills training and a practised understanding of the human condition who is encouraging a couple to agree. For many different disputing scenarios in which a third party is present to assist negotiations, attaching the tag of mediation would not evoke a serious outcry of mislabelling.

In theory and in practice, mediation or "third-party assisted negotiations" have such a high degree of built-in definitional flexibility that a process can be termed mediation in a broad range of circumstances. Once the malleability of the actual mediation process itself was understood, resistance based on views that mediation was soft, naive, unstructured, too structured, too time-consuming, or non-legal dissipated. A dispute resolution process called mediation could be constructed to avoid unwanted process concerns while at the same time retain sufficient party decision making and third-party helper characteristics to remain classified as mediation.

In addition to procedural flexibility, mediation also offers goal flexibility, which contributes to its present popularity in resolving disputes. The goals of mediation, like the goals of ADR, can be narrow or broad, progressive or conservative. Mediation offers to assist under-siege legal institutions, deficit-stricken governments, and profit-conscious businesses to reduce the cost of disputing. On the other hand, mediation also purports to be transformative, empowering the individual, the community, and even the global village by changing the dispute and the views and attitudes of the disputants. In between, mediation proponents claim that mediation can preserve continuing relationships, provide privacy, identify underlying interests, discover integrative or win-win solutions, result in long-lasting agreements, prevent violence, and generally avoid the downsides associated with more adversarial approaches to dispute resolution. Mediation did not need to be "given the boot" because its promised benefits were fanciful, unattainable, unwanted, or unfamiliar. The acceptance of mediation only required adoption of goals that made sense to the person or organization doing the accepting. Cheaper and faster, without additional benefits, could have widespread appeal.

Linked to the diversity of the mediation process and its goals is another factor that has made embracing mediation much easier. If the initial resistance to mediation, in part, was based on competing ideologies of dispute resolution — mediation being perceived as a challenge to the disputing status quo — was mediation's ideology as malleable as the mediation process itself?

The answer seems to be yes. Like the ambiguities around the ideology of ADR discussed in chapter 1, what mediation proponents wanted to prescribe as normal, natural, and essential about dispute resolution was not written in stone. In fact, the many ways of mediation and the myriad voices telling the mediation story opened up opportunities and motives to construct mediation in a shape, form, and function that did not seriously conflict with one's world view of disputing. Ideologically, mediation models could be seen as follows:

- **purely facilitative** — the third-party neutral helps the parties to arrive at their own solution although it is rare for mediators not to intrude, to a lesser or greater extent, in the substantive decision;

- **evaluative** — a hybrid of mediation and arbitration where the solution remains technically in the hands of the parties but the mediator provides information on legal or legislative outcomes, financial data or advice, advocacy or negotiation training, and even suggests possible outcomes or solutions;

- **transformative** — seeks to change the dispute or the disputants or even the wider community;

- **bureaucratic** — occurs in court or other institutional settings that can control or limit the process used or outcomes reached as a result of standardized training, procedural protocols, formalism, or other bureaucratic constraints;

- **open or closed** — determined by how much control the parties have over the process as opposed to the outcome, moving between the parties exercising a high degree of choice about ground rules and other process aspects to the mediator dictating absolute process rules and routines of practice (one should not interrupt another party; one should speak directly to the other party);

- **activist or accountable** — the mediator, not always with the understanding or agreement of the parties, not only orchestrates who will participate in the mediation but also can be a main developer of the dispute's outcome;
- **community** — often presented as a less-professionalized, lay, community-controlled mediation process that seeks to recreate a greater sense of community homogeneity;
- **pragmatic** — "on-the-spot" mediation that is highly instrumentalist and agreement-oriented where mediators will do whatever is necessary, often disregarding particular procedural niceties, to end hostilities, avoid violence, and promote peace.[10]

In a variation of these themes, Bush and Folger suggest current tendencies in the field of mediation could be grouped into four great accounts:

1. **The Satisfaction Story** — Mediation is a tool that promotes the satisfaction of the genuine interests of the disputing parties through cooperative and integrative solutions to problems. Mediation distances the parties from adversarial, distributive bargaining schemes with their win-lose outcomes and encourages win-win types of solutions as well as reducing the cost of dispute resolution.

2. **The Transformation Story** — Mediation transforms the character of people and society as a whole by letting disputants define their problems and goals in their own terms within the full context of their lives; by allowing parties to self-determine, develop more self-respect, self-confidence, and self-reliance; by giving parties a non-coercive chance to humanize themselves to one another and express, despite their differences, a mutual acknowledgment and concern for each other as human beings who deserve this type of recognition.

3. **The Social Justice Story** — Mediation is a way to enable the organization of people around common interests and thereby encourage the formation of stronger community ties and structures. The development of community organization through mediation can be a key factor in limiting the exploitation and abuse of the less powerful in society.

---

10 Above note 1 at 228–30. Riskin helps to explain different mediator styles depending on whether they take a "broad" or "narrow" view of the goals of the process and whether they use a "facilitative" or "evaluative" approach in intervening. See L.R. Riskin, "Understanding Mediators' Orientations, Strategies and Techniques: A Grid for the Perplexed" (1996) Harv. Negotiation L. Rev. 7.

4. The Oppression Story — Despite good intentions, mediation has
become a tool that allows the strong to oppress the weak. The informality, privacy, consensuality and neutrality of mediation accentuate power imbalances between parties and contribute to the privatization of public interest problems.[11]

In an ideological characterization that presents mediation in a manner meant to temper much resistance, Menkel-Meadow calls mediation
"*educational*. At its best we learn about other people, other ways to conceptualize problems, ways to turn crisis into opportunities, creative new
ways to resolve complex issues and interact with each other. And we
learn about ourselves and, perhaps, new ways to negotiate our next
problem," and she describes mediation as "an important *democratic process*. At its best, it allows parties to talk directly to each other and arrive
at solutions to problems that would not be possible in other fora."[12]

Opposing mediation because it is better than the courts or threatens the economics of law practice is unnecessary if mediation can be
reconstructed in a shape designed to reduce court delays, can be
annexed to the courts, and can utilize mediators who are primarily
lawyers and judges. Bureaucratic mediation turns legal opposition into
support. Transformative mediation can be wildly applauded or, if necessary, ignored or not treated as normal, natural, and essential. Like
ADR, the meaning of mediation leaves much room for manoeuvring.

The variability, inconsistency, and indeterminacy of mediation, its
process, and its goals, consistent with similar comments about other
aspects of ADR, do provide challenges for the mediation student, practitioner, or participant, particularly around the question of what makes
up the practical knowledge and skills necessary for proficiency in
mediation. But part of the response or answer is to acknowledge, not
deny, the amorphous nature of mediation. What is right in mediation
depends on the context of the dispute for which mediation is used. It
depends on the nature of the mediation process and the goals the mediators hope to achieve. It particularly depends on what is presented as
natural, normal, and essential about mediating and whose voices do
this presenting, now and in the future. If mediation, like ADR, is
mainly about economic efficiency, one can expect to see such underlying values built into mediation processes or structures. If mediation is
mostly meant to be a process to encourage interest-based bargaining to
the exclusion of other orientations to negotiation, this particular way

---

11   See R.A.B. Bush & J. Folger, *The Promise of Mediation: Responding to Conflict
through Empowerment and Recognition* (San Francisco: Jossey-Bass, 1994).
12   Above note 1 at 240 [emphasis added].

of reaching consensus will be highlighted in mediation training and practices. If mediation is to transform individual or societal ways of thinking about dispute resolution and eventually about each other, mediation programs and practices should exhibit characteristics that reflect this transformative outlook.

The modern evolution of mediation has reflected and confirmed that mediation is a dispute resolution process with many possible faces. In any discussion or practice of mediation, careful and critical attention must be given not only to the form this face has taken and why but also to the look of mediation that may have been missed.

C. MEDIATION: WHAT DOES A MEDIATOR DO?

Imagine hearing the following conversation in a commercial mediation:

> The plaintiff, Paul, points to the defendant, his former business partner. Paul's voice quivers as he says, "I trusted him. I trusted him and he double-crossed me. You have no idea what it's like to have someone you trust take advantage of you." Paul leans back, even more visibly angry than before. Both parties turn expectantly to the mediator. The mediator judges that it is important for her to address the plaintiff's feelings immediately. She decides that she wants to try to demonstrate an appropriate level of empathy, allowing the plaintiff to feel heard and understood, while not jeopardizing her neutrality in the eyes of the defendant. She thinks for a moment, and then says, "Paul, it sounds like this has been a very difficult experience for you." She pauses, and the plaintiff nods. After a moment longer, the mediator says, "I can imagine that it must be difficult for you to talk about all of this. I would like to understand the situation better, though. Can you tell me more?"

Or this version:

> Okay, I hear a lot of emotion in your voice, Paul, and I'm afraid that if I leave it unaddressed, it will impair our ability to proceed. So what I'm going to do is try to show some empathy by expressing my understanding of your feelings. I hope to make you feel acknowledged, understood, respected and comfortable in going forward with the process. At the same time, I need to make sure that I don't offend the defendant. So, here goes: Paul, it sounds like this has been a very difficult experience for you.[13]

---

13   From M. Moffat "Casting Light on the Black Box of Mediation: Should Mediators Make Their Conduct More Transparent" (1997) 13 Ohio St. J. on Disp. Resol. 1 at 1–2.

1) The Search for Skills

Whatever shape mediation takes, one question is often asked: What exactly is it that mediators do? The interest behind this question is usually in learning about mediator knowledge and skills (how to think like a mediator) in order to become a mediator. But, learning to be a mediator, certainly studying mediation, requires close attention not only to relevant knowledge and applicable skills but also to the choices mediators make about what is said or done. How are choices made about addressing feelings, setting ground rules, caucusing, moving a party off an unrealistic position, or transforming the disputants? Sometimes a simple question can hide a more complicated answer.

As the modern evolution of mediation suggests, there can be no single or right answer to the question — what does a mediator do? A court-annexed mediation program, designed primarily to reduce court delay, mostly using mediators who are judges with limited training in the mediation process, will require different mediator attributes to be successful than a victim-offender reconciliation program for healing differences between the victim and offender in serious criminal cases using mediators with extensive backgrounds in criminal justice theories and counselling. Similarly, a mediator searching for consensus in a multi-party dispute around logging or not logging an old growth forest will need mediator capacities that only remotely resemble the qualities of a good labour mediator who brings a warring union and company together on a two-year collective agreement. The knowledge and skills traditionally needed by First Nations elders or village headmen in Asia to mediate a dispute to maintain harmony in their communities will not be the same knowledge and skills used by recently trained volunteer mediators in a North American community justice centre who seek to strengthen the disputants' self-reliance and consideration for others and to help the disputants deal with similar problems in the future as integral parts of the mediation process. A family mediator helping spouses to make decisions about their parenting plans would need to know and do different things than mediators involved in peace talks with divided factions in a country.

All these examples can fairly be termed mediation. But the knowledge and skills needed by a good mediator will depend on the context in which the mediation occurs, on the nature of the mediation process used, on the goals that the parties or the mediator hope to achieve, and especially on the ideological shape or structure that is given to this form of consensual dispute resolution.

Accordingly, setting down in writing what a competent mediator must know and be able to do in all circumstances would not seem possible, given mediation's diverse uses, unless artificial limits could somehow be imposed on how mediation is practised, or unless uniform standards existed or could exist among the many mediators who help people make up their minds around the world. Considering mediation in all its local and global applications, the production of an exhaustive, cross-contextual, and practically useful list of mediation standards would not appear feasible.

What would be possible and useful, as discussed for negotiation in chapter 3, would be the opportunity to analyze mediation in its various contexts and to determine what works or doesn't work in these settings. The results would likely be a panoply of context-specific truths and understandings about mediation that mirrored mediation's process, goal, and ideological malleability rather than a fixed, consistent, and coherent set of objective standards for most situations.

However, pressures have mounted for the articulation of mediator standards on local, national, and international scales. The exponential growth of mediation, the increasing initiatives to institutionalize mediation within public disputing systems like the courts, the multiplying voices of individuals and organizations who see an expanding market for mediation, the calls for mediation to be a new profession or part of existing professions, and other factors have fuelled efforts to concretize what it is that mediators do. The rationale usually given for wanting more clearly defined mediator standards is that these standards would provide the tools for selecting, training, and evaluating mediators; for protecting consumers of mediation services; for facilitating accreditation, licensing, or certifying of mediators; and generally for ensuring quality and integrity in the developing mediation and ADR fields.

These desires for standards come from various quarters in spite of the fact that mediation can be understood and practised well in almost an endless variety of ways for a vast number of reasons. Characterizing a matter as a family dispute, a commercial dispute, or a public policy dispute does not make mediation or its goals and procedures uniform within that specific category. Efforts to even out this practice and to establish exactly what a competent mediator must know and be able to do in a generic sense undoubtedly will give a shape to the process of mediation. Accordingly, in assessing the statements of standards that make up the mediation process, careful scrutiny needs to be given to why a particular form of mediation was chosen, who did the choosing, and why other shapes have been discarded.

In the search to define what mediators need to know and be able to do, three guiding principles have been dominant:

- that no single entity (rather, a variety of organizations) should establish qualifications for neutrals;
- that the greater the degree of choice the parties have over the dispute resolution process, program or neutral, the less mandatory the qualification requirements should be; and
- that qualification criteria should be based on performance, rather than paper credentials.[14]

In a 1995 follow-up report, the Society of Professionals in Dispute Resolution (SPIDR) went on to say that "if no single entity should certify general dispute resolution competence, then it is critical for those interested in qualifications to work collaboratively with [one another] to develop standards and models of best practice."[15]

These principles are intended to introduce a kind of rational logic and credibility to identifying mediator standards and are designed to strike a balance between the competing concerns over setting mediator standards such as concerns around restricting the development of varied mediation practices; concerns about the differing needs for, and methods of, consumer protection; concerns with limiting entry into the mediation field; concerns about preserving the integrity of a developing profession; and, to some extent, concerns about the viability of setting standards for such a diverse process.

2) Best Practices in Mediation

The concern about setting mediation standards, as discussed above, has been met generally by asserting, fairly explicitly, that certain mediation knowledge and skills transcend context. One approach has been to suggest "there are core skills, knowledge and other attributes necessary for competence (in mediation) that generally apply across most contexts and processes."

---

14   Society of Professionals in Dispute Resolution (SPIDR), *Qualifying Neutrals: The Basic Principles: Report of the SPIDR Commission on Qualifications* (Washington, DC: National Institute for Dispute Resolution, 1989) at 11.

15   SPIDR, *Ensuring Competence and Quality in Dispute Resolution Practice, Report No. 2 of the SPIDR Commission on Qualifications* (Washington, DC, 1995) at v.

(1) General

   (a) ability to listen actively;
   (b) ability to analyze problems, identify and separate the issues involved, and frame these issues for resolution or decision making;
   (c) ability to use clear, neutral language in speaking and (if written opinions are required) in writing;
   (d) sensitivity to strongly felt values of the disputants, including gender, ethnic, and cultural differences;
   (e) ability to deal with complex factual materials;
   (f) presence and persistence, i.e., an overt commitment to honesty, dignified behavior, respect for the parties, and an ability to create and maintain control of a diverse group of disputants;
   (g) ability to identify and to separate the neutral's personal values from issues under consideration; and
   (h) ability to understand power imbalances.

(2) For mediation

   (a) ability to understand the negotiating process and the role of advocacy;
   (b) ability to earn trust and maintain acceptability;
   (c) ability to convert parties' positions into needs and interests;
   (d) ability to screen out non-mediable issues;
   (e) ability to help parties to invent creative options;
   (f) ability to help the parties identify principles and criteria that will guide their decision making;
   (g) ability to help parties assess their non-settlement alternatives;
   (h) ability to help the parties make their own informed choices; and
   (i) ability to help parties assess whether their agreement can be implemented.[16]

Training programs can break down these cores into teachable microskills. For example, having an "ability to help parties to invent creative options" might be made up of brainstorming skills, being able to go outside the square[17] and other problem-solving behaviours.

---

16 *Ibid.* at 17–18.
17 Going outside the square or box seems to originate from a game where you are asked to draw a line through nine small circles arranged in three rows and columns, horizontally and vertically. You can only use four straight lines and you cannot lift your pen from the paper while drawing the four lines. The problem can only be solved if you go outside the box.

A similar perspective is to acknowledge that mediators take many different approaches to their role, but some common elements can be observed in experienced mediators. Genevieve Chornenki describes fourteen skill sets:

1. Create an atmosphere conducive to discussion;

2. Encourage the parties right away to agree on the goal of the session and on the rules that they will abide by, which might include speaking in turn, without interruption, and without personal attacks;

3. Elicit factual information about the conflict;

4. Understand the dispute from each party's perspective and communicate that understanding so that each party feels "heard";

5. Manage the interplay between the parties — at some points engineering civility in their communications, and at others allowing them to vent;

6. Help the parties identify the strengths and weaknesses of their case, often by playing devil's advocate;

7. Work with the parties to go beyond their positions to discover their underlying interests, and to talk about them;

8. Smooth communications between the parties in many ways — by listening to a "loaded" or angry statement made by one party and reframing it to convey the essential information to the other party without the potentially distorting emotional overlay, or by acting as the courier for information when the parties are physically located in separate caucus rooms, to name just two;

9. Provoke the parties to be creative in generating options for settlement that go beyond what could be ordered by a judge trying the matter, but which make sense and create value for these parties with these interests;

10. Assist the parties to analyze and assess their alternatives to a negotiated resolution to the dispute;

11. Control the pace of the negotiation to enable the parties to reach the moment of resolution on each point at the same time;

12. Keep the parties working and focused on the future and on their goal of resolving their differences;

13. Ensure that the parties' efforts are productive in moving them ever closer to that goal; and

14. Display endless optimism that an agreement can be achieved, and sustain commitment to the effort of its achievement. Good mediators do not give up easily.[18]

A further tact has been to identify the tasks performed by mediators and then to set out the knowledge, skills, abilities, and other attributes (KSAOs) that make it possible for a given person to perform those tasks. A sample list of mediator tasks and KSAOs is outlined by Chris Honeyman:

Tasks

A.   Gathering background information

B.   Facilitating communication

C.   Communicating information to others

D.   Analyzing information

E.   Facilitating agreement

F.   Managing cases

G.   Documenting information

Knowledge, Skills, Abilities and Other Attributes

1. Reasoning: To reason logically and analytically, effectively distinguishing issues and questioning assumptions.

2. Analyzing: To assimilate large quantities of varied information into logical ideas or concepts.

3. Problem Solving: To generate, assess and prioritize alternative solutions to a problem, or help the parties do so.

4. Reading Comprehension: To read and comprehend written materials.

5. Writing: To write clearly and concisely, using neutral language.

6. Oral communication: To speak with clarity, and to listen carefully and emphatically.

---

18   G.A. Chornenki & C.E. Hart, *Bypass Court: A Dispute Resolution Handbook* (Toronto: Butterworths, 1996) at 89–90.

7. Non-verbal communication: To use voice inflection, gestures, and eye contact appropriately.

8. Interviewing: To obtain and process information from others, eliciting information, listening actively, and facilitating an exchange of information.

9. Emotional stability/maturity: To remain calm and level-headed in stressful and emotional situations.

10. Sensitivity: To recognize a variety of emotions and respond appropriately.

11. Integrity: To be responsible, ethical and honest.

12. Recognizing Values: To discern own and others strongly held values.

13. Impartiality: To maintain an open mind about different points of view.

14. Organizing: To manage effectively activities, records and other materials.

15. Following procedure: To follow agreed-upon procedures.

16. Commitment: Interest in helping others to resolve conflict.[19]

In a similar vein, Boulle and Kelly[20] suggest that "in reality, each mediator can have only a limited 'tool-box' of skills and techniques"[21] depending on their training, experience, and personal attributes. To suggest otherwise would "imply that only divine beings could qualify for the role."[22] Selection from the toolbox of skills would be made at the mediator's discretion to further one or more of the functions of mediators and assist the mediating parties in making sound decisions. Boulle and Kelly[23] describe eleven mediator functions:

- develop trust and confidence
- establish a framework for cooperative decision making
- analyze the conflict and design appropriate interventions

---

19   C. Honeyman (Director, Test Design Project), *Performance-Based Assessment: A Methodology for Use in Training and Evaluating Mediators* (Washington: National Institute for Dispute Resolution, 1995).

20   L. Boulle & K.J. Kelly, *Mediation Principles, Process, Practice* (Toronto: Butterworths, 1998).

21   *Ibid.* at 163.

22   *Ibid.*

23   Adapted from *ibid.* at 136.

- promote constructive communication and modelling
- facilitate negotiation and problem solving
- educate the parties
- empower the parties
- impose pressure to settle
- promote reality
- advise and evaluate
- terminate the mediation

and provide a selection of skills and techniques[24] relevant to these functions:

- organizational skills and techniques, such as
  - supervising arrivals and departures
  - arranging seating
  - improving the emotional climate
  - presenting material visually

- facilitation skills and techniques, such as
  - converting concerns to issues
  - dealing with emotion
  - managing the process

- negotiation skills and techniques, such as
  - emphasizing common ground
  - increasing the issues
  - making and responding to offers
  - linking one negotiation issue with another
  - brainstorming
  - dealing with deadlocks

- communication skills and techniques, such as
  - developing appropriate verbal communication
  - listening effectively
  - reframing
  - reading and understanding non-verbal communication
  - questioning
  - paraphrasing
  - summarizing

- avoiding mediator traps, such as
  - being inadequately prepared
  - losing control of the process

---

24   Above note 20 at 164–96.

- losing impartiality
- ignoring emotions
- moving too quickly into solutions
- being too directive

Some suggest competency in mediation requires a certain quantity of skills training and experience. For example, the British Columbia Mediation Roster Society, formed to certify mediators for certain government-mandated mediation programs, requires

- 80 hours of core education in conflict resolution and mediation theory and skills training;
- 100 additional hours of related professional training such as law, psychology, and social work;
- 20 hours per year of ongoing professional development or continuing education; and
- knowledge of, or training in, civil procedure.

In addition, a roster mediator must

- have completed ten mediations as a sole mediator;
- provide two positive credible references;
- have liability insurance; and
- subscribe to standards of conduct.

Other statements on what mediators should do or can't do can be contained in Codes of Conduct for mediators as part of an ethical exercise. See section (F), "Mediation Ethics," in this chapter. For example, a mediator should avoid conduct that gives the appearance of partiality, should disclose all actual and potential conflicts of interest reasonably known, and must not engage in sexual intimacies with mediation participants.

Despite variations, the above statements of standards are useful descriptors. They provide a practical and learnable image, or even several images, of what it is that good mediators need to know and be able to do when helping disputants reach agreement. They draw the links between the art and science of negotiation and mediation practices. They point in a helpful way to the specific skills and the important knowledge that would have to be part of any credible mediation training program. The skill descriptions can also lead to an easier understanding of how the skills would be applied in practice.

For example, consider a tense and heated neighbour dispute. One neighbour's cat has really upset another neighbour with its habits. The neighbours have not been able to work it out themselves. Fortunately they agreed to meet with a mediator. The following dialogue from several mediation sessions illustrate how various mediator skills might be used.

Sally: You have no right to interfere with my cat. I'm not breaking any laws. It isn't bothering anyone else!

Fred: If you don't keep that animal inside, you won't have a cat!

Mediator: Well, let me jump in here if I can. [Managing the process — the mediator intervenes to improve the communication process]. I can see that the situation is quite upsetting for both of you and it must be quite frustrating to have to deal with your concerns on a day-to-day basis. [Active listening — the mediator acknowledges what appears to be the feelings of the disputants in order to show the disputants that they have been heard and to help build trust and rapport].

Sally: Right. It's crazy.

Fred: She shouldn't have a cat in the first place. The courtyard is too small for pets.

Mediator: Well, I'm glad you both decided to come to mediation. Working out solutions to problems often can be hard work especially when a mutually satisfying solution doesn't appear obvious. However, it seems to me that the use and enjoyment of the courtyard is important to both of you. [Reframing — the mediator identifies a common interest and restates the interest in a non-positional way]. [more dialogue . . .].

Fred: The cat has to go!

Mediator: I know getting this matter resolved satisfactorily is important to you [More reframing]. Before we look too closely at possible solutions, it might help me if I knew more about what exactly are your concerns. How would you describe them? [Questioning — the mediator seeks to identify the underlying interests behind the stated position].

Fred: Besides the smells, it's ruining my flowers. And she [pointing at Sally] is so arrogant — she thinks because she's half my age she can ignore me. Well, she's dead wrong!

Mediator: So one of the important issues you might like to see addressed in the mediation is the question of respectful relations between neighbours, both in terms of past events and future ones? [Converting concerns to issues — the mediator reframes a concern into an issue for negotiation].

Fred: Yes [more dialogue . . .].

Mediator: Let me see if I can summarize the agreement. Sally has apologized for her words and actions in the past that were less than respectful. She particularly regrets making the statement about your age, Fred. Fred, you have accepted the apology. I want to commend you both for these steps. Sometimes they are the most difficult to take. You've both agreed to treat each other with kindness and respect in the future. Sally, you've agreed to have litter available in the apartment so that outdoor habits should be reduced substantially. You'll pick up any outside waste that either you or Fred spot. Fred, you've agreed to provide some "tasteful" deterrence for any animals/birds getting into your flower beds and Sally has agreed to start her own flower or vegetable bed adjacent to her apartment. We are hoping that Tabatha, who I should note has attended this last session, will be trained to do any outside business in Sally's bed. The final point is that Fred will help Sally with setting up and maintaining her bed and I get a sense there may be a friendly rivalry as to who will grow the sweetest roses. Does that pretty much capture it?

Sally: Yes. Thank you, and thank you, Fred, for your patience.

Fred: Yes. Thank you. I'm glad it worked out this way. I was almost at my wit's end.

The above examples and listings of mediator skills clearly are not exhaustive, but they do represent practical illustrations of much of what mainstream mediators learn to do. The listed mediator tasks, skills, and educational requirements also provide several important insights about modern-day mediation practice.

First, the search for core, common, or always-present mediator skills, although necessary, cannot ignore the reality of mediation practice. The knowledge and skills needed by good mediators is going to depend on a careful understanding of the full context in which the mediation takes place, the goals that mediation hopes to achieve from both mediator and disputant perspectives, and, significantly, on what is said to be normal, natural, and essential about best mediator practices. Since the context, goals, and ideology of mediation are not necessarily uniform or consistent, and may even be conflicting, from one place to another, competent mediation practice must have an enormously high degree of flexibility. Even within particular mediation programs or initiatives, differences in mediator tasks and skills will exist.

Second, while competent mediation practice may defy precise pronouncement except in localized contexts, what a mediator needs to know and be able to do surely surpasses common sense. Mediators do perform certain tasks. They may allow adequate time for a disputant to tell her story or create a safe and comfortable negotiation environment for a divorcing couple. Mediators also use various skills, at times observing and interpreting non-verbal behaviour in the mediation or asking questions to elicit more detailed descriptions from the participants. Thinking of good mediation as only common sense avoids a more in-depth and critical understanding of what constitutes mediation practice and also hides the fact that common sense can mean different things to different people.

Third, while new and developing programs that offer multidisciplinary degrees or diplomas in dispute resolution or mediation may increasingly provide opportunities to acquire the necessary knowledge and skills to be a good mediator in context, the above lists suggest other paths can be followed to attain mediator competency. For example, a combination of life skills, work experience, personality traits, education, and cultural mores has been a formula for mediator credibility and success in specialized settings such as labour relations, community issues, and international affairs. There is no reason why this latter route to mediator effectiveness, which probably tends to be more contextualized and less formalized, could not be successfully duplicated in other settings.

Finally, the relationship between initiatives articulating core or fundamental mediator knowledge and skills and the professionalization of mediation needs to be clear. As the demand for mediation services expands, in both public and private settings, there is growing interest in seeing this market serviced by competent mediators. Clearly prescribed and core mediator attributes are necessary for mediation to fit into the classical definition of a profession: "Professions were organized bodies of experts who applied esoteric knowledge to particular cases. They had elaborate systems of instruction and training together with entry by examination and other requisites. They normally possessed and enforced a code of ethics."[25]

---

25   A. Abbott, *The System of Professions: An Essay on the Division of Expert Labour* (Chicago: University of Chicago Press, 1988) at 4.

With organized bodies of mediators emerging, education and training opportunities expanding, and codes of ethics developing, all that remains to satisfy the classical tradition of the profession is to construct the knowledge and skills that professionals apply to individual cases. This last step to professionalization is impossible to take if mediator knowledge and skills are variable, dependent on context, ideologically constructed, and perhaps indeterminate. The concept of prescribed and core mediation knowledge and skills, for the general mediation practitioner, with more specialized skills needed for the specialist in certain cases, helps to take that necessary step in the professionalization direction. Professional mediators will bring considerable benefits to the practice of mediation but the professionalization of this informal and flexible process can raise concerns about market closure and other adverse consequences.

D. MEDIATION: THE PROCESS

Neighbours choose mediation to settle a dispute about a falling-down fence on a shared property line. Lawyers recommend mediation to spouses contesting child custody. Businesses pledge to give mediation a chance in a multimillion dollar lawsuit. Multiple parties want to try mediation to resolve their concerns over the proposed siting of a halfway house in a residential part of town. Children in a schoolyard call on a peer counsellor to mediate a dispute involving a racial slur.

When the mediation process is chosen, what happens next?

The course of the mediation in any of the above scenarios will depend, in large part, on the exact nature of the mediation process used in each of these situations, on the goals being pursued by the parties, the mediator or the institutional actors promoting the mediation, and on the general ideological shape that mediation is given. The course of the mediation will also depend, as discussed in chapter 3, on negotiation-related variables. After all, a major activity in the mediation will be the "assisted negotiations." The disputants' fluency in the language of negotiation; the type of negotiation strategies used; the tactics employed; the degree of planning or analysis undertaken by the disputants; how power is perceived, used, and responded to; culture; and more will have an important impact on what happens next in any mediation as the parties negotiate. The involvement of a helping and neutral third party, the mediator, using core or other knowledge and skills to assist the negotiations seems to further suggest that what happens next in any mediation must be dynamic, diverse, unique to the setting, and somewhat unpredictable.

1) Mediation as a Staged Process

However, developments in thinking about mediation as a staged process that relies on interest-based bargaining add structure to what happens next. Consistent with, and complementary to, efforts to set mediator standards, seeing mediation as constructed of a number of carefully sequenced steps or events that allow for principled negotiations to take place makes for a more refined and respected picture of this process. The following are examples of practical descriptions of mediation as a structured process. These process descriptions allude to what might be appropriate mediator skills. The benefits to thinking of mediation as a structured process are discussed thereafter.

a) Twelve-Stage Model

First, Christopher Moore in *The Mediation Process: Practical Strategies for Resolving Conflict*[26] describes twelve stages of mediator moves and critical situations to be handled. Within each stage is a general checklist of the steps to be taken by the mediator:

Stage 1: Establish Relationship with the Disputing Parties

- make initial contacts with the parties
- build credibility
- promote rapport
- educate the parties about the process
- increase commitment to the procedure

Stage 2: Select a Strategy to Guide Mediation

- assist the parties to assess various approaches to conflict management and resolution
- assist the parties to select an approach
- coordinate the approaches of the parties

Stage 3: Collect and Analyze Background Information

- collect and analyze relevant data about the people, dynamic, and substance of a conflict
- verify accuracy of data
- minimize the impact of inaccurate or unavailable data

Stage 4: Design a Detailed Plan for Mediation

- identify strategies and consequent non-contingent moves that will enable the parties to move towards agreement

---

26   Adapted from above note 8 at 66–67.

- identify contingent moves to respond to situations peculiar to the specific conflict

Stage 5: Build Trust and Cooperation
- prepare disputants psychologically to participate in negotiations on substantive issues
- handle strong emotions
- check perceptions and minimize effects of stereotypes
- build recognition of the legitimacy of the parties and issues
- build trust
- clarify communications

Stage 6: Begin the Mediation Session
- open negotiation between the parties
- establish an open and positive tone
- establish ground rules and behavioural guidelines
- assist the parties in venting emotions
- delimit topic areas and issues for discussion
- assist the parties in exploring commitments, salience, and influence

Stage 7: Define Issues and Set an Agenda
- identify broad topic areas of concern to the parties
- obtain agreement on the issues to be discussed
- determine the sequence for handling the issues

Stage 8: Uncover Hidden Interests of the Disputing Parties
- identify the substantive, procedural, and psychological interests of the parties
- educate the parties about each other's interests

Stage 9: Generate Options for Settlement
- develop an awareness among the parties of the need for options
- lower commitment to positions or sole alternatives
- generate options using either positional or interest-based bargaining

Stage 10: Assess Options for Settlement
- review the interests of the parties
- assess how interests can be met by available options
- assess the costs and benefits of selecting options

Stage 11: Final Bargaining
- reach agreement through either incremental convergence of positions, final leaps to package settlements, development of a consensual formula, or establishment of a procedural means to reach a substantive agreement

Stage 12: Achieve Formal Settlement

- identify procedural steps to operationalize the agreement
- establish an evaluation and monitoring procedure
- formalize the settlement and create an enforcement and commitment mechanism

b) Six-Stage Model

In a related way, mediation often is presented as a staged model that reveals reliance on an interest-based approach to the negotiations. Consider the following six- stage model of mediation:[27]

Stage I: Introduction

1. Introduce yourself and any co-mediator and take questions about your status or credentials, as necessary.
2. Explain clearly the mediation process and the philosophy of disputant responsibility for settlement.
3. Set a positive, future-focused tone.
4. Set ground rules and take questions.
5. Ensure disputants understand process and clarify if necessary.
6. Obtain a commitment to the process.

Stage II: Gather the Facts

1. Confirm disputants' willingness to proceed.
2. Have the parties give a synopsis of the facts of the dispute and encourage delineation of the issues.
3. Ensure disputants are listening and understanding.
4. Enforce ground rules as necessary.
5. Summarize what the disputants have said.

Stage III: Issue Clarification and Development

1. Identify and emphasize commonness of issues.
2. Link issues that are inseparable or strategically interrelated.
3. Fractionalize (break) compound issues into more manageable parts.
4. Frame the issues until you obtain joint affirmation.

Stage IV: Identify Interests

1. Use open questions.
2. Manage emotions and accusations.
3. Move the disputants from their positions to interests.
4. Summarize lists of interests.

---

27   Adapted from the Continuing Legal Education Society of British Columbia, Family Law Mediation, materials prepared for a training workshop, 12–16 June 1990.

5. Avoid premature proposals.
6. Formulate a neutral goal statement.

Stage V: Generate Options and Select a Solution
1. Summarize areas of present agreement.
2. Generate options: the "easy fix," brainstorming, past successes, hypotheticals.
3. List objective criteria against which options can be measured.
4. Seek solutions to maximize mutual gain and meet joint goals.
5. List and evaluate options and encourage fair, agreeable solutions.
6. Reality-test solutions by raising hypotheticals over implementation.
7. Avoid imposing own view or opinion.

Stage VI: Formalize Agreement in a Clear, Comprehensive, Accurate, Enforceable Way
1. Consider the state of the parties' representation and elect how to proceed.
2. Consider referrals to other professionals.
3. Convert the parties' consensus into written format.
4. Review the document with the parties.
5. Consider independent legal advice, if necessary.
6. Address problems of implementation and evaluation.

c) Interest-based Mediation Models
The following two narratives describe similar stages in the mediation process in more detail and demonstrate clearly the prevalence of interest-based bargaining within the various stages:

Excerpt from Chornenki and Hart, *Bypass Court: A Dispute Resolution Handbook*:[28]

> The mediation process used in court-connected projects and in many private mediations generally moves through several predictable stages. The first session is often a joint session in which all the parties and their professional advisors meet together with the mediator. This may not be possible if there are a large number of parties and space limitations prevent them from meeting in one room. In family mediations, the first session is typically with the parties individually. After introductions and the mediator's opening, involving what to expect of the process, comes the opening statements by the parties. These can be made either by the party representative or its professional advisor, but the latter is more typical in court-connected mediations. The

---

28   Above note 18 at 91–92.

statement is usually quite brief. It tells the mediator and the other parties about the dispute from each party's perspective, and typically outlines the positions taken on the outstanding issues.

Following the opening statements, the mediator will often have questions of the parties that may be designed to clarify certain facts or issues, or may be intended to begin the involvement of the parties themselves, if they have done none of the talking up to that time. This can be the point at which the mediator will work with the parties to create an agenda of what will happen in the course of the mediation.

The mediator will then start to move the discussion from positions to interests (the needs, motivations or concerns underlying the dispute). At some point, when the mediator decides that the joint session is no longer productive, the mediator will meet with each side separately, in a private or caucus session. It will generally be established at the beginning of the joint session what use the mediator may make of information learned in the caucus session in talking to the other party in the mediation. The two common models are either the mediator may take nothing out without the party's express permission, or the mediator may take anything out that has not been flagged as confidential by the party in the caucus session. If parties have a preference, they should speak up as it is their process.

The number of caucus sessions will vary with the mediation. In some cases the parties will not meet together again until they are very close to or have reached agreement. Other mediations are conducted almost entirely in joint session. All sorts of permutations and combinations are possible and valid. What the mediator is doing in trying to identify each party's interests is to give the parties more possibilities that can meet their needs. This moves a simple choice of opposites (positions) into a problem-solving exercise around a "how-to" question.

Many mediations will end with a joint session. If a settlement is concluded, the parties will generally be asked to write down and sign a memorandum of settlement. If the agreement needs ratification (e.g. by a board of directors or a municipal council), the negotiator for that party will often be asked to endorse on the memorandum that she or he recommends the proposed settlement to the ratifier. If there is no settlement, the last joint session is often used to summarize the progress that has been made and to agree on the next step or on an agenda for future resolution.

Excerpt from Janet Walker, "Family Mediation"[29]:

> The first step in mediation is crucial to the establishment of a relationship which will facilitate the rest of the process. Described by Haynes as the "intake" process, the emphasis is on describing what mediation is, how it works, what is expected of the couple and setting some ground rules. Folberg and Taylor, who call this initial stage "creating trust and structure," use it to gather relevant information about the participants' perceptions of the conflict, their goals and expectations, and the situations in which the conflict manifests itself.
>
> Part of the mediator's task is to gather data which can be used to assess the parties' motivation and ability to negotiate together. They include information about communication styles and patterns; the extent and level of conflict; incidents of domestic violence and abuse; the preparedness of each partner for the decision to separate; parental functioning; and financial, emotional and social resources. This initial stage is complete when the mediator has a clear picture of the manifest and underlying issues, and the couple have a clear understanding of mediation and can determine if they wish to proceed.
>
> *Fact-finding and planning the agenda*
> Although much relevant information will have been shared during the engagement phase, the next step is to ensure that all the data relevant to the case is "on the table." From the mediator's perspective, knowledge about family composition, living arrangements, and the steps either or both might have made to seek a divorce and obtain legal advice, needs to be clarified. The mediator helps each partner to describe the conflicts and disputes between them, to assess their immediacy, duration, intensity and to discern areas of potential rigidity in the position each of them holds. Clarifying areas of agreement and disagreement in this way enables the mediator, in collaboration with the couple, to set the agenda for mediation.
>
> *Exploring options and alternatives*
> According to Taylor the key question in this stage is "How can you do what you want to do in the most effective way?" To answer it, each party is helped to articulate the options they know or want, and to develop new alternatives. These then need to be assessed and evaluated by anticipating their implications, workability, limitations, and

---

29   J. Walker, "Family Mediation" in J. Macfarlane, ed., *Rethinking Disputes: The Mediation Alternative* (Toronto: Emond Montgomery Publications Limited, 1997) at 67–70.

costs and benefits to each party and to their children. Mediators need to be both facilitative and creative during this part of the process. Taylor describes the mediator as a resource person, an expert who can suggest new options based on a more extensive knowledge and experience of divorce and its effects. Mediation moves to the next phase when there has been a full discussion of all the possible options, without prejudicial or judgmental attitudes impeding it.

Negotiation and decision making

Having explored all the options, the couple are helped to negotiate towards making some decisions, which frequently entails compromise on both their parts. What matters is that both can accept the decisions, even if they are not what they had hoped for originally, and believe them to be fair and just. It is in this phase of mediation that negotiation and bargaining take place with the intention to reach a win-win solution. Maintaining some sort of balance and equality in communication is essential to effective bargaining, as is resisting the urge to reach settlements too hastily. The mediator needs to ensure that each party is ready to make a decision.

Clarifying and summarising agreements

This stage in the mediation process has as its goal the production of some sort of document or draft agreement, frequently referred to as a Memorandum of Understanding in England. It is a summary of the agreements reached and not reached which should be capable of forming the basis of court orders if necessary, and of being used as a working document for the parties concerned. Most importantly, the document is not a legal one, it is written in everyday language, and it should be open to modification as circumstances change. The signing of the document by each party is a symbolic step and provides tangible evidence of cooperation and closure. Sometimes children are invited to mediation at this point so that their parents can talk through the arrangements they have made. Not only does this ensure that children are properly and adequately informed of decisions affecting their lives, but also it can be very reassuring for them to see their parents cooperating and planning their future jointly.

Review

Mediators are well aware that the best negotiated plans may still falter in practice. Time is often given to the couple to try arrangements out and then to review them. Each may wish to take legal advice about the settlements to ensure that they are not seriously prejudicial to one person's best interests. In England, the majority of those mediating their disputes seek independent legal advice before and/or after the mediation process. Since it is not usual for advising lawyers to attend the mediation sessions, mediators always encourage their clients to take the Memorandum of Understanding to their lawyers for scrutiny. Our research indicates that this acts as a safeguard against either party making agreements which could have unforeseen adverse consequences, and is much appreciated by the users of mediation. In practice, few agreements get unpicked by lawyers at this stage.

Some people refer back to their lawyers throughout the mediation process. Although a few of the early court-based schemes encouraged the attendance of advising lawyers at mediation, this model has largely disappeared. Most mediators do not want parties' lawyers to be quite so influential during the mediation, but welcome the support they offer their clients before and after.

Implementation and reviewing agreements

Many mediators will not expect to see a couple again if their respective lawyers are content with the agreements reached and they are capable of being put into practice. For most couples, the mediation process ends with the review stage. For others, however, mediators may offer a follow-up appointment some months on. They recognise that the weeks and months after mediation are likely to be difficult and may involve several transitions in living arrangements. At the very least, each party has to adjust to new situations and arrangements which may be strange and emotionally painful. Rarely does everything run smoothly, hence the offer of a further appointment to review the outcomes of mediation. Such a practice can, in Taylor's experience, "put out brushfires of discontent and provide positive reinforcement for the continuance of the mediation plan." In her view, mediation is unique among conflict resolution processes because it can create a process for future review and revision regardless of whether there are any problems or concerns. Of course, people are encouraged to return to mediation at any time if concerns, problems or further disputes emerge. The door to mediation is always left open. Divorce requires families to manage and adjust to a series of transformations each of which may be complex and stressful. Mediation must, therefore, be flexible and sensitive to individual needs, and most mediators emphasize the importance of process and not merely outcomes.

2) Open Consensual Mediation

Another approach to the idea of mediation as a staged process is to honour more stringently the concept of consensus. Rather than being driven by the assumption that interest-based bargaining is the superior negotiating strategy, the mediation process could be practised according to the consensus of the parties involved. In open consensual mediation, the decision makers might be the mediator and two disputants. There might be many parties and multiple mediators who decide. The State or a public agency could also be a party. But the guiding principle that determines the structure of the mediation process would be party consensus. The disputants, their representatives if agreed, the mediator, and others to be decided would have to negotiate and reach agreement on how they wanted to conduct the mediation. The disputants and others would not only have the authority to make substantive decisions (should access to the children be restricted? how much money should be paid? will the culturally modified tree be cut?) but also have the power, subject to any legislative enactments, to make the process decisions that mattered. These process decisions could include the following: Where do we meet? What ground rules, if any, are to be set? How would the disputants prefer to negotiate? Should there be an explicit attempt or not to engage in interest-based bargaining? Should there be caucusing? Should the mediation be open or closed, confidential or not? Who should participate? What does consensus mean?

The mediator would be an obvious party and would need to agree to any process decision. If the mediator is not in agreement with the parties on what steps are to be taken and why, the process might not work. Also, there may be times, because of the mediator's experience or knowledge, when mediator input on what happens next will be extremely useful and save time. But, obviously, the more the mediator determines or strongly influences the actual process outcomes, the more the mediation does not resemble open consensual mediation. The parties may still have authority to make substantive decisions about the problem (should the access be monthly or weekly?) and hence be clearly mediation. But, at some point, too much exclusion of the disputants from involvement in deciding key process matters (will we try to encourage principled negotiation even though other orientations might work equally well? will we speak to each other?) means the mediation is not open and consensual.

Open consensual mediation could be a form of transformative mediation, but it need not be. The self-determination in open consensual mediation might, directly or indirectly, lead to mutual understandings, respect, a shared sense of responsibility, and an increased capacity for constructive conflict resolution in the future in much the same way as might occur in transformative mediation. But open consensual mediation might just as easily not incorporate these goals or values into the process. It would depend on the consensus of the parties. The divorcing couple might make an informed decision to set a strict time frame for the negotiations and agree to hard but not destructive bargaining over who gets what. Two businesses in conflict, parties interested in the construction of a dam, and neighbours with a disputed property line might take the same approach. Then again, they might not. Some might like the sound of trying interest-based bargaining with the mediator leading the way. Some may prefer to be transformed. Consensual mediation, its process, its goals, and its very ideological make-up would serve the needs of the parties in the context of their problem.

This kind of consensual mediation might be more time-consuming and more difficult than the many mediations already taking place, but it might not. Open consensual mediation could be faster and easier. Early agreements between the parties on process issues might have a positive influence on later decision making that can get difficult. Going slow at the start could mean going faster later on. And it is probable that many process decisions (how long will the sessions last?) would be made quite expeditiously. However, some agreements on structuring the mediation process would take time and effort and be contentious. But this approach would allow for the decisions about the look and feel of mediation and all its possibilities to be made by the parties to the mediation rather than having mediation's process, goals, and ideology, and ultimately the dispute's consequences, imposed by someone else.

Open consensual mediation therefore might only have two clear steps or stages:

Step 1: Commitment

The mediator would determine if there was party commitment to open consensual mediation. For reasons of bureaucratic convenience, legislative imperative, program goals, or mediator or party comfort levels, the structure of the mediation may be preset or be left mostly up to the individual mediator. In this stage, the mediator would provide a general overview of an open consensual approach to mediation and answer any questions.

Step 2: Processing

What would occur in this stage would depend on context. The parties might begin by telling their respective stories to the mediator and each other. However, they might decide instead to create an agenda of the issues to be discussed. Or they might prefer to concentrate on the reasons why they have not been able to negotiate a solution themselves. The mediator's main function in this stage is to make sure that progress is being made and to maintain the commitment to open consensual mediation.

3) Benefits of Structuring Mediation

The benefits to thinking of mediation as a staged process are similar to those suggested for negotiation in chapter 3. Most parties have chosen mediation because they have not been able to work out a problem themselves, and other options, such as abandoning a claim or going to court, are not seen as attractive alternatives. The parties will be expecting some guidance in the mediation process beyond the mediator saying "let's negotiate" or "how can I help you?" Taking the parties through a staged or step-by-step process can help keep negotiations on track, can highlight actions and skills that are necessary for negotiation success, can convey a sense of progress to the parties, can provide a framework to move off a difficult point and on to an easier one, and generally can give the parties a sense they are taking a new approach to the issues in dispute.

Structuring the mediation process also makes sense when problem-solving or interest-based bargaining is commonly presented as the preferable method of negotiation to be followed in the mediation. By emphasizing interest-based bargaining in mediation, it is only natural, for example, to proceed through the process in a way that encourages the parties to discover their underlying interests before talking about possible positions. In mediation, framing neutral goal statements that encompass the parties' interests must come *after* a thorough exploration of what is important to the parents who are disputing custody and *before* win-win options are generated and reviewed in the mediation. For example, how can we decide on parenting responsibilities that ensure the children maintain strong relationships with both parents, that avoid or minimize disruptions to the children's schooling and social activities, and that are flexible enough to accommodate the parents' busy work schedules? Similarly, setting ground rules to encourage the parties to participate in problem-solving behaviour logically must come at the front end of a process that promotes this type of bargaining strategy over a more adversarial approach.

Emphasizing a staged approach to mediation also appears to be an echo of the economics behind the demands to articulate the core knowledge and skills required for all mediators. Clearly defined and mainly mandatory mediation stages are an integral part of the professionalization mandate for mediation. Thinking of mediation as a step-by-step process that can be studied and learned is much like the approach taken to structuring the professional tasks of doctors, lawyers, dentists, accountants, airline pilots and others. The professional look of mediation is enhanced when the stages of mediation map neatly onto the descriptions of the fundamental and core skills that professional mediators require. A more general, variable, and unpredictable mediation road map that allowed for, or even encouraged, twists and turns of every kind would mean that mediator skills could be too general and variable, dependent on context, and uncertain. This uncertainty and imprecision in process and skills would leave mediation with the same status as negotiation — or parenting, partnering, communicating — an often-used and highly complex process but not a profession; practised successfully in many different ways by many different people; capable of inquiry and analysis but not naturally amenable to generalizations out of context. The stages of mediation allow for a process that can be studied and applied more conveniently.

E.   CHOOSING THE MEDIATION PROCESS

Choosing the mediation process is an important decision. Because the exact course that any dispute takes is not usually fixed or certain, choosing to mediate, rather than going to court, negotiating, avoiding the dispute, or taking matters into your own hands will obviously result in changes to the way in which the dispute is processed and probably to the eventual outcome.

The consequences of choosing mediation over another disputing process may be dramatic. A mediated agreement in a custody case may be fundamentally different and longer lasting than any decision a judge might have made in court if litigation had been chosen. As a result, the children may experience completely different lives. The mediation of a will dispute might result in new understandings and relationships emerging among family members that would not have developed if only lawyer-to-lawyer negotiations had been resorted to or if the testamentary controversy had been ignored. Choosing mediation might mean much less money is expended, time is saved, privacy is maintained and agreements are honoured. If the critics of mediation are consulted, mediation might also mean a single disputant does not despair but an important precedent is never set.

For the lawyer or her client, for any specific disputant, or for an institution or a government considering making mediation part of a permanent problem-solving structure, choosing the mediation process probably will depend on how a number of factors are understood and assessed.

1) When to Choose Mediation

Much like choosing to negotiate, choosing to mediate can involve weighing the advantages and disadvantages of mediation, compared with other methods of dispute processing, vis-à-vis goals. Is mediation more likely to result in a disputant or an organization achieving their disputing goals? Determining whether mediation will help to achieve these goals or not is a complicated decision for at least two reasons.

First, the substantive, procedural, or personal goals that individual disputants or institutions are pursuing will vary from one disputing context to the next. A manufacturer of an allegedly defective product might want to prolong proceedings to deter present and future claimants and to limit their ultimate exposure to financial liability. However, the officers of another company, faced with a similar situation, might see benefits in settling quickly to reduce publicity and to preserve their business reputation. A plaintiff in a personal injury case may want to settle for as much as possible for the pain and suffering whereas a similar claimant may be willing to settle for a more modest amount so he can get on with his life. Governments and businesses may want speedy, credible, and cost-effective dispute resolution, and an efficient order, while other public and private institutions may have dispute resolution goals to produce a more peaceful world and an end to violence. What the parties to a dispute are pursuing and why they are pursuing these goals will be enormously varied. Specific disputing goals need to be understood in context before it is possible to say that mediation will, or will not, be helpful in achieving them. A disputant who wants to drag out the litigation, win as much as he can, avoid responsibility, practise deceit, punish his partner or otherwise be oppressive probably will find mediation is less useful for these goals than a disputant with opposite aims. On the other hand, mediation, depending on its form, might well serve a disputant's desire to oppress.

Second, whether the mediation process helps to achieve these varied goals also depends on the shape and structure that the mediation process is given. All mediations and mediators are not created equal. The strengths and weaknesses of mediation referred to in this chapter and more fully described in chapter 2 are neither uniformly present nor consistently assessed from one mediation scenario to the next. What may be an obvious mediation advantage in one setting may be non-existent or only marginally important to a disputant in another.

For example, a divorcing couple who are angry with each other may still want to maintain a positive working relationship for the benefit of their children. The couple may find that choosing mediation to resolve their disputes over property, support payments, and custody can help preserve their relationship. But this conclusion presumes that the mediator they use and the actual mediation process are responsive to this need. A judge who is trained in, or supportive of, a mostly evaluative or bureaucratic approach to mediation, acting as mediator in a mandatory settlement conference, may be helpful at pushing the parties to a legally fair agreement but be uncomfortable with, or not capable of handling, the relationship issue. On the other hand, a contractor being sued for defective work by a customer may find that the speedy mediation conducted by a judge in a settlement conference suits his desire for a quick and inexpensive resolution. A mediation with a transformative or healing focus between the same contractor and customer held over several hours or days in a community justice centre may be ill-suited to the contractor's needs. A mediator insisting that an interest-based bargaining approach be followed in a mediation may help the parties in a wrongful dismissal dispute who want to resolve both an economic interest (how much severance should be paid) as well as a reputation concern (how to minimize barriers for the dismissed employee to re-enter the workplace). However, this type of mediation process may be unfamiliar to, unsatisfying, and even counter-productive for parties who see the dispute as a purely distributional one, who want to negotiate adversarially, or whose culture makes the concept of interest-based bargaining an artificial construct for them.

Because the mediation process and the disputants' goals will vary considerably, it can be problematic to mechanically match the mediation process to a particular type of dispute or conclude mediation is a helpful process in almost all cases. Choosing to mediate depends more on a careful consideration of whether mediation *in the specific context* will help a disputant achieve desired goals in the resolution of the dispute.

a) Mediation Agreements: Examples

In addition to evaluating the advantages and disadvantages of mediation in context, disputants who choose the mediation process are often required to enter into a written agreement to mediate. The primary purpose of such an agreement is to ensure that the participants understand, at least in a general way, what is involved in the mediation process they have chosen.

This type of agreement is not unusual. Lawyers typically must get clear client instructions before they file a lawsuit, negotiate resolutions with the other side, or take significant steps to resolve a client's problem. In obtaining these instructions, the lawyer will want to be assured that the client is fully informed about the consequences of the actions being taken. For parties considering mediation, the terms of an agreement to mediate also need to be carefully considered and factored into the decision-making process. The agreement can deal with issues around fees, disclosure and confidentiality of information, independent legal advice, and other matters that are clearly relevant when considering the utility of mediation. These agreements to mediate also can indicate whether the approach being taken by the mediator is likely to help a disputant achieve the goals that are important to them in the dispute resolution process.

Consider the following two examples of terms from agreements to mediate and how these terms might affect the decision to use mediation:

Example 1[30]

Terms of Mediation

1. Mediation is a voluntary and informal settlement process by which the parties try to reach a solution that is responsive to their joint needs. Their participation in the process is not intended to alter their existing rights and responsibilities unless they expressly agree to do so.

2. The mediator is a facilitator only, is not providing legal advice, legal representation or any other form of professional advice or representation and is not representing the party. The mediator's role is to assist the parties to negotiate a voluntary settlement of the issues if this is possible.

3. The parties will send to the mediation representatives with full, unqualified authority to settle and understand that the mediation may result in a settlement agreement that contains binding legal obligations enforceable in a court of law.

4. The parties will discuss the matter with the mediator individually or together, in person or by telephone, with a view to achieving settlement.

5. If the matter cannot be settled voluntarily and if the parties agree, a memorandum listing areas of agreement or disagreement may be prepared by the mediator to facilitate future attempts at settlement.

---

30   Above note 18 at 126–27.

6. Throughout the mediation the parties agree to disclose material facts, information and documents to each other and to the mediator, and will conduct themselves in good faith.

7. Statements made by any person, documents produced and any other forms of communication in the mediation are off-the-record and shall not be subject to disclosure through discovery or any other process or admissible into evidence in any context for any purpose, including impeaching credibility.

8. The parties will deliver to the mediator and exchange with each other a concise statement of the issues and the problem as they see it not less than five (5) days before the start of the first meeting.

9. No party will initiate or take any fresh steps in any legal, administrative, or arbitration proceedings related to the issues while the mediation is in progress.

10. Either during or after the mediation, no party will call the mediator as a witness for any purpose whatsoever. No party will seek access to any documents prepared for or delivered to the mediator in connection with the mediation, including any records or notes of the mediator.

11. Other than what is stated above, the mediation is a confidential process and the parties agree to keep all communications and information forming part of this mediation in confidence. The only exception to this is disclosure for the purpose of enforcing any settlement agreement reached. The mediator will not voluntarily disclose to anyone who is not a party to the mediation anything said or done or any materials submitted to the mediator, except:

    a. to any person designated or retained by any party such as a professional advisor, as deemed appropriate or necessary by the mediator;
    b. for research or educational purposes, on an anonymous basis;
    c. where ordered to do so by a judicial authority or where required to do so by law;
    d. where the information suggests an actual or potential threat to human life or safety.

12. The parties are responsible for obtaining their own independent professional advice, including legal advice or representation, if desired; the mediator is not providing same. The mediator has no duty to assert or protect the rights of any party, to raise any issue not raised by the parties themselves or to determine who should participate in the mediation. The mediator has no duty to ensure

the enforceability or validity of any agreement reached. The mediator will not be liable in any way, save for his or her wilful default.

Example 2[31]
The parties wish to resolve specific issues between them by way of mediation and will employ the mediator named below to assist them. THEREFORE both parties understand and agree as follows:

1. The parties appoint and retain [ ] to act as mediator of the issues between them.

2. The parties understand that mediation is a process whereby the parties attempt, with the assistance of an impartial third party, to reach a consensual settlement of specific issues between them.

3. The parties acknowledge and agree that full disclosure of all relevant information is essential to the mediation process. Accordingly, there will be a complete and honest disclosure by each of the parties to the other and to the mediator of all relevant information and documents. It is agreed that the mediator may disclose fully to each party all information provided to him by the other party, or any other information of which he becomes aware, which is relevant to the issues being mediated.

4. It is understood and agreed that while the mediator is a lawyer, he is not acting as legal counsel for either party throughout the mediation process. It is understood that the mediator must remain neutral in all contacts with the parties and that he will not advance the interests of one party over the other.

5. The parties agree that insofar as the mediation process is part of an attempt to settle differences between the parties, all communications between the parties or with the mediator are made on a without prejudice basis and are privileged. Any information, communication, documentation, or correspondence of any party arising out of the mediation sessions shall be treated by all parties as confidential. Accordingly, the mediator shall not be asked or required by either party to provide information or give evidence in any legal proceedings with respect to any such information, communication, documentation or correspondence.

---

31   An agreement made to conform with the Law Society of British Columbia's ruling on Family Law Mediation. See *Professional Conduct Handbook*, Appendix 2.

6. The parties are aware that the confidentiality and privilege referred to above could potentially be breached in the following circumstances:

   a. the mediator is obliged by law to report to the Superintendent of Family and Child Services any information arising out of the mediation process which gives him reasonable grounds to believe that a child may be in need of protection;
   b. a court of law has the discretionary power to require one of the parties or the mediator to give evidence.

7. The mediation process shall continue until terminated by any of the parties or the mediator or until the parties reach an agreement on the issues and this agreement is reduced to writing and signed.

8. It is agreed that the mediator will be paid [ ] plus disbursements for all work done including meetings, telephone calls, correspondence, drafting and reviewing of documents and other necessary services.

9. The parties agree that each will be responsible for a portion of the said fees of the mediator. The fees will be payable by each party within 30 (thirty) days of the rendering of any interim or final accounts.

10. It is also understood that each of the parties will likely incur further expense with respect to independent legal advice. Each party will be responsible for her or his own costs incurred with respect to independent legal advice.

11. The parties confirm that the mediator has given them no legal advice with respect to this Agreement to Mediate. Each is encouraged, if he or she has any questions or concerns, to review this agreement with independent legal counsel.

12. The parties understand that they may have adverse interests. They are strongly encouraged to retain individual lawyers, of their choice, to secure independent legal advice regarding their individual interests, rights and obligations arising out of the issues between them. In the event that an agreement is reached, each party agrees to retain separate legal counsel for independent legal advice and to execute the agreement before such independent legal counsel.

2) When Not to Choose Mediation

In considering the mediation process, are there occasions when mediation is never going to be appropriate?

Although the previous discussion suggests that choosing mediation depends on context, some say that mediation should never be used in disputes where there is a history of violence or abuse between the disputants.[32] Disputes involving spousal abuse, sexual abuse, sexual assault, incest, sexual harassment and other forms of harassment would fit this description.

There are several related reasons for this direction to avoid mediation.

- Mediation is an informal and private ordering process and not subject to external scrutiny. The due process protections that are available in public disputing systems, like the courts, are absent in most mediations.
- The fact that mediation takes place behind closed doors may be attractive to some disputants but victims of abuse may be further victimized by the continued privatization of the violence perpetrated against them.
- Mediation tends to focus on the psychological "interests" of the disputants and pays less attention to legal rights and facts. This inattention to the rights of victims of violence or abuse and to the details of these actions is particularly problematic.

---

32 For an entry into the critiques of mediation in cases of violence or abuse, see S.A. Goundry, et al., *Family Mediation in Canada: Implications for Women's Equality* (Ottawa: Status of Women Canada, 1998); J. Pearson, "Mediating When Domestic Violence is a Factor: Policies and Practices in Court-based Divorce Mediation Programs" (1997) 14 Mediation Q. 319; B. Landau, "Qualifications of Family Mediators: Listening to the Feminist Critique" in C. Morris & A. Pirie, eds., *Qualifications for Dispute Resolution: Perspectives on the Debate* (Victoria, BC: UVic Institute for Dispute Resolution, 1994); L. Perry, "Mediation and Wife Abuse: A Review of the Literature" (1994) 11 Mediation Q. 4; K. Fischer, N. Vidmar, & R. Ellis, "The Culture of Battering and the Role of Mediation in Domestic Violence Cases" (1993) 46 SMU L. Rev. 2117; J. Kelly & M. Duryea, "Women's and Men's Views of Mediation in Voluntary and Mandatory Mediation Settings" (1992) 30 Fam. & Concil. Crts. Rev. 34; P.E. Bryan, "Killing Us Softly: Divorce Mediation and the Politics of Power" (1992) 40 Buff. L. Rev. 441; A. Gagnon, "Ending Mandatory Divorce Mediation for Battered Women" (1992) 15 Harv. Women's L.J. 272; B. Whittington, *Mediation, Power and Gender: A Critical Review of Selected Readings* (Victoria, BC: UVic Institute for Dispute Resolution, 1992); T. Grillo, "The Mediation Alternative: Process Dangers for Women" (1991) 100 Yale L. Rev. 1545; N.Z. Hilton, "Mediating Wife Assault: Battered Women and the 'New' Family" (1991) 9 Can. J. Fam. L. 29; L. Girdner, "Mediation Triage: Screening for Spouse Abuse in Divorce Mediation" (1990) 6 Mediation Q. 365; M.J. Bailey, "Unpacking the 'Rational Alternative': A Critical Review of Family Mediation Movement Claims" (1989) 8 Can. J. Fam. L. 61; M. Shaffer, "Divorce Mediation: A Feminist Perspective" (1988) U.T. Fac. L. Rev. 162; L. Lerman, "Mediation of Wife Abuse Cases: The Adverse Impact of Informal Dispute Resolution on Women" (1984) 7 Harv. Women's L.J. 57; J. Rifkin, "Mediation from a Feminist Perspective: Promise and Problems" (1984) 2 Law & Inequity 21.

- There is no mechanism in mediation to hold an abuser truly accountable for his actions. This can send a message to the participants and to society that violence is condoned and that the victim may be partly responsible for its occurrence.
- Mediation to be fair and effective requires a level playing field on which the parties can negotiate. The presence of violence or abuse, real or threatened, makes it impossible to bargain equally, and any agreement reached will necessarily reflect the power imbalance between the parties, whether the agreement can be legally challenged or not.
- Women who have experienced abuse are more likely than other women to have established a pattern of deferring to their abusers in disagreements.
- Victims may be too intimidated to give an informed and voluntary consent to mediation.
- Most women in a patriarchal society are not equal to their male partners in bargaining power and experience, or financial resources.
- The existence of violence or abuse is an indicator of a larger systemic or structural problem in society that the private, individualized mediation process cannot address or ignores.
- Face-to-face meetings in mediation exacerbate the abuses of power that are at the base of disputes that involve violence or abuse.
- No amount of skill or training can make up for the control that an abuser exerts over his victim.
- Mediation of cases involving violence or abuse send a signal to other survivors and society at large that these types of cases are not taken seriously.

The above reasons suggest that any advantages of mediation can never outweigh the disadvantages to the victim and society at large when there is a history of violence or abuse between disputants. However, some mediation proponents suggest there should be a rebuttable presumption that mediation is inappropriate in cases of abuse.[33] The problem is not with mediation *per se* but with potential deficiencies in how mediation handles cases involving violence or abuse. Through careful screening, changing the structure of the mediation process, using shuttle diplomacy, employing a range of empowering communication skills, ensuring a party's safety during the mediation process, terminating the mediation appropriately including referrals to other

---

33 See Landau, *ibid.* at 44.

resources, more extensive mediator training, and other measures, victims of violence or abuse may be able to participate in mediation.

3) Mandatory Mediation

Contrasted with the idea that mediation must never be used in certain situations is the issue of whether mediation should always be utilized. In an increasing number of disputes, mediation is being made mandatory. Either through legislation, regulation, or a judge's direction, parties with certain disputes are being required to participate in mediation before they are able to proceed further in the formal justice system or other dispute resolution procedure. In mandatory mediation, the choice of mediation has already been made for the disputants. A government or organization overseeing a particular area of activity will have made a policy decision that certain benefits of mediation (e.g., speedy, inexpensive, relationship maintaining, transformative, educational, peaceful) outweigh any costs (slower, more expensive, oppressive). The move to mandatory mediation might also be made to institutionalize a particular ideological form of dispute resolution as discussed in chapter 1. Whatever the motivation, mandatory mediation takes away the individual choice that in most cases accompanies the use of mediation.

Mandatory mediation raises many vexing questions, some of which relate to procedure. When should mandatory mediation be scheduled? Where should it be held? How long should it last? Who should attend? Who should be the mediator? Who pays the costs? Is it necessary to screen cases for mandatory mediation? What does good faith participation in mandatory mediation require? Some questions are more substantive. What types of cases or issues are appropriate for mandatory mediation? Can involuntary mediation ever be successful? Why should mediation be made mandatory? The answers to these and other questions along with descriptions of several mandatory mediation schemes are discussed in chapters 6 and 8 below.

F. MEDIATION ETHICS

The concept of ethics can bring to mind the existence of certain duties or standards that morally right people ought to adhere to and exhibit. Ethics can create distinctions between what is right and what is wrong; about what is good and what is bad. These moral obligations can be formally set out in laws or statutes that apply to everyone (the prohibition against murder in Criminal Codes) or, quite commonly, ethics can be part of a community or family's customs or values (always tell the truth, avoid violence). Of course, there can be disputes between people and within communities and countries about what is morally correct behaviour on issues such as abortion, euthanasia, reproductive technology, world trade, civility, and other matters. There also can be controversy about which variables influence, or should be made to influence, how we understand or approach moral questions and moral development.

The legal profession has long been accustomed to ethics. Canons of Ethics or Codes of Professional Conduct that prescribe duties and describe standards of professional behaviour have been promulgated for lawyers. For members of the legal profession, these canons and codes invariably place their emphasis on lawyers establishing and maintaining a reputation for both integrity and high standards of legal care and skill. As a hallmark of a profession, the primary purpose of ethical enactments is the protection of the public interest. Links between professional ethics and more public ethical imperatives are common. For example, the usual requirements that a lawyer's conduct towards other lawyers be characterized by courtesy and good faith, and that quarrels between lawyers which cause delay and promote unseemly wrangling should be avoided, reflect standards of civility expected in many quarters outside the legal profession. Violations of professional standards can lead to disciplinary action including removal from the profession.

Mediation ethics have emerged with the modern evolution of mediation. A number of mediation-focused organizations around the world have promulgated ethical codes. No one code dominates and, as might be expected, there are differences between and among these statements of what it is that mediators are bound to do or not do. A sampling of extracts from a number of the ethical standards or codes of professional conduct for mediators follows.[34] This sampling provides an opportunity

---

34   The extracts are from American Arbitration Association, American Bar Association, Society of Professionals in Dispute Resolution, *Model Standards of Conduct for Mediators*, 1995; Association of Family and Conciliation Courts Symposium on Standards of Practice, *Model Standards of Practice for Divorce and Family Mediators*, August 1999; Arbitration and Mediation Institute of Canada Inc., *Code of Ethics*; Centre for Dispute Settlement and The Institute of Judicial Administration, *National Standards for Court-Connected Mediation Programs*, 1992; Family Mediation Canada, *Code of Professional Conduct*, 1996; Mediation Development Association of British Columbia, *Code of Professional Conduct for Practising Mediators*; Mediation UK, *Practice Standards*, July 1993; Victoria Dispute Resolution Centre, *Code of Conduct for Mediators*; Canadian International Institute of Applied Negotiation, *Code of Conduct for Registered Practitioners in Dispute Resolution*, 1997; Law Society of British Columbia, Appendix 2, Family Law Mediation, *Professional Conduct Handbook*.

to get a grasp of what are being billed as mediation ethics, see the potential influence of ethical provisions on the meaning of mediation and its goals and consider how these standards might affect the practice and development of mediation skills. The extracts are listed under headings similar to those usually found in mediation codes. Following these extracts is a commentary on the issues and concerns raised by mediation ethics and how such issues and concerns are to be resolved.

1) General Definition

Family Mediation Canada:
For the purpose of this Code, "family mediation" is defined as a cooperative, problem-solving process in which a qualified and impartial third party neutral, the mediator, assists mediation participants to resolve their disputes by mutual agreement. The resolution is to be voluntary and based upon sufficient information and advice for each person involved in the dispute.

Model Standards of Practice for Divorce and Family Mediators:
Divorce and family mediation ("family mediation" or "mediation") is a process in which an impartial third party — a mediator — facilitates the resolution of a dispute between family members by promoting their voluntary agreement (or "self-determination"). The family mediator facilitates communications, promotes understanding, focuses the family members on their interests and seeks creative solutions to problems that enable the family members to reach their own agreements.

Mediation Development Association of British Columbia:
"*Mediation*" is defined as a cooperative, consensual process in which a qualified, impartial third party, the mediator, with no power to impose a resolution, works with the disputing participants, to assist them in determining whether and how to reach a voluntary, mutually acceptable resolution of some or all of the issues in the dispute. Mediation involves an interplay between process, relationship and content management skills. These skills are continuously and often simultaneously in use during a mediation.

2) Confidentiality

Canadian International Institute of Applied Negotiation; also in SPIDR Ethical Standards of Professional Responsibility, 1986:
Maintaining confidentiality is critical to the dispute resolution process. Confidentiality encourages candour, a full exploration of the

issues, and a practitioner's acceptability. There may be some types of cases, however, in which confidentiality is not protected. In such cases, the dispute resolution practitioner must advise the parties, when appropriate in the dispute resolution process, that the confidentiality of the proceedings cannot necessarily be maintained. Except in such instances, the practitioner must resist all attempts to cause him or her to reveal any information outside the process. A commitment by the practitioner to hold information in confidence within the process also must be honoured.

Model Standards of Practice for Divorce and Family Mediators:
A family mediator should maintain the confidentiality of all information acquired in the mediation process, unless the mediator is permitted or required to reveal the information by law or agreement of the parties.

D. The mediator shall disclose a party's threat of violence against another party likely to result in imminent death or substantial bodily harm to the threatened party and the appropriate authorities.

E. If the mediator holds private sessions with a party, the obligations of confidentiality with regard to those sessions should be discussed and agreed upon prior to their being undertaken.

Model Standards of Conduct for Mediators:
Confidentiality: A Mediator Shall Maintain the Reasonable Expectations of the Parties with Regard to Confidentiality.

The reasonable expectations of the parties with regard to confidentiality shall be met by the mediator. The parties' expectations of confidentiality depend on the circumstances of the mediation and any agreements they make. The mediator shall not disclose any matter that a party expects to be confidential unless given permission by all parties or unless required by law or other public policy.

Mediation Development Association of British Columbia:
The mediator shall not voluntarily disclose, directly or indirectly, to anyone who is not a party, or represents a party, to the mediation, any information or documents from the mediation except:

(a) with the written consent of the parties to the mediation contract;
(b) when ordered to do so by an authority with jurisdiction to compel such disclosure, or required to do so by legislation or other law;
(c) non-identifying information for research or educational purposes;
(d) when the information discloses an actual or potential threat to human life or safety.

3) Impartiality

Model Standards of Practice for Divorce and Family Mediators:
A family mediator should conduct the mediation in an impartial manner.

A. A mediator should avoid conduct that gives the appearance of partiality towards one of the parties.

B. A mediator should guard against partiality or prejudice based on the parties' personal characteristics, background or performance at the mediation.

C. A mediator should exercise best efforts to insure that the mediation proceeds as expeditiously as possible and to not allow a mediation to be unreasonably delayed by the parties or their representatives.

Mediation Development Association of British Columbia:
1. The mediator has a duty to conduct, in word and action, the mediation process in an impartial manner.
2. The mediator must disclose to the participants biases s/he has relating to the participants, issues and circumstances of the dispute.
3. The mediator shall disclose to all participants any significant prior personal or professional involvement between the mediator and any of the participants and shall provide mediation services only if all participants consent to the mediation.
4. The mediator shall decline to serve or withdraw from serving as a mediator in a dispute if:
   (a) either participant perceives the mediator may be partial toward one of the participants or the issues in dispute; or
   (b) in his/her own judgment believes there may be a reason which may compromise the impartiality of the mediator.
5. The mediator shall exercise due regard for the appearance of impartiality in establishing new relations with the participants following the conclusion of the mediation.

Model Standards of Conduct for Mediators:
A Mediator Shall Conduct the Mediation in an Impartial Manner.

The concept of mediator impartiality is central to the mediation process. A mediator shall mediate only those matters in which she or he can remain impartial and evenhanded. If at any time the mediator is unable to conduct the process in an impartial manner, the mediator is obligated to withdraw.

Family Mediation Canada:

1. A mediator has a duty to act with impartiality in relation to the participants. Impartiality means freedom from favoritism or bias either in word or in action; or the appearance of such favoritism or bias.
2. Notwithstanding the above, a mediator has a duty to assist participants to reflect upon and to consider how their proposed arrangements realistically meet the needs and best interests of other affected persons, especially vulnerable persons.
3. The perception by one or both of the participants that the mediator is partial does not in itself require the mediator to withdraw, but in such circumstances, the mediator must remind both parties of their right to terminate the mediation.
4. A mediator must disclose to the participants any biases he or she has relating to the issues to be mediated and any circumstances which might constitute or cause a conflict of interest, real or perceived, to arise. Such disclosure must be made as soon as the mediator recognizes the potential for any bias becoming operative or any conflict of interest arising.
5. A mediator must disclose any prior or current professional or personal involvement between the mediator, or any associate of the mediator, with one or more of the participants. The mediator must refrain from mediating unless every participant expressly consents to the mediation after there has been full disclosure. In this case, the role of the mediator should be carefully distinguished from the prior relationship.
6. Mediators must not provide any professional services to only one participant during mediation.

4) Qualifications

Model Standards of Practice for Divorce and Family Mediators:
A family mediator should be qualified by education and training to undertake the mediation.

A. To effectively perform the family mediator's role, a mediator should:

1. be knowledgeable about family law;
2. be aware of the psychological impact of family conflict on parents, children and other family members, including education and training in domestic violence and child abuse and neglect;
3. have special education and training in the process of mediation.

Family Mediation Canada:

1. Family mediators must perform their services in a conscientious, diligent and efficient manner in accordance with this Code.
2. It is the obligation of a member acting as a family mediator to ensure that he or she is qualified to deal with the specific issues involved. Mediators shall have acquired substantive knowledge and procedural skills as defined by the Standards and Certification Committee and adopted by the Board of Directors of Family Mediation Canada.
3. While family mediators may have a diversity of education and training, a family mediator must refrain from rendering services outside the limits of his or her qualifications and competence.
4. Family mediators must engage in continuing education to ensure that their mediation skills are current and effective.

Model Standards of Conduct for Mediators:
A Mediator Shall Mediate Only When the Mediator Has the Necessary Qualifications to Satisfy the Reasonable Expectations of the Parties.

Any person may be selected as a mediator provided that the parties are satisfied with the mediator's qualifications. Training and experience in mediation, however, are often necessary for effective mediation. A person who offers herself or himself as available to serve as a mediator gives parties and the public the expectation that she or he has the competency to mediate effectively. In court-connected or other forms of mandated mediation, it is essential that mediators assigned to the parties have the requisite training and experience.

Mediation Development Association of British Columbia:

1. It is the obligation of every MDABC practising mediator to provide mediation services consistent with this Code.
2. Every MDABC practising mediator shall:
   (a) maintain professional competency in mediation skills;
   (b) ensure that s/he is qualified to deal with the specific issues in a dispute and that s/he has the appropriate skills to work with the particular participants;
   (c) decline to provide service outside the limits of his/her qualification and competence; and
   (d) upgrade his/her skills on an ongoing basis.

Arbitration and Mediation Institute of Canada Inc.:
A Member shall ensure that the parties involved in an arbitration or mediation are fairly informed and have an adequate understanding of the procedural aspects of the process and of their obligations to pay for services rendered."

5) Conflict of Interest

Model Standards of Practice for Divorce and Family Mediators:
A family mediator should disclose all actual and potential conflicts of interest reasonably known to the mediator. The parties can choose to retain the mediator by an informed, written waiver of the conflict of interest, unless it is so significant that informed waiver offends public policy. The need to protect against conflicts of interest also governs the conduct that occurs during and after the mediation.

Mediation Development Association of British Columbia:
1. The mediator shall, as far as possible, disclose all actual and potential dealings or relationships with the participants that are known to the mediator and which could reasonably be seen as a conflict of interest which might impair the professional judgment of the mediator or in any way risk exploiting the participants.
2. The mediator shall not establish a professional relationship (such as counsellor or lawyer) with any of the parties in a related matter or in an unrelated matter under circumstances which may compromise the integrity of the mediation process, unless all the participants consent.

Family Mediation Canada:
1. Mediators must avoid any activity that could create a conflict of interest. They must not become involved in relationships with the clients which might impair their professional judgment or in any way increase the risk of exploiting clients. Except where culturally appropriate, mediators must be cautious about mediating disputes involving close friends, relatives, colleagues, supervisors or students.

Model Standards of Conduct for Mediators:
A Mediator shall disclose all actual and potential conflicts of interest reasonably known to the mediator. After disclosure, the mediator shall decline to mediate unless all parties choose to retain the mediator. The need to protect against conflicts of interest also governs conduct that occurs during and after the mediation.

A conflict of interest is a dealing or relationship that might create an impression of possible bias. The basic approach to questions of conflict of interest is consistent with the concept of self-determination. The mediator has a responsibility to disclose all actual and potential conflicts that are reasonably known to the mediator and could reasonably be seen as raising a question about impartiality. If all parties agree to mediate after being informed of conflicts, the mediator may proceed with the mediation. If, however, the conflict of interest casts serious doubt on the integrity of the process, the mediator shall decline to proceed.

A mediator must avoid the appearance of conflict of interest both during and after the mediation. Without the consent of all parties, a mediator shall not subsequently establish a professional relationship with one of the parties in a related matter, or in an unrelated matter under circumstances which would raise legitimate questions about the integrity of the mediation process.

6) Other Issues

Family Mediation Canada:
In keeping with the expanded objects of Family Mediation Canada, "family mediation" focuses upon a broad range of areas in which families experience conflict including intra or inter family conflicts as well as conflict between families and other agencies or organizations. For example, divorce and separation, post divorce, parents/child, inter-generational, elder care, pre-nuptial, child welfare, adoption, wills, family business, schools and neighbourhood conflicts and other interpersonal disputes.

Mediation Development Association of British Columbia:
1. It is the duty of the mediator to suspend or terminate mediation whenever continuation of the process is likely to harm or prejudice one or more of the participants.
2. The mediator must suspend or terminate mediation when it appears that further discussion between the parties is unlikely to be productive.

Model Standards of Conduct for Mediators:
Mediators are regarded as knowledgeable in the process of mediation. They have an obligation to use their knowledge to help educate the public about mediation, to make mediation accessible to those who would like to use it, to correct abuses and to improve their professional skills and abilities.

The primary purpose of a mediator is to facilitate the parties' voluntary agreement. This role differs substantially from other professional-client relationships. Mixing the role of a mediator and the role of a professional advising a client is problematic, and mediators must strive to distinguish between the roles. A mediator should, therefore, refrain from providing professional advice.

Law Society of British Columbia:
Without limiting the generality of the foregoing, "family law mediation" includes one or more of the following acts when performed by a lawyer acting as a family mediator:

(i)   informing the participants of the legal issues involved,
(ii)   advising the participants of a court's probable disposition of the issue,

(iii) preparing any agreement between the participants other than a memorandum recording the results of the mediation,

(iv) giving any other legal advice.

Model Standards of Conduct for Mediators:
A mediator shall work to ensure a quality process and to encourage mutual respect among the parties.

Model Standards of Practice for Divorce and Family Mediators:
The mediator should be sensitive to the impact of culture and religion on parenting philosophy and other decisions.

A family mediator should recognize a family situation involving domestic violence and take appropriate steps to shape the mediation process accordingly.

Mediation Development Association of British Columbia:
It is a violation of this Code to engage in sexual intimacies with mediation participants.

Victoria Dispute Resolution Centre:
It is a violation of this Code to engage in sexual intimacies with mediation participants within a 2 year period of the last mediation session.

Mediation UK:
The mediator(s) will try to ensure that the mediation is a comfortable and constructive experience.

National Standards for Court-Connected Mediation Programs:
Mediation services should be available on the same basis as are other services of the court.

7) The Resolution of Mediation Ethics

The need to articulate ethical guidelines for mediators has been identified with increasing frequency. Professor Bush, one of the leading advocates for a code of ethical behaviour, has said, "if identifying and solving [ethical] problems . . . is left to the ingenuity and conscience of the individual mediator, without coherent and programmatic guidance, there is serious cause for concern."[35] Likewise, Bishop warns that "for divorce mediation to endure . . . those of us who are its adherents have a responsibility to create and employ standards that function as internal

---

35   R.A.B. Bush, "The Dilemmas of Mediation Practice: A Study of Ethical Dilemmas and Policy Implications" (1994) J. Disp. Resol. 1 at 43–44.

safety mechanisms,"[36] and Salem states that "guidance for mediators facing ethical dilemmas is long past due."[37] However, there have been conflicting and questioning voices. Stamato argues that "promulgating rules for dealing with ethical dilemmas and rooting them formally in policy and procedure is not the right course. Not only would it be difficult to promulgate such rules, it would be undesirable."[38]

To consider the fundamental question of the desirability of codes of ethics for mediators and issues raised by mediation ethics it is necessary to examine three questions: What is the meaning of ethics in the mediation context? What are the difficulties in trying to create a code of ethics to guide mediators? Is there a best ethical response?

a)   The Meaning of Ethics in the Mediation Context

A central issue whenever ethics is being debated is identifying a coherent and useful understanding of what the term "ethics" means. In the mediation context, one approach is to identify those dilemmas faced by mediators which constitute ethical dilemmas.

The most comprehensive examination of what constitutes an "ethical dilemma" in the mediation context is provided by Bush, who broadly identifies an ethical dilemma as "a situation in which you felt some serious concern about whether it was proper for you as a mediator to take a certain course of action, i.e., where you were unsure what was the right and proper thing for you as a mediator to do."[39] In other words, whenever the action to preserve one value involves the undermining of another, a mediator is in an ethical dilemma that, if it is to be resolved, requires ethical action.

Bush concludes that mediators face ethical dilemmas in nine different situations. For example, a typical ethical dilemma that mediators face is the situation where they may be required to act outside the area of their competence. What should mediators do when a situation requires a skill outside of their competence? Bush provides an instructive example:

> In a landlord/tenant mediation, Tenant, who has appeared "normal" in the session, tells the mediator in caucus that the reason he is late with payments sometimes is that "the voices from the transmitter in

---

36   T.A. Bishop, "Mediation Standards: An Ethical Safety Net" (1984) 4 Mediation Q. 5 at 6.

37   A. Salem, "Ethical Dilemmas or Benign Neglect" (1994) J. Disp. Resol. 71.

38   L. Stamato, "Easier Said Than Done: Resolving Ethical Dilemmas in Policy and Practice" (1994) J. Disp. Resol. 81.

39   Above note 35 at 7.

my neck get me confused sometimes." Assuming it is clear that Tenant is not referring to a real medical implant, does such a remark indicate a lack of mental capacity. Should the mediator, lacking any special training in diagnosis of mental incapacity, play it safe and assume incapacity whenever any suggestion of it arises? If so, he avoids the risk of noncomprehension in some cases, but runs the risk of disempowering parties in others.[40]

Another common ethical dilemma faced by mediators involves ensuring that they preserve their impartiality during the course of the mediation. How does a mediator remain impartial? Bush gives the following examples of situations where the appearance of mediator impartiality could be threatened.

> In a community mediation over damage to property, one of the parties is white and one Hispanic, and the mediator is Hispanic. Should the mediator do anything to directly address the possible appearance of partiality, even if neither party raises any questions? If the mediator asks the white party if he objects, that party may be offended at the question, or embarrassed to respond honestly. But if the mediator says nothing, the white party may in fact suspect partiality.
>
> One of the parties is the manager of the mediator's condominium complex. (The dispute has nothing to do with the complex.) This fact is disclosed and the other party has no objection and is willing to proceed. But the mediator is concerned whether, if he has to engage in persuasion with that party later in the mediation, the party will wind up being suspicious because of the relationship, despite his present unconcern. The question is: should the mediator ever refuse to serve because of a prior relationship, even though the parities know and want him anyway? If he does, he protects the parties from possible future regrets, but he deprives them of their choice of mediator, an important element of control over the process.[41]

The above examples illustrate the types of situations that Bush identifies as posing ethical dilemmas for mediators. The following chart[42] summarizes all of these situations.

---

40   *Ibid.* at 11.
41   *Ibid.* at 12–13.
42   Adapted from *ibid.* at 9–10.

Figure 4.1   Types of Dilemmas

Mediators encounter situations presenting dilemmas about the following:

A. *Keeping Within the Limits of Competency*

    1. When diagnostic competency is lacking
        (a) to diagnose a history of violence
        (b) to diagnose mental incapacity
    2. When substantive or skill competencies are lacking

B. *Preserving Impartiality*

    1. In view of relationships with parties or lawyers
        (a) after disclosure and waiver of objections
        (b) when relationships arise *after* mediation
        (c) when class or group "relationships" exist
    2. In view of a personal reaction to a party in mediation
        (a) antipathy to a party
        (b) sympathy for a party

C. *Maintaining Confidentiality*

    1. Vis-à-vis outsiders
        (a) reporting allegations of violence or crime
        (b) communicating to a court or referring agency
        (c) communicating to a party's lawyer
    2. Between the parties
        (a) when disclosure would prevent "uninformed settlement"
        (b) when disclosure would break "uninformed" impasse

D. *Ensuring Informed Consent*

    1. In cases of possible coercion of one party
        (a) by the other party
        (b) by the party's own lawyer/adviser
        (c) by the mediator's "persuasive" measures
    2. In cases of party incapacity
    3. In cases of party ignorance
        (a) of factual information known to the mediator
        (b) of legal/expert information known to the mediator

E. *Preserving Self-Determination/Maintaining Nondirectiveness*

    1. When tempted to give the parties a solution
        (a) at the parties' request
        (b) on the mediator's own initiative

2. When tempted to oppose a solution formulated by the parties
   (a) because the solution is illegal
   (b) because the solution is unfair to a weaker party
   (c) because the solution is unwise
   (d) because the solution is unfair to an outside party

F. *Separating Mediation from Counselling and Legal Advice*

1. When the parties need expert information
   (a) therapeutic information
   (b) legal information
2. When tempted to express a professional judgment
   (a) therapeutic advice
   (b) legal advice
3. When a party needs a therapist or advocate

G. *Avoiding Party Exposure to Harm as a Result of Mediation*

1. When mediation may make a bad situation worse
2. When mediation may reveal sensitive information
3. When mediation may induce "detrimental reliance"

H. *Preventing Party Abuse of the Mediation Process*

1. When a party conceals information
2. When a party lies
3. When a party "fishes" for information
4. When a party stalls to "buy time"
5. When a party engages in intimidation

I. *Handling Conflicts of Interest*

1. Arising out of relations with courts or referring agencies
2. Arising out of relations with lawyers/other professionals

While the Bush classification system of ethical dilemmas is quite comprehensive, there are a number of other perspectives on the meaning of ethics that help inform the mediation context. Gibson suggests that to fully identify the ethical dilemmas that mediators face, the ADR field must first gain an understanding of the different philosophies of existing ethics. Gibson states: "Until mediation practitioners and theorists distinguish the type of ethical assumptions made and begin to use very precise language, they will be unable to sort out the issues within each arena of debate."[43]

---

43 K. Gibson, "The Ethical Basis of Mediation: Why Mediators Need Philosophers" (1989) 7 Mediation Q. 42 at 50.

Similarly, Grebe, Irvin, and Lang describe the understanding of the philosophies of ethics that mediators have in the following manner:

> Mediators and many other service-providing professionals do not have much background in philosophy or the philosophy of ethics, nor do they engage in philosophically informed discussions of the dilemmas they encounter. It is not part of their training as mediators, nor is it usually part of the training they received in the previous discipline. They are often uncomfortable about certain aspects of cases they encounter and use the wisdom learned from their present profession and their own personal biases and values to make their decisions. Family mediators practice an institutional approach to ethics, rather than an analytical one.[44]

Gibson identifies three groups of philosophies of ethics that mediators should investigate and understand: utilitarian theories, virtue theories and deontological theories. Utilitarian theories centre around the belief that "a right act is one in which we are able to maximize the good or minimize the bad."[45] Virtue theories state that the determination of what is ethical is dependent upon the character of the person doing it. Deontological theories argue that the value of an action, the determination of whether it is ethical or unethical, depends upon the motives that guide the action. Another name for deontological theories are rights-based theories or duty-based theories.

Another factor that many authors argue should help to identify the meaning of ethics in the mediation context is the concept of professionalization. They argue that codes of ethics are outgrowths of the notion and ideology of a profession, and as such should reflect the norms of what it means to be a profession as much as the nature of mediation itself. Pavalko identifies this relationship between professionalization and the meaning of ethics:

> The extent to which groups have developed codes of ethics, whether written or unwritten, is another measure of where they are on the occupation-profession continuum. Generally codes of ethics tend to be found more in the professional end, and the complexity, kinds of behavior they cover and their enforceability are a matter of degree.[46]

---

44 S.C. Grebe, K. Irvin, & M. Lang, "A Model for Ethical Decision-Making in Mediation" (1989) 7 Mediation Q. 133 at 136.

45 Above note 43 at 43.

46 R.M. Pavalko, *Sociology of Occupations and Professions* (Itasca, IL: F.E. Peacock Publishers Inc., 1971) at 25.

Grebe expands on this by suggesting that by thinking of mediation as a profession, we can identify the situations that give rise to ethical dilemmas and the responses that would constitute ethical behavior. She identifies the principles of *beneficence* (working to advance someone's legitimate interests without being inconvenienced too much) and *non-maleficence* (doing no harm) as the universal guiding principles of all professions. Consequently, an ethical dilemma for a mediator would arise when an action could possibly cause harm to a party or require a major inconvenience to be born by the other party and/or the mediator.

With mediation becoming more international, Morris[47] questions whether Western theories will dominate talk about mediation ethics and points out that ethical issues are often addressed from cross-cultural and cross-religious perspectives.[48] However, Morris goes on to suggest that "the most important point for discussion of ethics in mediation is the fact of human interdependence" and "it is increasingly obvious that the whole world community shares in this interdependence."[49] Relying on the notion that there are three universal principles — respect, caring, and procedural fairness — needed in all conflict resolution, Morris concludes that ethical policy in mediation will depend on asking what mediator and process qualities engender trust and demonstrate respect, caring, and fairness in context while avoiding ethics that emphasize individuals over communities and individual rights over responsibility to others.

As the above examples illustrate, ethical dilemmas will arise in mediation, but what is identified as an ethical dilemma and how that situation is discussed and responded to can vary depending upon the approach taken. Practitioners and students of ADR will be assisted in understanding the ethical dimensions of mediation by being aware of both mediation-specific and traditional approaches to the meaning of ethics.

b) The Difficulties in Identifying the Ethics of Mediation

Although it is generally agreed that ethical dilemmas will arise in the practice of mediation, a problematic task is trying to identify what the ethics of mediation should be. Some accept that the various codes of conduct for mediators have settled or will settle this matter. But in

47   C. Morris, "The Trusted Mediator: Ethics and Interaction in Mediation" in J. Macfarlane, ed., *Rethinking Disputes: The Mediation Alternative* (Toronto: Emond Montgomery Publications Limited, 1997) at 301.

48   One example is J. McConnell, *Mindful Mediation: A Handbook for Buddhist Peacemakers* (Bangkok: Buddhist Research Institute, 1995).

49   Above note 46 at 347.

addition to concerns over what it is that is actually driving the move to mediation ethics, there also are a number of theoretical and practical difficulties in identifying the ethics of mediation.

i) Theoretical Difficulties

The primary theoretical concern is that we cannot determine what the ethics of mediation should be until we are clear what the role of a mediator is. But what if no common conception of the mediator's role exists at the present time. If the role of mediators were to be defined as one of empowerment and relationship building, as Bush argues it should, then a basis for a code of ethical conduct could be that "the mediator will . . . do everything possible to ensure that the parties are empowered to exercise their autonomy and self-determination."[50] However, if on the other hand the role of the mediator were defined as providing more efficient justice, then the basis of an ethical code would be the cost and time that certain actions would entail.

A second theoretical difficulty with identifying the ethics of mediation is that the notion of ethics is a relative one. A situation that poses an ethical dilemma to one mediator may pose no difficulty of any sort to another. As Stulberg argues, how a particular mediator views the process of mediation and his role in it "is a necessary condition for assessing whether or not some practice or situation presents a dilemma let alone an ethical dilemma."[51]

A third theoretical concern is that mediation is too complex a process to have general rules of conduct enunciated for it. Mediation is a flexible process that will vary dramatically depending on a number of variables. Are the parties capable of driving the process forward in an effective manner? Are lawyers involved? Are the disputants from different cultures? What is the background of the mediator? What if the process is a *self-determined* process that the parties are to define and bring forward? Any code of ethical conduct will represent an infringement on the autonomy and freedom of the parties to drive the process forward. Codes of conduct will act as barriers that prevent the parties from resolving a dispute in a manner they feel is most appropriate.

A fourth theoretical concern is the debate over the status of mediation as a profession. Historically, a sign of being a profession is that there is self-regulation of the members of the profession, which often includes the enforcement and application of a code of ethics. Many

---

50   R.A.B. Bush, "Efficiency and Protection, or Empowerment and Recognition? The Mediator's Role and Ethical Standards in Mediation" (1989) 41 Fla. L. Rev. 253 at 277.

51   J.B. Stulberg, "Bush on Mediation Dilemmas" (1994) J. Disp. Resol. 57 at 62;

practitioners and academics argue in favour of the creation of codes of ethics for mediators to position mediation as a profession. Codes of ethics allow for self-regulation rather than having the regulation, and consequential loss of true professional status, imposed externally. But if constructing mediation as a profession is not necessary or counter-productive, professional mediation ethics is a non sequitur. As for other complex activities such as parenting, communicating, and nego-tiating, there might be norms, values, attitudes, beliefs, customs, laws, or regulations that guide behaviour but, as is the case for these other activities, there would be no comprehensive ethical codes.

A final theoretical concern centres around the identification of what the ethical goals of mediation should be. Cooks and Hale[52] iden-tify four issues that would be at the heart of any code of ethical behav-iour for mediators: preserving self-determination, ensuring informed consent, mediator impartiality and mediator neutrality. However, they go on to illustrate that our ways of talking and thinking about these four goals render them irreconcilable objectives. In other words, a code of ethics for mediators could not enunciate rules to protect these four goals because these goals will always be in conflict with one another. For example, a code could state the general rule that the parties must be left free to self-determine the process of mediation. However, does this mean that a mediator should not be concerned with the fairness of the outcome of the process? If the answer is yes, then mediation is ren-dered problematic because mediators would not act when an unfair resolution occurred because of a lack of information being possessed by one party or power disparity between the other parties. On the other hand, if a mediator is to be concerned with ensuring a fair outcome, isn't the goal of mediator neutrality undermined?

Thus, Cooks and Hale conclude that to enunciate a coherent and internally consistent code of ethics for mediators, the debate must include a discussion of new approaches to studying communicative action. Our current ways of thinking and talking about ethics and mediation has resulted in an irreconcilable set of ethical goals being positioned at the core of an ethical code. Until this discourse over eth-ics matures and develops, any attempts at enunciating ethical codes will be doomed to failure.

---

52   L.M. Cooks & C.L. Hale, "The Construction of Ethics in Mediation" (1994) 4 Mediation Q. 55.

ii) Practical Difficulties

Practical difficulties involve identifying who should create the codes of ethics, whom they should apply to and how they could be applied and enforced.

The most debated practical difficulty with proposals for codes of ethics revolves around who should be creating the codes. Because mediation is not a self-regulating profession at this time, there exists no authoritative body of mediators to articulate a code of ethics. Further, considering the complexities of the ideology of professionalism, it is arguably undesirable that such a body emerge. Consequently, it appears that if a code of ethics were to emerge to regulate mediators in a province or a state at the present time, it would likely have to originate with the makers of public policy. This reality has been the cause of much discomfort and anxiety by mediators. The concerns are not only that government officials will intrude on the professionalization process but also that they will have problems in determining standards that clearly reflect the values central to the mediation process.

A related issue to who should create the code of ethics is whom the code should apply to. Should different forms of mediation (e.g. employment versus family) have different ethical standards? Should court-appointed mediators be held to a different standard than private mediators? Should one code of ethics be applied universally? There can be strong suggestions that standards for the conduct of mediation practice must apply to all mediators regardless of background and should cover the majority of situations confronted by mediators. Others can differ and suggest that in different forms of mediation and where mediation is court-associated, there will be different values at stake, and codes of ethics must consider and contemplate these differences.

A final practical difficulty that deserves comment is how a code of ethics will be enforced. If mediation does not emerge into a unified self-regulating profession, the duty of enforcement will probably fall onto the courts and government. As Stulberg points out, the cost of articulating and implementing such a system would be immense and perhaps remove many of the benefits that courts saw mediation bestowing. The alternative, at the present time, is to have a code of ethics without a system of sanctions, but the usefulness and effectiveness of this would be highly questionable.

c) A Best Ethical Response

The existing systems of regulating mediator behaviour are likely to continue particularly as mediation puts on more of a professional face. Codes or guidelines, primarily made by associations of mediators, will be supplemented by codes of conduct that regulate a profession of which a mediator may be a part. A lawyer as a mediator would not only be bound by the legal profession's ethical prescriptions but also subject to the particular set of mediation standards that might be applicable.

However, while the dominant sources of ethical guidelines remain professional associations of mediators and the professions that mediators belong to, it should be noted that the movement to government-created and enforced codes of ethics has begun. For example, in 1992 the Florida Legislature provided that the Supreme Court shall establish minimum standards and procedures for professional conduct and discipline for mediators. The Court then established a Standing Committee on Mediation and Arbitration Rules, which subsequently had its proposals adopted as the *Florida Rules for Certified and Court-Appointed Mediators*. The Florida scheme includes a system of sanctions and the establishment of a board to endorse observance of the rules, which sets it apart from the rules promulgated by professional associations. The success of the scheme in regulating mediation without interfering with the essential informality of the mediation process will determine whether the Florida model will be followed elsewhere.[53]

The final look of mediation ethics is not clear. There may be a universal code that covers the general types of ethical questions present in all forms of mediation. There may be more individualized forms of regulations developed for particular types of mediation. Lawyer-mediators and lawyers who act for clients in mediation will need to be aware of any potential conflicts between codes of mediation ethics and existing ethical dictates that lawyers are bound to follow. The resolution of the ethics of mediation is very much a part of, and helpful to, an understanding of ADR.

FURTHER READINGS

BOWLING, D., & D. HOFFMAN, "Bringing Peace into the Room: The Personal Qualities of the Mediator and Their Impact on the Mediation" (2000) Negotiation J. 5

DARLING, C.R., ed., *Turning Conflict into Consensus: Mediation Theory, Practice and Skills* (Vancouver: Continuing Legal Education Society of British Columbia, 1998)

---

53   For a description, see R.B. Moberly, "Ethical Standards for Court Appointed Mediators and Florida's Mandatory Mediation Experiment" (1994) 21 Fla. St. U. L. Rev. 702.

FOLBERG, J., & A. TAYLOR, *Mediation: A Comprehensive Guide to Resolving Conflicts without Litigation* (San Francisco: Jossey-Bass, 1984)

IRVING, H., *Divorce Mediation: The Rational Alternative* (Toronto: Personal Library Publishers, 1980)

IRVING, H., & M. BENJAMIN, *Family Mediation: Theory and Practice of Dispute Resolution* (Toronto: Carswell, 1987)

KOLB, D.M., *When Talk Works: Profiles of Mediators* (San Francisco: Jossey-Bass, 1994)

LANDAU, B., M. BARTOLETTI, & R. MESBUR, *Family Mediation Handbook*, 2d ed. (Toronto: Butterworths, 1987)

LEMON, J.A., *Family Mediation Practice* (New York: Free Press, 1985)

MACFARLANE, J., ed., *Rethinking Disputes: The Mediation Alternative* (Toronto: Emond Montgomery, 1997)

MOORE, C.W., *The Mediation Process: Practical Strategies for Resolving Conflict* (San Francisco: Jossey-Boss, 1996)

MOSTEN, F.S., *The Complete Guide to Mediation: The Cutting-Edge Approach to Family Law Practice* (Chicago, IL: American Bar Association, 1997)

NOBLE, A., L.L. DIZGUN, & D.P. EMOND, *Mediation Advocacy: Effective Client Representation in Mediation Proceedings* (Toronto: Emond Montgomery, 1998)

ROGERS, N.H., & C.A. McEWEN, *Mediation: Law, Policy and Practice*, 2d ed. (St. Paul, MN: West Publishing, 1994)

CHAPTER 5

ARBITRATION AND THE ADR INFLUENCES

A. INTRODUCTION

Arbitration was not at the forefront in the modern emergence of alternative dispute resolution for obvious reasons. The process of arbitration, in which parties agree or are compelled to submit their dispute to a neutral person or group of persons whose function is to receive proofs and arguments more or less formally and then render a binding decision based on objective standards, resembled too closely for comfort the process of court adjudication. Consider a standard clause in many arbitration contracts:

> Any controversy or claim arising out of or relating to this contract, or the breach thereof, shall be settled by arbitration in accordance with the Commercial Arbitration Rules of . . . , and judgment upon the award rendered by the arbitrator(s) may be entered in any court having jurisdiction thereof.

ADR's early emphasis on mediation and other forms of consensual decision making and the implicit and often explicit criticisms that ADR directed at the courts meant that arbitration initially did not fit easily into the new ADR vocabulary. Arbitration did not appear to be a process that could further ADR goals.

However, as discussed in chapter 1, with the meaning of alternative dispute resolution no longer restricted to non-court activities, the goals of ADR open to broader interpretation, and with the process of arbitration more closely examined and understood, arbitration can no longer be regarded by ADR students and practitioners as a separate entity to be studied and applied primarily in the special contexts of labour relations, commercial matters, or international trade. In fact, for the ADR student or practitioner, the subject of arbitration presents unique opportunities to consider the ways in which this process fits within, and contributes to, the developing meaning of alternative dispute resolution; recent developments in the use of arbitration to resolve disputes beyond arbitration's more traditional boundaries; when to resort to the arbitration process to deal with important controversies or conflicts; the knowledge and skills required for this adjudicative process; and the future potential of this disputing method in ADR developments.

B. THE PROCESS OF ARBITRATION: KEY FEATURES

Arbitration has a long lifeline. Frances Kellor's introduction to the history behind the American Arbitration Association[1] illustrates the staying power and values that have been hallmarks of arbitration through the centuries.

> Of all mankind's adventure in search of peace and justice, arbitration is among the earliest. Long before law was established, or courts were organized, or judges had formulated principles of law, men had resorted to arbitration for the resolving of discord, the adjustment of differences, and the settlement of disputes.
>
> Out of the dim recesses of fable and mythology, it appears that upon Mt. Ida the royal shepherd Paris was called upon to deliver a famous award. The dispute concerned the competing claims of Juno, Pallas Athene and Venus for the prize of beauty. All other means of settlement having failed, Paris, by agreement of the parties, decided the issue.
>
> If the course of arbitration, begun presumably on Mt. Ida, could be traced through the centuries, it would be found in the most primitive society as well as in modern civilization. Commercial arbitration was known to the desert caravans in Marco Polo's time and was a common practice among Phoenician and Greek traders.

---

1   F. Kellor, *American Arbitration* (New York: Harper and Brothers Publishers, 1948).

Civil arbitration also flourished. In the Homeric period, chiefs and elders held more or less regular sittings in places of assembly to settle the disputes of all persons who chose to appear before them. In the middle of the sixth century B.C., Peisistratus, the Athenian tyrant, furthered his policy of keeping people out of the city by appointing justices to go on circuit throughout village communities. They were authorized to give binding decisions if they failed to effect a friendly settlement.

International arbitration was also known to the ancient world, for many political disputes seem to have been thus settled. In a controversy between Athens and Megara, about 600 B.C., for the possession of the island of Salamis, the matter was referred to five Spartan judges who allotted the island to Athens. A dispute between Corinth and Corcyra for the possession of Leucas (480 B.C.) was settled by Themistocles as arbitrator. A boundary in dispute between the Genoese and Viturians was settled by arbitration (117 B.C.), the decision having been recorded upon a bronze tablet unearthed near Genoa. There are also instances in which a third strong power compelled other powers to resort to arbitration. Sometimes the arbitrator was an individual as Themistocles; or an institution such as the Areopagus at Athens; or a state. The tribunal might, therefore, be an individual, a group of individuals, a state, or a large number of citizens chosen from within a state.

Industrial controversy was also arbitrated in such matters as master and servant relations, terms of employment, working conditions and wages. One of the first disputes submitted to the earliest known American arbitration tribunal, organized in 1786 by the Chamber of Commerce of New York, involved the wages of seamen.

It is important to recall these early uses of arbitration at this time when, in the midst of a rising tide of controversy, doubts arise and arbitration is sometimes thought to be something new and untried and hazardous to good public relations; or when its organization seems to be detrimental to judicial institutions that seem older but are in reality next of kin.

So soundly was arbitration then conceived, and so generally was it applied to all kinds of controversy, that little change in its fundamental principles has taken place over the centuries. Despite efforts to narrow the early concept or to put its practice in a legal strait jacket, arbitration remains the voluntary agreement of states or persons to submit their differences to judges of their own choice and to bind themselves in advance, to accept the decision of judges, so chosen, as final and binding. This natural right of self-regulation is a precious possession of a democratic society, for it embodies the principles of independence, self-reliance, equality, integrity, and responsibility, all of which are inestimable value to any community.

Whether arbitration had its genesis in ancient Greece or was an obvious and well-used mechanism for dispute resolution with first peoples in other parts of the world, typically arbitration is regarded as an adjudicatory process. The disputants, in general terms, follow the traditional adversarial model associated with litigation in an effort to ultimately convince a third-party decision maker — the arbitrator — that their claim or that of their client should prevail over that of an opponent. The rules of the arbitration process and how an arbitration unfolds are not so much relaxed from the rules and procedures of court as they are modified. In the final analysis, arbitration incorporates substantially the same operating assumptions as the judicial adversarial process and reflects the essential elements of court adjudication — evidence is submitted by the disputants or their advocate to a neutral third party who has the power to issue a binding decision.

Although arbitration may have been regarded with some disdain by original ADR enthusiasts, it is interesting to note several key features of the process of arbitration that existed when ADR emerged in the 1970s. As Kellor states, these features are not new, but when closely examined, they tend to illustrate the many benefits that can accrue to disputants who decide to choose arbitration over another disputing process. These disputing qualities point to the potential for arbitration to become a major contributor, much in the same manner as mediation, to the meaning of the ADR field and to future ADR developments. The features of arbitration that should be understood are discussed below.

1) The Knowledgeable Arbitrator

Similar to decision making in the courts, a neutral third party to the dispute is given authority to render the decision in arbitration. But the character of the decision maker in arbitration bears a marked difference to that of her judicial counterpart. Although the manner in which judges are appointed varies from jurisdiction to jurisdiction, judges are almost always lawyers who are selected because of their experience in practising, sometimes teaching, law and who are regarded as having the skills and savvy to hear and make decisions about the wide range of disputes that come before them. The higher the court, the more closely scrutinized the proposed judge's background will be because Courts of Appeal and Supreme Courts are the final arbiters of many important disputes that occur in a society.

Whatever the selection process, most judges are generalists. Whereas some judges sitting in specialized courts such as unified family courts or youth courts may develop a certain expertise in dealing with a particular type of problem, the demands of judging in modern civil societies most often require judges to be able to figure out what has happened and what should be done under the law equally well in all manner of cases. Whether the dispute revolves around the complications on a construction site, the details of a surgical procedure, or competing claims to the ownership of a popular melody, judges are expected to be able to grasp the contextual complexity surrounding these disputes and then be able to apply sound legal principles objectively to arrive at a fair and just solution.

More often than not judges meet these challenges. With the assistance of learned counsel, a variety of witnesses, and various institutional support persons, the judicial process unfolds. The story is told, the issues are narrowed, the law is expounded, the arguments are made, and eventually a judgment is rendered. However, the difficulties in accomplishing these tasks in an adversarial setting for judges with limited or no experience with the actual industry or subject matter in dispute point to a real advantage of arbitration. Unlike the judge, the arbitrator can be an expert, knowledgeable, or fluent in what really makes up the case. Whether an arbitrator is appointed by government under existing legislation, chosen by an overseeing organization or body concerned with the dispute, or selected by the disputants themselves, the arbitrator can bring to the decision-making process an expertise that can go a long way to ensure that nuances, complexities, or other insider aspects of the dispute are not missed or given inappropriate attention in the adjudicative process. The delays involved in educating the decision maker about what is at stake can be avoided.

The expertise of the arbitrator can extend beyond the normal judging skills of being fair-minded, familiar with the relevant legal frameworks, able to conduct a hearing in accordance with established rules of procedure, and practised at applying law to facts. Hand-picked arbitrators can have important industry knowledge. The arbitrator may be an engineer or architect who understands and has worked with the technical drawings that are at the heart of the construction dispute. The labour arbitrator, who may have been a long-time player in the specific labour relations area, knows exactly what the economic consequences of a 2 percent wage increase or a ten million dollar salary will be. A problem that would be presented to a judge in court as an intellectual property dispute may be best decided by an arbitrator with a law and technology background who knows a lot about intellectual property law and procedure and also understands fully the biogenetics associated with the cloning controversy in issue.

The advantages of having an expert as arbitrator are not limited to decision making in individual cases. There can be a broader or systemic good in arbitration. Having an expert or a group of experts regularly rendering decisions in a particular field also can tend to create a high degree of certainty and confidence around dispute resolution for the parties who are engaged in activities in that field. These benefits accrue because the number of decision makers can be kept small, the specialized arbitrators are less likely to go on a frolic of their own by missing or misinterpreting important information, and a workable jurisprudence can be developed by the arbitrators that covers the entire field. These positives do not mean that disputants will never need to adjudicate issues from time to time or that every arbitration outcome can be forecast. However, the expert or knowledgeable arbitrator can help to avoid unpleasant surprises that might otherwise taint the process or the result.

2) Flexibility of Process

Flexibility of process does not mean that the process of arbitration is simple or straightforward. When the stakes are high, as they often are, and consensus can't be reached, persuasive argumentation in an adversarial atmosphere and workable quasi-judicial proceedings require clearly delineated and sophisticated rules so that the disputants and their representatives can put their best case forward as efficiently and effectively as possible. For this result to occur, it has been common for jurisdictions to enact arbitration legislation. This legislation normally would set out a general framework for the submission of a dispute to an arbitrator and provide for matters such as the production of documents, power to subpoena witnesses, removal of arbitrators, and the power of the courts to review arbitral awards.

However, the highly detailed and mainly mandatory specifics of procedure that are spelled out for courtroom adjudications are absent from the arbitration legislation. The determination of the actual details of the arbitration process is left to the arbitrator and the parties to work out. As a result, there are considerable opportunities to craft the arbitration process in a flexible format that would be responsive to the particular context of the dispute and the needs of the parties and that would, as far as possible, avoid replicating the litigation process and its downsides for disputing. Thus, for example, in some instances uniform arbitration rules have been established for all disputes in a particular industry. Participants in areas such as building construction agree to have a fixed set of delineated rules govern arbitrations to which they submit. In other cases, the rules of arbitration vary in formality and comprehensiveness depending on the complexity of the dispute, the nature of the issues in question, and the amount of money involved. The parties to a dispute over the distribution of massive mineral rights or the quantification of damages in a failed merger may rely on several common arbitral procedures but fine-tune the process to meet the individual requirements of the specific case. Other arbitrations, when appropriate, can resemble or be likened to the informality of a job-site or boardroom meeting where the task of the arbitrator is to encourage a relaxation in procedural and evidentiary rules to promote greater disclosure and discussion and to promote a speedy hearing or, perhaps, even a settlement. A continued focus on the flexibility of the arbitration process can lead to a fuller appreciation of arbitration's potential.

3) Privacy and Confidentiality

Arbitration is usually private and confidential. Unlike the courts, which are almost always open to public scrutiny and whose decisions are regularly reported, read (at least by lawyers) and frequently commented on in the press, arbitration hearings and awards are rarely the subject of much public attention. This can be a major benefit for disputants who may worry that publicity about their involvement in a dispute could negatively affect their reputation, name or goodwill. The subject matter of the dispute could be embarrassing or of a personal nature. Even being seen to be in a debate over a particular matter could be problematic. The disclosure of financial or technological information in a public dispute resolution process could be damaging to a disputant's competitiveness in a particular market or do other economic harm. Being able to channel a dispute that might otherwise attract a good deal of public interest into a private setting where the proceedings and the arbitrator's decision can commonly be kept private and confidential may make the arbitration process much more attractive than going to court or even commencing a judicial proceeding with the expectation of settling out of court.

4) Time and Cost Effectiveness

As a result of the ability of the disputants to appoint an expert arbitrator and the flexibilities inherent in the arbitration process, arbitration can be a time- and cost-effective way to process a dispute. Unlike in the courts, disputants who choose arbitration are not usually faced with lengthy pre-hearing proceedings or long waits for trial.

Depending on the nature of the case and the arbitration rules being used, pre-hearing matters involving an exchange of pleadings, replies, agreed statements of facts, documents, correspondence and other relevant material, on-site inspections if needed, and any pre-hearing conference can be completed expeditiously. However, there will be pre-hearing steps that must be taken in every arbitration process. Any time savings associated with arbitration would quickly disappear if these procedures were allowed to consume as much time as pre-trial litigation proceedings would for the same case. As a result, the time taken to prepare a dispute for an arbitration hearing can be shortened by either imposing strict time frames for the completion of a pre-hearing procedure or by dispensing with a pre-hearing matter altogether. However, pre-hearing procedures often can serve to narrow the issues, get agreements on facts, obtain admissions, or otherwise help prepare the case for adjudication. Inappropriately eliminating or shortening pre-hearing discovery procedures to save time in arbitration can mean that the actual hearing will be lengthier as a result.

Disputants who choose arbitration also do not usually have to endure a lengthy wait to have their case heard once the pre-hearing procedures are completed. Again, depending on the case, there may be some delays in establishing a hearing date to accommodate the schedules of the arbitrator, the disputants, their lawyers, and any witnesses to be called. This courtesy in date setting is not usually extended as easily in the formal justice system. The timing of the trial mostly depends on the availability of a judge and courtroom and no irreconcilable conflicts in the lawyers' schedules. However, the demands on judicial time and court resources are such that the earliest possible trial date that can be set for the disputants usually allows them plenty of time to get ready for the ensuing trial. Even with the delays inherent in an arbitration system where the parties generally agree on a hearing date, the time spent waiting will be shorter to have a dispute adjudicated by an arbitrator than to have the same case heard by a judge in court. In fact, given the conceptual similarities between arbitration and court adjudication, disputants who choose arbitration are privately paying to jump the courthouse queue that can often take litigants two, three, or more years to pass through in large urban centres, compared with perhaps a few months for an arbitration.

The cost savings of arbitration are related to the time savings. Normally, if the disputants and arbitrators are able to prepare for and conduct the arbitration hearing in a time-efficient way, cost efficiency will follow. In many cases, this will mean that the costs of arbitration can be lower than the cost of taking the same case to court. However, in the courts, many costs are publicly subsidized. The judge and other court officials are not paid for by the disputants. The courtroom is not rented. In private arbitrations the parties are responsible for the fees charged by the arbitrator and any reporter and for the rental of a hearing room. These costs need to be considered when assessing the cost advantages of arbitration over court. In public arbitrations, which are discussed later, the cost of the arbitrator and the institutional support for the arbitration process are borne by the state. Cost advantages vis-à-vis the courts also will be affected by the length of time required for the actual hearing. Complex cases or adversarially contested issues may be just as expensive to adjudicate before an arbitrator as in front of a judge in court.

5) Ongoing Relationships

In addition to striving for speed, cost savings, flexibility and responsiveness, predictability and credibility, arbitration can help to preserve ongoing relationships. The source of this goal, in part, comes from the features of arbitration already discussed. Here is a dispute resolution process, often of a voluntary nature, that can help the disputants get a solution from a respected and party-selected decision maker, inexpensively, privately, and without resort to the adversarialness of the courts. These process characteristics can themselves do much to maintain positive relationships between or among parties. The personal stresses and strain of seeing one another on a regular basis or having to work together under the cloud of a continuing and murky conflict can be ameliorated somewhat by the process features of arbitration. A final and binding arbitral award that is made quickly can allow parties to get on with their businesses or personal relationships and put past differences, resolved by the arbitrator, behind them. This built-in respect for relationships is not normally seen as being present when disputants go to court. As discussed in chapter 2, part of the reason for this is the adversarial thinking or win-lose approach associated with litigation. Dispute resolution in the adversarial atmosphere of the courtroom can often push parties apart, cause suspicions, exacerbate existing differences, and even create new conflicts for the disputants to deal with. But these types of consequences are not necessarily absent from many arbitral proceedings. After all, arbitration is an adjudication, and the process provides plenty of opportunities for the disputants to argue back and forth about whose claim has the most merit and about who should win. The features of arbitration described above act as a kind of mutually agreed upon damper on the degree of adversarial zealousness allowed. By agreeing to do things more quickly, less expensively, privately, and away from the courts, the parties to arbitration can de-emphasize or minimize the adverse impact on relationships that can flow from the more protracted, bitter, costly and public battles that take place in litigation. However, the more that arbitration procedures resemble adversarial court proceedings in content and tone, obviously the less likely will arbitration work to maintain positive future relationships between the disputants.

Apart from the process features of arbitration that can help to ensure the relationships among disputants come out none the worse for wear, arbitration, despite its adjudicatory nature, also can have relationship maintenance as a clear outcome goal. Arbitration can strive not to make these disputes personal or worse. In addition to the general and laudable goals of the courts to provide a just, speedy, and inexpensive determination of every proceeding on its merits, arbitration can go one step further. Arbitration can regard disputing as more matter of fact. Arbitration can be presented as an efficient, effective, and credible dispute resolution process that parties can resort to when there is need to have a third-party neutral make and impose a decision in a manner that can be accepted as mutually satisfying whatever the result. This does not mean that the party ordered to compensate the contractor, to pay the higher salary, or to reinstate the employee as a result of arbitration may not be disappointed. But the arbitration process can be seen as a necessary and positive mechanism to deal with the inevitability of disputes in our society. Provided that all the disputants are given a fair opportunity to prepare and present their case and the expert arbitrator carefully weighs the evidence and gives a reasoned decision, there may be no reason to consider changes to ongoing relationships. The dispute has been settled. It is time to move on.

6) Judicial Deference

A final feature of arbitration focuses on the interrelationships that exist between arbitration and the courts. Based on the previous discussion of the arbitration process, many of arbitration's advantages as a disputing mechanism depend on features that stand it apart from court adjudication. The expert arbitrator is contrasted with the generalist judge. Flexible rules of procedure in arbitration vary from broadly applicable, comprehensive, and complex court rules. Arbitration may be less expensive and yield faster results than going to court. Arbitration can nurture and maintain continuing relationships whereas the litigation process can pull people apart and cause irreparable damage to disputant connections.

Arbitration's advantages fade as the process of arbitration comes to resemble closely the judicial process. Indeed, one of the criticisms often levelled at some labour arbitrations is that these proceedings have become so highly adversarial, so dominated by lawyers and legal thinking, and so costly and time-consuming, there is little in substance that distinguishes them from court adjudication. But the advantages of arbitration also can crumble if the courts ultimately are able to assume jurisdiction over disputes that may be or actually are submitted to arbitration.

The former category — disputes that may be submitted to arbitration — is probably small. If the parties want to submit a dispute to arbitration for resolution, there are few legal restrictions. Most arbitration legislation defines an arbitral submission as a written agreement to submit differences or a matter to arbitration. If the parties agree, the dispute can go to arbitration because "broadly speaking, arbitration is a contractual process."[2] Although some courts have not always supported private disputing arrangements, worried that private arbitration agreements allowed the parties to circumvent their jurisdiction, court interest in disputes destined for arbitration has waned, particularly with the enactment of arbitration legislation that supports arbitration and deals with concerns that agreements to arbitrate were contrary to public policy because they purported to oust the jurisdiction of the courts.[3] Public policy grounds would undoubtedly raise legitimate fears for disputes going for final decision in arbitration in cases where the contractual agreement to arbitrate was problematic, such as disputes involving children, persons under a disability or other matters that impinge on the agreement. But apart from these types of cases, judicial interception of disputes destined for arbitration would be rare.

Courts assuming jurisdiction over the second category of disputes — disputes that are now in arbitration — could be more problematic. The benefits associated with arbitration could vanish depending on how the court intervenes.

---

2   M. Domke, *Domke on Commercial Arbitration (The Law and Practice of Commercial Arbitration)*, rev. ed. by M.W. Gabriel (New York: Clark, Boardman, Callaghan, 1997) at 1.

3   In fact, the early enactment by the United States Congress in 1925 of the *Federal Arbitration Act* was "to reverse the longstanding judicial hostility to arbitration agreements . . . and to place arbitration agreements on the same footing as other contracts." See *Gilmer v. Interstate/Johnson Lane Corp.*, 500 U.S. 20 (1991). The law on when courts enforce arbitration agreements by "staying" court proceedings is generally in accord with the expression of public policy that encourages arbitration agreements. The exact test for staying cases thereby requiring them to be heard in arbitration will depend on why the agreement is being challenged.

The exact role that the courts play in the actual arbitration process varies from one jurisdiction to the next. However, there are fundamentally three ways in which the courts can be involved in the arbitration of disputes. First, the written agreement to arbitrate or the enabling legislation establishing the arbitration program may provide for an *appeal* to the court. The grounds for appeal might be on questions of law and/or fact, arguing that the arbitrator made a substantive and serious error. Rarely would the appeal to the court be to hear the matter afresh. Second, by agreement or statute the court may be given power to judicially *review* the arbitration process to determine if the arbitrator made a procedural error, exceeded his jurisdiction, or otherwise misconducted himself. Third, again through the parties' agreement or as set out in the relevant legislation, the parties to arbitration may make a decision to *refer* a question or issue to a judge for decision. This reference might raise a legal question for the judge to answer but it may also put a factual issue or process matter before the court for judicial determination. The reason for the reference to the court may be to bring in the extra expertise of the judge if needed on a more purely legal question or perhaps to acknowledge, indirectly or directly, that the arbitrator is not the best person to make that particular decision.

Whatever way the court becomes involved in arbitration, careful judicial deference is needed to preserve arbitration's advantages vis-à-vis the courts. This can be a fine balancing act. If a judge on appeal mostly substitutes her opinion for that of the arbitrator, the advantage of having an expert arbitrator may be lost. Extra time and money will be spent. If a judge undertaking a judicial review chastises an arbitrator for omitting a fairness step, the consequences in terms of lost time, money, and especially flexibility may make arbitration less appealing. The more occasions that the court substantively and procedurally replaces the arbitration process with the judicial process, the more risk there is that arbitration duplicates the eventual resolution of the problem by the court or becomes an expensive and time-consuming add-on.

The degree of deference that the courts will show to these expert decision makers in an arbitration obviously will depend on a number of factors. The nature of the subject matter, the magnitude of the decision, the type of error complained of, the terms of the arbitration agreement or legislation setting up the arbitration process, the presence of any privative clause purporting to oust the jurisdiction of the court, and the position of arbitration in the ADR field can all be influencing factors. If there is an obvious intention on the part of the parties or the enabling legislation to make the expert arbitrator's decision final and binding, that intention should be respected by and large. A pragmatic and functional control by the courts would be the desired standard, as is the case in general with the court's supervision of administrative agencies. However, the arbitration process can clearly include a place for a judicial supervisory role or for the courts to act as an appellate check on the fairness and accuracy of proceedings. In these latter cases, the additional costs, time, and other consequences associated with using the courts can be seen less as a diminution of arbitration's advantages and more as a further strengthening of the decision-making process that has been agreed upon, a process that includes some limited judicial checks. How the agreement is reached about the appropriate nature and scope of this further strengthening is an important ADR question.

C. DEVELOPMENTS IN ARBITRATION

Although interest in mediation may have surpassed the attention awarded arbitration as ADR became popular, recently the full potential of arbitration to be a fast, inexpensive, and just dispute resolution process has been examined more closely. Developments in arbitration are now a part of the overall ADR scene. In much the same fashion that improvements have been made to the ways in which the courts adjudicate disputes, there also have been improvements in recent years in the arbitration process. For example, in Canada, arbitration legislation, which had been modelled on the English *Arbitration Act, 1889,* has been generally modernized. Many procedural problems that created disincentives to participate in arbitration have been remedied. Federal and provincial legislation also has been enacted to facilitate international commercial arbitration by implementing international conventions on the recognition and enforcement of foreign arbitral awards and by adopting model laws on international commercial arbitration.[4] There have been centres established to provide support and supervision for domestic and international arbitration. There also has been increased attention given to the education and training that arbitrators need.

However, there are four other developments in arbitration that are worth noting in more detail. These developments are significant because

---

4   The international arbitration statutes adopted by Canada and the provinces and territories are modelled on the *Convention on the Recognition and Enforcement of Foreign Arbitral Awards* (adopted by the United Nations Conference on International Commercial Arbitration, 1958) and the UNCITRAL *Model Law on International Commercial Arbitration* (adopted by the United Nations Commission on International Trade Law, 1985).

they are examples of the ways in which the arbitration process may position itself to be a major dispute resolution player outside of its more traditional uses in labour, commercial, and international trade disputes.

1) Rent-a-Judge

California and other U.S. states are generally given credit for popularizing the concept of channelling disputes, primarily of a commercial nature, to private referees or arbitrators. Under these initial schemes, parties to a dispute would agree to petition the court for an order submitting their dispute to a referee. The referees, who were typically retired judges, could hear the dispute at a convenient place and time. The referee's report would be filed with the court and essentially then be treated as a judgment of the court. The early goals of these reference procedures were primarily directed at permitting inexpensive and expeditious settlements of disputes.

However, with enhancements made to the rules and procedures under which arbitrations take place, private judging did not need to depend on court approval for its viability. As a result, there has been some proliferation of California's rent-a-judge experiment in which organizations or individuals, often legally trained and having judicial experience, offer an adjudicative alternative to the courts. In essence, this development promotes private arbitration as an effective, efficient, and viable option to the traditional litigation process for all types of disputes.

Seeing arbitration as a readily accessible process option for dispute resolution of the widest array of problems is what really may distinguish rent-a-judge offerings in the ADR field. Although arbitration in the modern ADR era will continue to play an important role in its comfortable labour, commercial, and international enclaves, the promulgation of an adjudicative system that promises to deliver all the benefits associated with arbitration for a broad cross-section of disputes is a major development. Whether the dispute involves disagreement over damages in a motor vehicle accident or medical malpractice case, the interpretation of a clause in a contract, questions over the sale of stocks by a brokerage firm, who gets what when spouses separate, or what style of fence is chosen by neighbours for the common property line, any of these disputes could be submitted to a private arbitrator for decision if the disputants viewed adjudication as the preferred dispute resolution method. The disputes suitable for this type of private judging would not necessarily need to be private in nature. Any civil case that judges now hear could be decided by a private arbitrator, particularly if that arbitrator was a former judge. Although there might likely be some hesitation in transferring complete jurisdiction on public policy grounds for certain cases, these limits would not need to be unduly inhibiting if the disputants are themselves in agreement on using this particular type of process.

Of course, criticisms can be directed at rent-a-judge programs. They can be seen as promoting a two-tiered system of justice much as has been happening in health care. For the wealthy, there will be speedy access to accomplished arbitrators who can provide all the natural justice that is needed for the parties to feel they have had a fair and impartial hearing. For those who cannot afford this private process, there will have to be resort to the courts with their delays, costs, and other ills for many adjudicated decisions. Keeping justice private also may inhibit the systemic changes that can occur when courts make their decisions public. Judicial precedents often shape the future behaviour of individuals and organizations. Court cases can be the impetus for new and improved governmental legislation and policy. The common law —the law developed and applied by the courts — is an important source of the ways in which individuals in society order their affairs. The remedial dimension of the public lawsuit may be lost, diminished, or at least delayed if litigants and their lawsuit are diverted in large numbers to private arbitrators. The public review of judges and their decision making, often revealing and provocative, also would likely be absent or at least privatized in the arbitration process. The privacy and confidentiality that cloaks arbitration would mean that any concerns about adjudicator bias, insensitivity, or inappropriate behaviour would essentially be left to the parties themselves to handle. In some situations, leaving the monitoring of arbitrator competencies to market forces may be effective. But in other cases, the subtle and nuanced concerns about adjudicative decision making may never be raised in an arbitration hearing.

The extent to which private judging develops further will depend on various factors. Is there a supply of quality arbitrators? Do the relevant rules for arbitration provide an effective and efficient dispute resolution process? Can the disputants afford to rent-a-judge? How will the criticisms of private adjudicative programs be addressed? However, the role that private judging plays in modern alternative dispute resolution developments also will depend on its impact on the courts. Private judging initiatives are essentially private courts or commercial chambers. As these private arbitration processes expand, they will come into more direct competition with the courts. While the demand for court time is presently high, the pressures on, and criticisms of, the courts that gave rise to alternative dispute resolution in the first place are likely to continue. The increasing availability and marketing of an alternative adjudicative mechanism that is, in essence, a streamlined version of the courts and that even uses retired judges may spawn judicial resistance in much the same manner that mediation first caused some legal backlash. The end result may be that the two offerors of justice, one public, the other private, will share the adjudicative pie. Alternatively, the ADR-inspired changes that are taking place in court systems and discussed in chapter 8 — particularly those procedures that allow for flexibilities in procedures and summary or expedited judgments — may make many privatized justice options redundant or less attractive when compared with the public disputing system.

2) Public Arbitration Models

In contrast to private judging developments, there also have been advancements in public arbitration models. Public arbitration can be defined as any government-mandated or government-provided adjudicative process outside of the courts. This definition, on its face, would include the mass of administrative agencies and tribunals that are called upon daily to adjudicate thousands of disputes covering matters such as cable rates, human rights, refugee status, welfare benefits, and more. Several developments in dispute resolution involving administrative bodies are discussed in chapter 6, "ADR in Practice." Although the dispute resolving functions of administrative agencies have been the subject of ADR's scrutiny, there also has been interest in the potential for establishing public arbitration schemes for disputes that might otherwise end up in the courts for adjudication. The example of landlord and tenant disputes demonstrates the kind of general ADR goals that can underlie the public policy decision for this type of dispute resolution arrangement. This example also illustrates the possibilities for a greater growth of this kind of public dispute resolution mechanism.

In many jurisdictions, legislation prevents landlords and tenants who have a tenancy dispute from going to court. To have the dispute adjudicated, the matter must be referred to an arbitrator or referee for resolution. The conflict might involve the responsibility for damages to residential premises, the obligation of the landlord to provide appropriate heating and lighting, pets, the number of tenants permitted to reside in an apartment, the level of noise allowed, establishing grounds for eviction or proving damages for wrongful eviction. Where rental accommodation exists, these and other kinds of disputes between landlord and tenant, tenant and tenant, tenant and neighbour, and the other combinations of parties are regular occurrences. There also could be controversies of a larger scale that involve governments or agencies responsible for housing, human rights, or other residential tenancy-related matters. When the money involved in these disputes was small, small claims courts were a possible adjudicative forum into which the disputes could be taken if the disputants were not able to work out a satisfactory solution on their own. But the problems with using the courts to resolve residential tenancy disputes were much the same ones as other parties experienced when using the courts. Although costs in small claims courts would be lower than in superior courts, time was still a huge hurdle. A landlord, whose other tenants were complaining about the excessive noise coming from a certain suite, could not afford to wait six or eight months or even longer to get an order that the noise was unlawful. A needy tenant could not wait several months or longer to find out whether the damage deposit was wrongly retained. In addition to the delay in individual cases, opening up the courts to hear innumerable landlord-tenant cases also meant that other types of cases in small claims court would experience a consequential type of delay. Channelling landlord-tenant disputes into public arbitration created an opportunity not only to eliminate delay in particular cases but also to free up court time to concentrate on the other cases before the court.

The exact details of the public arbitration models that exist for landlord and tenant disputes may vary but the essential attributes of arbitration are constant. A third party in a relatively informal atmosphere hears arguments from the parties and then renders a binding decision. The arbitrator will usually be appointed by the state. He or she might be a person with a legal background or have familiarity with residential tenancy affairs. In many cases the arbitrator is chosen for the ability to be a trusted decision maker. In other words, because of the person's background and experience, it is likely that he or she will be able to conduct a fair hearing and make an order that is consistent with existing laws and applicable norms. The requirement for a full-fledged judge with a legal background is not normally needed or seen to be needed for these types of problems.

The goals behind this public arbitration approach to landlord and tenant disputes usually relate to speed, cost and credibility. As mentioned, handling these types of disputes in the courts would, in almost every case, be too slow and perhaps too costly. Even the simplest matter would be able to use up significant court time. Arbitration provides opportunities for a more time-efficient dispute resolution process because many formal procedures of the courts, both before and during adjudication, can be dropped or amended. Evidentiary quarrels that can erupt in the court can be avoided by relaxing the rules of evidence in the arbitration. Even the full panoply of procedures that might normally occur in arbitration can be revised if speed is a major process objective. Pre-trial discovery can be jettisoned or kept to a succinct written statement to save time. Cost savings can follow the time efficiencies, and the public support of the system can eliminate or reduce the costs borne by the disputants, depending on the level of user fees. If the dispute requires the involvement of lawyers in landlord-tenant disputes because the money is important, the questions are legal, or the client otherwise needs legal representation, the costs will increase, but the truncated procedures in residential tenancy arbitrations do not have to make this dispute resolution process inaccessible because of legal fees. Finally, the credibility or public acceptability of landlord-tenant arbitration schemes can depend on many factors. But if the system is running well administratively, has credible arbitrators, allows some access to the courts as discussed above, meets modest requirements for fairness in procedure, and provides answers at a reasonable cost to disputants in a timely way, there is generally no outcry that public arbitration is not appropriate.

State-provided or public arbitration may gnaw at the concept of arbitration as a private contractual process and seem out of step with the right of self-regulation that accompanies the flexibility of arbitration. Public arbitration may also be seen as an example of second-class justice where the frequent users can have significant advantages over the one-time participants. However, using state power to mandate public arbitration as the preferred ADR approach for large classes of disputes raises one other related concern. What will be the policy goals that determine whether a particular group of disputes must go before a public arbitrator? The articulated answer to the question — speed, cost saving, peace, or other — will inevitably create a tension with other goals that might also be put forward for dispute resolution. Will the move to be fast jeopardize justice that might be achieved if more time were taken for discovery? Is the desire to have the dispute resolved more important than one or both of the disputant's desire to spend more time and money in conflict? Do the social and economic costs of imposing arbitration exceed the benefits, particularly where the benefit is mostly money. Which factors influence a policy to move to state-provided or mandated arbitration are bound to depend on the many factors that can shape government or organizational policy. Many types of disputes might be eligible for this type of dispute processing. Choices to make public arbitration the sole adjudicative mechanism for a certain class of disputes is part of, and related to, other ADR developments.

3) Hybrid Arbitration Processes

A third development in arbitration illustrates the benefits of viewing arbitration as a flexible process that need not be restrained completely by its adjudicatory foundation. In some cases hybrid processes have been developed that merge arbitration with other ADR techniques to provide more responsive, efficient, and effective dispute resolution. Three examples are mediation-arbitration, the mini-trial and circle sentencing.

a) Mediation-Arbitration

In mediation-arbitration or med-arb, consensual decision making and adjudication are combined in one process. The process commences as a mediation of a dispute by a neutral third party. If the mediation does not succeed, the third party takes on the role of arbitrator and imposes a decision upon the parties. Typically, the decision is binding. This approach has some obvious advantages. Rather than having to re-educate the arbitrator or reintroduce evidence, the parties from a failed or stalled mediation can go directly by agreement or legislation to arbitration. They can recast the mediator as arbitrator who could then, potentially, substantially shorten any adjudicative process. Whether the arbitration would involve process steps other than the making of the arbitrator's decision would depend on the mediation-arbitration rules established. In certain med-arb cases, the arbitrator might have heard enough in mediation. Other circumstances may require resorting to a more fully fledged arbitration hearing to reflect the change from a collaborative settlement focus to a much more adversarial process. In these latter cases, there would still be opportunities for some time and cost savings. There would be benefits associated with each of these processes, as well as the additional advantage of the parties themselves often creating and agreeing to the rules of how this process would be played out. Some disadvantages are obvious: the tendency to be wary of a mediator who might turn instantly into your judge, the potential intrusions into mediator neutrality, the character and skills needed to wear the dual hats, laws about confidentiality when the confidential listener becomes the decision maker and other worries about role incompatibilities. However, the creativity in combining such disparate disputing methods, active in small claims cases in New Zealand to big business dealings in New York, begins to hint at the endless possibilities for consciously adding structure to dispute processing in ways that disregard rigid boundaries to the major disputing methods. Mediation-arbitration also shows the strengths that an arbitration process can bring when paired with other disputing processes.

b) The Mini-Trial

The mini-trial, discussed further in chapter 6, provides another mirror into arbitration's flexible make-up. The mini-trial was developed by the Center for Public Resources (CPR) in New York as an aid for large corporations involved in complex and potentially costly disputes. In a mini-trial, typically the disputants' lawyers or representatives will make submissions to a panel of the disputants' key decision makers, and, if seen as helpful, to a neutral third party. The submissions can include the oral examination of witnesses. The neutral third party might render a non-binding advisory opinion on the merits of the case. This process allows the senior representatives of the disputants to see the strengths and weaknesses in their respective cases and to make an informed decision regarding settlement. Rules of Court in some jurisdictions also can provide for a mini-trial of different sorts to be held. For example, the British Columbia Rules of Court provide "where a judge or master orders or directs that the parties attend a mini-trial, the parties shall attend before a judge or master who shall, in camera and without hearing witnesses, give a non-binding opinion on the probable outcome of a trial of the proceeding."[5] Depending on the form it takes, a mini-trial can combine advocacy, negotiation, mediation, and non-binding arbitration to determine whether settlement is possible. With the inherent flexibility in the mini-trial process where the parties themselves decide on the general procedure, there are many ways in which the legal advocacy, the panel as negotiators and the neutral third party might interact to achieve a broad range of disputant goals beyond saving time and money. The non-binding opinion might be used to jump-start the negotiations. The neutral third party might act more like a mediator than an arbitrator. However, the use of arbitration-like features in the mini-trial is another tribute to the shifting way in which an arbitral process can be employed creatively in a hybrid ADR process.

c) Circle Sentencing

Circle sentencing may be an example of arbitration's earliest roots if this idea is correctly attributed to the communal disputing traditions of Aboriginal peoples in which elders often were the final arbiters of tribal disputes. Circle sentencing practices vary and there can be no precise or all-inclusive definition.[6] Essentially, circle sentencing is an attempt

---

5   British Columbia, Rules of Court, r. 35(5), B.C. Reg. 221/90, as amended.

6   For a judicial account of sentencing circles, see B.D. Stuart, "Sentencing Circles: Making 'Real Differences'" in J. Macfarlane, ed., *Rethinking Disputes: The Mediation Alternative* (Toronto: Emond Montgomery, 1997) at 201. See also chapter 6.

to add more dispute resolution goals to those already being pursued in the criminal justice system or improve the chances of achieving already set objectives. Instead of having a judge in court impose a sentence on an accused person convicted of, or pleading guilty to, a crime, circle sentencing alters the decision-making process. A circle of people would be formed to hear and decide or advise what should happen next. The people in the circle might be the victims of the person's crime, community members interested in criminal justice, community elders, members of the accused's or victim's family, the judge who heard the case, lawyers or others.

Circle sentencing can be viewed as adding arbitration features to the traditional adjudicative functions of a judge alone. Instead of important decisions being made by the judge, these decisions or persuasive opinions on these decisions are made by individuals who have been selected because of their abilities to contribute constructively to the dispute resolution process. If a defining feature of arbitration is the presence of a neutral third-party decision maker outside the formal confines of a courtroom, the participants in the circle, who listen to relevant matters and then decide or advise, fit an arbitration-type mould.

4) Mandatory Arbitration Clauses

The potential benefits of arbitration over litigation have spurred interest in the idea of making arbitration mandatory when there is a claim arising out of a contract. In other words, when parties enter into a private contract, they also agree to include a binding arbitration clause that not only can require the parties to resort to arbitration but also can establish the rules of procedure to be followed. For example, the arbitration clause can set out where the arbitration must take place, limit recourse to the courts on appeal, and set out procedural safeguards. The arbitration clause could require all or only selected future disputes to be arbitrated under the rules of a popular or hand-picked arbitration organization. Accordingly, binding arbitration clauses are becoming a more common feature in banking, insurance, health care, communication, and other types of service contracts, as well as showing up in agreements for the purchase of consumer goods.

This type of pre-dispute agreement appears unproblematic where the parties to the contract actually agree on the form of the mandatory arbitration provisions. The parties who have consented to this type of arrangement are resorting to a form of preventative dispute resolution, agreeing in advance that arbitration and its benefits will be the preferred process. However, there can be worries when the contract terms providing for mandatory arbitration are contained in a form contract and the issue of contractual consent is disputed. In *Allied-Bruce Terminix Companies. Inc. v. Dobson*,[7] the United States Supreme Court overrode a state consumer protection statute that made written pre-dispute arbitration agreements invalid and unenforceable. The Dobsons had purchased a house that had been inspected for termites. Although the extermination company pronounced the house free of termites, the Dobsons found the house "swarming" with them. They sued for damages in state court but Allied-Bruce moved to enforce an arbitration clause in the service contract. The Supreme Court found that the state law did not override section 2 of the *Federal Arbitration Act (FAA)*, which provides that written agreements to arbitrate "shall be valid, irrevocable, and enforceable, save upon such grounds as exist at law or in equity for the revocation of any contract."[8] Although the case turned, in part, on the constitutional coverage of the *FAA* (the transaction in question was substantially interstate commerce), the Court in Allied-Bruce reaffirmed its previous endorsements of arbitration as a mode of dispute resolution[9] and made it difficult for states to impose any requirements on arbitration clauses even as consumer protection responses.

The use and expansion of mandatory arbitration clauses in the consumer context will need to respond to the criticism of unfairness. Companies may resort to mandatory arbitration clauses because this dispute resolution device can give businesses the advantages of arbitration already alluded to in the event of a dispute. However, the advantages may not accrue equally to both the business and the individual consumer in cases where the business is an experienced repeat player, the arbitrator is selected only by the business, the forum of the arbitration is inconvenient to the consumer, and, fundamentally, the consumer has not participated in the construction of the clause.[10] Apart from legal questions as to whether the mandatory arbitration clause will form a part of the contract if it was not brought to the consumer's attention, there will be disputes about the fairness in businesses man-

---

7   513 U.S. 265 (1995).

8   *Federal Arbitration Act*, 9 U.S.C. 2 (1994).

9   See *Gilmer v. Interstate/Johnson Lane Corp.*, above note 3 (an employment form contract provided for mandatory arbitration between employer and employee. Gilmer, fired when he was sixty-two years old, was unable to sue the employer under the *Age Discrimination in Employment Act*).

10   For a recent comment, see J. Senderowicz, "Consumer Arbitration and Freedom of Contract: A Proposal to Facilitate Consumers' Informed Consent to Arbitration Clauses in Form Contracts" (1999) 32 Colum. J.L. & Soc. Probs. 275.

dating this type of dispute resolution process and the eventual enforceability of such clauses to finally handle consumer complaints.

D. ARBITRATION KNOWLEDGE AND SKILLS

Much the same as for negotiation and mediation, a certain knowledge and a range of skills are needed to participate effectively in arbitration. For the disputants and their representatives, while dependent on the goals being pursued in the arbitration, the knowledge and skills will be primarily related to effective advocacy. The pre-hearing preparation, the discovery, the presentation of evidence, the cross-examination, and the arguments are mostly carried on in a classical adversarial pattern. There may be occasions where the job-site, boardroom, or dispute-specific arbitration, despite its name, resembles mediation or negotiation more than arbitration and the adversarial approach could be suitably tempered. Also, as discussed, there will be many arbitrations in which the adversarial zealousness commonly displayed in the courtroom and the associated behaviour of the parties will be less in evidence so that the process can be fast, inexpensive, and, as far as possible, satisfying. But essentially in arbitration, the parties and their representatives will be concerned with good advocacy.

On the other hand, a competent arbitrator will be thinking about how to be a good judge for the parties, which can be a difficult job. However, having competent decision makers as arbitrators is not a new thought. In fact, an advantage of arbitration is that in many circumstances, an expert familiar with the subject matter of the dispute can be placed in the arbitrator's chair. This qualification, combined with cases where the parties actually agree on who the arbitrator will be, means that as much as possible, competency to make a credible arbitral award is assured. Yet, as arbitration takes on a higher profile as a well-used and accessible dispute resolution process, more attention will likely focus on arbitrator training. What are the knowledge and skills needed by a competent arbitrator? Do the knowledge and skills depend on the type of arbitration and the goals being pursued? Are the knowledge and skills any different than what a judge needs in court? This latter question arises inevitably as private arbitrators handle cases that would, except for the parties' choice of venue, be decided in court.

The concern for arbitration is that, heretofore, the arbitration and judicial worlds had been reasonably separate. Except for the court's appeal, review, and reference jurisdiction over arbitration cases, arbitration and courtroom litigation kept to themselves. Motor vehicle accident cases went to court. Baseball salary disputes were arbitrated. Some business conflicts were decided by judges but many ended up in arbitration. The expanded concept of arbitration as an appropriate process for almost any kind of problem can create more of a competitive tension between arbitration and courtroom adjudication, especially if the arbitrators and advocates are non-lawyers. Worries about the abilities of arbitrators could be a legitimate concern as the quasi-judicial process of arbitration expands.

The knowledge and skills needed to be a good judge in arbitration, much like in negotiation and mediation, would be difficult to list. Although arbitrators in many contexts can receive training in adjudicating as do judges, there has been limited attention given to a thorough analysis of what arbitrators need to know and be able to do to judge. Much like judges, the appointment of arbitrators has been largely linked to their past reputation and what in that reputation indicates that the person would be a good decision maker. Certainly, all arbitrators, like judges, need to be able to conduct a fair hearing. They must also understand the various laws or principles that are relevant to the decision and to the hearing. Finally, arbitrators must apply these laws or principles to the facts of the case and then decide.

The knowledge and skills necessary to undertake any of these tasks will vary from context to context. A fair hearing may be well defined in a typical labour arbitration and can always include such steps as issuing subpoenas to witnesses, allowing cross-examination and written submissions and ruling on adjournments and objections. The arbitration of a tenant-landlord dispute over soiled carpet may be perceived as fair but lack all of the above procedural protections. The arbitrator needs to know the elements of fairness or due process that are required in the specific case.

However fair is understood, conducting a fair hearing requires additional arbitrator skills. Sometimes the implementation can be straightforward once the procedure is clarified. Giving a party the opportunity to be heard may be accomplished by just asking for oral or written submissions. However, determining what is fair can sometimes be a difficult decision as new types of disputes engage the arbitration process or as fairness demands begin to have an adverse impact on desired arbitration goals. For example, will allowing cross-examination or lawyers to be present provide a better result? Getting through the process can be tricky for the arbitrator.

Knowing what laws or principles apply also can be challenging. If a lawyer is appointed as arbitrator, there would not be any general concern that the new appointee did not have a grasp of the relevant substantive and procedural law. Lawyers' experience in the law is actually what equips them with the requisite legal knowledge to conduct fair hearings and make sound decisions. Non-lawyer arbitrators would require some education and experience to come up to the legal standard, and the lack of law might be a determining factor in the choice of arbitrator where the rule of law was a dominating force in the dispute. However, in arbitrations where formal law may be less important, and even in arbitrations where law plays a critical role, non-legal acumen may be the real key to arbitrator competency. A philosophy of labour relations for a region or country may be as important to bring to bear on a question around the decertification of a union as are the formal laws on the subject. The long-term economic foundation for a professional sport and the nature of the working relationship between the owners and players may be paramount concerns for an arbitrator although lip service will be paid to the strict legal notion of contract which might be relevant in the individual arbitration. The national reputation of a university in all its permutations may be a more essential ingredient of an arbitrator's decision than the strict legal interpretation of the tenure document when determining whether a senior faculty member, convicted of an indictable criminal offence, should be fired. Identifying, understanding, and applying these extralegal considerations to the decision-making process are important tasks for arbitrators.

Finally, arbitration is an adjudicative process and arbitrators must decide. Some decisions are easily made. The precedent may be so clear or the facts so obvious that any opposing point of view to the arbitrator's decision is perverse or patently unreasonable. An obvious choice is not likely to be challenged on appeal. But when the process yields a possible decision that is not quite perverse, not so unreasonable, or balanced with an opposing point of view, how do arbitrators decide? What is required to be a good decision maker when the decision is difficult?

Part of the answer is for the arbitrator to determine why the decision is hard to make. Despite the expertise of the arbitrator, the facts may not be clear. The evidence may be incomplete. The arbitrator may need time to digest the materials and law that have been presented or require further submissions. But, there may be conflicting evidence. Experts may disagree. Issues of credibility may have arisen with respect to one or more witnesses. The precedent may be ambiguous and its application to the facts of the case uncertain. There may be competing legal and policy claims that point to irreconcilable or opposed outcomes. There may be no right answer to the problem and a logical answer may tug at the arbitrator's own sense of justice or other deeply held values.

Recognizing a credibility issue, knowing the experts are in disagreement, or otherwise spotting the difficulty in deciding does not usually end the matter. One person's version of events must be favoured over another. Differences of opinion need to be split or reconciled. The difficulty in making a decision must be overcome by the arbitrator. Sometimes the answer may be to make more inquiries or to look to a wider range of factors that can assist in choosing between competing versions of the facts. Sometimes the answer is in preferring a result that as much as possible fulfils the goals of that particular arbitration process. Often the answer can be a credible compromise because perfect justice is unattainable. Arbitration does its best as do the courts. Giving some sort of logical or other form of reasoning for the result reached that is in general accord with the disputants' and the industry's expectations or norms may be what good arbitrators do best.

The skills involved in making important decisions, whether as a judge or arbitrator, are enormous. It is hard work to conduct a fair hearing, understand and apply the relevant legal and non-legal norms and values, determine and interpret what is relevant, and make a decision in an acceptable way, all when it matters most to the disputants. The movement to more arbitration, with the consequent narrowing of a skills gap between judges and arbitrators, will result in continuing looks at what arbitrators (and judges) do. This examination likely will show that what arbitrators, like negotiators and mediators, need to know and be able to do is highly contextualized.

FURTHER READINGS

ALVAREZ, H.C., "The Role of Arbitration in Canada — New Perspectives" (1987) 21 U.B.C. L. Rev.

COULSON, R., "The Decisionmaking Process in Arbitration" (1990) 45 Arbitration J. 37

FAURE, J.E., "The Arbitration Alternative: Its Time Has Come" (1985) 46 Mont. L. Rev. 199

HURLBURT, W.H., "New Legislation for Domestic Arbitrations" (1992) 21 Can. Bus. L.J. 1

MCNEIL, I.R., American Arbitration Law: Reformation, Nationalization, Internationally (New York: Oxford University Press, 1992)

RAYNER, W.B., "Arbitration: Private Dispute Resolution as an Alternative to the Court" (1984) 22 U.W.O. L. Rev. 33

CHAPTER 6

ADR IN PRACTICE

A. INTRODUCTION

For many of the same reasons that make the meaning of alternative dispute resolution complex and ambiguous, ADR in practice defies precise pronouncements. Part of the challenge lies in the fact that the ADR field is rapidly expanding. Many initiatives from legal and non-legal sources, vie for ADR status often without clear coordination. New pilot projects and experiments with ADR labels focus on an increasing number of disputing subject matters. The popularity of ADR also is not confined to a single community, region or country. ADR has made inroads not only in North America but also in England, Australia, New Zealand, Europe, Asia, and South America, not to mention the new frontiers of space and cyberspace.[1] ADR has become an area of practice of enormous magnitude — its sheer size makes description difficult.

More than ADR's scope complicates the task of describing ADR in practice; it also depends on how ADR is defined. Some versions of ADR will be at a higher level, go beyond technique, and be about re-engaging the wisdom. Other understandings of ADR may be less expansive

---

1   For the new frontiers, see K.H. Brockstiegal, "Settlement of Disputes Regarding Space Activities" (1993) 21 J. Space L. 1; and several articles on ADR in Cyberspace in (2000) 15 Ohio St. J. on Dis. Res.

and more constrained. Differing ADR interpretation also will result in varying ways of how the same disputing practice, say a mediation session, is understood, discussed, and evaluated. For these reasons, a description of ADR in practice can be not exhaustive enough for some and too subjective for others.

Despite these words of warning, an overview of several disputing practices in selected settings is a useful and rewarding exercise. This analysis can highlight ADR innovations, compare ADR practices across contexts and point to emerging or dominant ADR themes. A careful look at ADR in practice can aid in understanding why ADR is being used in certain situations and not in others, highlighting ADR strengths and weaknesses in particular applications. A description of ADR practices also can point to the required knowledge and skills that work best in these areas. A critical examination of ADR in practice can further contribute to an appreciation of ADR's meaning and its developing ideology. Each of the following sections provides a general overview of key contextual features that need to be well understood, followed by a description of, and commentary on, several ADR practices in that setting.

B. LABOUR DISPUTES

Labour relations disputes provide a particularly poignant and compelling focus for the study of ADR practice because of the importance and complexity of these types of disputes. The importance of labour disputes is due, in part, to the enormity of the enterprise. There are large numbers of labour participants, both employers and employees. The scope of their activities is wide and labour unrest is a common and frequent event. It is difficult to imagine a subject matter that is more omnipresent. Labour relations disputes are also important because of the significant impact they have on society as a whole. Labour disputes and how they get resolved affect income and employment levels, standards of living, working conditions, health and safety, costs of goods and services, market structures, the distribution of wealth, and so on. As well, labour relations disputes touch more people than just the immediate parties. Strikes, lockouts, layoffs, slow-downs, work stoppages, and even violence, as responses to labour disputes, can impose serious and lasting economic and social consequences on governments, businesses, communities, and many individual members of the public who rely on a stable labour environment for their well-being. Finally, labour relations disputes generally involve parties who are in a continuing relationship, often over an extended period of time. The dynamics of the relationship can be compared to marriage or long-term partnerships. Disputes that occur within these ongoing relationships cannot easily be ignored, and the manner in which they are resolved, or not, can have profound personal repercussions.

Disputes in the labour context are not only very important but also, in a related way, very complex. Government regulation of labour is not always confined to a central or single body. Discrepancies and differences in labour laws among jurisdictions can exist, not only nationally but also internationally. In addition, the various laws that govern labour relations and their disputes are constructed from competing and often conflicting economic, political and social policies. These policies derive from such highly nuanced notions as democracy, capitalism, corporatism, social justice, environmental sustainability, equality, the marketplace, and, more recently, concepts such as free trade, globalization, restraint, recession and deficit reduction. Dispute resolution in such a milieu cannot be ordinary. What is causing the labour dispute can go beyond wages and overtime to fundamental beliefs and values that will define not only the future of labour relations but also the shape of other societal structures. Finally, labour relations disputes are not isolated from the long and global histories of labour movements, trade unionism, collective bargaining practices and related detail. These rich histories and their resulting traditions and influences shape the players and the organizations, the expectations, the hierarchical structures, and the communication lines involved in labour relations worldwide, making labour disputes that much more contextually complicated to understand and to follow.

The importance and complexity of labour relations disputes, not surprisingly, have resulted in considerable attention being given to how these disputes are best resolved. In fact, the modern history of ADR generally and the evolution of mediation in particular often refer to positive influences and even the need for more guidance from established dispute resolution practices in the labour field.

The disputing regimes in place to resolve labour relations disputes, particularly in North America, reflect a palpable tension. This tension revolves around the twentieth-century search for the ideal of labour-management cooperation in dispute resolution and the practical matter that most often labour disagreements are viewed or responded to adversarially, treated as distributional or "dividing up the pie" problems. Much like the contrary notions of adversarial and non-adversarial thinking discussed in chapter 2, the theory of how labour disputes should or could be stands in stark contrast to how labour disputes really are. While the resolution of labour disputes strives for coopera-tion, this effort is made in a decidedly competitive environment.

On the one hand, bargaining or negotiation between employer and employee is, and has long been, an obvious fixture in the resolution of labour disputes. Whether the dispute revolves around attempts to reach a first collective agreement or concerns specific issues between employ-ees and employer during the life of a collective agreement, negotiation is regularly resorted to by the parties. In many cases, legislation requires the parties to engage in "good faith" bargaining before utilizing any other dispute resolution processes. The emphasis on reaching negoti-ated agreements is intended to foster harmonious labour-management relations, minimize disruptions in the workplace, ensure workable agree-ments, and generally avoid the disadvantages associated with non-con-sensual dispute resolution methods and the costs of prolonged labour strife. On the other hand, the general approach to labour negotiations has not normally been characterized by the problem-solving strategies discussed in chapter 3. Labour negotiations are more typically con-ducted in competitive ways using tactics that suit a zero-sum game and an overall attitude designed to maximize gains and minimize losses. Positions are presented; interests are hidden; communications are antagonistic. As a result, it is not uncommon, even predictable, that there will be regular breakdowns in these negotiations and that the res-olution of labour disputes will require, in many cases, more than a reli-ance on direct bargaining among the parties.

If negotiations fail or are not productive, dispute resolution mecha-nisms exist in the labour field that either provide assistance to get the negotiations back on track or offer an acceptable adjudicative process to expeditiously resolve the problem. Both approaches involve the intervention into the dispute of a third-party neutral.

1) Mediation and Conciliation

The labour field has processes in place, some of which are long-standing, to provide negotiating assistance, reinforcing the premium attached to cooperation and consensual decision making. This assistance usually takes the form of conciliation, mediation, or even fact-finding. Labour mediation or conciliation can take place while the parties are still in the process of negotiating a new agreement. More recently, grievance mediation procedures have been developed to respond to particular disputes relating to the interpretation, application, administration, or alleged violation of an existing collective agreement. In some cases, the conciliation or mediation will be compulsory. The disputing parties must go through these assisted negotiations before engaging in any work stoppage or other action, with the conciliator or mediator often being appointed by the responsible government department. Again, the motivation behind these compulsory schemes is to ensure that as much support as possible is provided to the parties to cooperatively reach their own agreement.

The role of the labour conciliator or mediator, whether compulsory or not, can reflect the system's emphasis on, and hope for, negotiated agreements. Unlike mediators in other areas who may be less interventionist regarding the actual outcome, labour conciliators and mediators can often be highly instrumental in shaping the final terms of any agreement and in modelling a more evaluative or activist mediation orientation. Usually these third-party neutrals are trusted by both sides and in many cases the mediators will have extensive backgrounds in labour law or the labour movement. As a result, their views carry weight. Because of their experience and knowledge, labour mediators may make recommendations on how the dispute might best be resolved. Although these recommendations are not necessarily binding and may even be an obvious compromise, a respected labour mediator's suggestions can allow the disputing parties to move from their public positions without losing face or appearing to be weak. In other cases, the labour conciliator, shuttling back and forth between the parties, may have acquired confidential information that indicates a negotiated agreement is possible. For example, the mediator may discover that the union, although publicly demanding a 3 percent increase in wage level, is willing to settle for as little as 1 percent. The company, insisting in public meetings that 0 percent is their final offer, tells the mediator that it would be prepared to go as high as 2 percent. Only the mediator really knows that a settlement is possible and what that settlement or deal might be. Although the mediator cannot disclose this zone of possible agreement, she or he will often encourage, cajole, prompt and push the parties towards that zone of agreement.

2) Adjudication

Adjudication also plays a key role in the resolution of labour disputes. Despite the fundamental distinction between adjudicative processes and consensual processes, labour adjudication is generally intended to complement, not conflict with, the negotiating process. This dispute resolution fit is sought to be achieved in two ways. First, there has been a clear movement away from the adversarialness of the courts to labour relations boards to deal with certain unresolved labour disputes. These specialized administrative tribunals were to be faster and less formal, less costly, and less confrontational than the courts. Although the courts would still maintain jurisdiction respecting board decisions, this jurisdiction was often in the nature of judicial review only, and unless the board's decision was patently unreasonable or otherwise in excess of its jurisdiction, judicial deference to administrative decision making was expected. Second, arbitration was to be regularly used when the parties could not agree on the terms of a collective agreement (interest arbitration) and for disputes arising under an existing collective agreement (grievance arbitration). Although these arbitral processes were again adjudicative in nature, they also were intended to be a natural extension of the negotiation process. If the parties were unable to negotiate an agreement in good faith, an arbitrator experienced in labour matters and often hand-picked by the disputants would give the parties an informal but fair hearing and then render a decision as quickly as possible. The arbitrator's decision would represent, in essence, a neutral third party's opinion of what would have been a reasonable negotiated agreement or which one of the parties' final negotiating positions was most reasonable if final-offer arbitration was used.

Although labour's adjudicative measures were developed to provide a fast, inexpensive, informal, and credible alternative to the courts — while at the same time not damaging labour's long-term relationships — problems common to adjudicative processes persist. What might have been intended as a more mediatory and flexible style of arbitration and decision making seems to have been eclipsed in many jurisdictions by a more adversarial version of arbitration. In practice, labour arbitrations can be unduly legalistic, slow even when expedited, cumbersome, expensive, and conservative, "less a vehicle for developing a 'common law of the shop,' and adjusting the contract to fit unexpected circumstances, than a procedure for transferring income from workers and their employers to arbitration and labour lawyers."[2]

3) Work-Site Strategies

Although the long history of labour dispute resolution has provided inspiration and insight, ADR also has sought to make new contributions to labour's disputing practices. The modern development of grievance mediation; preventative mediation programs (involving the

---

2   Canadian Bar Association Task Force on Alternative Dispute Resolution,
     Alternative Dispute Resolution: A Canadian Perspective (Ottawa: Canadian Bar
     Association, 1989) at 11.

permanent use of mediators on a work site to help develop communication between employers and employees so that future problems are better handled); quality of working life programs (QWL — to encourage employee involvement in workplace design, task assignments and other work-related decisions); and employee ombudsperson programs (to resolve or manage work-site issues not covered by collective agreements) can all be linked to the general ADR movement.

4) Mutual Gains Approach

There also have been efforts to alter collective bargaining behaviour by introducing mutual gains strategies into labour negotiations. "Mutual gains" is another way of saying win-win and mirrors an interest-based or principled approach to negotiation rather than a separate or distinct negotiation orientation. The assumptions behind this ADR initiative are that the chief obstacle to win-win agreements in labour disputes is a lack of certain negotiating skills and knowledge on the part of the negotiators at the bargaining table, and that labour disputes include issues and elements that clearly lend themselves to an integrative solution. Given the increasing economic pressures felt by companies competing in a more international marketplace, the benefits generally associated with interest-based bargaining would accrue not only to the direct participants in labour disputes but also to the many parties adversely affected by unresolved labour strife.

There are examples of successes in mutual gains approaches to labour disputes,[3] as well as increasing instances of training in mutual gains techniques and the facilitation of actual labour negotiations. However, there also are suggestions that interest-based bargaining in the labour context "is intuitively nonsensical, despite the appeal of the claim."[4] Although skills training and active facilitation may continue to occur, the notion will tend to degenerate over time, the argument goes, because these ADR interventions seek to change labour-negotiating behaviours while disregarding the very structures that determine the nature of these behaviours.

A closer look at the context of labour negotiations reveals fundamental and long-established features that present challenges to mutual gains approaches. In practice, the course of most labour negotiations is

---

3   C. Heckscher & L. Hall, "Mutual Gains and Beyond: Two Levels of Intervention" (1994) 10 Negotiation J. 235. Also see R. Paquet, I. Gaétan and J.G. Bergeron, "Does Interest-Based Bargaining Really Make a Difference in Collective Bargaining Outcomes? (2000) 16 Negotiation Journal 281.

4   *Ibid.*

heavily constrained by factors beyond the bargaining table. Labour negotiators represent a constituency whose members normally are not at the table. Effective communication with these constituencies and getting instructions or mandates on short notice can be difficult, particularly during the actual negotiations. Labour negotiators must also represent multiple views. The success of the negotiations and even the careers of the negotiators depend on a majority of these views being satisfied. But these views can often be conflicting and unclear. This negotiating infra-structure therefore tends to encourage positional bargaining with a focus on a few clear and simple issues. Major movements are difficult to make. Inventing creative new options at the bargaining table, which principled negotiators do, can be unrealistic. The long-time presence of mistrust between labour and management groups and, in some cases, between a constituency group and its own negotiators can nurture more non-cooperative negotiating behaviour. Mutual gains bargaining and its calling for inclusive language, if not well understood and endorsed, can exacerbate the level of mistrust. Whereas the use of negotiating teams in labour disputes can provide effective links back to union or manage-ment members, negotiating teams lined up physically on opposite sides of the table can emphasize divisions and discourage the expression of internal differences. The need to maintain team coherence and solidarity makes offer and counter-offer and demands and rejected demands nor-mal negotiating behaviour as opposed to the more open dialogue asso-ciated with mutual gains bargaining and interest identification.

In a related way, all labour negotiations are also, at a basic level, about power structures in the workplace. Part of what determines power in the workplace is the distribution of the economic returns of produc-tion in the form of profits, wages, benefits, working conditions and so on. Minimum wage laws, health and safety standards, and other labour laws predetermine in some cases the costs of production and how the economic power is to be shared. But in labour relations, more often than not, there will still exist a great deal of discretion and uncertainty around how the pie is best divided, particularly in new and developing indus-tries and businesses. In addition, developing understandings of deficit reduction, free trade, global competition, and new technologies that give companies the ability to move their capital and production to locations around the world with lower labour costs and no organized workforce, add to the uncertainty around who gets what. Labour negotiations are, in part, directed at clarifying this economic uncertainty for the life of any agreement and, in some cases, much longer.

In addition to determining economic power, modern labour nego-tiations are equally concerned with structural power — the power to make decisions. Although much weight rides on the essentially economic terms of the collective agreement such as wage rates, salary caps, job security, and the like, perhaps more important are the explicit and implicit issues about who has the power to make or impose these economic decisions. Labour negotiations clear this up or at least signal the different strengths that labour and management can bring to bear on decision making. The union may use the threat of a strike or other job action to obtain an acceptable agreement. The company may rely on superior economic resources or threats to shut down operations to persuade the union to agree. Management may go to court to seek injunctive relief or consider dismissing non-unionized professional employees who are attempting to influence stalled salary negotiations by withholding their services. Both sides may use the media to garner public support. Although these negotiating tactics are designed to achieve substantive results, they also can forcefully demonstrate who has the stronger voice in the negotiation and who might prevail in future decision-making processes. Labour negotiations can say as much about decision-making power as they do about money.

Mutual gains bargaining will be challenged to address the power dynamics at work in labour negotiations. This is not to suggest that sharing information, mutual respect, open dialogue, and understanding interests cannot be part of a labour negotiation. But fundamental or even incremental changes in the economic and decision-making power structures that often are at the foundation of labour disputes are difficult to reach by consensus, except grudgingly and adversarially. These types of profound structural or value changes are more likely to be imposed by legislation, by more unilateral acts or threatened acts on the part of one side or the other, if possible, or through some type of adjudicative mechanism rather than ADR processes stressing cooperation and consensus.

C. FAMILY FIGHTS

The family can conjure up many images, one being that of loving relationships. But another equally compelling picture that comes to mind is the image of a fight. In families, there are fights between parents and children about curfews, clothing, and cars; about music, drugs, and sex; and about respect and responsibility. Siblings fight over attention, television and sharing. Spouses or partners fight about money and more. There are increasingly heated fights about the meaning of the family and who is entitled to enjoy the benefits commonly associated with being a family member in a society.

When families change, more fights ensue. Family members fight about inheritance and the cost of nursing homes, about independence, about childhood and elder abuse, about maintaining traditions in a new society. The decision to end a family relationship can result in further fights over child custody, support payments, and division of property, which often precipitate or depend on factual fights about who did what to whom during the relationship. When blended families emerge from divorcing families, there can be fights over who is mom and who is dad and a whole host of other matters.

Family fights, whatever the focus, take many courses. They can be highly public or held behind closed doors. Some are short and sweet, while others can seem as long or violent as a war.

Much like labour disputes, the resolution of family disputes had attracted considerable attention well before the modern emergence of ADR. This attention was partly attributable to the pervasiveness of these disputes, particularly those disputes related to divorce and separation whose rates had soared in the 1970s and 1980s in North America. Family disputes also were likely to be highly emotionally charged. Whether it was over the children or the visionware, the boyfriend or the tattoo, the car or the condom, anger, upset, frustration, despair, resentment, guilt, rage or other strong feelings would commonly be a part of the search for solutions around these controversies in the family. The expression of such feelings would sometimes help but often emotional outbursts would disrupt discussions or encourage destructive disputing behaviours. Although a few family fights might be obvious test cases with their resolution providing guidance and precedents for future events, most family disputes were intensely private and personal. They were disputes about what mattered most in people's lives — relationships, children, security, well-being, happiness, community, values and more. In these charged settings, the potential for irreparable harm was always present, particularly for the least powerful family members. And so in family disputes, children were often caught in the middle and hurt, and women — more than men — suffered physically and economically. In many cases, the family disputants could not simply walk away from the problem or treat a resolution as the end of the matter in the same way that might occur for the disputants in a motor vehicle accident case or for a retailer writing off a bad debt. The best interests of the children, economic and emotional ties and cultural constraints, often meant that a continuing relationship between family disputants was a necessary requirement in any satisfactory solution.

Finally, unresolved or poorly resolved family disputes were also a threat to a society at large that counted on family stability to help maintain other social orders and structures. Effective, efficient, and lasting dispute resolution for family matters was an important affair.

Although all these reasons explain the interest in family dispute resolution, they also begin to disclose the challenges associated with constructing disputing mechanisms for these types of conflicts. Family disputes were widespread, over anything and everything, heated and highly personal, often the powerful against the least powerful, and mirroring obvious and ignored systemic inequalities in society. These disputes were complicated to unravel, difficult to understand and predict, at times seemingly never-ending, and yet their satisfactory resolution was almost always of critical importance to the disputing partners, their children, friends and the surrounding community.

Before the modern emergence of ADR, there was a heavy reliance in many quarters on formal systems of justice and legal resources for the resolution of these myriad family fights. Family disputes, along with motor vehicle accidents, would commonly account for the largest percentage of all cases heard by the courts. Many more family conflicts would find their way into lawyers' offices to be settled out of court or quite often on the courthouse steps. Although these cases were not adjudicated by judges, they depended on the hallmarks of the justice system for their eventual outcomes — adversarial bargaining, legal precedents and formal enforcement mechanisms.

Although the extensive use of courts, judges and lawyers was a common feature of family dispute resolution in North America, this approach attracted a great deal of criticism despite efforts, such as specialized family courts and family court judges, to make litigation more sensible and sensitive for family disputants. Four problems were usually cited, all by-products of an adversarial system. First, court adjudication was too expensive and took too long. Often the assets necessary for the parties to support their children or make new lives for themselves were depleted by the legal costs incurred in lengthy court battles. Second, the results of each court adjudication included, almost always, a winner and a loser. Building a future continuing relationship or maintaining commitments on this win-lose result could be difficult. At times even the winners lost when losers refused to accept or comply with court-ordered solutions. Third, the adversarial nature of court proceedings or lawyer-to-lawyer negotiations would tend to keep parties apart and exacerbate the hard feelings already present in the dispute. As a result, personal tragedies for the parties or their lawyers during litigation became far too common occurrences. And finally, the

answers to child custody and access disputes, support payment controversies, and division of assets questions were seldom black and white.
Even with court-appointed experts, child advocates, legal precedents,
legislative guidelines and other resources, were judges the best persons
to make discretionary calls on matters that often defied a right answer
and on issues that usually displayed more complexity in them than a
formal legal judgment could accommodate?

Despite these challenges, or perhaps because of them, alternative
dispute resolution found a fertile field in family disputes. Claims that
ADR with its emphasis on mediation would relieve court congestion as
well as undue cost and delay, facilitate access to justice, empower the
disputing parties to make their own decisions, and increase the satisfaction of the parties in the outcomes of the disputes seemed to meet
head on the criticisms directed at the court adjudication of family disputes. For these reasons, family disputes were an early and obvious
focus for ADR proponents. In particular, mediation was touted as the
preferred ADR process for family disputants to use.

A review of the various ways in which family mediation is practised
raises a number of interesting questions, some of which reflect issues
around ADR in general. Where are we going with this dispute resolution process? What are its underlying goals? Is family mediation good
for the family or does it disguise a coercive nature? What does family
mediation say is normal, natural and essential about resolving family
fights. Other questions about the practice of family mediation are
extensions of the questions asked of mediation in general. What makes
a family mediator competent? Why is there a preference for interest-
based bargaining in good family mediation? Why is family mediation,
for all its purported benefits, not used more frequently? What is the
ideological picture of mediation that is being painted?

Most of these questions cannot be answered easily or unequivo-
cally. Family mediation is still developing both outside and inside the
formal justice system. Much like the ADR field, many factors are driving this growth — governments wanting to reduce the public costs of
disputing, the burgeoning supply of newly-trained family mediators,
the quest to create a new profession, courts trying to shed unwanted
reputations, and human desires and hopes for a more peaceful future.
The final shape of family mediation practice is not yet settled. However, given the complexity and volatility of family disputes and the significant consequences associated with their resolutions, it is likely that
only a form of mediation that is responsive to the real-life characteristics of family fights will gain the long-term acceptance of the parties
that matter most — the family disputants themselves.

Family mediation cannot be conveniently discussed under any one heading. As discussed in chapter 4, the form and function of mediation will vary from one mediator to another and from one location to another. However, the present practice of family mediators can be better understood by briefly describing four structures within which family mediation practice generally occurs: private, mandatory, court-connected and specialized.

1)　Private Family Mediation

Private family mediators provide mediation services to family disputants usually for a fee. These family mediators may provide comprehensive mediation services for all issues in dispute or they may limit the focus of the mediation to one issue or another such as disputes over property or parenting issues. In private family mediation, unlike other mediation settings, lawyers typically are not present with their clients. This practice is predicated on several ideas. First, solutions reached in family mediation likely will be more satisfying and longer-lasting if the parties themselves without their lawyers present are empowered to work out the details. Second, the issues in family disputes almost always will involve facts or interests that are not always legally relevant but nevertheless are important to the parties and possible outcomes. Finally, the process will be more efficient if lawyer input for the participants is coordinated by the mediator by encouraging the parties to seek independent legal advice (even if the lawyer-mediator is permitted to give legal information or advice[5]) at appropriate times during the course of the mediation.

It is not uncommon for a private family mediator to be a lawyer, social worker, psychologist, psychiatrist, family counsellor, therapist or other person with experience or interest in working with families in crisis. Many professionals, as well as people with varied life experiences see themselves, at times with no specific mediation training, as being able to contribute ideas and skills to effective mediation practices. In addition, helping family members solve problems is, and has long been, a part of many people's work with families. Moving their

---

5　For example, the Family Law Mediation ruling (Appendix 2) in the *Professional Conduct Handbook* of the Law Society of British Columbia defines family law mediation to include the following acts when performed by a lawyer acting as a family mediator: informing participants of the legal issues involved; advising the participants of a court's probable disposition of the issue; and giving any other legal advice.

work into an obvious mediation mode was either a mere matter of semantics or a logical extension of the work. The fact that anyone, in many jurisdictions, can call themselves a family mediator also contributes to the array of backgrounds found in private family mediators.

This multidisciplinary mix of family mediator profiles raises several practice points. First, co-mediation involving mediators with differing skills and experiences can be particularly helpful in family mediation. For example, the lawyer-mediator might be taking the lead in assisting the parties to tell their stories by using familiar questioning techniques. The co-mediator with a master's degree in psychology might be listening and observing during this time to interpret any key non-verbal communication, identify underlying interests, or spot subtle signs that might suggest a power imbalance needs to be addressed. Having coordinated and competent co-mediators with complementary strengths can help considerably to ensure that the family fights being mediated get all the attention they deserve. Second, if co-mediation is not available or affordable, family mediators might specialize along disciplinary lines. Lawyer-mediators might in some cases see their strengths in helping family disputants work out mutually satisfying agreement on what to do about assets and how to arrange financial responsibilities. Family mediators from the helping professions such as social work might be most comfortable working with spouses on parenting responsibilities or exploring reconciliation opportunities. Although agreements in family disputes will eventually need to be comprehensive, channelling specific issues in dispute to family mediators with the requisite knowledge and skills is a common occurrence. Third, the question of qualifications for mediators, discussed in chapter 4, is particularly relevant in family mediation since so many individuals are aspiring or could aspire to be a family mediator. The demand for private family mediation has grown rapidly, but the supply of mediators is generally understood to have eclipsed this growth and, without restrictions, the potential for others to enter the field is great. Although this type of competition in other settings is often encouraged and left to market forces to work out, a great deal of attention in private family mediation has focused on recognizing family mediation as a profession and consequently restricting entry into the profession to those persons with appropriate qualifications. However, for the complex world of family disputes, standardizing the knowledge and skills needed by a competent mediator is a daunting task. Model standards or best practices for private family mediators will continue to emerge, and it is likely that one or two sets of standards prepared by family mediation organizations will come to dominate thinking about what it is that a good family mediator needs to know and be able to do. These standards and the resulting form of family mediation will need to meet the needs and wishes of an enormously diverse group of family disputants if private family mediation is to flourish.

Drawing generalized conclusions about private family mediation can be misleading, but a fly-on-the-wall watching such a mediation take place would normally see a facilitative approach being implemented and the mediator encouraging the parties to use an interest-based or principled negotiation strategy. The reasons for these observations are twofold. First, this mediation philosophy and negotiation orientation are most likely to provide the greatest benefits to the family disputants who have ended up in mediation. These are the family fights that the parties or their lawyers have not been able to resolve by negotiation or other disputing process. The nature of the issues at stake, the emotional climate, and the consequences of failure can combine to point to the obvious rationale for taking a collaborative problem-solving approach. Cooperation, not competition, makes most sense. Second, family mediators are usually trained to follow this path. So the spouse who insists in mediation that access to the children must be curtailed (positional bargaining) is assisted by the skilful mediator to explain her fears, for example, about the influence of a new "girlfriend" on the children so that a solution can be crafted to meet these concerns (a family conference to learn more about each other and guidelines to provide consistency in parenting roles). The approaches taken to mediation may vary in court-connected or specialized settings, but training programs and accompanying ethical standards for private family mediation make an interest-based method of dispute resolution the norm.

2) Mandatory Family Mediation

There are long-standing examples of making mediation mandatory for family disputes.[6] These mandatory mediation models generally prohibit family disputants from proceeding past a certain stage in the formal justice system unless mediation is first attempted. In other words, the courts will not adjudicate until the parties have tried to negotiate a resolution with the assistance of a mediator. This type of mandatory mediation may be required only when child custody or access is in dispute or it may apply on a more comprehensive basis. In Canada, mandatory mediation of family disputes has generally not been promoted.

Imposing mediation on disputing parties may seem at odds with mediation's goal of promoting party autonomy and the philosophy of voluntariness associated with this consensual process of decision making. However, the thinking behind mandatory mediation appears to be based on two assumptions. First, certain disputes will be better off being channelled into mediation before taking further adjudicative and publicly financed steps. Rather than leaving the choice of mediating or not to the individual disputants or their lawyers, mandatory mediation schemes institutionalize an approach to dispute resolution that emphasizes the merits in attempting to reach a consensual resolution before resorting to the costlier, more time-consuming and win-lose characteristics of the civil justice system. For family disputes, mandatory mediation has the potential to eliminate many of the problems associated with this formal adjudication. Second, mandatory mediation will help to reduce court congestion and delays. At a structural level, mandatory mediation could improve the efficiency and effectiveness of the formal justice system by removing a large chunk of cases that would otherwise have to be decided in court.

As discussed further in chapter 8, it is not clear that these outcomes have been achieved. There are certainly cases that have been resolved satisfactorily through mandatory family mediation; however, it is difficult to empirically demonstrate that mandatory mediation has changed settlement rates. Approximately 90 to 95 percent of family cases settle without trial in any event. Whether mandatory mediation produces an earlier, less costly, or better settlement is difficult to say because one never knows what course the dispute might have taken but for the mediation.

Mandatory family mediation also may not have significant impact on court caseloads. To substantially reduce the backlogs and delays associated with going to court, mandatory family mediation would have to either resolve some of the small percentage of these cases that would otherwise go to trial or result in the settlement of family cases on the trial list at a faster rate than is presently the case.

---

6   For details, see H. McIssac, "Mandatory Conciliation Custody/Visitation Matters: California's Bold Stroke" (1981) 19 Conciliation Cts. Rev. 73; D.T. Saposnek, J. Hamburg, C.D. Delano, & L. Michaelsen, "How Has Mandatory Mediation Fared? Research Finding of the First Year's Follow-up" (1984) 22 Conciliation Cts. Rev. 7, 18; J. Orbeton, "California's Answer: Mandatory Mediation of Child Custody and Visitation Disputes" (1985) 1 Ohio St. J. on Disp. Resol. 149; L. Clark & J. Orbeton, "Mandatory Mediation of Divorce: Maine's Experience" (1986) 69 Jud. 310 (1986); L. Silberman & A. Schepard, "Court-Ordered Mediation in Family Disputes: The New York Proposal" (1986) 14 N.Y.U. Rev. L. & Soc. Change 741; N.G. Maxwell, "Keeping the Family Out of Court: Court Ordered Mediation of Custody Disputes under the Kansas Statutes" (1986) 25 Washburn L.J. 203.

There are other concerns about mandatory family mediation. Not all disputes are right for mediation. As discussed in chapter 4, choosing to participate in a consensual decision-making process — most often with the parties being face to face and outside the due process protections afforded by the courts — is an important and complex decision. For many family fights, mediation may make a positive contribution to a highly constructive outcome. Imposing mediation on these disputants may be for their own good. However, for other family disputants, mandatory mediation may be a serious problem. Imbalances of power based on economic, educational, and other systematic inequalities will make private bargaining on a level playing field impossible. Histories of violence and abuse may result in mediation re-victimizing the spouse who has been brave enough to finally leave the oppressive relationship. If a state-imposed mediation requirement seeks to achieve goals such as healing and transformation, mandatory mediation might not mesh with the parties' expectations in cases where they themselves want only to sever their ties or keep their continuing relationship around the children confined to what they decide is needed and legal for their children's best interests.

If family mediation is prescribed by legislation and imposed on disputants, concern for mediator competency usually is not left solely to the private sector to resolve. The usual practice is to develop rosters of mediators from private practice who hold the qualifications that have been determined to be those that a qualified family mediator must possess.

3) Court-connected Conciliation Services

Related to mandatory mediation, court-connected conciliation services allow judges to refer family disputants to mediation services in the middle of a court proceeding or in some cases before the parties ever get to court. Referrals are usually voluntary, at least on their face. The conciliators who deliver the mediation services may be full-time court counsellors who are adding mediation to the other types of assistance they would provide families going through the courts. However, court-connected conciliation programs can rely on existing community agencies, social work students or volunteers to assist families in conflict.

4) Specialized Family Mediation

Although the civil courts are commonly called upon to adjudicate on a wide array of family conflicts, certain conflicts in the family receive special attention. Most jurisdictions have developed specific rules and procedures for dealing with cases of spousal abuse. Other family fights that result in criminal offences such as murder, assault, kidnapping, harassment or theft would be handled by the criminal justice system. Spouses who default on support payments face an increasing number of enforcement mechanisms not usually available to other creditors. When children are involved in family break-ups, privately negotiated separation agreements are subject to approval by a judge to ensure that the interests of the children are protected.

With the explosion of family mediation, it is not surprising that mediation has been used for some family disputes that had previously been given special treatment. One such category of disputes is worth describing briefly as an example of the potential of the mediation process applied to family disputes and the challenges of applying mediation to highly complex family problems.

In some family settings, children are at risk. The risk may come from parents or others who are physically or sexually abusive to the child or from parents or other caregivers who are unable or unwilling to provide the child with the support and resources necessary for the child's healthy development. A family conflict in these situations may exist between spouses or with other family members. But when a child is in need of protection, the conflict also must involve the state. To protect children at risk, jurisdictions normally have legislative schemes in place that allow children in need of protection to be removed from the family setting, that provide an opportunity for an adjudication on whether the child is at risk, and, if the child is at risk, that allow the adjudicator to order alternate care for the child. Because of the severe consequences associated with a wrong decision or, indeed, any decision about a child in need of protection, these disputes inevitably are protracted, emotional, and highly adversarial.

Child protection mediation schemes allow for the mediation of most issues relating to the safety or care of a child who may be at risk, including terms of a plan of care, services to be received by a family, living arrangements for a child, the terms of a supervision or access order, or other similar issues. In British Columbia,[7] there are provisions for a mandatory mediation session or case conference to be held before a date can be set for any contested protection hearing. Judges who have received mediation training conduct these conferences, which are usually attended by the parents, the parents' lawyers, a social worker assigned to the case and a government lawyer. The mediation is

---

7   See the *Child, Family and Community Service Act*, R.S.B.C. 1996, c. 46.

intended to be interest-based and to explore early resolution to the issues surrounding the child apprehension. However, because all child protection cases will not be amenable to consensual resolution, judges have discretion in how they conduct the case conference including making an assessment as to whether to attempt to mediate the conflict at all. Mediation may also occur outside the mandatory case conference. Under the legislation, the parties can also voluntary agree to mediate, in which case a mediator will be chosen from a roster of government-approved mediators.

D. CRIMINAL ACTS

Criminal codes and penal statutes define behaviours and activities that are prohibited in a society and then provide mechanisms to prosecute and punish persons and organizations that allegedly have committed these criminal or quasi-criminal acts. Not surprisingly, at every stage in the criminal justice system, disputes involving the accused, the prosecutor, the state, victims of crime and even the public are frequent. A person accused of a crime denies his or her guilt. The accuracy of the victim's memory is challenged. The admissibility of police wiretap evidence or a confession is contested. Lawyers argue about proof beyond a reasonable doubt. There are charges of police brutality and submissions that an accused's constitutional rights have been violated, such as the right to retain and instruct counsel without delay, to obtain legal aid, to be secure against unreasonable search and seizure, or to have a trial in a reasonable time. Appeals are made that an innocent person has gone to jail, that a sentence is too harsh or too lenient. Minority groups say they are invisible and that the system discriminates. Victims of crime state they want a say in the resolution of criminal prosecutions. The death penalty is opposed or supported.

The resolution of these types of disputes in democratic societies increasingly relies on procedures and principles that attempt to strike a balance between important interests — the protection of individual rights and the preservation of broader social values that sustain a free and democratic society. But the balance is not always easily struck. How much power do the police need to investigate crime? When does free speech become hateful? What are the limits on the right to bear arms? Where is the criminal line drawn and who does the drawing for issues such as abortion and euthanasia? Is an honest mistake a defence to sexual assault? Is self-defence available when a woman shoots her abusive husband in the back of the head? What should the response be when a juror has an affair with the accused? Can a nine-year-old commit a crime? How are retribution, deterrence and rehabilitation balanced in sentencing? Are there ever times when someone should be locked up and the key thrown away?

Criminal dispute resolution is not only a challenge by virtue of the great difficulty in balancing these individual and collective interests that are in themselves complex, often competing, open to interpretation, and, in many instances, still evolving. Finding answers to criminal disputes is also complicated because the answers, almost always, create winners and losers, usually with considerable consequences. An accused person, ultimately, is convicted or acquitted, guilty or not guilty, goes to jail or is set free, loses a job, a family, a place in the community, or not. Even outcomes that might seem less onerous — probation, conditional discharges, community work, electronic monitoring, parole — still carry a good deal of sting, particularly if they come with a hefty legal bill, plenty of publicity or a criminal record. Essentially the mainstream criminal justice system in Western societies has focused on imposing punishment or on granting absolution as its defining moment. Retributive justice has been the norm. As a result, decision making in the resolution of criminal disputes is a weighty matter for all concerned.

The win-lose outcomes of criminal disputes, when paired with the issues in dispute that are complex and controversial, have pushed much criminal dispute resolution to become highly technical, adversarial and legalistic. Contested court cases are common and the presumption of innocence for all accused, whether they did it or not, requires the Crown to prove every element of the offence beyond a reasonable doubt. Defence lawyers are hired to prevent undesirable results from happening if at all possible. Although plea bargains out of court are often made, this consensual form of dispute resolution is still about imposing a penalty or not and the bargainers, usually the prosecutor and the defence lawyer, will be zealously protecting the interests of the constituencies they represent.

Criminal dispute resolution with its emphasis on an adversary system and a reliance on lawyers and judges has suffered, not surprisingly, from all the ailments associated with court adjudication. In criminal cases, there are high legal costs, lengthy delays, protracted proceedings, concerns about accessibility to, and understanding of, the court system and dissatisfaction with court-imposed outcomes. Although legal aid schemes, a clearly stated constitutional right to a speedy trial, Crown disclosure requirements, technology in the courtroom and improvements in case management techniques have reduced costs, saved time and generally improved access to the system, the fundamental features of criminal dispute resolution remain unchanged. The contextual complexity of these matters and the punitive nature of the burdens sought to be imposed on accused persons continue to support a heavy reliance on adversarialism in criminal dispute resolution.

The ways in which criminal disputes are resolved has not been overlooked by ADR proponents. There have been suggestions that there is scope for improvements and reforms in the process of negotiations or plea bargaining that takes place between an accused and the prosecution mindful that "fears of closed door negotiations, arbitrary deals and expediency at the expense of justice may outweigh potential benefits."[8] The negotiation and mediation potential in pre-trial conferences in criminal proceedings also has been explored. This pre-trial procedure brings the accused, the accused's lawyer, and Crown counsel together with an experienced judge with opportunities to exchange information, evaluate issues, and assess outcomes not only to assist in trial efficiency but also, potentially, to promote a settlement of the case. Case management initiatives, technology, and changes in legal aid funding also provide opportunities to improve the ways in which criminal cases are processed. An essential goal of all these developments is to create conditions for more productive and earlier settlement discussions between the prosecutor and the accused's lawyer around the disposition of the case. Rather than maintaining the trial-by-ambush outlook, more open routes to negotiations and private settlements are available.

However, there have been other ADR-inspired efforts to process criminal cases in ways that take them further out of the normal court processes and further emphasize the negotiation and mediation processes.

1) Diversion

In diversion, cases in which criminal charges have been laid — and even in some situations where no charges have yet been approved — are referred or directed to an alternative mechanism for decision making. The decisions are normally around how the accused or wrongdoer will assume responsibility for his actions and not about whether responsibility or guilt is being legally admitted or denied. In diversion programs, negotiation and mediation processes are used to reach these decisions. The parties involved in the process of diversion can include the victim of the alleged crime as well as other involved community members.

---

8   Above note 2 at 17.

2) Victim-Offender Reconciliation Programs

Victim-Offender Reconciliation Programs (VORP) can be either pre-or post-charge and even post-conviction. These programs are a type of diversion but they specifically seek to shape or influence the relationship between offender and victim. The change to the relationship may seem modest. The victim now understands that nothing she said or did contributed to the decision to break and enter her home, or, more monumental, the victim is able to truly forgive the serious offender for what he has done and the offender sees the light and is, as a result, truly rehabilitated. VORP goals can vary depending on program and personnel.

3) Circle Sentencing

In circle sentencing, changes are made to the usual sentencing procedures. Instead of a judge alone imposing a sentence (fine, imprisonment, discharge, electronic monitoring, community service, restitution or other) with certain terms and conditions ($5,000, five years, absolute or conditional, in the home, 1,500 hours, repay the damage or more), a circle of people make contributions to the final outcome. The participants in the circle are there because of their involvement with the case as friends, family, adviser, legal representative or interested community members. Their contribution may be significant although the judge retains both authority and jurisdiction to impose whatever sentence the judge decides. Rather than focus on punishment, the goals of circle sentencing are to bring a wider range of perspectives to the sentencing process and to restore and empower offenders, victims and the community at large.

Stuart J. concludes the process contains the potential to

- engender moral growth among all participants;
- foster positive attitudes about others;
- empower individuals, families and communities to take responsibility for conflict in their lives and constructively resolve differences with others;
- generate innovative, enduring solutions;
- remove underlying causes of crime;
- build a sense of community;
- create safe and healthy communities;
- educate participants about causes of crime and the importance of community prevention.[9]

---

9   B.D. Stuart, "Sentencing Circles: Making Real Differences" in J. Macfarlane, ed., *Rethinking Disputes: The Mediation Alternative* (Toronto: Emond Montgomery, 1997) at 230.

He notes in *R. v. Moses*,[10] where a sentencing circle was used that "by changing the process, the primary issues changed, and consequently, the decision was substantially different from what might have been decided had the usual process been followed."[11]

Because sentencing circles are a relatively new criminal law innovation, courts have made it clear that "the judges of courts utilising this new process should formulate rules, so that the public will understand the basis upon which individual judges are appearing to depart from the practices followed in all other cases."[12] In *R. v. Morin*,[13] the Saskatchewan Court of Appeal articulated seven criteria, the seventh most discretionary, to be considered in determining whether use of a sentencing circle is appropriate in a given case:

(1) The accused must agree to be referred to the sentencing circle.

(2) The accused must have deep roots in the community in which the circle is held and from which the participants are drawn.

(3) That there are elders or respected non-political community leaders willing to participate.

(4) The victim is willing to participate and has been subjected to no coercion or pressure in so agreeing.

(5) The court should try to determine beforehand, as best it can, if the victim is subject to battered spouse syndrome. If she is, then she should have counselling made available to her and be accompanied by a support team in the circle.

(6) Disputed facts have been resolved in advance.

(7) The case is one in which a court would be willing to take a calculated risk and depart from the usual range of sentencing.[14]

---

10 (1992) 71 C.C.C. (3d) 347 (Y.T. Terr. Ct.).

11 *Ibid.* at 350.

12 *R. v. Johns*, [1996] 1 C.N.L.R. 172 at 180 (Y.T.C.A.), McEachern C.J.B.C. Chief Justice McEachern went on to call circle sentencing "a salutary practice in some kinds of cases," which was some kind of departure from the judge who had earlier "put the boots to ADR."

13 [1995] 4 C.N.L.R. 37 (Sask. C.A.).

14 *Ibid.* at 44.

4) Restorative Justice

The above examples — diversion, VORP, circle sentencing — are being viewed increasingly as part of a larger dispute resolution change taking place in the criminal justice system. Rather than isolated acts, these initiatives represent a shift in philosophy. The shift is to a concept called restorative justice. The idea of restorative justice appeared on the ADR scene as an alternative to retributive justice. Restorative justice was aimed at repairing the harm caused by a wrongful act and restoring a balance in the community affected by the crime.

> The overall purpose of restorative justice is not to inflict punishment in proportion to the seriousness of the offence, or to incapacitate offenders so that they pose no further risk to the public, but the restoration into safe communities of victims and offenders who have resolved their conflicts.[15]

The overarching principle of restorative justice, matched with purpose, is that the most important task of criminal justice should be the restoration of stable relationships. Because crime affects more than the individuals directly involved and the state, restorative justice seeks to re-establish healthy communities by treating governments and the wider communities as active partners with victims and wrongdoers in restoring relationships and in maintaining harmony and social stability. Additionally, restorative justice stresses that a consensus approach to justice is the most effective response to crime. A sampling of what can be seen comparatively through the retributive and restorative lenses makes each of these orientations to justice clearer:[16]

Retributive Lens	Restorative Lens
Blame-fixing central	Problem-solving central
Focus on past	Focus on future
Needs secondary	Needs primary
Battle model; adversarial	Dialogue normative
Emphasizes differences	Searches for commonalities

---

15 B. Hudson, "Restorative Justice: The Challenge of Sexual and Racial Violence" (1998) 25 J.L. & Soc'y 237 at 241.

16 H. Zehr, *Changing Lenses: A New Focus for Crime and Justice* (Waterloo, ON: Herald Press, 1990) at 211–14.

Retributive Lens	Restorative Lens
Imposition of pain considered normative	Restoration and reparation considered normative
One social injury added to another	Emphasis on repair of social injuries
Harm by offender balanced by harm to offender	Harm by offender balanced by making right
Focus on offender, victim ignored	Victim's needs central
Victims lack information	Victim and offender are key elements
Restitution rare	Restitution normal
Victims' "truth" secondary	Victims' suffering lamented and acknowledged
Action from state to offender; offender passive	Offender given role in solution
State monopoly on response to wrongdoing	Victim, offender and community roles recognized
Offender has no responsibility for resolution	Offender has responsibility in resolution
Outcomes encourage offender responsibility	Offender has responsibility in resolution
Rituals of personal denunciation and exclusion	Rituals of lament and reordering
Offender denounced	Harmful act denounced
Offender's ties to community weakened	Offender's integration into community increased
Offender seen in fragments, offense being definitional	Offender viewed holistically
Sense of balance through retribution	Sense of balance through restitution
Balance righted by lowering offender	Balance righted by raising both victim and offender
Justice tested by intent and process	Justice tested by its "fruits"
Justice as right rules	Justice as right relationships
Victim-offender relationships ignored	Victim-offender relationships central
Process alienates	Process aims at reconciliation

Retributive Lens	Restorative Lens
Response based on offender's past behaviour	Response based on consequences of offender's behaviour
Repentance and forgiveness discouraged	Repentance and forgiveness encouraged
Proxy professions are the key actors	Victim and offender central; professional help available
Competitive, individualistic values encouraged	Mutuality and cooperation encouraged
Ignores social, economic and moral context of behaviour	Total context relevant
Assumes win-lose outcomes	Makes possible win-win outcomes

The strengths of restorative justice are said to be (1) that it makes a perpetrator face the fact that real harm has been done to an actual victim; (2) that a perpetrator who is a party to the outcome is more likely to display remorse for his or her actions than resentment at the punishment; and (3) that restorative justice can provide for a balance between the needs and rights of both offenders and victims. Restorative justice approaches may also be particularly advantageous, it is argued, in cases were traditional criminal justice has failed to provide effective responses, such as violence against women, children and ethnic minorities.

Restorative justice, like ADR itself, is not a brand new idea. Some see connections to the European abolitionist movement, which has campaigned for the rights of prisoners, improvement in prison conditions, as well as for reductions in the use of imprisonment. As with ADR, proponents of restorative justice found examples of this philosophy of punishment in some Aboriginal healing traditions and the non-retributive responses to harmful acts advocated by several faith communities. Developments in ADR in North America for non-criminal disputes also influenced the modern formulation of the term. Whatever its source,[17] restorative justice has focused attention squarely on the idea of punishment itself.

---

17   For some historical analysis of the roots of Restorative Justice, see J.J. Llewellyn & R. Howse, "Restorative Justice: A Conceptual Framework" and "From Restorative Justice to Transformative Justice" (Ottawa, 1999) available at <www.lcc.gc.ca>; and for a recent critique, see R. Delgado, "Goodbye to Hammurabi: Analyzing the Atavistic Appeal of Restorative Justice" (2000) 52 Stan. L. Rev. 751.

Although the full history of restorative justice is beyond the scope of this book, the links between restorative justice and ADR deserve comment. Much like the politics and contradictions of ADR discussed in chapter 1, the meaning of restorative justice in practice needs to be carefully examined. Like ADR, there may be conflicting and competing goals for restorative justice. Circle sentencing may not be about empowerment but about allowing the informality of this process to conceal the continuing oppression that is taking place, particularly for Aboriginal members of society. Diversion programs may be mostly about saving time and money or expanding state control and have little to say about reconciliation or healing. Restorative justice may be second-class justice or a way to strengthen, not change, the existing system by siphoning off for restoration the cases that expose flaws in the present structures. Restorative justice may be billed as being a common-sense way to provide accessibility and be inclusive, safe, fair, and cost-effective, or another contribution to harmony ideology at the expense of legal rights or the more vigorous legal action needed to effect progressive change in an imbalanced world. Or, restorative justice may be a step to enlightenment. Like ADR, there will be several sides to the story.

E. BUSINESS AFFAIRS

Disputes from the world of business might, at first glance, appear tame when compared with the vehemence in a contested divorce, the turmoil around a labour strike, or the drama of a criminal case. Many business disputes do get resolved quickly and easily. The supplier of a defective product returns the purchase price or replaces the goods when the defect is traced to the manufacturer. The deadline for completion of the project is extended when the reason for the delay is explained and further delays are not anticipated. The amount of the disputed bill is reduced by the architect to acknowledge the client's concerns with the design process. Time after time, without great fanfare, business people successfully negotiate solutions to the thousands of issues that naturally arise from business intercourse.

The reasons for this dispute resolution success depend on context. Some business disputes are minor and lend themselves to quick fixes. Some business people are marvellous negotiators. Maintaining business relationships, keeping markets open, preserving reputations, avoiding publicity, and saving time and money are other factors that can encourage speedy settlements when businesses disagree. In many cases, the alternatives to fair agreement will not be palatable.

But business disputes, in some cases, can fall at the other end of the disputing spectrum. They can display all the emotional intensity and turbulence of a mean-spirited family break-up, the antagonism and hardened positions of a long labour-management clash and the suspense and seriousness of the criminal process. In these cases, the resolution of business disputes will not be quick and easy. The solution to the problem will not be obvious or affordable or one that can be entered into voluntarily. To the disputants, the issues will be major, perhaps going to the long-term economic security of a company, questions of a CEO's competency or integrity, a clash of personality types, marketplace or political power, ambition or greed, enormous wealth or financial ruin, success or failure or the bottom line.

Where a business dispute falls on the disputing spectrum and whether it is easily resolved or not cannot depend on pre-set notions. A million-dollar claim may be settled in a moment with a single handshake, while a hundred-dollar difference can become a principle that has to be litigated. Wrinkles in a takeover bid can be ironed out or last for years. Disputed words in a contract can result in allegations and counter-allegations about who said what to whom and the pleading of the parole evidence rule in a subsequent lawsuit. Conversely, the same contractual words can be ignored or changed. The make-up of a business dispute and the course it takes depend on context. Clearly, many business disputes do present challenges for their successful resolution.

When the parties to a business dispute have been unable to negotiate a satisfactory resolution themselves, there often is recourse to court adjudication, which produces certain benefits. Individual cases are resolved, or at least the parties receive and accept a binding decision from a neutral party to the dispute. In addition, the business law jurisprudence developed by the courts provides guidance and precedents so that other businesses can adjust their practices and avoid the same problems in the future. The students, lawyers, judges and other individuals who read and rely on these court decisions understand both the extent and the significance of these judicial decisions.

But the common complaints associated with court adjudication can be particularly problematic for businesses going to court. High legal costs cannot always be easily absorbed or passed on in industries where margins are tight and profit levels are critical. Long delays in getting to trial can add burdensome layers of uncertainty to the need for business planning or financial flexibility. Pre-trial motions and conferences, discovery, and the trial itself can take key personnel away for lengthy periods of time from the critical day-to-day operations of the business. Having to sue another player in the same industry or your own employer often can do irreparable harm to long-term working relationships that need to be on solid ground after the particular dispute is over. Airing commercial controversies in the public domain also can impair business reputations and can compromise confidential information about finances, markets, product designs or other integral features of how the company works. Finally, leaving ultimate decisions about the dispute to judges who usually do not have experience in the complex and technical details of the industry can lead to impractical results that will not stand the test of time however legally sound they might be.

In addition to the courts, arbitration has been another dispute resolution process that the business community has regularly used to resolve differences between their members. As discussed in chapter 5, arbitration has a long history. The idea of having a neutral third party adjudicate disputes outside of any formal justice system certainly predates ADR's emergence. Over its history, this adjudicative process has been structured by legislation, court decisions and the business parties themselves to be a fast, cost-saving, flexible, responsive, relationship-preserving, predictable and credible contribution to the resolution of business disputes. In creating this dispute resolution mechanism for businesses that could not or perhaps would not agree, the arbitration process, at the very least, had to provide a viable option to the courts. In other words, arbitration had to offer benefits that could not be attained by going to court. In addition, arbitration benefits also had to outweigh any disadvantages associated with submitting the dispute to a neutral third party for decision. Although arbitration's popularity in the business community has been up and down, particularly in different sectors, there has been growing popularity with this adjudicative process as a dispute resolution option particularly in cases where the number or nature of the disputes make use of the courts undesirable. Recent developments in the use of arbitration for business disputes are discussed in chapter 5.

Although business disputes were not the main motivation for the modern emergence of ADR, the business community has not ignored claims that alternative dispute resolution procedures can save even more time and money while avoiding the combative characteristics of going to court, preserving and enhancing future relationships, ensuring privacy and generally providing better dispute resolution. The off-spring of this apparent match between the dispute resolution needs of business and what ADR had to offer have been a number of innovative disputing initiatives. ADR efforts to keep business disputes out of court dominate these developments. In addition to the arbitration processes described in chapter 5, business ADR efforts include commercial mediation, partnering, ADR contract clauses, the mini-trial, the ADR pledge and dispute systems design.

1) Commercial Mediation

Because the bulk of business disputes are resolved through direct negotiation processes, mediation has not always seemed necessary. Getting a neutral third party to assist deadlocked negotiations, or resorting to mediation without negotiating first, has not generally been the business instinct. Negotiating is generally what business people do for a living and if negotiations in one form or another are at an impasse, it is probably assumed that further assisted negotiations will be futile. This attitude is changing as instances of successful mediations of business disagreements are cited. There are examples of commercial mediations resulting in substantial savings of time and lawyers' fees, improved business relationships for the future and other benefits commonly associated with the mediation process.[18] The development of on-line commercial mediation services will likely accelerate as technology enables Internet communications to become more effective and efficient, particularly where the business parties are separated geographically and the nature of the controversy lends itself to electronic exchanges.[19] The continued use of mediation by businesses in dispute, whether Internet or interpersonal, will depend on a careful consideration of the factors discussed in chapter 4 for choosing mediation, including appreciation of the considerable negotiating expertise that can be brought to the table in a commercial mediation.

---

18   For example, see T.J. Stepanowich, "Beyond Arbitration: Innovation and Evolution in the United States Construction Industry" (1996) 31 Wake Forest L. Rev. 65.

19   For an introduction to this rapidly developing field, see S. Hardy, "Online Mediation: Internet Dispute Resolution" (1998) 9 Austl. Disp. Resol. J. 216; R.C. Bordone, "Electronic Online Dispute Resolution: A Systems Approach — Potential, Problems and a Proposal" (1998) 3 Harv. Negotiation L. Rev. 201; A.E. Almaguer & R.W. Baggott, "Shaping New Legal Frontiers: Dispute Resolution for the Internet" (1998) 13 Ohio St. J. on Disp. & Resol. 724; and M.E. Katsh, "Dispute Resolution in Cyberspace" (1996) 28 Conn. L. Rev. 965. Also click on Internet Neutral at <http://www.internetneutral.com> ; ClickNSettle at <http://clicknsettle.com>; Online Mediators at <http://www.onlinemediators.com>; CyberSettle at <cybersettle.com>; and a whole host of ADR business sites such as <Disputes.org/eResolution.ca>.

2) Partnering

Several businesses are set to embark on a joint project. The managers of the businesses are aware that disputes can often arise in this type of venture. The companies enter into an agreement, part of which follows:

> In order to complete this project most beneficially for all parties, the parties agree to form a Partnering relationship. This Partnering relationship will draw on the strengths of each party in order to achieve a quality project, on time and within budget. . . . Any costs associated with Partnering will be shared equally.

Partnering is a technique pioneered by the U.S. Army Corps of Engineers and is most commonly associated with the construction industry. Partnering can be defined as "an emerging alternative management process designed to help interdependent organizations identify common goals and objectives and manage conflict in joint undertakings such as large-scale construction projects and facilities services contracts."[20]

Although the partnering process is flexible, depending on the size and complexity of the project being partnered, partnering involves the collaborative development of a framework for preventing, managing and resolving disputes. With the help of a neutral facilitator, the stakeholders on a particular project can work to identify mutual goals, values, and philosophies associated with the collective endeavour. This type of team building is accompanied by structured mechanisms that can establish chains of decision making within organizations and time frames for action for any complaints or conflicts that arise. Lines of communication are clear, and issue-resolving power can be placed in the hands of people who are closest to the problem. Although partnering emphasizes dispute prevention, partnering arrangements can be extended to include understandings or agreements on what dispute resolution processes may be resorted to in the event an issue cannot be resolved through the negotiation process. Partnering does not usually prevent a party from litigating a dispute, but "litigious disputing is spiritually incompatible with the partnering ethos."[21]

---

20   R.A. Shearer, J.D. Maes, & C.C. Moore, "Partnering: A Commitment to Common Goals" (1995) 50 Dispute Resolution Journal [formerly Arbitration Journal] 30.

21   I.C. Szlazak, "Haven't Been There, Haven't Done That: An Exploration of Construction Industry Partnering and Further Applications of the Concept in Other Contexts" (1999) 41 C.L.R. (2d) 216 at 229.

3) ADR Contract Clauses

ADR contract clauses are written terms in business contracts that require the contracting parties to use specific dispute resolution methods in light of a likely problem. In addition to arbitration clauses that require the parties "to arbitrate any and all claims, controversies or disputes arising out of or relating to the contract," it also has become common for ADR contract clauses to refer to other disputing processes, most commonly mediation. For example:

> If a dispute arises out of or relates to this agreement, or the breach, termination, validity or subject matter thereof, or as to any claim in tort, in equity or pursuant to any domestic or international statute or law, the parties to the agreement and to the dispute expressly agree to endeavour in good faith to settle the dispute by mediation [administered by Ö] before having recourse to arbitration or litigation.[22]

The rationale behind ADR contract clauses revolves around understanding the reality that disputes are likely to occur, even with partnering structures in place. Permitting the parties to pre-select and define a preferred method or methods of dispute resolution can avoid delays or other consequences in deciding what to do in the moment when a dispute has arisen. The details in the ADR clauses will vary from one case to another. Some clauses may favour mediation while others may sequence or stage the dispute resolution steps to be taken, requiring resort to one or more dispute resolution methods before commencing formal legal proceedings.

There can, however, be disputes about the interpretation and application of these ADR clauses. In *Toronto Truck Centre Ltd.* v. *Volvo Trucks Canada Inc./Camions Volvo Canada Inc.*,[23] the parties had agreed it was in their mutual interests to avoid litigation if a business dispute arose. To maintain respect, trust and confidence, the parties had committed to mediation to resolve their disputes. However, when the manufacturer purported to cancel a dealership agreement because of an alleged misrepresentation about finances, the dealer had to take the manufacturer to court to enforce participation in the mediation process.[24]

---

22 L. Boulle & K.J. Kelly, *Mediation Principles, Process, Practice* (Toronto: Butterworths, 1998) at 277.

23 (1998), 163 D.L.R. (4th) 740 (Ont. Gen. Div.).

24 For a further commentary on this case, see chapter 8, "The Law of ADR: Legislation, Cases, and the Courts" at 315.

4) Mini-Trial

A mini-trial, as described in chapter 5, is not a short trial. Rather, the mini-trial is a label for a union of several different disputing approaches to give disputants, often business disputants, the most attractive result. The mini-trial may be privately arranged or court sponsored. In a private mini-trial, the parties and their lawyers generally understand that the purpose of the mini-trial will be to inform key management representatives of the central issues in dispute and the reasons for the dispute. The mini-trial protocol will set out the necessary (and shorter than a trial) procedures — presentation of respective positions identified in the schedule, submission of written summaries of evidence and argument and role of the neutral adviser regarding the procedural parts of the mini-trial. Mini-trials usually combine selected elements of negotiation, mediation, arbitration and advocacy. Typically, there will be an abbreviated presentation of the case by counsel and the parties to a panel of senior executives from opposing sides and often also to a neutral third party. Some witnesses might be called to highlight orally the evidence they would give at trial and, if necessary, these witnesses may be cross-examined. There may be written summaries of other evidence submitted. After the case has been presented as persuasively as possible, the high-level representatives of the parties who have authority to decide will engage in a negotiation process often with the guidance of a third-party neutral. The third-party neutral, probably chosen because of his evaluative mediator qualities or past judging experience and expertise in the subject matter of the dispute, may also assist the negotiations by rendering a non-binding opinion on the merits of the case. If the mini-trial is court ordered, the process will take place before a judge who then would be disqualified from presiding at the trial unless all the parties consent. Rules of Court can place restrictions on the procedures to be followed in a court-directed mini-trial such as hearing oral evidence.

Whether privately agreed to or court sponsored, an effective mini-trial can highlight the strengths and weaknesses in each side's case, provide a sense of how the dispute would unfold in a courtroom, and put the disputing parties in a position to assess whether a settlement would be a better alternative than going to court or taking other action. These strengths need to be balanced with concerns that a mini-trial, despite its good intentions to assist the negotiations in complex cases, may not avoid unnecessary formality and adversarial attitudes. If no agreement is reached, in addition to the costs incurred and time lost, a party may be prejudiced by disclosures made in the course of the mini-trial even if the mini-trial agreement specifies that the entire process is confidential and any statements made in the mini-trial are inadmissible in any subsequent proceeding.

5) ADR Pledge

The ADR Pledge is a variation on putting terms in business agreements that legally obligate the contractual parties to use certain dispute resolution mechanisms, such as arbitration or mediation, in the event of a contract conflict. The pledge is a commitment, the equivalent of a businessperson's handshake, to use ADR if appropriate.

The original ADR Pledge (the Corporate Policy Statement on Alternatives to Litigation developed by the CPR Institute for Dispute Resolution in New York) referred to a moral commitment made by a group of Fortune 500 and mid-size companies to use ADR as a starting point for any business disputes between or among the signatories to the pledge. Rather than moving too quickly to the courts or engaging in adversarial approaches to dispute resolution, companies pledged that they would attempt to resolve their differences by using more collaborative and consensual dispute resolution processes before pursuing litigation. The pledge declared:

> We recognize that for many disputes there is a less expensive, more effective method of resolution than the traditional lawsuit. Alternative dispute resolution (ADR) procedures involve collaborative techniques which can often spare businesses the high costs of litigation.
>
> In the event of a business dispute between our company and another company which has made or will then make a similar statement, we are prepared to explore resolution of the dispute through negotiation or ADR techniques before pursuing full scale litigation.

Whether the pledge was a radical departure or just the sign you would expect in modern times from a serious negotiator, the pledge idea still attracts attention. Four thousand parent companies and operating subsidiaries still agree to explore ADR in disputes with other signers. In addition, approximately 1,500 law firms have signed the CPR Law Firm Policy Statement on Alternatives to Litigation, which commits them to be knowledgeable about ADR and to counsel clients about ADR options where appropriate. The Canadian Foundation for Dispute Resolution encourages corporations and law firms to sign a similar Dispute Resolution Protocol that commits signatories to willingly consider and suggest alternative dispute resolution processes in appropriate situations before turning to the courts. The language of the

Millennium Accord[25] is another example of the corporate pledge. Anticipating Y2K problems had not been fully solved, signatories to the Millennium Accord agree to support dealing with any millennium problem on the basis that:

- a millennium problem is a mutual problem not a competitive opportunity;
- a mutual problem may be solved faster and more cost-effectively by communication and co-operation rather than confrontation;
- timely dispute prevention is preferable to retrospective redress;
- communication and co-operation enhance timely dispute prevention;
- any differences or dispute ought to be resolved without resort to adjudicative resolution methods ("ARMs" — e.g. litigation or arbitration) by using the Millennium Accord Procedure ("the Accord Procedure").

If, however, an Accord Signatory does resort to ARMs it should immediately initiate the Accord Procedure to run concurrently and, if feasible, stay the proceedings pending the outcome of the Accord Procedure.

A "millennium problem" is any problem arising out of the failure of technology systems to cope with the millennium transition, up to, during and beyond the year 2000.

This declaration is not intended to create legally binding obligations, or to override any obligations of a professional adviser to its client.

Analogous to the pledge, various government offices and departments also make commitments to ADR. As an example, the federal Department of Justice in Canada has developed a Policy on Dispute Resolution which requires employees and legal counsel to integrate appropriate dispute resolution not only into legislative, policy and program initiatives but also contracts involving the federal government.

6) Dispute Systems Design

Dispute systems design (DSD) has attracted considerable attention particularly from businesses engaged or about to engage in long-term rela-

---

25   Six ADR bodies (Canadian Foundation for Dispute Resolution; Centre for Dispute Resolution, London, Europe; JAMS/Endispute, Washington; LEADR, Sydney; Hong Kong International Arbitration Centre; and Singapore Mediation Centre, Asia) were going door to door on the Web and through other networks for signatories to the Millennium Accord.

tionships. The commercial arrangements might involve joint ventures, product purchasing, the provision of a wide range of services, money lending, or even non-consensual situations such as competing business organizations who share the same market. As companies recognize that disputes between them are inevitable, there is the increasing understanding that ad hoc dispute resolution or undue reliance on one disputing method or another may not fully serve the business needs.

> The task for parties who can reasonably anticipate a stream of disputes between them is to go beyond settling those disputes one at a time and to go beyond selecting one procedure to resolve all disputes. Their goal should be to design a comprehensive and effective dispute resolution system.[26]

Goldberg, Brett and Ury describe six basic principles of dispute systems design:[27]

1. **Prevention** — Dispute prevention may take many forms. However, when one party to a relationship is contemplating taking some action, notification (an advance announcement) and consultation (discussion of proposed action) should proceed any action. Prevention might also involve institutional changes to product design, communication methods, behaviours, or other areas that are diagnosed as causing the conflict.

2. **Put the focus on interests** — The emphasis in dispute resolution systems is to fully utilize procedures that assist the parties to reach an interest-based solution. Contract clauses might specifically provide for negotiation to be the first step in settling a dispute and, even if unsuccessful, direct further negotiations to take place at a higher level in the organizations involved. Mediation using insider employees or outside neutrals trained in interest-based approaches could also be mandated.

3. **Build in "loop-backs" to negotiation** — When interest-based negotiations fail because perceptions of legal rights or who is more powerful make it difficult to reconcile interests, design procedures to provide the parties with information about their realistic alternatives

---

26   S.B. Goldberg, F.E.A. Sander, & N.H. Rogers, *Dispute Resolution: Negotiation, Mediation and Other Processes*, 3d ed. (New York: Aspen Publishers, Inc., 1999) at 338.

27   S.B. Goldberg, J. Brett, & W. Ury, "Designing an Effective Dispute Resolution System" in J. Wilkinson, ed., *Donovan Leisure Newton and Irvine ADR Practice Book* (New York: Wiley Law Publications, 1991).

to a negotiated agreement (the likely court outcome) without actually going through a contested and lengthy court proceeding. With this information about their rights and power in hand through the mini-trial, non-binding arbitration, early neutral evaluation, independent legal advice or other process to obtain a credible, neutral opinion, the system encourages the parties to loop back to negotiation.

4. **Provide low-cost rights and power backups** — In cases where consensual agreement is not attainable, an effective dispute resolution system will provide time-and cost-efficient methods for the parties to obtain a final and binding resolution to the dispute. Conventional, expedited, or final offer arbitration might be employed, or any type of decision-making board where the decision is accepted as essentially the last word on the issues.

5. **Arrange procedures in a low-to-high cost sequence** — Without minimizing the utility of the initial efforts at dispute resolution, the system can structure the sequence of procedures to encourage cost efficiencies.

6. **Provide the necessary motivation, skills, resources, and environment** — To avoid resistance to the change that will be brought about by DSD, appropriate actions need to be taken to manage this change. The change management moves might include training key personnel in the necessary dispute resolution skills and making needed resources (such as mediators, technologies) available.

Whether DSD is used before disputes arise or when an existing system is plagued with problems, the idea of designing an effective dispute resolution system or "a conflict management system"[28] for business or others in long-term relationships may encourage innovations in the processes that already exist for these disputers. All the systems that result, private and public, will be influential in contributing to the shape of ADR.

---

28 C. Costantino & C. Merchant, *Designing Conflict Management Systems* (San Francisco: Jossey-Bass, 1996). The change in language from DSD to "interest-based conflict management systems" reflects criticisms that DSD is too dependent on expert designers, too linear and mechanistic, and is not attentive enough to prevention and organizational dynamics. Conflict management systems "walk the talk" by involving all relevant participants in a meaningful way so that any disputing system will be durable and actually used.

F. ENVIRONMENTAL CONCERNS

Dispute resolution in environmental matters has been described as

> a decision-making process that is based largely on the adversarial view of society. It utilizes courts, adjudicative bodies and commissions to set policy and resolve disputes. . . . The present adversarial and hierarchical structure of adjudication and decision-making seems to impress environmental issues with a competitive stamp. Litigants do not come to court seeking cooperative solutions to environmental problems, they come seeking victory over their opponents.[29]

Various factors help to explain this picture of environmental dispute resolution. First, there is history. Confrontational clashes between supporters and opponents of activities around land use, natural resource management, water and air quality, waste disposal and other related matters have been common. Much like labour discords, the hallmarks of environmental dispute resolution have developed over time to include furious opposition, entrenched positions, glaring mistrust, appeals for public support, government lobbying, blockaded roads, court injunctions and various win-at-all-cost actions.

Second, the stakes are high in environmental disputes. There may be millions or billions of dollars, thousands of jobs and other economic benefits resting on a single decision of whether to log or not. In opposition there may be further risks to an endangered species, irreversible damage to natural habitat, destruction of ecosystems or an Indigenous people's way of life, contributions to ozone depletion, global warming or other unnatural and undesired results.

Third, environmental disagreements are often framed as value disputes that cannot be sorted out by the convenient application of scientific or technical data to reach a right decision. Whether to log an old growth forest, build a golf course on farmland, drain a mangrove swamp for a shrimp farm, flood traditional territory to produce more electricity or create a national park instead of a copper mine are said to be as much about conflicting values as about economic or scientific controversies.

---

29 D. P. Emond, "Environment Law and Policy: A Retrospective Examination of the Canadian Experience" in I. Bernier & A. Lajoie, eds., *Consumer Protection, Environmental Law and Corporate Power* (Ottawa: University of Toronto Press, 1985) 89 at 162.

Fourth, there is often a great deal of indeterminacy in the resolution of environmental disputes. Does deforestation contribute to global warming? Is the species endangered? Will the pipeline interfere with the migration patterns of the caribou? How much will it cost? Is it sustainable? Scientific answers to these questions are often not reliable because there are concerns about buying expert evidence — experts often disagree and the necessary empirical data is not always agreed upon or readily available. The enormity of the questions being posed makes certain answers difficult.

Fifth, environmental disputes almost always have a public policy element to them. Claims to represent the broader "public interest" in environmental disputes (including the interests of wildlife, inanimate objects and unborn generations) create controversy and complexity not only around who has standing but also around what exactly is the public interest.

Finally, environmental disputes often pit powerful economic entities interested in exploiting or harvesting the wealth in the environment against individuals and organizations with less economic clout. This economic imbalance does not mean the stronger economic interests always prevail in environmental disputes or that there is necessarily an overall power imbalance. It does mean, however, that strategies such as civil disobedience, protests, media campaigns designed to discredit corporate practices or activities and calls for boycotts of certain products often are employed to counter one party's superior economic strength. These strategies can exacerbate strained relations and contribute further to the intense adversarial, win-lose nature of environmental disputes.

Given these factors, environmental dispute resolution efforts have not been completely successful. Attempts by governments to set environmental standards, policies, rules, codes or regulations so that disputes are prevented in the first place, provided the rules are followed, have been plagued by disputes about what the rules should be and also by inadequacies in the bureaucratic processes used to set these standards. Even when such regulations are in place in the form of forest practices codes or environmental protection legislation, violations occur, conflicting interpretations are raised and enforcement is questioned. Sending environmental disputes to the courts or to specialized administrative agencies such as environmental assessment appeal boards results in binding decisions by neutral third parties, but these adjudicative processes often are criticized as too adversarial, too time-consuming and costly, too harmful to future relationships, too distant from the communities most directly affected by the dispute and often too inflexible to adequately address the issues in dispute or come up with anything other than a win-lose result.

Although developments in administrative procedures, the law of standing, funding for intervenors in important environmental cases and court procedures generally will improve the quality of how environmental disputes are adjudicated, the overall picture of environmental dispute resolution, much like labour controversies, may essentially remain a decision-making process that is based largely on an adversarial view of society.

However, the emergence of alternative dispute resolution has highlighted thinking that "consensual forms of dispute settlement, such as negotiation or mediation, are particularly appropriate in environmental cases because they focus on having all the key actors at the table and allowing a full hearing of all the relevant issues."[30] Two approaches to environmental dispute resolution deserve description: environmental mediation and negotiated rule making.

1) Environmental Mediation

Mediations of environmental disputes, in which the private and public stakeholders affected by land use, resource management or other environmental issues attempt to reach consensus on an acceptable outcome, have been reported in the United States since the early 1970s.[31] As with arbitration, the concept of a number of interested parties getting together to work out a solution as to who hunts where, fishes for what, builds when or responds otherwise to deal with environmental matters is not new. However, the rise of ADR did turn attention naturally enough to how environmental disputes were being resolved. The costs and challenges of successfully adjudicating these cases moved the focus quite quickly to environmental mediation.

Bingham and Susskind[32]chronicle a remarkable evolution in environmental mediation. From site specific and voluntary mediations involving a few stakeholders using well-intentioned but untrained mediators, environmental mediation is frequently used in a wide array of situations because it is now institutionalized in environmental protection or assessment legislation. For example, the *Canadian Environ-*

---

30   S.B. Goldberg, E.D. Green, & F.E.A. Sander, *Dispute Resolution* (Boston: Little, Brown and Company, 1985) at 404.

31   For examples, see G. Bingham, *Resolving Environmental Disputes: A Decade of Experience* (Washington, DC: Conservation Foundation, 1986); and L. Susskind & J. Cruikshank, *Breaking the Impasse : Consensual Approaches to Resolving Public Disputes* (New York: Basic Books, 1987).

32   *Ibid.*

mental Assessment Act, S.C. 1992, c. 37, provides that projects for which an environmental assessment must be done can be referred to a mediator by the government if public concerns warrant such a reference or if the parties agree. Other Canadian administrative tribunals within jurisdiction over the environment — such as the National Energy Board, Ontario Environmental Assessment and Appeal Board, Nova Scotia Environmental Assessment Board, Manitoba Clean Environment Commission and Alberta Environmental Appeal Board — use mediation to address environmental disputes.

The move to environmental mediation was made for many of the same reasons that encouraged the modern emergence of ADR: it would be faster and cheaper and also lead to enduring and satisfying results. More important, involving the affected stakeholders in a participatory process of consensus decision making would help to eliminate the adversarial mindset that could dominate decision making around these natural matters. The goal of replacing the adversarial and competitive with collaborative and cooperative approaches is often a distinguishing feature of environmental mediation, resulting in creative and integrative approaches to decision making and problem solving and ensuring the parties live up to the environmental accords reached.

There is no one model for environmental mediation. Much like the shape of mediation in general, environmental mediation will be structured in its particular context by a number of factors. First, there are the participants. A manageable number of stakeholders need to be chosen. However, selecting or soliciting participants to participate in possibly unfamiliar processes can be complicated by mistrust, tenuous past connections, money, schedules and more. Any party with the power to block the implementation of a mediated agreement should normally be at the table. Some parties may be obvious but if the stakes are high, deciding on others to be present can be tricky. Having representation from future generations and non-legal entities, like trees and fish, may not be impossible in mediation but it can be hard to get a handle on them.

Second, choosing a third party that is neutral about ozone depletion, clear-cutting, privatization, global trade development, civil disobedience, environmentalism and other such issues can be difficult. Environmental mediators must not let their personal views and values interfere with their tasks of moving the negotiation along and, if required, submitting a report to the appropriate government authority. As discussed in chapter 4, the moves of the environmental mediator and the stages of mediation will depend on the disputants' approaches to mediation, the goals that have been set for the mediation process and the type of the individual mediator.

Third, the actual mediation process can vary. Take, for example, its degree of openness or transparency. There is the argument that unless the process of making these public policy decisions in mediation is transparent, the results are not likely to be credible. However, there will undoubtedly be occasions when closed-door negotiations will be necessary. A development company may need to discuss confidential business arrangements. A personality dispute between opposing participants may have to be addressed. Privacy may be sought for one reason or another. Deciding when a very public environmental mediation process has to go private and for how long can yield different results. The pre-negotiation phase can be similarly varied. The number and type of private conversations that can take place while the parties are being canvassed by an agency, firm or official may be crucial to the final outcome. Like the subject it serves, environmental mediation is subject to change and a shaping to suit the circumstances. There is finally the decision making at the end of the process. The results of environmental mediation are rarely legally binding contracts. Most environmental mediations will produce recommendations that then must be acted upon by a government or a regulatory authority. The weight of the recommendations can depend on whether and to what extent the legally mandated decision makers (the bureaucrat, agency head, politician) are represented in the mediation. If those with formal authority to decide are treated as important stakeholders, it would be expected that a recommendation produced by consensus would be adopted.

In the final analysis, the environmental mediations that occur in widening substantive areas are unique from a process perspective. They may share the mediation label but the details of the assisted negotiations can be as varied as the landscapes they deal with.

2) Negotiated Rule Making

The promulgation of environmental regulations or standards setting out permitted levels of emissions, protected areas and habitat, forestry practices, catalytic converter requirements, prohibited imports and other rules to be followed when natural resources are in question do not always prevent disputes from arising. There often can be disputes about the rules themselves. Industries may argue the standard is not economic in a global market. Environmentalists may predict dire consequences if the regulation is not strengthened. Even when the government agency or ministry has followed the traditional notice and comment approach to rule making and then decided and announced its decision after the fullest of deliberations, the parties affected may not all be satisfied.

In an effort to avoid these after-the-fact disputes, consensus-building negotiations to resolve environmental disagreements have been used. Negotiated rule making or "reg-neg" is a process in which

> the agency and the private parties with a significant stake in the proposed rule participate in facilitated face-to-face negotiations designed to produce a consensus. In these negotiations, they have the opportunity, lacking in the adversarial process, to explore shared interests and differences of opinion, collaborate in gathering and analyzing technical information, generate options, and bargain and trade across those options according to their different priorities. If agreement is reached, it is published as the agency's notice of proposed rulemaking, and then the conventional review and comment process takes over. Because, however, most or all of the interested parties have participated in framing the proposed rule, there should be little critical comment, and few judicial challenges.[33]

Although the structure of negotiated rule making is designed to deal with the challenges associated with the resolution of environmental disputes, much in the same way as environmental mediation, a recent study questions whether the benefits of regulatory negotiation are being achieved.[34] For example, Coglianese found only thirty-six final rules through federal agency negotiated rule making compared to 47,603 final rules by traditional notice and comment, no decrease in time for enacting final rules, significant costs associated with regulation-negotiation particularly for environmental groups, and a higher rate for litigation challenges of rules issued by negotiated rule making. The problems may lie with the current administration of negotiated rule making rather than the concept itself. Questions around how to convene a consensus process, overcoming bureaucratic resistance, defining consensus, managing power imbalances and recognizing the distributional aspects of the bargaining will need to be carefully considered to assess the future of this dispute resolution process.

---

33   Above note 26 at 502.
34   C. Coglianese, "Assessing Consensus: The Promise and Performance of Negotiated Rulemaking" (1997) 46 Duke L.J. 1255.

FURTHER READINGS

BACOW, L.S., & M. WHEELER, *Environmental Dispute Resolution* (New York: Plenum, 1984)

BLACKBURN, J.W., & W.M. BRUCE, eds., *Mediating Environmental Conflicts: Theory and Practice* (Westport, CT: Quorum Books, 1995)

CORMICK, G., N. DALE, P. EMOND, S.C. SIGURDSON, & B.D. STUART, *Building Consensus for a Sustainable Future: Putting Principles into Practice* (Ottawa: National Round Table on the Environment and the Economy, 1996)

EMOND, D.P., *Commercial Dispute Resolution* (Aurora, ON: Canada Law Book, 1989)

FENN, P., & R. GAMESON, *Construction Conflict: Management and Resolution* (London: Chapman Hall, 1992)

GALLAWAY, G. & J. HUDSON, *Restorative Justice, International Perspectives* (Monsey: Criminal Justice Press, 1996)

MESSMER, H., & H-U OTTOC, *Restorative Justice on Trial — Pitfalls and Potentials of Victim-Offender Mediation: International Research Perspectives* (Boston: Kluwer Academic Publisher, 1992)

SUSSKIND, L., P. LEVY, & J. THOMAS-LARMER, *Negotiating Environmental Agreements* (Thousand Oaks, Ca.: Island Press, 1999)

TAYLOR, M., et al., "Using Mediation in Canadian Environmental Tribunals: Opportunities and Best Practices" (1999) 22 Dalhousie L.J. 51

CHAPTER 7

ADR AND CULTURE

A. INTRODUCTION

Placing ADR alongside culture can bring to mind the following remarks on ADR and culture.

> "The establishment of ADR processes would benefit Nicaragua in both the short and long term. In the short term, ADR would lessen the pressure on administrative and judicial institutions by resolving current post-revolutionary property disputes. In the long-term, . . . ADR would bring more collaborative and problem-solving techniques to Nicaraguan society. . . . The team believes that a real window of opportunity exists to establish ADR in Nicaragua and make a long-lasting improvement in Nicaraguan society."[1]

> "The language was ours, to use as we pleased. The literature that came with it was therefore of peculiar authority; but this literature was like an alien mythology. There was, for instance, Wordsworth's notorious poem about the daffodil. A pretty little flower, no doubt; but we had never seen it. Could the poem have any meaning for us?"[2]

---

1   Newsletter of the Consortium of Georgia Universities for the Advancement of Conflict Resolution Theory and Education (Atlanta, GA: August 1995) at 3. It is now a common occurrence to read regularly about this Western phenomenon being applied successfully to long-standing problems around the globe.
2   V.S. Naipaul, "Jasmine," in R. Hamner, ed., *Critical Perspectives on V.S. Naipaul* (Washington, D.C.: Three Continents Press, 1977).

The expression "alternative dispute resolution" grew out of popular dissatisfaction with the administration of justice in the United States in the 1970s, but ADR developments have not been confined to that country alone. ADR ideas and practices are blossoming in Canada, England, Australia and New Zealand. Increasingly, ADR is being promoted in many regions and countries with cultures quite different from the dominant cultures of the areas where ADR first flourished.

Even within countries such as Canada and the United States that have remarkable cultural diversity, ADR is being institutionalized in formal justice systems; adopted for use within governments, businesses and other organizations; taught in primary, secondary, and post-secondary educational settings; and generally presented as a common-sense way of approaching disputes and their resolution.

The growing instances of ADR across cultures have resulted in important questions:

- What role does culture play in understanding and shaping disputing behaviour, theories, and structures?
- What is the relationship between ADR practices and culture?
- Are the disputing concepts that make up ADR transferable across clear cultural divides?
- Are there disputing practices that transcend culture?
- Should there be concerns about cultural diffusion?
- Can ADR have any meaning in different cultures?

This chapter provides an opportunity to consider these and related questions by reviewing the notion of culture, by considering how culture influences and is influenced by conflict and by assessing the impact of culture both on the meaning of ADR and on the ways in which ADR is practised. For the ADR student or practitioner, factoring culture into the ADR equation is an important assignment.

B. THE NOTION OF CULTURE

It is perhaps not surprising that the question — what is culture? — opens up complex and interdisciplinary lines of inquiry that reveal stark differences in perspective. In many respects the varied notions of culture that emerge from such an inquiry mirror the politics and contradictions in the meaning of ADR discussed in Chapter 1.

What is culture? The question provokes a bounty of definitions both in everyday usage of the term and in the literature of various disciplines. Some notions of culture clearly reflect the classical nineteenth-century definition that inspired the study of culture as a separate science: "Culture or civilization . . . is that complex whole which includes knowledge, belief, art, law, morals, custom and any other capabilities and habits acquired by man as a member of society."[3]

Included in this definition of culture are non-material products of social life such as folklore, traditions, mores and laws which emerge from social interaction and serve a normative function; material elements in forms ranging from arrowheads to automobiles to other artifacts that represent an obvious product of a society; and finally, the meaningful relationships between the parts of culture and the symbolic interpretations placed upon them. But eighty years later, Kroeber and Kluckhohn discovered over 160 different definitions of culture coined before 1950, as well as thousands of statements about culture.[4] None of these definitions or statements gained universal support; many conflicted with one another. The approaches to culture were not uniform.

1) Classical Definition of Culture

Some definitions of culture mostly enumerate or catalogue the various kinds of phenomena that different writers consider as cultural objects such as mental states and processes (knowledge, ideas, beliefs, attitudes, values, morals); patterns of behaviour (habits, customs); part mental and part material acquisitions (language, abilities, art); material and non-material products of human activity (tools, artifacts, songs, stories); and generalized behaviour (laws, marriage, religion). Culture from another vantage point can primarily depend on the empirical and theoretical criteria necessary to distinguish culture, such as objects or activities that are shared, accepted, acquired, or handed down. Some definitions of culture focus on the creation or survival of culture so that culture is artificial and transmitted independently of genetic inheritance or learned behaviour.

The differentiation between non-material products of group life and material elements was critical for still other definitions. Some writers stressed a unique feature of culture such as its symbolic aspects or its learned or intellectual quality. Parsons considered culture as a basic part of a "system of action." Culture "comes out of social interaction and is an important constituent in personality. The individual incorpo-

---

3   E.B. Tylor, *Primitive Culture* (London: Murray, 1871).

4   A.L. Kroeber & C. Kluckhohn, *Culture: A Critical Review of Concepts and Definitions* (New York: Vintage Books, 1952).

rates the culture of his society and develops a personality that is more or less adjusted to the demands of that society."[5]

Definitions that reduced culture to mental phenomena or to patterns of behaviour often vied for supremacy within this array of perspectives. These definitions separated human behaviour into concrete observable actions or into shared values, beliefs and ideas. Although differences in definition existed, classical sociological theory and classical social anthropology generally conceived of culture as made up of the shared values, norms, beliefs and attitudes of the entire population or subgroups within the population and especially the behaviour that accompanied these attributes. Culture classically consisted of how a people talked, walked, moved, related, created, acted and behaved. More important, culture was also coherent and consistent.

2) Critical Perspectives on Culture

New perspectives in the sociology of culture, strongly influenced by other disciplines such as anthropology, political science, literary studies, cultural studies, feminist studies, and ethnic studies and by insights from European sociological theory, challenge these classical orthodoxies of culture. This powerful body of work[6] rejects culture as a rather narrow ribbon of patterned behaviour that does not extend into social institutions and that is external to a powerful determining set of material constraints and forces. In fact, these perspectives suggest that theories of culture cannot be separated from cultural critique — that is, from the need to engage with specific cultural problematics in a way that underscores their relevance to the contradictory reproduction of social divisions and hierarchies across the social field.

---

5   T. Parsons, *The Social System* (Glencoe, IL: Free Press, 1951). See F.E. Merril, *Society and Culture: An Introduction to Sociology* (New Jersey: Prentice Hall, 1961) for a summary of these representative definitions.

6   For an introduction to this literature, see T. Bennett et al., eds., *Culture, Ideology and Social Process* (London: The Open University Press, 1981); R. Wuthnow et al., *Cultural Analysis: The Work of Peter L. Berger, Mary Douglas, Michel Foucault and Jürgen Habermas* (London: Routledge and Kegan Paul, 1984); M. Ryan, *Politics and Culture: Working Hypotheses for a Post-Revolutionary Society* (London: MacMillan Press, 1989); J.C. Alexander & S. Seidman, eds., *Culture and Society: Contemporary Debates* (Cambridge: Cambridge University Press, 1990); P. Scannell, P. Schlesinger, & C. Sparks, eds., *Culture and Power* (London: Sage, 1992); and D. Crane, ed., *The Sociology of Culture: Emerging Theoretical Perspectives* (Cambridge: Basil Blackwell Ltd., 1994).

Accordingly, culture is linked to social constructionism — the theory that much of what we take for granted as objectively real or necessary in social life is actually "constructed" through social relationships and social behaviour. Hence we see Berger and Luckmann's concern with the social construction of implicit culture (social behaviour).[7] European theorists, such as Foucault and Bourdieu,[8] emphasize the social construction of explicit culture such as the media, knowledge and science, as well as the ways in which these forms of recorded culture construct social roles such as class, gender and race. From these perspectives, science, technology, and knowledge generally cease to be viewed unproblematically as absolute or nearly absolute truths. They are the constructions of particular social groups and used as instruments of power for these groups.

Similarly, culturally oriented historical sociologists focus on cultural change and cultural control — how culture in conjunction with, or independently from, social structures has brought about changes in nation states, in relationships between or within social classes or ethnic groups, or in the conduct of everyday life.[9] A major theme in this work is that of a dominant class imposing a coherent worldview on the population, either in the form of an ideology or as hegemony, to such an extent that the worldview is accepted unquestioningly as common sense.

For cultural Marxists, like Louis Althusser, culture does not simply express and directly reproduce social power through a distribution of cultural capital. "Culture is the arena in which the contradictions that arise within a capitalist society are resolved in ways that assure the continuation of a ruling group's hegemony."[10] The althusserian theory sees culture more accurately as a function of power and assumes culture is something more than an expressive medium for extra-cultural social structures.

Swidler rejects the classical view of culture which sees the individual as a passive recipient of cultural influences that define goals and determine individual behaviour.[11] She argues that culture offers the

---

7   P.L. Berger & T. Luckmann, *The Social Construction of Reality: A Treatise in the Sociology of Knowledge* (New York: Doubleday, 1966).

8   For example, see P. Rabinow, ed., *The Foucault Reader* (New York: Pantheon, 1984); P. Bourdieu & A. Passeron, *Reproduction* (Los Angeles: Sage, 1977); and P. Bourdieu, *Distinction: A Social Critique of the Judgment of Taste* (Cambridge: Harvard University Press, 1984).

9   See E. Morawska & W. Spohn, "Cultural Pluralism in Historical Sociology: Recent Theoretical Directions" in Crane, above note 5.

10   Ryan, above note 5 at 11.

11   A. Swidler, "Culture in Action: Symbols and Strategies" (1986) 51 Am. Soc. Rev. 273–86.

individual a wide range of choices. Instead of defining goals, culture provides tool kits in the form of "symbols, stories, rituals and world-views" that people use to solve problems and to organize their activities. Although values may be shared, individual behaviour may be very different because the capacity to translate the same values into "strategies of action" varies. Not only do individuals use the same cultural components differently, Swidler also argues that culture is not a unified system that pushes action in a consistent direction. All real cultures contain diverse, often conflicting, elements.

Other works show culture as determining of materiality, as a force capable of reshaping social life. In Juri Lotman's semiotic theory, culture consists of "a hierarchy of semiotic systems" the purpose of which is "structurally organizing the world around man."[12] The Japanese cultural theorist Tetsuo Kogawa also presents a strong case for cultural determination.[13] Kogawa argues that the "Emperor System" in contemporary Japanese society reshaped social and bodily life along Western capitalist lines in the late nineteenth century and shows how the deliberate use of the emperor helped establish attitudes of discipline, respect, and obedience that were necessary to the process of modernization and industrialization.

Culture from these critical perspectives becomes inherently contradictory, inconsistent and complex instead of primarily a global unitary characteristic or set of characteristics of the society or group. Abandoning the reduction of culture to mental phenomena and to patterns of behaviour, new perspectives on cultural analysis break down the boundary between the traditional concept of culture and the supposedly extra-cultural realm of materiality, economics, and social reality. The notion of culture from a non-classical perspective focuses attention away from a fixed view of how to catalogue, compartmentalize, simply describe or accept what is culture. Culture from a contemporary vantage point involves a more critical and in-depth explaining or understanding of social structures and roles, hierarchies and hegemonies, power relationships and power imbalances, those who control and those who don't, as well as the changes, reproductions and interrelationships that take place between and within these structures, relationships and institutions.

---

12   J. Lotman et al., *Theses for the Semiotic Study of Culture* (Lisse: De Ritter, 1975).
13   T. Kogawa, *The Electronic State and the Emperor System* (Tokyo: Kawadeshoboshinsha, 1986).

C. CULTURE AND CONFLICT

The range of multidisciplinary perspectives on what culture is provides diverse and competing frameworks for conceptualizing culture. These frameworks also can provide the basis for understanding the influence of culture on conflict. When confronted with conflicts in differing countries and communities, conflicts about culture, cross-cultural conflicts, or indeed any conflict that extends into social institutions, roles, or hierarchical structures, the notion of culture will be invaluable to an ADR practitioner or student in analyzing the conflict, understanding the course that the conflict has taken, evaluating what type of intervention might be possible and generally having a greater appreciation of what is going on.

However, how culture is understood to influence conflict and the practice of ADR depends on how the notion of culture is defined. Much of the recent work on culture and conflict has opted for the classical definition, one that essentially ignores more contemporary and critical perspectives. In a highly regarded review of work on conflict and culture, culture is matter-of-factly Ralph Linton's 1945 version: "the configuration of learned behaviour and results of behaviour whose components and elements are shared and transmitted by the members of a particular society."[14] This definition is carried forward in a 1994 report on conflict and culture with the result that culture's fundamental implications are limited to "worldview, language, beliefs, values, concepts of space and time, religion and social and family relationships."[15] To understand conflict and dispute resolution, culture becomes, classically, shared behaviour, albeit broad-based behaviour.

---

14   M. LeBaron Duryea, *Conflict and Culture: A Literature Review and Bibliography* (Victoria, BC: UVic Inst. for Dispute Resolution, 1992) at 4, referring to R. Linton, *The Cultural Background of Personality* (New York: Appleton-Century, 1945). Some of the literature reviewed by Duryea that also appears to accept the classical view of culture includes: K. Avruch, P.W. Black, & J.A. Scimecca, eds., *Conflict Resolution: Cross Cultural Perspectives* (New York: Greenwood Press, 1991); S. Bochner, ed., *The Mediating Person: Bridges between Cultures* (Cambridge: Schenkman, 1981); P.H. Gulliver, *Disputes and Negotiations: A Cross-Cultural Perspective* (New York: Academic Press, 1981); J.P. Lederach, "Training on Culture: Four Approaches" (1990) 9 Conciliation Q. 6; and D.N. LeResche & J. Spruill, "Training on Culture: A Survey of the Field" (1990) 9 Conciliation Q. 2. See also M.H. Ross, *The Culture of Conflict* (New Haven: Yale University Press, 1993).

15   B. Lund, C. Morris, & M. LeBaron Duryea, *Conflict and Culture: Report of the Multiculturalism and Dispute Resolution Project* (Victoria, BC: UVic Inst. for Dispute Resolution, 1994) at 25.

By equating culture with behaviour, several models and theories about cultural behaviour have been relied on to explain how different peoples view and respond to conflict.

1) Individualist vs. Collectivist

The premise of the individualist versus collectivist model is that differences in cultural behaviour in general can be understood by the degree to which a culture has collectivist or individualist tendencies. Individualism refers to the tendency to be more concerned about one's own needs, interests and goals, whereas collectivism refers to the tendency to be more concerned about the consequences of one's behaviour for in-group members and to be more willing to sacrifice personal interests for the attainment of collective interests.[16] The common suggestion is that people from Western cultures tend to be more individualistic and those from Eastern and Southern cultures more collectivist.[17]

Duryea sets out some implications of this approach to understanding conflict behaviour and for encouraging successful dispute resolution, particularly through the use of mediation:

> Collectivists place more importance on resolving disputes amicably than do individualists.[18]

> For collectivists . . . more attention is paid to the context of the communication, including verbal associations, gestures, body postures, and the facial muscles of the other person.[19]

> Collectivists are more comfortable than individualists in hierarchical structures. This has implications for the role and acceptance of the third party facilitator.[20]

> Collectivists are more likely to agree that it is all right to show respect to people in authority and to direct the actions of those who are junior in age or status. They are also more influenced by familial, tribal or social group connections than individualists. First meetings with

---

16   *Ibid.* at 26–27, referring to H.C. Triandis, R.W. Brislin, & C.H. Hui, "Cross Cultural Training across the Individualism-Collectivist Divide" (1988) 12 Int'l J. Intercultural Relations 269.

17   Duryea, above note 13 at 39.

18   *Ibid.* at 40.

19   *Ibid.*

20   *Ibid.* at 41.

collectivists tend to be formal, and payment is frequently in kind rather than in monetary currency.[21]

[C]ollectivists are most comfortable sharing intimacies when the sharing is reciprocal.[22]

[E]vents accompanying marital or familial difficulties in a collective culture may be decided consultatively by relatives and elders in the community, not solely by the immediate parties. The parties, if they are quite traditional, may expect recommendations and decisions from the intervenor, as would occur from elders within their culture.[23]

[O]nce the parties are at the table, the procedural needs of the parties may vary considerably, with the collectivist expecting a broad, leisurely discussion and the individualist a tight, controlled atmosphere.[24]

[I]ndividualists may be slow to see common ground while those from collectivist cultures find this natural.[25]

Cultural norms for collectivists emphasize avoidance of confrontation as a means of preserving harmony while individualists value individualism and directness as signs of strength.[26]

Morris provides a more overarching view of the conflict perspectives of individualists and collectivists.[27] For the individualist she states:

Conflict is viewed as an expressed struggle to air out and resolve differences and is seen as both functional and dysfunctional. It is functional when it provides an opportunity to resolve problems. It is dysfunctional when not confronted and allowed to fester.

For the collectivist she asserts:

Conflict is viewed as dysfunctional. Conflict is seen as damaging to social harmony and should be avoided as much as possible. Conflict may be considered to indicate a lack of self-discipline and a sign of emotional immaturity.

---

21   *Ibid.*
22   *Ibid.*
23   *Ibid.*
24   *Ibid.* at 42.
25   *Ibid.* at 44.
26   *Ibid.* at 45.
27   C. Morris, "Dispute Resolution in the 1990s: An Overview of Principles and Practices in Canada" in Conference Materials, Dispute Resolution (Khon Kaen, Thailand, 8–9 June 1995) at 28.

2) Low Context vs. High Context

A second and similar model of cultural behaviour is the low context versus high context model.

> Low context cultures generally refer to groups characterized by individualism, overt communication and heterogeneity. The United States, Canada and central and northern Europe are described as areas where low context cultural practices are most in evidence. High context cultures feature collective identity-focus, covert communication and homogeneity. This approach prevails in Asian countries including Japan, China and Korea as well as Latin American countries.[28]

The distinction in cultures tends to suggest that low context cultures perceive conflict in terms of the individual and the striving for individual achievement through self-reliance. Conflict is thus more easily constructed as an "us versus them/me versus you" competitive exchange of adversaries. High context cultures, on the other hand, will perceive of conflict as the disruption of a state of harmony and balance in relationships and, as such, conflict is often seen as requiring the rebuilding and maintaining of relationships.

3) Universalist

A third model is the universalist model. Rather than emphasizing differences in cultural behaviour, this model looks for uniformity by positing that there are certain universal behavioural elements that apply to conflict resolution in all cultures. These elements are the universal need for respect, caring and procedural fairness. Although differences may exist in how conflict is understood, behaviour that embodies these three elements is desirable in the resolution of all conflict.[29]

4) Cultural Demands and Constraints

Ting-Toomey uses the idea of cultural demands and cultural constraints to explain conflict behaviour. Ting-Toomey claims these demands and constraints implicitly dictate what are the appropriate and inap-

---

28   Duryea, above note 13 at 39.
29   The idea that there are several overarching universal "principles" that apply in conflict resolution across cultures appears in Lund, Morris, & Duryea, above note 14 at 26. The thesis is that certain behaviours in conflict (e.g. respect, caring, fairness) are acultural and always desirable for good conflict resolution.

propriate ways of behaving and communicating in a conflict situation. For Ting-Toomey, the application of these cultural demands and cultural constraints depends on "the patterned ways of thinking, acting, feeling and interpreting that constitute the fundamental webs of a culture." Thus, in the classical tradition,

> cultural demands here refer to the set of cultural ideologies or implicit standards that a collective group of individuals more or less ascribe to. They pose as the "oughtness" of how things should be done. The term cultural constraints here can be divided into three types: cultural cognitive constraints, cultural emotional constraints and cultural behaviour constraints. Cultural cognitive constraints refer to belief systems or ideologies that prevent or discourage group members from cognitively thinking in a particular direction. Cultural emotional constraints arise from cultural norms that dictate what sorts of emotional expression (such as anger, frustration or grief) are acceptable or unacceptable to be outwardly displayed in the public cultural context. Finally, cultural behavioural constraints refer to cultural rules and codes that govern the behavioural appropriateness of a given gesture, or words or phrases in a given socio-cultural context.[30]

5) Cultural Values and Perspectives

In a related vein, Sunshine[31] suggests cultural values generate a cultural perspective, which in turn shapes the negotiating behaviour that takes place in international negotiations. Cultural values are, again classically, a society's basic beliefs, norms or standards of conduct and customs. Cultural perspective is a way of looking at, and interacting with, the world. Over time, perceptions become selective because we tend to filter out data that are inconsistent with our cultural values. Cultural perspective then influences the development of a shared and distinctive negotiating approach or style.

Relying on models of cultural behaviour may provide some insights that can help to explain or predict conflict responses but the approach appears highly problematic for two reasons. First, there is the concern

---

30 S. Ting-Toomey, "Toward a Theory of Conflict and Culture" in W.B. Gudykunst, L.P. Stewart, & S. Ting-Toomey, eds., *Communication, Culture and Organizational Processes* (Beverly Hills: Sage, 1985) at 73–74.

31 R.B. Sunshine, *Negotiating for International Development* (Dordrecht: Martinus Nijhoff Publishers, 1990).

that sweeping generalizations about how an entire country, region, or peoples will behave are no more than outdated and simplistic portrayals of stereotypes that do not reflect reality. Canada and the United States may be characterized as countries that are intensely individualistic. However, that characterization and the resulting assumptions about how Canadians and Americans will behave in conflict would not be accurate descriptions for many individuals in these diverse societies. Similarly, First Nations treaty negotiators may come from collectivist or high context cultures but be more than willing to use confrontation or tough negotiating tactics to gain advantage for their peoples. The thesis that behavioural attitudes can be generalized over large geographical areas or for large numbers of individuals based on their race, ethnicity, religion or other cultural characteristic may not be supported by the truth of everyday experiences.

Second, the above models of cultural behaviour appear to be inspired by the classical definition of culture. Culture continues to be equated with behaviour within these models. The models reinforce this close connection between culture and behaviour by positing that there are a number of limited categories that capture and explain much (if not all) of the conflict behaviours exhibited in a particular country or region or by a certain set of peoples. These classical models of cultural behaviour ignore the ideas that culture extends well beyond behaviour and that a focus on behaviour omits other contemporary perspectives on what makes up culture.

D. CULTURE, CONFLICT AND ADR

Understanding conflict and conflict resolution across cultures primarily in behavioural terms — how disputants perceive, approach, process and resolve conflict — meshes neatly with the understanding that ADR is primarily an assortment of common-sense processes, most often consensus-based, which disputants engage in to resolve conflicts. As ADR crosses paths with culture, the approach then can become one of adopting or adapting an existing ADR method or establishing a "made in the country" variation in ways that accommodate and respect the behaviour that has been discovered to be culturally correct in conflict settings. In this way, ADR has a stability and certainty that facilitates its transferability across clear cultural divides, provided the ADR process is culturally (read behaviourally) sensitive.

The benefit to this approach to ADR across cultures is that it acknowledges that behaviour is relevant to understanding conflict and conflict resolution and that the presence or absence of certain behaviours can be important to the course conflict takes. A particular Japanese businessperson may need to establish a certain type of trusting relationship with the Canadian negotiator before discussing the substantive merits of the joint venture. Efforts by the Canadian, or a mediator asked to assist negotiations, to push the agenda along too quickly may be counter-productive. Crossed legs may show disrespect in a business meeting in Thailand and jeopardize the negotiation of a successful agreement even though this posture may be comfortable to the unsuspecting negotiator and unobjectionable in another setting. An Aboriginal person may not make eye contact with the judge when giving evidence in a criminal case. This behaviour may have more to do with respect for authority and uncertainty over the trial process and little to do with the credibility of the evidence being given. Rigid class, religious or social hierarchies where extreme deference must be shown to those higher up may mean face-to-face meetings in mediation where everyone is expected to participate equally will be unrealistic or seriously problematic. Unintentionally invading a disputant's personal space or rejecting an offer on a holy day may be serious negotiation errors in one setting but be effective tactics in a different venue.

But these examples are no different in kind than the behavioural needs in every dispute. A university student may only agree to a mediation with the professor she has accused of sexual harassment if she can have a trusted advocate or lawyer with her in the mediation. In a business setting, a handshake may be highly significant to one negotiator but this same behaviour might carry very little weight with another. A disabled person's continued insistence that the corporate landlord issue a public apology as part of the settlement of a human rights complaint may jeopardize chances for any agreement. The crossed arms of the insurance company representative during a mediation may give the claimant in a motor vehicle accident case the impression that the representative is close-minded both to the proposed settlement and to the accident victim's overall circumstances. An intentional leak of confidential information to the media may result in increased public support for the union's position but it also may be viewed by the company as a breach of trust.

Behaviours are important in dispute resolution. The context of any dispute will dictate just how the various disputants should or must act in different situations and whether or not this behaviour is constructive or destructive. The challenge of understanding and recognizing these behavioural requirements and assessing their impact on the disputing process will depend on the degree to which the dispute's contextual features are appreciated, as discussed in chapter 1. The lawyer who is representing the native band needs to be aware that getting instructions to settle an important claim may take considerably more time than would be the case if the client was a non-native organization. The lawyers in a wrongful dismissal case will understand that an early and higher-than-expected offer to settle is influenced by the Asia-based company's desire to avoid confrontation and maintain harmony in its ranks.

However, as ADR expands into different countries, regions and situations and encounters peoples with other disputing traditions, the problem with understanding culture's impact on ADR primarily in behavioural terms lies in what this perspective fails to mention. Consider the use or establishment of ADR for American and Iraqi negotiators, the Israelis and Palestinians, Cubans and Americans, the Sikh denied entry into the war veterans' lounge unless he removes his turban as a sign of respect for the fallen soldiers, Quebec sovereigntists and nationalists, a neighbour of European descent quarrelling with a neighbour of Chinese ethnicity, opposing government parties seriously disagreeing on parliamentary reforms in Cambodia, or the people of Nicaragua. Culture can point to more than an inquiry into the way that unique and often demanding disputant behaviours, wherever located, fit or can be made to fit into existing ADR procedures. Culture from a contemporary vantage point can raise questions about the ADR movement itself.

First, there are the politics, contradictions and ambiguities of ADR discussed in chapter 1. Rather than asking whether North American notions of ADR can possibly have any relevance or utility for Nicaragua, Cambodia or other cultural context, when culture is equated with behaviour the question can be reframed, in a mediative manner, into a neutral goal statement that makes ADR appear culturally friendly. The question is obvious. How can the common sense of ADR — saving time and money, getting long-lasting and better results and other democratic goals — be realized while at the same time maintaining and respecting the behavioural requirements unique to the culture? ADR, aware of its essentially Eurocentric roots, offers to change shape somewhat to fit in so that any concerns of cultural insensitivity are met or minimized. The chameleon-like response is possible because ADR can be presented as an eclectic collection of many and varied neutral processes seeking to achieve a range of good and common-sense goals. If culture is primarily about behaviour, the only challenge for ADR is how to make its initiatives behaviourally correct in a specific cultural setting.

However, if culture is made up of more than learned or shared behaviour, the twin assumptions that ADR is common sense and that ADR can make long-lasting improvements, provided it is culturally sensitive, come under scrutiny. If the notion of culture has links to the construction of class, race, gender and power structures and is a force in shaping social life and society's institutions, the underlying ideology behind ADR's politics and contradictions, whatever it is, and not disputant behaviour, becomes a critical factor in deciding whether or not ADR is sensible and whether ADR procedures can offer any help to "cultural" disputes. The notion of culture points to the fact that what ADR presents as normal, natural and essential in disputing in a society is not neutral but must be highly relevant to, and implicated in, the course the dispute takes and its outcome. In fact, culture broadly defined draws attention to the symbiotic relationship between the structures, relationships, hierarchies and general ordering in a society and the dispute resolution methods and practices, including those classified as ADR, relied on to construct, maintain or change these orders.

The practical result is that culture complicates one's assessment and use of ADR. For example, the construction of a dam in Thailand, if approved, would create enormous wealth and produce a range of economic benefits, but the consequential flooding would displace villagers from their homelands and cause environmental damage. An ADR-inspired idea of mediating this dispute to prevent violence and arrive at a creative, win-win solution raises more than the procedural challenge of establishing a shared decision-making process in Thailand "in which, on a certain set of issues for a defined period of time, those with authority to make a decision and those affected by that decision are empowered jointly to seek an outcome that accommodates rather than compromises the interest of all concerned."[32] The broader notion of culture opens up questions about mediation's role in maintaining or exacerbating existing power differentials and other decision-making deficiencies, about the efficacy of consensual decision making in a society where structural inequalities predominate, about the consequences of using a private process to address the public problems that underlie the dam dynamics and about whether ADR in any shape can or should have meaning in a country with its own disputing traditions and histories.

---

32   This definition was coined for the British Columbia Commission on Resources and Environment (CORE) as the overarching framework for public participation in their environmental mediations.

Consider also treaty negotiations between Aboriginal and non-Aboriginal governments. Although the negotiation process will play a role in achieving enduring agreements on complex issues, successful negotiations will depend on more than ADR efforts to ensure negotiating behaviours do not clash in this cross-cultural setting. A First Nation's treaty negotiator may need to have the negotiations take place on traditional territories, to include certain ceremonies in the negotiations, to proceed at a certain pace, to have elders physically present and participating at length and to obtain community support for any proposed agreement. If accommodating these behavioural needs in an ADR-inspired negotiation model is all that is required, much may be missed. Culture in a critical light would show the interdependencies that must exist between and among (1) treaty efforts to share power, change structures of governance, provide compensation for past injustices and paint a bright future; (2) opposition to such efforts and the reasons for wanting to maintain the status quo; and (3) the actual disputing methods and dispute resolution goals being used to reach treaty accords. For some, the notion of culture may cast doubt on the utility of ADR-influenced ideas for treaty negotiations, help understand breakdowns in treaty negotiations and point to other disputing approaches as more likely to achieve the fundamental societal changes that lie at the heart of these conflicts.

In another example, thinking that culture equals behaviour would provide a limited focus to the conflicts that women have encountered in the military. Understanding a conflict (e.g. a woman pilot complains of harassment by military superiors) and pursuing its successful resolution will depend on much more than a main thesis that the woman pilot will be anxious or angry about bringing the complaint forward and the corollary to this behavioural conclusion that an effective dispute resolution process must be designed to make her feel comfortable. In this example, culture broadly defined would implicate the systemic nature of the problems faced by women in a male-dominated institution, would probably assume many more women have suffered similar fates, and might point to remedying the cultural conditions (sexism, power imbalances, too few women in top positions) that give rise to the conflict in the first place as part of any responsive disputing process. This critical perspective on culture might mean effective approaches to the conflict would be class actions, criminal charges, legislation, independent reviews, personnel changes, publicity or even education rather than efforts to accommodate the behavioural needs of the individual complainant in, for example, a mediation process. In this military conflict, the notion of culture provides opportunities for a more expansive examination of the situation and more focused responses.

There is a second and related area of omission when culture's impact on ADR is presented primarily in behavioural terms. The interest-based foundation of ADR that was described in chapter 3 also can avoid close scrutiny. The concept of collaboratively achieving consensus through interest-based approaches to dispute resolution has been a distinguishing and dominant feature throughout the modern emergence of ADR. An interest-based approach to dispute resolution essentially means that the disputants collaborate to uncover the needs, desires, concerns, fears and hopes that are motivating them in the dispute and then together develop creative and win-win solutions that satisfy these interests as far as possible.

When culture is equated with behaviour, ADR's interest-based foundation can be presented as posing no threat to cultural sensitivity. The argument usually made is that this approach works. Interest-based negotiation and mediation processes can result in the achievement of laudable and diverse goals including economic efficiency and personal transformation. There are numerous and increasing examples of services and programs that use this collaborative approach. There is a growing demand for training in interest-basing and an emerging new profession extolling the virtues of interest-based approaches to dispute resolution. Any concerns about cultural costs associated with this concept are met by offering analyses of similarities or common ground between interest-based consensual approaches to disputes and the specific culture's own traditional or customary methods of disputing. As well, there are observations that the values behind collaborative interest-based processes — respect, caring, trust, mutuality, harmony, relationship — are (or should be) universally desirable in dispute resolution.

However, with a more contemporary, complex and critical look to culture, two concerns can be raised about the assumption that ADR's interest-based foundation is transferable intact from one setting to another.

First, there are the goals behind interest-based approaches to dispute resolution. These goals are generally presented as incontrovertible and achievable. Reaching consensus through an interest-based bargaining process or facilitating resolution in mediation by encouraging the disputants to reveal the underlying interests behind their stated positions can save time and money, reduce court congestion, transform personal thinking about disputing, preserve continuing relationships, produce lasting agreement, eliminate violence, nurture democratic development and achieve other long-lasting improvements.

However, culture broadly defined forces one to evaluate whether the overarching goals of ADR generally and interest-based approaches to dispute resolution particularly come with too high a cost for many disputants. The concern is that interest-based dispute resolution processes shunt controversies into private settings without formal due process protections. In these circumstances, there is a risk that existing power imbalances can be exploited and structural inequalities can be difficult to address or change. For many women, the poor, Indigenous peoples, minorities and others who generally have been disadvantaged in a society, the widespread promulgation of private, interest-based approaches to their disputes may offer little assistance and may in fact cause great harm. Power imbalances and structural inequalities are often the real cause of a conflict for these people. The conflicts are difficult to resolve through interest-based consensual approaches because the more powerful party has little incentive to negotiate in good faith, often has a better alternative than voluntarily giving up power, or can impose an inequitable solution. Thinking that culture's main contribution to the resolution of these types of disputes is ensuring respect for, and sensitivity to, proper interest-based behaviour has the potential to make matters worse by discouraging disobedience, protests, activism or other approaches to dispute resolution designed to change settled structures. Consensual or interest-based dispute resolution may not get to the crux of the matter.

A second concern goes beyond the efficacy or achievability of disputing goals to what it is that really drives the theory of interest-based dispute resolution processes. If the notion of culture is central to how social institutions and structures are shaped and ordered, an obvious point to consider is how the underpinnings of interest-based approaches to dispute resolution fit the social shaping and ordering that make up culture.

Interest-based approaches to dispute resolution did not magically materialize in *Getting to Yes* with the rise of ADR. The concept has an interesting background.[33] In part, the theoretical framework of interest-based bargaining derives from the work of American legal realists who criticized legal doctrine and rights talk. These theorists tried to build a more realistic jurisprudence through closer attention to behaviour, empirical data, facts and "the actual doings of judges."[34] Interests or preferences "seemed to more forthrightly demand and empower empirical demonstration and would therefore provide the basis for a more realistic legal science."[35]

---

33   Silbey and Sarat provide insights into what helped shape the concept: S. Silbey & A. Sarat, "Dispute Processing in Law and Legal Scholarship: From Institutional Critique to the Reconstruction of the Juridical Subject" (1989) 66 Denver U. L. Rev. 437 at 479.

34   *Ibid.* at 480.

35   *Ibid.*

Vilhelm Aubert, a Norwegian sociologist, differentiated between conflicts of interest and conflicts of value.[36] Essentially, conflicts of interest derived from competition over scarce resources. These conflicts could be resolved through the market or through mechanisms that compromised the demands, gains and losses to each side and "minimized the likelihood of maximal loss."[37] Solutions to interest conflicts would involve what Aubert called "a natural adjustment of needs."[38] Conflicts of interest "emphasized the similarity of the contestants, their common needs and aspirations."[39] In contrast, conflicts of value arose not from competition but from "dissensus" or disagreement "concerning the normative status of a social object."[40] For dissensus and conflicts of value, Aubert suggested that law and courts would provide the most appropriate mode of conflict resolution. Conversely, he hypothesized that law and formal conflict resolution institutions would transform conflicts of interest into conflicts of value making compromise solutions less possible. Aubert's analysis borrows from standard conceptions of economic markets but adds to the usual variables. At the heart of the dispute decision model is the "conception of the dispute as an arena of competitive decision-making by rationally calculating individuals motivated by utility maximization."[41]

More comprehensive theories of needs have added another layer of complexity to interest-based approaches to dispute resolution. The fundamental premise of these theories is that disputants share essential human requisites and capacities. Based on the work of Ardry and Wilson in sociobiology, Maslow in psychology, as well as stimulus response behaviourism, fundamental human needs are identified which collectively constitute human nature. For example, Maslow identified a hierarchy of basic needs that influence behaviour from lowest (or most basic) needs such as food, shelter, safety to highest (or least basic) needs such as aesthetic demands or wants. Burton and Sandole[42] identify needs such as a need for consistent response, a need for stimulation, a need for security, a need for recognition, a need for dis-

---

36   V. Aubert, "Competition and Dissensus: Two Types of Conflict and Conflict Resolution" (1963) 7 J. Conflict Resol. 26.

37   *Ibid.* at 29.

38   *Ibid.* at 34.

39   *Ibid.* at 29.

40   *Ibid.*

41   Above note 32 at 484.

42   J.W. Burton & D.J.D. Sandole, "Generic Theory: The Basis of Conflict Resolution" (1986) 2 Negotiation J. 333.

tributive justice, a need to appear rational, a need for meaning in response and a need for role defence.[43] Successful dispute resolution, it is said, must explore these fundamental, deep-seated human needs or "underlying interests." Attention to these needs will reveal grounds of interdependence, reciprocity and compatibility as well as show that solutions based on needs are not limited and may expand through interaction and exchange. This focus on allegedly universal and core human attributes also raised suggestions that cooperative approaches to dispute resolution meet all people's psychological needs for harmony, peace, autonomy, integrity, dignity, trust and relationship.[44]

These intellectual underpinnings that an apparently essentialist view of human needs that transcends contextual differences rests at the core of interest-based approaches to dispute resolution. Whatever the traditional or dominant disputing mores, there is an assumption behind interest-based dispute resolution of a "better," more essential approach to expressing and realizing our needs. Interest-based dispute resolution also assumes the disputants begin at, or aspire to, a condition of perfect competition for maximizing preferences. Identifying important bundles of interests or needs, attaching utility to them and working together to create mutually satisfying solutions is an efficiency-maximizing process. Focusing on interests in this manner can point more easily to Pareto efficient or optimal exchanges in a negotiation. The negotiation outcome is Pareto efficient if it makes at least one party better off and the other parties concerned no worse off than they were before the exchange was made. Where no further improvements can be made to Pareto efficiency, the exchange is said to be Pareto optimal. There is additionally the inevitable dependency on expert helpers who will specify and service human needs. There is a consequential denying of legitimacy to those who disagree about what is needed or who is needy. There is the claim that all problems are solvable because a dispute involves the technical and individual problem of matching available means to essential needs. Interest-based inspired dispute resolution becomes a technocratic activity[45] that is apolitical and relatively uncontroversial.

For the range of countries, regions and peoples to which ADR is being promoted, the theory underlying interest-based approaches to dispute resolution may make sense. But the reverse may also be true. When compared with a country, region, or people's own psychological,

---

43   Ibid.
44   Above note 32 at 486–88.
45   Ibid. at 495.

sociological, anthropological, legal, customary or other relevant disciplinary ideas of disputes and disputing, the theory and practice of interest-based bargaining may have little meaning and may even smack of neocolonialism and ethnocentric biases.

The frequency of ADR being tested across cultures, both within and between countries, is likely to increase because of advances in communications technology, globalization efforts, world trade organizations, the proliferation of ADR supporters, a steady supply of complex and costly "cultural" disputes that existing structures seem ill-equipped to handle and ADR's many promises of help. ADR advancements are likely to assist in the achievement of long-lasting improvements in these cultural settings. However, if the impact of culture on conflict is understood primarily to mean that effective dispute resolution needs to respect and accommodate the learned and shared behaviour of a society or people, the most challenging questions associated with ADR across cultures may be overlooked or dealt with superficially. There are real risks that cultural diffusion, complaints of neocolonialism, more marginalization for minorities and the least powerful in society, missed opportunities, and perhaps ultimately failure will be the true legacies left behind from ADR's journeys into the culture and conflict terrain.

E. CULTURE AND NEW APPROACHES TO DISPUTE RESOLUTION

A practical cultural dispute might involve lawyers representing relatives wanting to keep a child from returning to his father in another country; a mediator working to ease tensions between Aboriginal and non-Aboriginal fishers; a consultant helping teachers, parents and children to eliminate violence in an inner-city school; or an ombudsperson investigating allegations of racial discrimination in hiring practices. Understanding and working with the complexity of "cultural" disputes requires new approaches to dispute resolution. Rather than mechanically adopting or adapting ADR, the student or practitioner's approach to dispute resolution could be informed and guided by the following points:

- **Context matters most.** As discussed in chapter 1, a dispute, the course it takes, and its eventual outcome depend on the interplay of many real-world details. Culture as a concept can provoke a critical look at these contextual details, can provide a basis for a more in-depth analysis of the situation, and can aid in indicating which dispute resolution initiatives might help or hinder. In many respects, culture in its contemporary perspective is context. Culture essentially covers the where, who, what, when and why of disputing. Thinking of culture primarily in behavioural terms gives a blinkered outlook on the context of conflict. Culture as context opens up more possibilities. **Culture will influence disputing behaviour in one way or another.** The aggressive moves, the backing down, the compromises, the respect for authority, the indirectness, the formality and the informality may be better understood and anticipated by knowing the disputant's culture. But culture may have more important contributions to make: it may explain what is actually in dispute. Culture may point to the parties who are (or should be) concerned with a particular problem. Culture may be particularly helpful in showing why a dispute has finally emerged or why it is proceeding in a particular direction. When culture is equated with the myriad real-world details that shape and determine what happens next in any dispute, the notion of culture must also encompass the range of dispute resolution processes and practices that are applied to these disputes. Rather than ADR being separate from culture and somehow culturally neutral, ADR is an obvious contributor to culture in the ways that it calls for, encourages, mandates or actually influences how disputes come forward and are addressed and in the ways that ADR affects the real and substantive changes that come out of disputing. Adapting ADR to fit a particular culture may seem possible. But this adaptationist approach is not a compulsory one and it largely ignores the idea that ADR is itself an integral and key element in the cultural makeup.

- **ADR is (mostly) a Eurocentric construct.** The history of ADR has some roots in the disputing traditions of non-European peoples and societies. However, for the most part, ADR has been constructed using North American notions of dispute resolution with significant help from a Western-based legal profession needing to remedy flaws in the adversarial approach to resolving disputes. The result is a mostly mainstream movement that is solidly grounded in processes, skills, values and beliefs that express Eurocentric and increasingly legal approaches to dispute resolution. The history of ADR means that ADR may not make much sense for certain conflicts. For example, the idea of mediation as a mandatory process in which the disputants meet face-to-face and go through a structured negotiation with a heavy emphasis on interest-based bargaining may not be what many disputants would favour, be comfortable with, or expect if they had a choice. The market forces that seem to underpin the essentialism of principled negotiation may be incongruent with what motivates a wide range of disputants or their understanding of what it is that shapes and influences the course of a dispute. The ADR admonitions to avoid court and resort to consensual approaches to dispute resolution may be surprising or even oppressive to disputants who need to show a strong deference to authority figures, who look to elders for authoritative advice or who regard the courts as appropriate and needed arbiters of conflicting rights.

- **ADR is linked to comparative studies.** The unreflective promulgation of ADR across diverse cultures can raise more than cries of cultural imperialism, colonialism or cultural diffusion. These concerns are chilling enough but the idea of widely promoting a Eurocentric concept of disputing across cultures really requires one to appreciate that this is not an isolated example. At one level, the instances of ADR in Nicaragua, South Africa, China, Thailand, Cambodia and elsewhere are unremarkable. It would be surprising if ADR theories and practices were not shared and compared given globalization, trade agreements, advances in communication technologies and other factors. It would be unusual if there was not worldwide interest in a disputing movement that makes so many promises. It would be unrealistic to think that ADR could be hidden or should be hidden from world view. Certainly, the exchange of information is common currency in other areas such as law, economics, politics, religion, and engineering. Accordingly, truly understanding the example of ADR across cultures with its Western traditions requires generally an understanding of, and approach to, comparative studies. This subject is beyond the scope of this book but an example is illustrative. In law, comparative legal studies has a long history. Over time, laws from different countries, regions, and communities have been compared, contrasted, and considered, and, in this exchange, many examples have emerged of laws from one region being transferred and transnationalized, or at the very least influencing legal development in another region. However, there are different approaches to considering this phenomena. Some approaches were inspired by a vision of a common law of mankind or a policy of legal harmonization in designated areas of common purpose. Worldwide conventions on human rights and certain global trade rules are examples of this industry. Other approaches to comparative legal studies, such as the law and development movement; law and society and legal history studies; or critical legal theory challenged programs that depended on the use of Western models of law as a vehicle to achieve modernization and suggested instead the exploitative, oppressive and coercive nature of such programs. Although legal development occurs, how it is viewed very much depends on how it is analyzed. Assessing the merit of ADR across cultures will depend on exactly the same factors.

- **The notion of culture reaffirms the indeterminacy of dispute resolution.** Predicting what will happen next in a conflict or deciding which resources might best suit a conflict situation are challenging enough tasks. Culture complicates this work for alternative dispute resolution theorists and practitioners by introducing variables that strongly influence the course of conflict but that can be difficult to understand or even identify. What will continue to happen in disputes such as those between the United States and Iraq, the Israelis and Palestinians, Indigenous peoples worldwide and the non-Indigenous governments they must deal with, pro-choice and pro-life factions, and sovereigntists in Quebec and those who oppose Quebec's separation? Culture is a notion that pervades all these disputes as well as the processes that seek to resolve them. A consideration of culture will undoubtedly influence disputing decisions. These decisions, in turn, will affect the course that these conflicts take. But it is unrealistic to think that cultural considerations can be used to fully remove the indeterminacy that is a normal part of most dispute processing.

- **The real promise of ADR is its inspiration.** The notion of culture adds another layer of considerable complexity to the theory and practice of alternative dispute resolution. The efforts to date to unravel the mysteries of conflict and culture have been successful in discovering more to explore. The real promise of ADR may be its encouragement to take on and not to ignore these challenges. Despite its history, politics, contradiction and ambiguities, alternative dispute resolution has inspired much thinking in many quarters about the world of disputes, about the numerous ways in which disputes are or can be processed, and about the practical principles, skills and hunches that help resolve problems. ADR, at its best, has opened up a field of inquiry of enormous potential, fundamental importance and untapped potential. ADR can encourage the reflective, critical, and multidisciplinary work necessary to explore the complex interrelationships between culture and conflict. The result may be a new world order for disputing. But it is likely that analyses of culture and conflict will produce a mosaic of approaches to dispute resolution that are as varied, complex and contradictory as culture itself. There will no doubt be well-known institutionalized disputing structures, like the courts, which will be designed to be accessible to all and which, to one degree or another, will reflect a dominant cultural view of appropriate disputing practices. But in the same way that the courts are the final arbiters of only a small percentage of disputes that arise in society, institutionalized or formal dispute resolution procedures will not likely displace the enormously diverse array of ways in which disputes emerge and are processed in real life. ADR should not be seen as illustrative of the only way to dispute. Culture in its broadest sense pushes the field of ADR to be about inspiring individuals, organizations and governments to search for the most desirable outcomes we can imagine.

FURTHER READINGS

AVRUCH, K., P. BLACK, & J. SCIMECCIA, *Conflict Resolution: Cross-Cultural Perspectives* (New York: Greenwood Press, 1991)

BARNES, B.E., "Conflict Resolution across Cultures: A Hawaii Perspective" (1994) 12 Mediation Q. 117

CARTER, J., *Keeping Faith: Memoirs of a President* (New York: Bantam Books, 1982)

LEDERACH, J.P., *Preparing for Peace: Conflict Transformation across Cultures* (Syracuse, NY: Syracuse University Press, 1995)

ROSS, M.H., *The Culture of Conflict* (New Haven: Yale University Press, 1993)

CHAPTER 8

THE LAW OF ADR: LEGISLATION, CASES AND THE COURTS

A. INTRODUCTION

Few people would be surprised to find there exists a large body of law on subjects such as contracts, torts, property, business associations, the constitution, the family, crime and trusts, to name a few. One source of this law comes from the decisions of judges regarding disputes that have gone to the courts for adjudication. The disputes may have been about such issues as whether there was a need for independent legal advice before the elderly person signed the bank guarantee, whether a psychiatrist owed a duty of care to warn the target of his patient's rage, whether the chief executives are personally liable for a crime committed by their company or whether sexual orientation is relevant in deciding what is in the best interests of the children. Court decisions on these and other disputes, along with their interpretation and application to future cases that come to court, make up the powerful and evolving legal standards or common law that lawyers employ to advise clients what can, cannot or might be done in specific situations.

The law also includes legislation enacted by federal, state, territorial or provincial governments. This legislation may, for example, establish guidelines for support payments in divorce proceedings, require sustainable practices to be followed when harvesting timber, make certain conduct criminal, fix income tax rates, provide protection against unfair trade practices or regulate the price of oil and gas. Legislation can actually prevent some disputes from arising by making it clear what behaviours or which standards are to be followed. Legislation also can be a way of resolving an ongoing dispute by setting out a legislated solution.

Although this law may be expected, the law of ADR may be a surprise. After all, alternative dispute resolution emerged as a movement that stood in stark contrast to court adjudication. ADR proponents saw a need to avoid the undue cost and delay of litigation. They extolled the virtues of non-adversarial approaches to dispute resolution. Negotiation, mediation and other forms of consensual decision-making were a first focus of ADR and informal justice and informalism were defining characteristics in ADR's early days. ADR and formal law more resembled antonyms than anything else in contemporary dispute resolution conversations.

A number of factors have combined to change this picture. As discussed in chapter 1, the meaning of ADR has come to include how litigation is managed with a focus on the appropriate method for resolving any given dispute. The space that initially existed between ADR and the court is no longer as yawning. There are increasing examples of ADR initiatives, such as mandatory or court-connected mediation, being implemented within the very formal justice system that ADR first stood in opposition to. An ADR movement that had attracted hostility and criticism from the legal profession is now being heartily embraced by most lawyers. ADR practices and procedures are presented as an integral part of what it is that good lawyers do. Along with this legal acceptance, there have been increasing examples of ADR being formally institutionalized by governments and organizations into existing societal systems and structures. Not surprisingly, disputes about ADR use have come with these developments. Some disputes have been principled and about important policy issues such as qualifications. But other disputes have been more pragmatic and pressing, requiring a more immediate reply.

- Should a government endorse ADR in this legislative session? What should the endorsement say?
- Should ADR be spelled out for pupil and school disputes as well as for funeral home operators and their clientele?
- Can a party be exempted from attending mandatory mediation?
- Are communications made in mediation privileged?
- What is the scope of judicially assisted dispute resolution?
- When should a judge order a mini-trial to be held?
- Can a mediator be negligent?

It perhaps should not be a surprise that the law of ADR is also developing.

The theory and practice of ADR now are informed by the law of ADR. Understanding the law of alternative dispute resolution is important because this law — whether it is judge-made law or legislation — can directly affect and even dictate what should or must be done in best ADR practices. In a related way, the law of ADR and how this law develops have enormous potential to shape the ideological meaning of ADR by creating these legal frameworks for what is normal, natural, and essential in disputing practices and by having the courts resolve the disputes that arise about the meaning of ADR and how it should be practised. A critical eye on the law of ADR provides opportunities to see what components of disputing the legal frameworks and judges favour and what parts may be ignored or left behind.

The law of ADR can be conveniently examined by considering selected ADR legislation, judicial decisions involving ADR and ADR in the courts.

B. ADR LEGISLATION

As the use of ADR became popular, governments began increasingly to see opportunities to apply ADR processes to public disputing scenarios. The business of running democracies was always filled with controversy. Governance disputes, whether about the siting of a new waste management facility, regulating fisheries, taxing decisions, making modern treaties or international trade agreements, choosing parks over industrial plants, criminalizing the right to die, or pepper-spraying protesters tended to be costly, time-consuming, and often hard to settle. Shielding difficult public policy decisions and the decision makers by closing Cabinet doors, relying mostly on a bureaucratic analysis, providing varying degrees of fairness in administrative hearings, or making and defending town hall–type announcements was being viewed as unsatisfactory by many people affected by the issues at hand. More openness and transparency in good government were being demanded. The emergence of ADR was particularly timely for besieged and cost-conscious governments. ADR developments in the private sector raised an awareness that better options might be available to enhance or improve public dispute resolution as well.

Several governmental responses to ADR have been referred to earlier, the most significant of which has been the institutionalization of ADR in the form of ADR legislation. In the United States, there are over two thousand federal and state statutes regulating the field. In Canada and other countries, the number is substantially smaller but growing steadily. ADR legislation generally takes two shapes.

The umbrella-type legislation promotes the use of alternative dispute resolution in much the same manner as is done in dispute resolution clauses in private contracts or in partnering arrangements. For example, the *Alternative Dispute Resolution Act of 1998* requires every federal district court in the United States to establish ADR programs and requires litigants in each case to consider the use of ADR at the appropriate time. The *Administrative Dispute Resolution Act of 1990* provides a similar exhortation for federal administrative agencies in the United States. The *Negotiated Rulemaking Act of 1990* authorizes and encourages agencies to use negotiated rule making or neg-reg to set standards, policies or other rules instead of the traditional decide-announce-defend practices. The *Civil Justice Reform Act of 1990* and the Federal Rules of Civil Procedure changed the definition of ADR from "extrajudicial procedures" to "special procedures to assist in resolving the dispute when authorized by statute or local rules" and reiterated the view that district courts use ADR.[1] A uniform mediation Act is being developed to help clarify, among other things, some disclosure disputes that can arise when mediation is used.

In Canada, the *Divorce Act* imposes a duty on every lawyer or advocate who acts on behalf of a spouse in a divorce proceeding to discuss the advisability of negotiating support or custody matters in dispute and to inform the spouse of mediation sources that might be of assistance in negotiating such matters. There is also the *North American Free Trade Agreement (NAFTA)* that requires each of the signatories to encourage and facilitate the use of arbitration and other means of ADR for the settlement of international commercial disputes between private parties in the free trade area.

Apart from umbrella-type coverage, ADR legislation can be more specific. This type of legislation will provide for mandatory or discretionary resort to specific ADR processes in certain situations. For example, regulations to the *Homeowner Protection Act*, S.B.C. 1998, c. 31, provide that any party to a residential construction lawsuit can serve a notice to mediate on the other side and, unless exempted, the other side would have to attend at a mediation session.

Under the *Funeral Directors and Establishments Act*, R.S.O. 1990, c. F.36, the Board established to regulate the practices of funeral directors and establishments is given the authority to mediate complaints between consumers and licencees. If a mediator is appointed to assist the parties to resolve a dispute under the *Agricultural Operations Act*, S.S. 1995, c. A-12.1,

---

1   For other examples of U.S. legislation, see N.H. Rogers & C.A. McEwan, *Mediation: Law, Policy, and Practice*, 2d ed. (St. Paul, MN: West Publishing, 1994).

evidence of anything said or arising from anything said is declared by the legislation to be not admissable in any proceeding before a court unless the mediator and all parties consent in writing. Under the *Courts of Justice Act*, R.S.O. 1990, c. C. 43, as amended, the Ontario Judicial Council may establish a mediation process for complainants and for judges who are the subject of complaints but must ensure complaints are excluded from the mediation process if, among other things, there is a significant power imbalance between the complainant and the judge. The *Residential Tenancies Act*, S.N.B. 1975, c. R-10.2 gives a rentalsman the power to mediate disputes between landlords and tenants.

Examples of ADR legislation in Canada with references to ADR terms or processes are listed in Appendix 1 with their relevant clauses. These selections further illustrate how governments can incorporate ADR into a wide variety of contexts in which disputes have a public side and show the type of impact that legislation can have on the form and function of ADR.

Two observations can be made about ADR legislation in Canada. First, the institutionalization of ADR in Canada appears mostly to occur in the form of mediation. Although labour legislation will often refer to the arbitration process, legislative provisions permitting mediation to be attempted in a wide range of subject areas under federal or provincial jurisdiction are becoming common. In a manner of speaking, this statutory encouragement of mediation is analogous to umbrella-type legislation for the many ways in which mediation could be practised.

Second, in some cases, however, there are specific legislative prescriptions for what must or must not happen in the mediation process. Apart from making mediation mandatory, the statute may impose time limits on the mediation, refer to necessary mediator qualifications, require good-faith bargaining in mediation or create a statutory privilege for the communications taking place. This latter standard — making admissions or other communications in the course of a mediation inadmissible in a subsequent court proceeding unless the parties consent — reaffirms the general ethical rule that the mediation process is confidential. Although there have been (and will likely continue to be) cases challenging this rule, in which mediators are subpoenaed to give evidence regarded as essential for the court to effectively adjudicate, imposing a statutory privilege may be unnecessary given common law developments (see below section (C), "Judicial Decisions and ADR"). A statutory privilege for all mediations may also not be needed if the common law exceptions to the law of privilege, to be decided upon by the courts on a case-by-case basis, could be a usual and important part of the mediation process without unduly interfering with the openness and candour desired in such a process. Care will need to be taken that the legislative detail required to encourage or provide for mediation or other ADR mechanisms does not prematurely close the debates on important matters of disputing policy.

C. JUDICIAL DECISIONS AND ADR

From one vantage point, all judicial decisions are a part of ADR. These cases represent the results of the formal adjudication of particular disputes by judges. As ADR precedents, they may illustrate the features of disputes most amenable to disposition by the courts or be analyzed to determine whether negotiation, mediation or other ADR approaches might have helped.

However, some judicial pronouncements are more about ADR than others. Disputants often will take ADR to court. In some cases, judges are asked to make decisions about the forms and functions of various disputing processes. For example, there is an extensive body of law on the procedures and practices that must be fairly followed by administrative agencies when these bodies are adjudicating disputes. The courts have had a significant influence on what is a fair process in most regulatory regimes. Similarly, as referred to in chapter 5, the courts also have made decisions that determine the detail of the general arbitration processes provided for in arbitration legislation and in private arbitral agreements. Courts also adjudicate disputes about their own procedure.

The judicial impact on ADR has not been limited to these examples. As ADR and its various disputing processes flourish, there have been other instances when judges have been asked to make decisions about specific ADR-related matters. These decisions are becoming part of the growing law of ADR.

Disputants are resorting to the courts to settle ADR disputes for three reasons. First, some ADR disputes, much like the other disputes that end up in court, can be difficult to settle consensually. A mediation participant feels she was not well served by the mediator and sues him or her for breach of contract, breach of fiduciary duty or for being negligent. A party from an unsuccessful mediation subpoenas the mediator to give important and otherwise unobtainable evidence in the subsequent court proceeding when the statute is silent on mediator compellability. Aboriginal peoples see the government is not engaging in treaty negotiations in good faith and ask the court for a remedy. A party asks to be excused from attending a mandatory court-annexed mediation session or complying with a clause in a business contract requiring mediation. These types of ADR disputes are naturally emerging. Getting to yes, as in other instances, will not always be possible. Second, as ADR becomes more closely connected to the courts, the adversarial process, and lawyers, some mutual adjustments are bound to be made. One of the adjustments has been a formalizing of ADR's informalism. With more formal and written requirements for ADR, such as British Columbia's Notice to Mediate regulations, the opportunities to question and query the exact meaning of these ADR guidelines and how they should be applied will arise. Because of the imprecision of language, conflicting interpretations can be made. It will be natural for lawyers or their clients to ask the courts to resolve some of these differences.

Finally, as mentioned in chapter 1, what happens in dispute resolution does matter. The arrangements made by the divorcing couple around their property and children will stay with them for the rest of their lives. How the siblings work out the operations of the family business when their parents die intestate will be influential for other generations in the family. The settlement of a serious personal injury case may be the most important decision the plaintiff has to make. In these and other cases, the resolution of controversies around ADR can have significant consequences on the parties and the outcome of the case. When the answers to the ADR controversies are not clear, judges may be asked to adjudicate. Should the mediator have adjourned the meeting or further encouraged independent legal advice? What is the legal basis for mediator liability? Is protecting confidentiality in mediation in the absence of a clear statutory privilege more important than the interests of the children? Is a refusal to negotiate when litigation is ongoing a sign of bad faith? How private should ADR be? Can a court effectively control private bargaining? The evolution of ADR raises thorny questions whose answers can mean quite a lot to disputants, particularly those questions that go to the fundamentals of how the disputing process unfolds. When more than one answer is possible to questions going to the very foundations of ADR, it would be surprising not to have the courts involved in the debate even in a field emphasizing consensus.

1) ADR Case Notes

The following case notes provide you with entry points into the developing law of ADR. The notes are not an exhaustive compilation of all ADR cases but are summaries of several important and interesting ADR disputes that ended up being adjudicated in court. They are intended to illustrate the potential for judicial influence on the meaning of ADR, most obviously mediation, and to make the point that the courts and lawyers are likely to continue to play major roles in the shape of ADR to come.

a) Exemptions from Attending Mandatory Mediation

In *Ross* v. *Seib* [2] the court refused to grant an exemption from mandatory mediation provisions. The action arose out of a motor vehicle accident in which the plaintiff allegedly sustained whiplash-type injuries among others. The defendant admitted liability but put in issue the quantum of damages. The plaintiff and the defendant consented to the exemption from the requirement to attend on the basis that the examinations for discovery had not yet been held and there was no point in mediation until this step was completed. In an affidavit filed in support, the plaintiff swore: "I am confident that mediation would not be necessary in order to achieve a settlement of the matters in issue in this action." The mandatory mediation legislation required the parties to attend mediation after the close of pleadings and before taking any further step in the matter.

The court held that the fact of the parties consenting to an exemption from mediation "is not a compelling reason to grant the request" and that "the courts should not sanction a circumvention of the project except on a sound basis." The court referred to one objective of early mediation being reduced costs of litigation and "this objective would be frustrated where mediation is delayed until after discoveries." While dismissing the application for exemption, the court noted:

> It may well be that the usual whiplash actions should be exempted from early mediation and that the court should postpone the requirement. Commonly, the injuries require some years of assessment after the defence has been filed, and settlement discussions at the close of pleadings would be futile. Where that is the case, the material tendered to the court on the exemption or postponement application should be focused accordingly.

In *Agriculture Credit Corp. of Saskatchewan* v. *Olson*,[3] *The Queen's Bench (Mediation) Amendment Act* required the court registrar to arrange for the parties to attend a mediation session before taking any further steps after the close of pleadings. The court could, on application, exempt the parties from this requirement. The plaintiff had sued the defendant for a liquidated demand arising from a livestock cash advance and the defendant filed a perfunctory statement of defence denying the claim and alleging that a third party had agreed to assume the debt. The plaintiff brought an application for summary judgment and an order that the parties be exempted from attending the mandatory mediation

---

2   (1996), 145 Sask. R. 62 (Q.B.).
3   (1995) 135 Sask. R. 319 (Q.B.).

session, arguing that the requirement for mediation was redundant if the defence had no legal effect or was a simple denial of the debt.

The court held that it had discretion to override the mandatory mediation requirement, once it was set, "if the party seeking an exception could demonstrate they were unable to attend for medical reasons or that the cost of attending was prohibitive or raise any other reasonable excuse for not attending." The court found the plaintiff's submission "tends to put the cart before the horse" particularly when the regulations set out specifically a number of situations exempted from mandatory mediation. An application for summary judgment was not included in the exemptions. Although commenting that the drafters of the mediation legislation may have created an anomaly in the statute, the court ordered that the dispute must first be submitted to mediation.

b) Liability of the Mediator

In *Lange* v. *Marshall*,[4] a lawyer agreed to act as a mediator for close personal friends who were ending a long marriage. A settlement agreement was reached in a psychiatric hospital room where the plaintiff had been admitted. Before the agreement was judicially approved in divorce proceedings, the plaintiff had second thoughts. She consulted another lawyer and ten months later, after contested proceedings, she received a more favourable settlement. She sued the mediator for negligence and alleged, *inter alia*, that the mediator did not advise her she would get a better settlement if she litigated and did not negotiate for a better settlement for her.

The Appeal Court did not resolve the issues around the exact status of the mediator and the duties associated with that status but found that none of the mediator's actions was a proximate cause of the damages (lawyer's fees, no support for ten months) alleged to be suffered in waiting and preparing for the eventual settlement.

c) Enforceability of Agreements to Mediate

In *Toronto Truck Centre Ltd.* v. *Volvo Trucks Canada Inc./Camions Volvo Canada Inc.*,[5] a Dealer Sales and Services Agreement between a truck dealer and the truck manufacturer provided that the agreement would terminate automatically without notice if the dealer misrepresented a material fact to the manufacturer. The manufacturer, after auditing the dealer's records, concluded that a misrepresentation had been made

---

4   622 S.W.2nd 237 (Mo. App. 1981).
5   (1998), 163 D.L.R. (4th) 740 (Ont. Gen. Div.).

that induced the manufacturer to lower the cost of various trucks. The manufacturer sought to terminate the agreement.

However, the agreement contained a dispute resolution clause:

VIII. Dispute Resolution Process

The Company and the Dealer agree that mutual respect, trust and confidence are vital to the relationship between the Company and the Dealer. So that such respect, trust and confidence can be maintained, and differences that may develop between the Dealer and the Company may be resolved amicably, it is agreed that it is in the best mutual interest of the Company and Dealers to avoid costly litigation. Therefore, at Dealer's option, Dealer may elect to resolve disputes in accordance with the Dispute Resolution Process, a copy of which is attached to this Agreement.

The actual Dispute Resolution Process provided first for an internal review of any manufacturer decision at the request of the dealer, and second, if the dealer did not accept the decision, the dealer "may advance its interest by engaging mediation as a preferred course of resolution." The agreement stated that mediation was "binding" but also stated the "mediator shall not be authorized to impose a decision on the parties. Its primary task is to impartially and effectively bridge the positions taken by the parties in order to reach an accord." The parties agreed that any dispute shall be settled by the said process and "such a settlement shall prevail as a final remedy over any other available actions."

The dealer applied for an interlocutory injunction to prevent the manufacturer from terminating the agreement. The court held that the three-stage test necessary to issue an interlocutory injunction had been satisfied and issued an order requiring the manufacturer to submit to the dispute resolution process. The court did not find there was a fundamental breach of the agreement which entitled the manufacturer to refuse to participate in the dispute resolution process.[6]

---

6   The term "binding mediation" caused confusion. The parties clearly intended any settlement reached through mediation to be binding and to resolve all issues constituting the dispute. However, the agreement clearly stated that the mediator was not authorized to impose a decision on the parties. The court, however, regarded its order to participate in mediation as finally disposing of the action and that participation in binding mediation would require final resolution of the differences between the parties. Given the court found the dealership would continue pending completion of the dispute resolution process and given the time frame within which the mediation was to take place (no later than twenty-four days after the internal review was completed), the court-enforced mediation would have to resemble an arbitration to give effect to the court's interpretation of "binding mediation."

d) Duty to Negotiate in Good Faith

In *Gitanyow First Nation* v. *Canada*,[7] the plaintiff First Nation sought declarations that the federal and provincial Crowns had a legal duty to negotiate in good faith within the treaty process and that the defendants were in breach of that duty. Although the court refused to rule on the latter point on a summary application, it held that the Crown had entered voluntarily into the treaty negotiation process and had a legal duty to negotiate in good faith. Williamson J. declined to determine in a detailed way the content of the Crown's duty to negotiate in good faith, but stated that "in general terms, the duty must include at least the absence of any appearance of 'sharp dealing,' disclosure of relevant facts and negotiation 'without oblique motive'."

In *Delgamuukw* v. *British Columbia*,[8] the appellants, all Gitskan or Wet'suwet'en hereditary chiefs, claimed Aboriginal title over 58,000 square kilometres of the province. In allowing the appeal in part and ordering a new trial (the first trial through 1987 to 1990 had taken 374 days of court time), the Justices of the Supreme Court of Canada gave some ADR directions at 1123–24:

> Finally, this litigation has been both long and expensive, not only in economic but in human terms as well. By ordering a new trial, I do not necessarily encourage the parties to proceed to litigation and to settle their dispute through the courts. As was said in *Sparrow*,[9] at p. 1105, s. 35(1) "provides a solid constitutional base upon which subsequent negotiations can take place." Those negotiations should also include other aboriginal nations which have a stake in the territory claimed. Moreover, the Crown is under a moral, if not a legal, duty to enter into and conduct those negotiations in good faith. Ultimately, it is through negotiated settlements, with good faith and give and take on all sides, reinforced by the judgments of this Court, that we will achieve what I stated in *Vander Peet*,[10] *supra*, at para. 31, to be a basic purpose of s. 35(1) — "the reconciliation of the pre-existence of aboriginal societies with the sovereignty of the Crown." Let us face it, we are all here to stay.

---

7   [1999] 3 C.N.L.R. 89 (B.C.S.C.).

8   [1997] 3 S.C.R. 1010.

9   R. v. *Sparrow*, [1990] 1 S.C.R. 1075.

10 R. v. *Vanderpeet* (*sub nom. R. v. Van der Peet*), [1996] 2 S.C.R. 507.

and at 1134–35:

> On a final note, I wish to emphasize that the best approach in these types of cases is a process of negotiation and reconciliation that properly considers the complex and competing interests at stake. This point was made by Lambert J.A. in the Court of Appeal,[11] . . . , at pp. 379-80:
>
>> So, in the end, *the legal rights of the Indian people will have to be accommodated within our total society by political compromises and accommodations based in the first instance on negotiation and agreement and ultimately in accordance with the sovereign will of the community as a whole.* The legal rights of the Gitksan and Wet'suwet'en peoples, to which this law suit is confined, and which allow no room for any approach other than the application of the law itself, and the legal rights of all aboriginal peoples throughout British Columbia, form only one factor in the ultimate determination of what kind of community we are going to have in British Columbia and throughout Canada in the years ahead. [Emphasis added.]

e) Enforcing Mediated Agreements

In *Lenney* v. *Lenney,* [12] the parties had divorced and then agreed on joint custody of their two children. The divorce judgment contained a provision that "in the event that the parties alone cannot resolve a conflict they agree . . . the matter shall be referred to mediation. This procedure shall be followed through to its conclusion prior to either party seeking relief from the court." The mediation clause in the divorce judgment tracked terms set out in Minutes of Settlement that had been executed by the parties. The mother subsequently brought a motion for sole custody without going first to mediation.

Citing the rule that the courts generally recognize and enforce a contractual obligation to mediate or arbitrate in the commercial or business context, especially one that has been written into a judgment of the court, Veit J. held that a contractual obligation to mediate also will be enforced in a family law situation unless the best interests of the children required the court to deal with a matter before mediation ran its course. In other words, children urgently in need of intervention by the court constitute an even more important priority than the need to reinforce the importance of keeping promises set out in the contract. In this case, there was a formal, contractual obligation to mediate. The court decided "unless special circumstances exist, the court should

---

11   *Delgamuukw* v. *British Columbia*, [1993] 5 W.W.R. 97 (B.C.C.A.).
12   (1996), 194 A.R. 50 (Q.B.).

enforce the agreement between the parties to mediate." The court reached this conclusion even though the father, representing himself, had not raised the obligation to mediate.

f) Confidentiality in Mediation/Subpoenas to Mediators

In *Condessa Z Holdings Ltd. v. Rusnak*,[13] an elaborate settlement was reached in a pre-trial conference. Shortly thereafter, a disagreement arose between the parties about one of the items on which an agreement was thought to have been reached. An application was made to the court to enforce the pre-trial settlement as it was understood by one of the parties. A subpoena also was issued to compel the attendance of the judge who had presided at the settlement conference as a mediator. The Deputy Attorney General applied to set aside the subpoena.

In confirming that the subpoena should be set aside, the Court of Appeal held that the pre-trial judge is engaged in a judicial function notwithstanding the fact that the judge is a mediator who plays a role that is a departure from the traditional adversarial role of the parties. Judicial immunity pertaining to the exercise of a judge's judicial authority accrues to the judge qua judge and cannot be waived by the parties.

In *Pearson v. Pearson*,[14] a mediator was required to give evidence. In oral reasons, Kroft J. said:

This is an important issue and probably deserves more extensive comment than I am going to give it, but I will not serve anybody's interests if I delay proceedings to write learned reasons, even if I were capable of so doing.

I am satisfied from the evidence that I have received to this point, and particularly I might say the evidence of Ms. Lewis herself, that the mediation in question, when undertaken by her, related solely to the custody and access to the Pearson children and to the monetary matters related to support.

Ms. Lewis was not a mediator appointed by the Court pursuant to Section 43 of the Children's Act. Neither, it is clear to me, did she undertake a mediation directed towards reconciliation within the contemplation of the Divorce Act. Nonetheless, the function which she undertook was of a privileged nature and within the well established rules relating to such communications.

. . .

---

13 *Condessa Z Holdings Ltd. v. Brown's Plymouth Chrysler Ltd.*, [1993] 6 W.W.R. 544, (*sub nom. Condessa Z Holdings Ltd. v. Rusnak*) 104 D.L.R. (4th) 96 (Sask. C.A.).

14 [1992] Y.J. No. 106 (QL) (Y.T.S.C.).

The rules pertaining to privileged communications to which I have just referred are, of course, the four Wigmore rules. They have been considered in many contexts and in many cases.

. . .

The entire issue before me comes down to the fourth rule. That is to say, is there an overriding concern for the public interest of a nature that would justify my ordering Ms. Lewis to testify as to matters that would otherwise be confidential?

This kind of question, almost by definition, arises before one really knows the full story. Courts must and do proceed on the basis of there being a reasonable or probable concern, for there is nothing which, at the time the evidence is being sought, can be proved. If you required more, then you would get into a vicious circle of never being able to deal with the issue.

I have not received the whole explanation as to what risk the Pearson children are being exposed, if any.

I have, though, heard enough relating to pending criminal charges and observations of various authorities in the social welfare system who are concerned, to convince me that, at this stage of the proceedings it cannot be said that the fear of harm is unfounded. When there is a serious concern to be addressed pertaining to the safety of children, it is one of the most fundamental type of concerns that a court can have.

For those rambling reasons, I have come to the conclusion that, based entirely on the fourth of the Wigmore rules, the evidence which would clearly in other circumstances be of a privileged nature should be communicated to this Court; and I therefore order that the privilege claim be set aside and Ms. Lewis proceed to testify with respect to the matters pertaining to the mediation.

In *McDonald* v. *McDonald*,[15] a custody and maintenance action, McEachern C.J. was asked to order that all discussions in counselling sessions to be scheduled would be privileged. McEachern declined to create a new kind of privilege *in futuro* although he acknowledged that the communications made by the spouses if the process went ahead may be privileged under the general law relating to communications made for the purposes of settlement. For the process contemplated in this case, "whether it be called crisis counselling or mediation or therapy or anything else," Chief Justice McEachern decided it was "unnecessary to decide whether there is jurisdiction to create a blanket sort of privilege for an unascertained number of communications to be made by parties

---

15   (1987), 10 B.C.L.R. (2d) 257 (S.C.).

and others in futuro" and, in considering Wigmore's four principles, stated that "where a parent might admit serious parenting inadequacies, I doubt if any weighing of interests would support maintaining the confidentiality of such a communication . . . The creation of a broad, new privilege is more appropriately a function of the legislature rather than that of a judge sitting in chambers."

In *Sinclair* v. *Roy*,[16] a family court counsellor was assigned by the court to assist the parties through mediation to resolve their differences around custody and access. The mediator emphasized the confidentiality of the mediation process to encourage frank and open communications. The actual mediation took the form of a conciliation process in that the mediator did not meet with the parties together.

The mediation was not successful. The lawyer for the wife subpoenaed the mediator to give evidence respecting the wife's behaviour, condition and statements made during the mediation apparently for the purpose of rebutting the husband's argument that allegations of his abuse were recently fabricated by his wife.

The court set aside the subpoena on the grounds that the communications and observations in the mediation were statutorily privileged and the family court counsellor was not compellable as a witness.

In *Porter* v. *Porter*,[17] the report of a psychologist who had acted as a mediator in a custody and access dispute was sought to be introduced as evidence in a subsequent divorce proceeding. The joint letter of retainer sent to the psychologist by the parties' lawyers had indicated his recommendations would not be used in any court proceedings and he would not be called as a witness. The psychologist's report contained adverse findings regarding the husband's ability to have custody of his children.

The court considered whether Wigmore's four fundamental conditions, necessary to the establishment of privilege, were satisfied:

(1) The communications must originate in a *confidence* that they will not be disclosed.

(2) This element of *confidentiality must be essential* to the full and satisfactory maintenance of the relation between the parties.

(3) The *relation* must be one which in the opinion of the community ought to be sedulously fostered.

---

16   (1985) 65 B.C.L.R. 219 (S.C.).
17   (1983), 40 O.R. (2d) 417 (U.F.C.).

(4) The *injury* that would inure to the relation by the disclosure of the communications must be *greater than the benefit* thereby gained for the correct disposal of litigation.[18]

The court concluded that all the conditions were satisfied. With respect to condition No. 3, the court clearly took the view that it was "of great importance to the community that parties should be encouraged to resolve their matrimonial conflicts without resort to courts. Such efforts to settle might not take place if the parties could not rely on the confidentiality of their discussions." The court held that condition No. 4 was met because it is "of far greater importance that parties, with the aid of a mediator, are able to engage in frank and open discussion that can lead to agreed upon arrangements in the interests of children than that some information may be lost to a court in a subsequent proceeding."

On the basis that Wigmore's four conditions were satisfied and on the additional ground that the parties were engaged in "without prejudice" negotiations for settlement of litigation, the mediator's report was inadmissible.

In *Olam* v. *Congress Mortgage Co.*,[19] a dispute between a mortgagor and a mortgagee was settled by mediation. When the mortgagee sought to enforce the mediated agreement embodied in a memorandum of understanding, the mortgagor claimed undue influence and subpoenaed the mediator to give testimony about what happened during the mediation. Despite the fact that the *California Evidence Code* stated that any admission or writing made during the course of a mediation is not admissible or subject to discovery, the court held that the mediator's testimony would substantially contribute to a determination if there was undue influence in signing the mediation agreement and required the mediator to testify.

In *Foxgate Homeowners' Assn.* v. *Bramalea Cal. Inc.*,[20] the court ruled that a trial judge could consider a factual report from a mediator about conduct that occurred and statements made during a court-ordered mediation to determine whether a party or lawyer had violated an order to participate in the mediation in good faith. This ruling was made even though the state legislation had enacted what appeared to be a strict mediation privilege. The California Court of Appeals reasoned that the purpose in adopting the privilege was to make media-

---

18   Wigmore, J.H., *Evidence in Trials at Common Law (McNaughton Revision)* v. 8 (Toronto: Little Brown & Co., 1961) at 527.
19   68 F. Supp. 2d 1110 (N.D. Cal. 1999).
20   78 Cal. App. 4th 653 (2d Dist. 2000).

tions more productive. Good-faith participation in the process was necessary and "without [good-faith participation], there would be few if any confidential communications to protect." The legislature could not have intended that a party who had refused to participate in good faith use the privilege as a shield against detection and sanction.

D. ADR IN THE COURTS

> ADR is often supported by well-intentioned people who, for a variety of reasons, are anxious to reorganize society and procedures of courts with naive, theoretical concepts of humanity and efficiency . . . society's decent people need the no-nonsense, straightforward procedures of courtroom litigation to fight unreasonable claims and not the "soft" procedures ADR offers.[21]

Some judicial opposition to the first wave of ADR was entirely understandable. ADR began as a study of alternatives to the courts. Although long-standing criticisms that the courts were cumbersome, costly and slow had prompted various justice system reforms in the 1960s and 1970s, the ADR movement and its many non-lawyer supporters not only pointed out continuing troubles with court adjudication but also promised cost- and time-saving options to litigation. In addition, these alternative dispute resolution methods could result in disputant empowerment, preservation of ongoing relationships, win-win results, transformation in personal thinking and many more benefits, none of which were likely attainable when disputants took their cases to court. Simply put, ADR seemed superior.

Although the rejection of ADR by some judges and other members of the legal profession was by no means universal, the sentiments of Chief Justice McEachern did reflect the considerable dissonance in disputing views and practices that existed between judges in the formal justice system with its adversarial trappings and private mediators using the mostly consensual dispute resolution mechanisms of ADR.

The practical and philosophical differences between judges and mediators and between ADR and court approaches to dispute resolution may begin to explain the initial judicial reaction to ADR. What is more difficult to explain is why this reaction has changed. Today, the

---

21 A statement attributed to then Chief Justice A. McEachern of the British Columbia Supreme Court in "Chief Justice Puts Boots to ADR," *Lawyers Weekly* (26 October 1989).

gaps between ADR and the courts have been substantially bridged. ADR processes are often welcomed by the judiciary and judges are taking on mediators' roles. ADR principles and techniques are becoming increasingly integral and mandatory parts of how courts process disputes, with results labelled as judicial dispute resolution or JDR. Understanding the reasons for this judicial about-face, appreciating the roles that ADR now plays in the court adjudication of disputes and examining the impact of ADR's relationship with the courts on the meaning of ADR are important parts of an ADR study. Developing an informed perspective on ADR in the courts also will provide a basis for deciding whether or how to best utilize court-connected ADR resources and will point to the ADR skills needed in such a setting.

1) Changes in Judicial Opposition to ADR

The ADR movement provoked judicial opposition and critique for many of the same reasons that mediation met initial resistance from the legal profession. In the beginning, ADR was not particularly well understood by the bench. Additionally the multidisciplinary interest in alternative dispute resolution often meant that support for ADR was delivered in a language and style that was difficult for judges to translate or appreciate. Active listening, paraphrasing, reframing, refocusing, empowering, managing anger, interests, fears, hopes, "I" statements (I hear you saying that . . .) and the like were part of the ADR vocabulary but, without being carefully explained to judges, these words and expressions had the potential to portray ADR in such a touchy-feely, non-legal, and unfamiliar manner that some judicial rejection was almost a foregone conclusion.

In whatever form ADR was described, its methods and practices commonly were presented as incongruent with, and in opposition to, the adversarial thinking that dominated court adjudication. ADR also was promoted as a remedy for the ills that accompanied courtroom litigation. The ADR emphasis was not on hostility and fighting drawn-out, costly court battles but rather on negotiation, mediation, conciliation and other consensual forms of dispute resolution, which not only produced enduring agreements in timely and cost-effective ways but also other tangible benefits that courtroom combatants could not expect to achieve. Empowering disputants to make their own decisions was seen by ADR enthusiasts as more beneficial and laudable than relying on a stranger to impose a decision on the parties. These lines of logic were not lost on the judiciary. It was difficult for judges to accept the ADR antidote with its resulting paradigmatic shift away from the formalism of courts, where judges and lawyers were the dominant actors, to more informal venues where the parties themselves, with or without the help of a mediator, conciliator or facilitator, would be in charge.

Despite the substantially different worldviews of disputing held by the courts and early ADR proponents, several related factors have combined to enable ADR and the courts to end much of the animosity. First and foremost, the meaning of alternative dispute resolution has been and continues to be reformulated to help avoid a clash with the principles and practices of court adjudication. Rather than focusing primarily on alternatives to court, ADR is being seen as "an umbrella term which encompasses litigation, focusing on the appropriate method for resolving any given dispute."[22] Instead of standing in opposition to adjudication, ADR has come to be viewed as a concept that points to the need for evaluating the entire continuum of dispute resolution techniques, skills, and resources before choosing the right disputing steps to be taken. Defined in this manner, ADR simply becomes an expression of commitment to fair, effective, and accessible dispute resolution. As a result, ADR principles and practices "will not be viewed as superior or inferior to, or indeed even separate from, court adjudication."[23] This legal recasting of ADR's shape meant that ADR no longer naturally posed a threat to the courts but could fit, with appropriate alterations, into the formal justice system that, after all, also was concerned with fair, effective and accessible dispute resolution.

A second related factor also helped to eliminate judicial intolerance of ADR. With ADR redefined as the way for lawyers to fulfil their primary responsibility as problem solvers, as essentially about better dispute resolution, the impediments to legal acceptance of ADR disappeared. As a Canadian Bar Association report on ADR stated, "ADR is not a new idea but rather a modern reflection of the . . . legal profession's long standing support for quality legal services. Attempts to separate ADR from other dispute resolution processes or to value one process over another will be counter-productive."[24] As a result, more and more members of the legal profession, including senior members of the bar, were

---

22 *Charting the Course, Report of the Canadian Forum on Dispute Resolution* (Ottawa: Department of Justice, 1995) at 12.

23 Canadian Bar Association Task Force on Alternative Dispute Resolution, *Alternative Dispute Resolution: A Canadian Perspective* (Ottawa: Canadian Bar Association, 1989) at 4.

24 *Ibid.* at 4–5. The integration of ADR broadly defined into the legal profession and an emphasis on the problem-solving role for lawyers is followed through in the report of the Canadian Bar Association Task Force on Systems of Civil Justice, below note 25.

able to provide support for one ADR process or another, encourage its growth and openly practice ADR. Accordingly, ADR activities flourished within the legal profession. Lawyers took mediation courses and became mediators. Conferences on ADR for lawyers multiplied. Sections were organized within the legal profession for lawyers working with ADR. Lawyers advertised and held themselves out to the public as suppliers of ADR services. Cases that would otherwise have gone to court were successfully mediated. Bar admission courses added training in ADR skills to their curricula. It became important for lawyers to be well versed in ADR. A movement that had initially met resistance and rejection from the legal profession now found itself in high demand. The burgeoning acceptance of ADR within the legal profession meant that carefully infusing ADR into how the courts adjudicated disputes was a natural next step.

ADR also was able to fit into the formal justice system for purely pragmatic reasons. In the 1970s and 1980s, courts in North America were under attack. Many courts, especially those courts in large urban centres, were clogged. There were long delays in getting cases to trial. The cost of going to court was prohibitive for many litigants and high legal fees led to startling conclusions that claims under $40,000 or $50,000 were not economical to litigate. Quite often it appeared that the win-lose results of a court adjudication didn't end matters. Court-imposed orders often were ignored by the parties, or the disputants would continue their fight until their next court appearance. These court complexions exposed a potentially fatal flaw in the judicial make-up. How could a formal justice system be the backbone for order in a society when the justice system's basic mechanisms weren't working or weren't seen to be working and, in addition, were either inaccessible to, or perceived as irrelevant by, a large segment of society. As the 1996 report on the civil justice system in Canada said, "[m]any Canadians feel that they cannot exercise their rights effectively because using the civil justice system takes too long, is too expensive, or is too difficult to understand."[25]

However, with ADR now cast comfortably as a project long pursued by members of the legal profession and being increasingly touted by them, ADR was an obvious candidate to help cure the ailments that plagued the courts. The challenge would be to appropriately adapt ADR for use within the formal justice system so that the benefits associated

---

25   Canadian Bar Association Task Force on Systems of Civil Justice, *Report of the Task Force on Systems of Civil Justice* (Ottawa: Canadian Bar Association, 1996) at 11.

with its use outside the courts — such as saving time and money, reaching win-win results, making lasting agreements, reducing recidivism and increasing disputant satisfaction with results — also would accrue to disputants who used the courts to resolve their problems.

Even given a more court-friendly definition of ADR, its widespread and expanding use by lawyers around the world, and an apparently perfect fit between the benefits of ADR and the troubles with court adjudication, this combination of factors did not automatically ease judicial concerns that ADR could be naive compared to the court's no-nonsense, straightforward procedures and that ADR might be too soft to fight unreasonable claims. What disappeared with ADR's new meaning and acceptance within the legal profession was any practical possibility that ADR in the courts could be, or could be seen to be, in a form that would allow criticisms of naivety or softness to be levelled. The ideology of ADR that made its union with the courts possible was not an image of ADR made up of legally unfamiliar alternatives to the harsh realities of courtroom litigation being pushed forward as an anti-legal movement mostly by non-lawyers. Rather, what changed judicial opposition to ADR was the presentation of ADR as a lawyer-led, naturally occurring, timely, and responsible affirmation of the legal profession's modern quest, inside and outside the courts, for the just, speedy, and inexpensive resolution of all disputes on their merits, and assertions that appropriate ADR innovations within the court were possible.

2) The Roles of ADR in the Courts

Describing the precise roles that ADR now plays in the courts is a difficult task for two reasons. First, the activities that qualify as judicial ADR depend on the meaning ascribed to ADR. Disagreements on what constitutes ADR can lead to conflicts on whether a particular dispute resolution plan or initiative in the court system should be regarded as ADR or not. Second, much like the current state of ADR in practice, ADR in the courts is rapidly expanding. The growing popularity and frequency of these developments make it a daunting challenge to set out fully ADR's place in the formal justice system.

Despite these two limitations, reviewing the impact that ADR developments have had on the courts and considering the reciprocal effect that the justice system has had on ADR's character provide important insights into understanding ADR theories and practices as well as an indication of where ADR may be heading in the future.

a) ADR's Impact on the Role of Judges

The embrace of ADR as appropriate dispute resolution by the legal profession and the apparent match between ADR's promised benefits and the court's needs made the entry of ADR into the formal justice system seem possible. But the use of ADR in the practice of law, where more than 90 percent of all cases settle out of court and where negotiation and mediation had reasonable roots, was one thing. ADR alongside judges, inside the no-nonsense, straightforward procedures of the adversary system, was quite another. To be accepted, ADR, at minimum, had to complement, not conflict with, the role that judges generally played.

The role of a judge in an adversary system traditionally has been limited to deciding issues that have been presented to her or him. This role is in accord with the two principles discussed in chapter 2 that support disputing practices in an adversary system. First, the parties to a dispute or their lawyers are responsible for defining the problem and putting forward their case. Party autonomy means that the judge's role is primarily to judge. Although the scope of this judging can traverse a broad range of matters surrounding a dispute — such as whether the case has been commenced in a timely manner, whether full particulars of the factual allegations have been disclosed, whether interim protection should be ordered pending a full trial, whether questions can be asked or answered, whether a fact has been established or not or whether a claim or defence is legally valid — it is the parties who raise these issues and who ask the judge to make a decision on them. Unlike the role of a judge in an inquisitorial system where direct involvement by the judge in the preparation and presentation of a dispute is expected, the judge in an adversary system, is normally expected to respect the autonomy of the disputants during the course of the litigation. Second, in an adversary system partisan representation is another key feature that defines the judge's role. With advocates representing each disputant and endeavouring to obtain for their clients the benefit of any and every remedy or defence that is authorized by law, the judge's role is focused on deciding matters on which these advocates have made full submissions. The primary task of the judge is to decide which of the submissions should prevail on a particular issue. A judge would not normally raise issues or make submissions for the parties.

The traditional view of the judge's role is also in line with, and determined by, a mainly traditionalist view taken of courts. A traditionalist view of courts is a perspective willing to examine what it is courts do, what functions are being confided to courts, whether incompatibilities exist in court demands and what a court is best equipped to do. Nevertheless, a traditional outlook continues to see the courts based on their special attributes and characteristics. Confining the judge's role to deciding issues is part of a court's structure. Altering this essential judicial element or any other integral court component beyond certain limits by assigning courts too broad a repertoire of functions or requiring different processes or skills for judges means that the institution will no longer be recognizable as a court. This traditionalist view of courts contrasts with a more adaptationist view that would explain and understand court structures and functions in different ways. The actual workings of a court would be based on historical perspective; social, economic and political context; and the courts' reciprocal interactions with other institutions, legislatures and executive agencies. Although not asserting that the capacity of the courts is unlimited, an adaptationist perspective would attach little or no significance to identifying essential characteristics of courts and would insist that whatever limitations exist on the court's role, these limits have not yet been reached. Whether courts work effectively from an adaptationist outlook depends more on the acceptance of their function and their actual decisions by society at large than on adherence to a formulaic concept of what courts can and cannot do.

However, tradition did not mean that judges' doors were completely shut to ADR. Describing a judge primarily as a decision maker did not always mean that judges were merely passive or disinterested listeners as the disputants presented their case. Casting judges as the ultimate deciders of questions of fact or law also did not necessarily imply that no judicial role flexibility was possible due to the constraints imposed by the adversary system's reliance on party autonomy and partisan representation and by commonly held views on how courts must function. At times, some individual judges displayed skills and practices in dispute resolution that were a step removed from the traditional judge's role. Although neither widespread nor uniform and largely dependent on administrative arrangements and judicial personality, a growing number of judges began to adapt a more active, managerial approach to their role. This more-than-traditional role was evidenced in the courts at both structural and individual case levels. At a structural level, many individual judges have been responsible for recognizing deficiencies in the adjudicative process and then actively promoting reforms. These reforms, when implemented, would have an impact on how the courts processed cases. Judges also have been known to directly intervene in individual cases. This intervention might be made in a pre-trial conference, pre-trial motion, or even during a break in the trial itself when the judge because of his or her experience, position, or assessment of the case is able to encourage or push the parties or their lawyers to rethink a position, drop a demand, make a concession, reassess damages, or otherwise substantially alter the presentation or progress of the issues and ultimately influence the resolution of the dispute itself. In some jurisdictions, judges also would be assigned as case managers for lengthy or complicated lawsuits. The assigned judge would usually preside at the trial of the action but also would be responsible for hearing all interlocutory applications, conducting case management conferences, and otherwise assisting the parties in the processing of the particular case.

Though this structural and case-specific influence is exerted within the boundaries of the adversary system, the judicial conduct illustrated that workable role demarcations were possible from the quarters to which judges were traditionally confined. The flexibility that the concept of managerial judges lent to the traditional judicial role permitted judges to consider comfortably how they would take on or adapt ADR practices in the courts. The evolution, in many cases, has been quite dramatic. From the earliest ADR days when Frank Sander urged a "multi-doored courthouse" and lawyer and litigant consideration of the "significant characteristics of various alternative dispute resolution mechanisms" within the courthouse confines,[26] Judith Resnick chronicles significant ADR influences on the changing role of U.S. judges to the point where she observes "the melding of ADR into adjudication" and a redefined role for judges as "judicial officers" to produce "contractual agreements among disputants."[27] In many jurisdictions, judges are taking on more managerial roles and more regularly referring parties to mediation if not mediating themselves.

Indeed, a most significant example of ADR now being part of a judge's role occurs when the judge acts as a mediator. This arrangement is often formalized in legislation, litigation rules of court, or in a practice direction from a court's Chief Justice. Judges will perform mediator-type functions as they try to help parties settle in a pre-trial conference, settlement conferences, during the trial itself, during specific settlement periods when concentrated efforts are made by the judiciary to clear up long backlogs of cases awaiting trial or at the request of litigants themselves. These activities can be called JDR or judicial dispute resolution.

---

26   F.E.A. Sander, "Varieties of Dispute Processing," 70 F.R.D. 111 (1976) from the 1976 Pound Conference.

27   See J. Resnik, "Many Doors? Closing Doors? Alternative Dispute Resolution and Adjudication" (1995) 10 Ohio St. J. on Disp. Resol. 211 at 248, 265.

Whatever the source of the judge's jurisdiction to act as mediator, it is likely that the enormous diversity in mediation processes described in chapter 4 will carry over in judge-conducted mediations. Even within the same jurisdiction, a fly-on-the-wall watching different judges mediate will observe variations in what is said and done by the mediator judge and the parties even if the actual cases are similar in nature. This result should not be surprising. In addition to the fact that the disputing context will be unique, individual judges will bring their own personal style and orientation to the mediation. Some judges may adhere to a purely facilitative model of mediation while others may be much more actively evaluative and highly instrumental in forging or dictating the dispute's outcome.

The future of judge-conducted mediations within the court structure depends on the answers to several questions.

- Will judges be viewed as possessing the necessary knowledge and skills that all other mediators increasingly are being required to have or will judges by virtue of their position and experience be deemed to be "natural" mediators or at least competent to conduct judicial mediations?
- Will long-time judges be comfortable acting as mediators with limited training?
- Will roster mediators who have been approved to mediate cases referred from the courts get better results because of more extensive training and less process constraints?
- Will private mediators be able to reduce court backlogs so that the waiting time and costs associated with going to court are brought down to acceptable levels and judges are no longer required to mediate?
- Will the private mediators who are lawyers demand these cases for primarily economic reasons?
- Will the development of judge-conducted mediations erode or alter the traditional role of the judge beyond acceptable limits, or will mediation, particularly mediation designed specifically to settle cases prior to trial, come to be firmly incorporated into the image of adjudication and the judicial repertoire?
- Will mediation developments outside the court expose flaws or deficiencies in judge-conducted mediations?
- Will judge-conducted mediations fit into, or conflict with, the developing ideology of ADR?

Whatever the eventual answers to these questions, the role of the judge has become inextricably linked to ADR, and particularly mediation, developments.

b) Rules of Court and ADR

In the civil justice system, Rules of Court are designed, as far as possible, to standardize the ways in which disputes are processed so that all disputants are treated equally. These rules require all disputants using a particular level of court in a specific jurisdiction to follow the same procedures at various stages of the lawsuit up to and including the trial. For example, a civil action must be formally commenced by filing a certain type of originating process with the court, such as a writ of summons, petition, third-party notice or statement of claim. The originating document must then be served on the opposing party. The Rules of Court set out what must be, and what cannot be, included in the pleadings — the documents that set out the legal claims, defences and remedies being pursued in the case. The rules also set out procedures and time limits for making changes or amendments to the pleadings including adding or dropping parties as well as directions on a party obtaining further and better particulars of the facts on which a party is relying. The rules delineate the manner to proceed if one of the parties wants to show, at an early stage in the action, that there is no defence to the whole or part of a claim, to apply for judgment without the necessity of going through a full trial, to dismiss the proceeding because there has been undue delay in moving the case along or to set down a point of law for hearing. Rules of Court set out which documents must be produced for inspection by the opposing parties and which documents are exempt from such production. There are procedural rules that allow a party to question, orally and in writing, any other party that is adverse in interest regarding any relevant matter in the action. The rules set out when and where this oral examination for discovery must take place. If the parties need to seek directions or an order from a judge or Master prior to trial, the rules dictate how this interlocutory application is to be made. The rules even prescribe the size and type of paper the disputants must use for documents prepared for the litigation.

The Rules of Court are the machinery of the civil justice system. This procedural machinery does not mean that all civil actions are processed in exactly the same way. Disputants and their lawyers must make many decisions during the course of a civil action that will differentiate one dispute from another. For example, one disputant, for a variety of reasons, might decide to make a settlement offer at an early stage in the proceedings whereas another disputant might determine that any offer to settle would amount to an unacceptable admission of guilt or responsibility. A party to an action might instruct his or her lawyer to bring a series of interlocutory motions that they know would put financial and emotional pressure on the opposing party. Another party or their lawyer might resist following such a strategy and instead be more inclined to stress the legal merits of their case to encourage a satisfactory resolution. Opposing lawyers in a case may be very effective negotiators and assist their clients in satisfactorily settling the outstanding issues. Different lawyers in the same case might mean that a negotiated settlement is unlikely. Simply put, the diverse contexts of disputes means that their course and their outcomes will vary even when these disputes must comply with uniformly applicable court rules.

The modern emergence of ADR and its acceptance within the legal profession focused attention on the role of the court rules in helping or hindering the resolution of disputes. With ADR recast as appropriate dispute resolution, the Rules of Court and their review and revision can now come under the ADR umbrella. With ADR no longer an opposing alternative to the court adjudication of disputes, how the rules shape and move cases towards trial, how they contribute to, or detract from, constructive dispute resolution, and how rules of civil procedure could be improved became fair questions for an ADR inquiry. The fact that over 90 percent of all civil actions settle without trial adds further weight to this reasoning.

A complete study of the Rules of Court and how these rules have been interpreted and applied in cases that have come before the courts is beyond the scope of this book even though such a study might now be legitimately labelled as ADR. However, a general overview of several procedural rules that can clearly influence or encourage the resolution of court cases, as well as recent innovations in procedural rules, provides a sampling of the use of ADR in court procedures. The rules relate to costs, pre-trial conferences and other early interventions, summary proceedings and mandatory mediation. These rules provide an indication of how court cases can be managed to help achieve just, speedy and inexpensive dispute resolution and may suggest how the judicial management of disputes might be improved.

i) Costs

The general rule of indemnity in Canadian civil courts and in some American jurisdictions is that costs follow the event — the winning party in a lawsuit is entitled to be paid costs from the losing party. This rule means that a losing party in a litigation is responsible not only for his or her own legal costs but also for a portion of the other side's legal costs. The amount of costs that is recoverable varies from jurisdiction to jurisdiction but a major part will be lawyer's fees. Usually the losing party is only required to pay a certain percentage of the winning party's legal costs. Occasionally, a losing party may be required to fully indemnify the winning party by paying the entire legal bill when there has been reprehensible, scandalous or outrageous conduct on the part of the losing party.

The historical rationale for this cost rule appears to have been to provide compensation based on fault (the loser pays), but the emergence of ADR has focused attention on the use of costs as an effective means for encouraging litigants to resolve their dispute. Apart from the obvious impact of the rule itself, two procedures that can significantly alter this rule and its cost consequences for negotiators are worth describing.

First, rules of civil procedure often provide that a party to a court proceeding may deliver to any other party in the litigation a written offer to settle any or all of the claims in dispute on terms specified in the offer. This procedure is open to both plaintiffs and defendants and also applies to other disputants making counterclaims or third-party claims in the same proceeding. This statutory offer to settle formalizes what takes place regularly in the negotiation process. However, making the right written offer can substantially alter the general indemnity rule about costs. For example, the plaintiff in a personal injury action instructs her lawyer to communicate a compromise offer: the midpoint between her initial demand and the insurance company's low opening offer. The plaintiff is willing to sacrifice some hoped-for compensation for an early settlement. The trial is two years away. The insurance company rejects the offer. After trial, the plaintiff recovers judgment for more than the compromise offer. To encourage the insurance company to accept what turned out to be a reasonable offer, the cost rule now would entitle the plaintiff to recover far more costs, often double, from the time the offer was made.

Although these statutory offers to settle can include non-monetary terms and can be made on a without prejudice basis, their effectiveness at promoting settlement depends on at least two variables. First, the risk of paying some additional legal costs pursuant to these rules must be significant enough to be a factor in persuading the opposite party to accept the offer. Given the general uncertainties around litigation and the difficulties in predicting judicial decisions, it is not clear that a risk of a greater cost penalty would be of much assistance unless the potential liability for higher costs was greater than the perceived benefits of not accepting the offer to settle. Second, the rule only works if the parties are negotiating effectively. An unrealistically high or low offer to settle as a negotiating tactic would not produce the desired results. The rule also requires that a party be able to formally present an offer to settle. Given the complexity of the negotiation process described in chapter 3 and the fact that many cases settle on the courthouse steps, it is questionable whether procedural provisions by themselves will be effective catalysts to encourage realistic negotiations. On the other hand, a skilful negotiator, who is able to determine at an early stage in the litigation what a reasonable settlement offer should be, could gain considerable benefits.

A second procedural rule is directed at eliminating unnecessary and unreasonable disputing costs. This goal is accomplished by making lawyers personally responsible for these costs. The rules allow a court to disallow fees and disbursements between a lawyer and client, order reimbursement by a lawyer of costs the client has had to pay to another party, and order a lawyer to be personally liable for costs in cases where the lawyer has caused costs to be incurred without reasonable cause, or has caused costs to be wasted through delay, neglect or some other fault.

These rules appear designed to reduce the high costs and delays associated with litigation by providing a judicial check on the quality of the disputing process prior to trial. However, the rule assumes that unreasonable, unnecessary, or improper lawyer behaviour contributes to these problems. This assumption may not be accurate. The culprit may be adversarial thinking, as discussed in chapter 2, which encourages a win-lose approach to dispute resolution and provides a high degree of autonomy and discretion to the parties and their lawyers to decide what steps are necessary. Even if there is anecdotal evidence that some lawyers and their clients waste time and money in the litigation process, the courts have set a high threshold for calling into question a lawyer's behaviour. In *Young* v. *Young*, the Supreme Court of Canada said:

> The basic principle on which costs are awarded is as compensation for the successful party, not in order to punish a barrister. Any member of the legal profession might be subject to a compensatory award for costs if it is shown that repetitive and irrelevant material, and excessive motions and applications, characterized the proceedings in which they were involved, and that the lawyer acted in bad faith in encouraging this abuse and delay . . . courts must be extremely cautious in awarding costs personally against a lawyer, given the duties upon a lawyer to guard confidentiality of instructions and to bring forward with courage even unpopular causes. A lawyer should not be placed in a situation where his or her fear of an adverse order of costs may conflict with these fundamental duties of his or her calling.[28]

---

28   [1993] 4 S.C.R. 3 at 135–36.

ii) Pre-trial Conferences and Other Early Interventions

Pre-trial conferences have a long history in both the United States and Canada. Their history illustrates a change in goals for these conferences from one of strict trial preparation, to case management, to settlement being a by-product of good pre-trial procedure, to active promotion of settlement. Obviously the impact of pre-trial conferences on the resolution of disputes will depend on what is the major focus of these conferences. However, ADR directed attention to the potential of these pre-trial meetings to help cases settle earlier than might otherwise be the case.

Pre-trial conferences that are focused primarily on trial preparation tend to be concerned with simplifying issues, ensuring pleadings are in order, obtaining admissions, determining the length of trial and the numbers of witnesses and discussing any other matters that might facilitate the trial. Settlement-focused pre-trial conferences, on the other hand, are more analogous to a negotiation. Settlement is the goal. The presence of an experienced judge to assist these negotiations and to help the parties explore all possibilities of settlement of the outstanding issues is seen as a benefit. The judge, having heard the parties and been apprised of the reasons for their inability to agree, can point out, among other things, how an experienced judge might deal with the issues. This fresh judicial look can be of assistance in helping the parties reassess their best alternatives to a negotiated agreement (BATNAs) or in moving a party off an honestly-held but unrealistic position.

Having a pre-trial conference with a settlement focus before a judge who is comfortable taking on the rule of a negotiation facilitator has led to several developments. First, because judges in settlement conferences are essentially neutral third parties assisting the negotiations, there have been initiatives to train judges in mediation theories and skills. Although the amount of mediation training provided to judges and the time available to conduct mediations have been limited, judges officially acting as mediators in settlement conferences is now not uncommon. Second, judges have been given jurisdiction to order that the parties attend a mini-trial in which a judge can give a non-binding opinion of the probable outcome of a trial in the proceeding. The judge might also refer the parties to a mediation process outside the court or make other orders vis-à-vis settlement that the judge considers just or necessary.

The ADR-inspired expansion of settlement conferences is related to several other procedures that are designed to encourage the early resolution of cases. Early neutral evaluation (ENE) or early intervention (EI) rules operate on the assumption that barriers to prompt and forthright communication and realistic case analysis contribute to litigation costs. Such barriers can include pleading practices, the failure of law-yers to develop theories of the case at the outset, unrealistic clients, time-management pressures on lawyers, the distancing of the parties in litigation, the real difficulties people have in making major decisions and the adversarial nature of litigation. Procedures that provide for an early meeting with the parties and a judge or other quality neutral can encourage realistic case analysis, provide an opportunity for each party to hear the other side, give the lawyers and parties a confidential, frank, and experienced assessment of the strengths and weaknesses of their positions, and especially, provide the parties with an early opportunity and a forum to negotiate a settlement.

The efficacy of procedural rules that provide opportunities for set-tlements prior to trial will depend on a number of factors such as the skill level of the judges involved, the weight given by the parties to judicial views expressed in these meetings, the level of preparation of the parties, the degree to which the parties participate in good faith and the general negotiating abilities of the parties. In addition, there is also the factor that these pre-trial meetings occur within the confines of the adversarial arena. A lawsuit is in process. There is a tension between the openness and disclosure explicitly and implicitly called for in these settlement-oriented encounters and the adversarial thinking about dis-closure that commonly accompanies litigation.

iii) Summary Proceedings

Various procedural rules operate to provide summary determinations of civil cases so as to avoid the costs associated with protracted pro-ceedings. Rules allow cases to be dismissed for want of prosecution where undue delay in moving the case forward by one party has caused prejudice to another party. Other rules allow pleadings to be struck out at any stage in a proceeding if they disclose no reasonable claim or defence; are unnecessary, scandalous, frivolous, or vexa-tious; may prejudice, embarrass, or delay a fair trial; or are an abuse of the process of the court. More rules allow the parties to state a spe-cial case to a judge involving a question of law or fact or to set down a point of law for hearing. The answer to the question or the decision on the point of law may substantially dispose of the whole action. There are rules that permit the parties to apply to the court for sum-mary judgment on the grounds that there is no defence or that there is no merit in the claims being made.

Each of these rules provides a mechanism for a summary determi-nation of the case without a full trial. In some cases, these procedures can be invoked at a very early stage in the legal proceedings. Although the rules offer disputants opportunities to save a great deal of time and money, the occasions when the rules apply are quite limited. For example, in order for a plaintiff's claim or a defendant's defence to be struck out as unreasonable or frivolous at the pleading stage, it has to be plain and obvious on its face that the claim or defence could not succeed. The court would assume that all the facts pleaded are true and the only question is whether the facts disclose a claim or defence. It would not require sophisticated drafting skills to avoid this type of challenge. Artful pleaders are usually able to avoid early dispositions. Similarly, in an application for summary judgment, the judge could not decide disputed questions of fact or law. The judge's function was restricted to determining whether there was a bona fide triable issue. Generally, courts are reluctant to deny litigants their day in court unless the eventual outcome of the case is clear and unequivocal.

However, recent rule changes have been designed to expand the situations in which summary proceedings can be taken. Essentially, these rules provide for truncated adjudications or summary trials. The rules give judges jurisdiction to grant judgment based only on affidavit evidence, interrogatories, examinations for discovery, or admissions in cases where the court is able to find the facts necessary to decide issues of fact or law. The general purpose of these types of rules is to provide a simplified procedure that will allow for a less expensive and more expeditious resolution of the case unless to proceed summarily would result in an injustice.

Rules that provide for summary trials raise the concern that justice may be sacrificed for expediency. This fear of second-class justice also has been raised for some ADR initiatives outside the court. Part of the response to this concern is to acknowledge that summary trial rules "may not furnish perfect justice in every case but that elusive and unattainable goal cannot always be assured even after a conventional trial."[29] In addition, summary trial rules usually give judges discretion to refuse to proceed if it would be unjust based on factors such as the amount involved, the complexity of the issues, the urgency of the matter, the likelihood of prejudice from delay, costs and the course of proceedings to date.

---

29   From Chief Justice McEachern's explanation of the workings of British Columbia's summary trial rules. See *Inspiration Management Ltd.* v. *McDermid St. Lawrence Ltd.* (1989), 36 B.C.L.R. (2d) 202 at 214 (C.A.).

Even if a judge is not able to grant judgment generally, summary trial rules usually give judges the power to make decisions on certain issues or to issue directions to expedite or clarify future proceedings. Accordingly, even if the full case is not disposed of, the determination of a critical issue or a judge's direction on proper process can assist the parties in reaching settlement.

The usefulness of summary trials seems to depend on establishing a fine balance between the luxury of a full trial with all its traditional safeguards and a less expensive and more expeditious procedure with fewer procedural protections.

iv) Mandatory Mediation

In an increasing number of cases, mediation is being made mandatory in the courts. This matter is briefly referred to in chapter 4, "Mediation: The Science and the Skills," and mandatory family mediation is referenced in chapter 6, "ADR in Practice." Generally speaking, mandatory mediation in the courts or court-connected mediation means that the parties to a civil suit cannot proceed past a certain point in the litigation process until mediation has been attempted. The requirement on disputants to participate in mediation may be imposed by rules of procedure that call for a mediation session to routinely take place at an early point in the lawsuit or at least before the trial of the action. Conversely, participation in mediation may be mandatory only if one of the parties to the civil action requests a mediation process.[30] Mandatory mediation may apply to all civil cases or only to certain types of cases such as custody disputes, motor vehicle accidents or construction matters.

The reasons to resort to mandatory mediation may vary. Mandatory mediation rules may be implemented by governments, with the support of the legal profession, to reduce the costs and delays associated with litigation. Although most civil cases settle without a trial, many of these settlements occur late in the litigation process. Settlements on the courthouse steps are common. By this time the parties will have incurred significant costs. Mandatory mediation could contribute to earlier settlements that would then result in cost and time savings for the disputants as well as improve trial management. In certain cases, such as custody disputes, mandatory mediation could help achieve more enduring resolutions in contrast to the cases where

---

30   Rule 24.1 in Ontario's Rules of Civil Procedure is an example of the former approach whereas British Columbia's Notice to Mediate regulations are an example of the latter.

judge-imposed orders around matters like custody and access do not always garner long-lasting support. Other benefits associated with the voluntary use of mediation, such as maintaining continuing relationships and teaching people how to constructively manage future disputes, can be part of the rationale for making mediation mandatory in the courts.

However, requiring litigants to mediate raises a number of questions. Some of the questions are purely procedural. When should mandatory mediation be scheduled? Where should it be held? How long should it last? Who should attend? How is the mediator chosen? Who pays the costs? Are some cases exempt? What does good faith participation in mandatory mediation mean?

There are no uniform or singularly right answers to some of these important procedural questions. For example, a mandatory mediation session may be counter-productive if it is scheduled to be held at an early date when the parties have not had the time to fully prepare for the negotiations. On the other hand, if the mediation is scheduled too close to the trial date, the potential time and cost savings may be insignificant. Similarly, the time prescribed for the parties to attend the mediation must be long enough to permit productive discussions to take place but not so long as to impose a cost hardship that would interfere with access to trial for less well-off litigants if settlement is not reached.

Other procedural elements in mandatory mediation schemes may be more uniform. It will be common for the parties to share the cost of the mediation equally unless the parties agree to some other cost-sharing arrangement. The parties also will commonly be given the opportunity to agree on the name of a mediator. If the parties cannot agree on a suitable person, a mediator from an approved list or roster will be selected by the coordinator or organization overseeing the administration of the mandatory mediation program. The court will usually be given discretion in limited circumstances to exempt parties from attending the mediation or to adjourn the mediation to a more appropriate time. Refusal by one party to attend the mediation will normally allow another party to ask the court to impose consequences such as staying the action until the defaulting party attends mediation, dismissing the action or striking out the defence, ordering a party to pay costs or making any other order that is just.

Mandatory mediation also raises a number of more substantive questions. These questions centre on the efficacy of a procedure that forces parties to participate in a consensual decision-making process but does not require them to reach agreement. In other words, does mandatory mediation work? Does it change the nature of the mediation process? Are there risks or downsides for certain disputants when mediation is made mandatory?

The research and experience with mandatory mediation[31] often provide conflicting or equivocal answers to these questions. Although there have been few studies comparing mandatory and voluntary mediation to determine whether any negative consequences occur when participation in mediation is required, research on mandatory mediation suggests that

- mandatory mediation did not reduce the rate of settlement;
- parties in mandatory divorce mediation were as likely to recommend mediation to a friend as those in voluntary mediation;
- the majority of parties responded favourably to mandatory mediation even if they had not settled or would have rejected mediation if given a choice;
- the manner in which the case entered mediation did not affect parties' ratings of whether they had a sufficient opportunity to express views;
- parties in mandatory mediation did not differ from those who chose to mediate in their descriptions of the mediation session; and
- no general pattern of differences was evident between men and women or between non-white parties and white parties in their responses to mandatory mediation.

On the other hand, compared with voluntary mediation, studies of mandatory mediation report that

- cases that the courts sent to mediation were significantly less likely to settle;
- small claims cases in which parties were required to mediate were marginally less likely to settle;

---

31   For recent examples, see G. Smith, "Unwilling Actors: Why Voluntary Mediation Works, Why Mandatory Mediation Might Not" (1998) 36 Osgoode Hall L.J. 847; R.L. Wissler, "The Effects of Mandatory Mediation: Empirical Research on the Experience of Small Claims and Common Pleas Courts" (1997) 33 Willamette L. Rev. 565; C.C. Hutchison, "The Case for Mandatory Mediation" (1996) 42 Loy. L. Rev. 85; R. Inglesby, "Court Sponsored Mediation: The Case against Mandatory Participation" (1993) 56 Mod. L. Rev. 441; J.B. Kelly & M.A. Duryea, "Women and Men's Views of Mediation in Voluntary and Mandatory Mediation Settings" (1992) 30 Fam. & Concil. Crts. Rev. 34; W.O. Simmons, "An Economic Analysis of Mandatory Mediation and the Disposition of Medical Malpractice Claims" (1996) 6 J. Legal Econ. 41.

- parties that reached a settlement in mandatory mediation were less likely to see the mediation process as fair or to be satisfied with the process;
- parties that did not settle were marginally more likely to feel that the mediator had pressured them to settle;
- parties that were required to mediate were less likely to report a willingness to use mediation again;
- parties whose cases did not settle were more likely to be very dissatisfied with the mediation process;
- in cases that did not settle, women were less satisfied with the mediation process than men;
- female plaintiffs were less likely than male plaintiffs to report they would recommend mediation to a friend or colleague; and
- non-white plaintiffs were less likely than white plaintiffs to report they would recommend mediation to a friend or colleague.

Given the many ways in which mediation is actually practised and the contextual complexity that accompanies all disputes, the above research findings may not apply to all mandatory mediation programs. Whether mandatory mediation works will depend on the nature of the mediation process employed and the specific goals sought to be achieved. However, existing research findings do raise concerns about mandatory mediation, particularly along gender and race lines, as well as the potential negative impact that non-settled cases may have on the mediation process.

FURTHER READINGS

BRAZIL, W.D., "Comparing Structures for the Delivery of ADR Services by Courts: Critical Values and Concerns" (1999) 14 Ohio St. J. on Disp. Resol.

MENKEL-MEADOW, C., "Pursuing Settlement in an Adversary Culture: A Tale of Innovation Co-opted, or 'The Law of ADR,'" (1991) 11 Fla. L. Rev. 1

SANDER, F., H. ALLEN, & D. HENSLER, "Judicial (Mis)Use of ADR? A Debate" (1996) 27 U. Tol. L. Rev. 885.

WALD, P.M., "ADR and the Courts: An Update" (1997) 46 Duke L.J. 1445

CHAPTER 9

ADR IN ACTION: CASE STUDIES AND PRACTICAL PROBLEMS

A. INTRODUCTION

Although most people recognize a conflict when they see one, what happens next is not always so clear. The process that conflicts take — including whether one is raised or not, as well as the prevention, management, or resolution of conflicts in their disparate and unequal forms — is a complicated affair. Rather than withdrawing from or ignoring the challenges in this uneven, uncertain, and for some, terrifying, terrain, the ADR theories and practices in the preceding pages can provide a range of insights into what is going on and how best to respond.

For lawyers, ADR perspectives will be most helpful. When a lawyer is retained to represent a client with disputing or problem-solving needs, is asked to act as a mediator, or otherwise is concerned with a dispute of some kind, the theory and practice of ADR will always be in play. What is the cause of the conflict, the conflict styles of the parties and the best alternative to a negotiated agreement (BATNA)? Is the problem an integrative or distributive one? Is this a case for mediation, arbitration, early neutral evaluation, a mini-trial, or would it be best for the client to walk away? What should be disclosed in a mandatory mediation session? Can you sue a mediator who has made a mistake? Who should make the opening offer? What are the risks of boulwareism? What should the mediator do when it appears the parties have reached an impasse? Are the ADR goals right for my clients? ADR offers resources to lawyers to answer these and other questions about disputing. The answers will be significant in shaping the ways in which lawyers, regardless of area of practice, then go about their jobs. As ADR has evolved into a full-fledged examination of all manner of disputing developments — including how lawyers can contribute significantly to constructive dispute resolution — the importance of the modern phenomenon of ADR to the practice of law has become clear.

This chapter focuses on how ADR can be applied in a practical way to real-life problems. In other words, how can the ADR theories and references to ADR practices in this book help lawyers and others be better dispute resolvers and effective problem solvers. Using two ADR case studies and several disputing scenarios as examples,[1] the chapter illustrates how an ADR analysis of a dispute can assist in deciding what to do next in any dispute. Considering these cases from a practical ADR vantage point also demonstrates the uncertainty and unpredictability that infuse dispute resolution. What happens next in any dispute depends on context. Part of that context is how ADR is used. The decision to mediate as opposed to avoiding or arbitrating the dispute may mean there will be a completely different outcome to the dispute.

The two case studies involve a major real estate transaction gone sour and a landlord and tenant controversy. The case studies begin with general facts that begin to disclose some of the context around the particular dispute. As you read these facts, you can consider how you might approach the problems presented from an ADR point of view. The general facts are then followed by an analysis and advice section drawing on references to the ADR ideas and practices contained in this book. This section can be compared with your own analysis and advice or used as a model for analyzing the six disputing scenarios following the case studies or for examining other real-life disputes with which you are familiar. What happens next is set out in the disputing developments section. This section may involve several different outcomes depending on the ADR advice that is given or followed. Based on what happens next — because different ADR actions can lead to different results — there can be opportunities for more ADR analysis and advice, followed by the final disputing developments.

The chapter concludes with general facts for six further disputing scenarios. These additional problems can be used by readers, whether student or practitioner, to complete their own ADR analysis and pro-

---

1   The actual case studies have been adapted from real disputes. To preserve confidences, names and details have been changed but in other respects these are practical problems of a type that could easily come your way. The disputing scenarios are fictionalized accounts of what could be real-life situations.

vide their own ADR advice. This chapter shows how ADR in action may actually work.

B. CASE STUDY ONE: THE EXPANSIVE OCEAN VIEWS

1) General Facts

John is a forty-five-year-old chiropractor. His wife, Philippa (Pippa to her friends) is thirty-five and is finishing her training to be a naturopath. John and Pippa have been married for five years and each hopes their relationship (the second marriage for both) will be a lasting one. They have no children yet but are planning to have a child within a year or two at the latest.

John and Pippa had moved three years ago to a mostly rural area, sixty kilometres away from the big city. John has worked hard to establish his practice in a small town that services the surrounding area. His practice brings in approximately $140,000 gross per year. Pippa hopes to join John in his practice shortly, although they both recognize that balancing their jobs and a child will be demanding. The decision to have the child took some time, primarily because John (who has a ten-year-old daughter from another relationship) was anxious about becoming a father again at his age. John and Pippa estimate they can together comfortably earn $160,000 to $200,000 per annum. They both want balanced lives. In fact, much of their professional work involves telling people to get a better balance in their lives to stay healthy.

It was this interest in a balanced lifestyle that attracted them to the fateful property in the first instance. One year ago and considering their plans for a family, John and Pippa decided they would buy a home. They began looking for a fixer-upper property with some potential to appreciate in value over time. They looked at several interesting real estate listings but none caught their eye. While they were visiting one property, their real estate agent advised them that a five-acre parcel with expansive ocean views had just been listed. They went to the property immediately. As they walked up a winding and somewhat rundown pathway into the property, they saw the expansive ocean views that unfolded like a painting in front of a tired but soundly built rancher sitting on a rising ridge. It was love at first sight.

The five-acre parcel with the house needing work and the expansive ocean views were exactly what they had been looking for. The property was being sold by Nancy who had lived in the area for the past fifteen years. She had planted and landscaped much of the five-acre parcel that was being sold and was also the owner of an adjacent thirty-acre parcel.

Unknown at the time to John and Pippa was the fact that Nancy was really a shrewd developer. She had parcelled off the five-acre property four years ago and expected to do the same dividing of the thirty-acre property. One of the big reasons that the five-acre parcel had not sold was that Nancy was unwilling to give any purchaser who asked a legal covenant prohibiting her or any subsequent owner of the thirty acres from building a house or other structure that blocked the expansive ocean views.

John and Pippa saw themselves fixing up the old house, with outdoor swimming pool, converting an old shed or two on the property into greenhouses and bringing back into organic production the various fruit trees on the property. There seemed to be a natural harmony to the property.

John and Pippa never met Nancy until after the sale was completed. John and Pippa agreed to pay $427,000 for the property (asking price was $435,000) and over time and with their improvements, they conservatively estimated that the property could eventually be valued at $800,000 to $1,000,000, providing them with a perfect, non-taxable capital gain for their retirement plans.

John and Pippa retained a real estate lawyer, George, to handle the purchase. There was nothing unusual to note in the entire transaction except two points. First, the real estate listing described the property in written material as "having expansive ocean views." Second, John asked the vendor's real estate agent if Nancy would be coming back and building on the adjacent thirty-acre property. The real estate agent said that "she would, in all likelihood, be returning." John said, "Will she build in front of us?" The real estate agent said "no." John and Pippa didn't think of asking for a legal covenant because they didn't know such a legal beast existed.

In the year after the purchase, John and Pippa began to make improvements to the property. It was hard work and expensive. However, they had budgeted for this time and expense and although they had to extend their line of credit for an initial $50,000 in renovations, they felt confident everything would work out fine in the end and this would be a dream home for them. They also expected to have a lot of visitors once the initial improvements had been made because the general area itself and the ocean below the ridge were popular vacation spots.

Nancy's call on Sunday to say that there would be construction starting on Monday seemed to come out of the blue. There had been some interaction between the parties after the sale. Nancy had asked if she could continue to store some of her belongings in the sheds. John and Pippa had agreed. Nancy had also asked if she could use John and Pippa's laneway to get access to her property because it would be more convenient. John and Pippa had agreed. However, these concessions were later withdrawn in a slightly heated exchange between John and Nancy when John felt that Nancy had been less than honest about her reasons for needing to store the belongings in the shed.

On Monday, the day after Nancy's telephone call, the early arrival of heavy earth-moving machinery broke the morning tranquillity. John and Pippa soon saw that construction was starting on a two-storey home being built on the thirty-acre parcel still owned by Nancy. The home was being built on Nancy's property but it was situated only thirty metres from John and Pippa's house, the only other house on the entire thirty-five acres! The house being built would itself have expansive ocean views but the construction would ruin the views from John and Pippa's property.

There was a heated exchange between John and Nancy at the construction site. Indirect threats were exchanged. John soon discovered that Nancy was in complete compliance with all relevant building by-laws. It seemed to John and Pippa that Nancy's actions were being done in spite because there were other equally good building sites on the thirty-acre property.

John and Pippa are unsure about what to do. John wants to take immediate action and has even contemplated taking the law into his own hands. Efforts to lobby the municipal council have proved to be a waste of time. John is upset and angry. Pippa is frustrated and would just like the problem to go away. Her initial thinking is to landscape so that the new house is blocked from view. She is opposed to confronting Nancy any more.

2) ADR Analysis and Advice

Consider what the following ADR analysis and advice might mean to what happens next.

a) The Analysis

i) The Cause of the Conflict
Even with limited information, it is not difficult to understand that there may be several causes of the dispute. Identifying these causes may help to

- better understand what is really underlying the conflict;
- bring forward all the issues that are at stake;

- identify effective interventions;
- craft solutions suited to the real problem;
- promote constructive conflict; and
- recognize that some conflicts are difficult to resolve by the parties themselves.

John and Pippa clearly see several important interests being interfered with. Their economic interest in the property appreciating in value will not be satisfied if the construction proceeds. The loss of the expansive ocean views will no doubt also be a psychological blow to their desire for a balanced lifestyle through country living. There also may be a data dispute around whether Nancy is legally permitted to build in that location, given the statements made by her real estate agent. This data dispute may focus on who said what to whom if the real estate agent denies making the statement. The reason Nancy is building in that location may be because there is a relationship dispute arising out of John's manner of cancelling her right or permission to still use the five-acre property. The relationship dispute may be complicated by the manner in which the construction started and the "heated exchanges" that have taken place. Because Nancy was the original owner of the property and sees herself as still "connected to the land," value and structural disputes may also be present. How land is used, particularly by rural neighbours, and how these decisions get made, may be significant.

Unknown at this time to John and Pippa, which is common in disputing, are other potential causes for conflict from Nancy's perspective. Nancy obviously has a significant economic interest at stake in her development of the thirty-acre parcel. John and Pippa's economic concerns may pale in comparison. If John and Pippa challenge the building, economics are sure to fuel Nancy's reaction. Also, opposing the building may create a structural dispute between simple landowners (John and Pippa) and a developer. The power relationships between these parties and how development business generally is done could come into sharp conflict if John and Pippa voice opposition.

Thinking about what can cause conflicts appears to show that this dispute may be quite complicated and difficult to resolve, particularly by consensual methods of dispute resolution.

ii) Destructive and Constructive Conflict

There are indications that the dispute, whatever its causes, is already beginning to take a destructive course. The communication between the parties has become unreliable. There is evidence of suspicious and hostile attitudes that accentuate differences and minimize similarities.

There has been talk of actions that would escalate the dispute. At this point, the elements associated with constructive dispute resolution (common problem, open and honest communication, trust, creativity) are absent. Shifting away from a destructive approach may be challenging in these circumstances.

iii) Conflict Behaviour

Analyzing conflict from a behavioural perspective can be tricky, but focusing on what the parties have done can help to understand what has already happened and what might occur in the future.

In this case, Nancy appears to be exhibiting a highly competitive conflict style. The decision to build in that location and to give one day's notice appears to be entirely self-interested. Although John appears ready to lock horns, Pippa is demonstrating classical avoidance behaviour. She is not able at this point to be assertive about her own needs and has already expressed a desire to walk away from the problem and to take whatever steps are necessary to block out the view of the offending house.

These differing behaviours may point to a very adversarial showdown, a walking away from the problem or that John and Pippa may have difficulties in negotiating a joint course of action.

iv) Power

At first glance, Nancy may appear to be in the driver's seat. She has a building permit and has complied with all relevant by-laws regarding the type of construction she is engaging in. She is wealthy. There is no legal covenant that prevents her from building on that site. Time seems also to be on Nancy's side. The further the construction proceeds, the more difficult it will be in a practical way to make the necessary changes to get back the expansive ocean views. Although John and Pippa had the ability to lobby informally with local politicians, these efforts have not made a dent in Nancy's plans. It seems clear that unless there is a change in the power dynamics, there will be no opportunity for John and Pippa to respond effectively.

v) Interest/Legal Rights

ADR, with an interest in consensual methods of dispute resolution, can bring out the distinction between the interests or needs of the disputants and their legal rights. Several of John and Pippa's interests in any eventual resolution have already been noted. Nancy's desires to build also have been alluded to. At this point, a common interest in having neighbourly relations in the future does not seem to exist or even seem desirable. The legal rights, on the other hand, are less clear. Although Nancy has complied with relevant building laws and by-laws, there appears to be an issue about whether Nancy, through her real estate agent, contracted not to build so as to block the expansive ocean views. If there was a collateral contract of this nature, or these representations induced John and Pippa to buy the property, John and Pippa could have a legal right to stop the building. This legal right depends on a legal analysis of the events leading up to the purchase and sale of the property. If the representations of the real estate agent are denied, as they likely will be, the ascertainment of the various legal rights can get complicated. Nancy may be entitled to build on the site she has chosen and John and Pippa may only have a claim for damages against the real estate agent for negligent misrepresentation.

b) The Advice

John and Pippa need to clarify their legal rights as soon as possible including the extent of their economic loss. Without this information, taking any step other than walking away from the dispute seems unlikely. What happens after obtaining the legal advice will depend on a number of factors, including the strength of the legal advice. In these circumstances, resorting to further informal negotiations or the parties somehow agreeing to mediation are not realistic options. Walking away from, or avoiding, the dispute, which is often a wise move, does not seem advisable here, although going to a lawyer can be a major hurdle to get over, given John and Pippa's different conflict styles.

3) Further Disputing Developments

a) Scenario A

Despite the advice, John and Pippa decide not to see a lawyer. The decision respects Pippa's aversion to confrontation. She is simply unwilling to devote the energy and time or pay the money to pursue a remedy. Even if there is a strong opinion from the lawyer that Nancy has no legal right to build in that location, it seems unlikely that Nancy would voluntarily stop construction. She would most likely hire her own lawyer. Pippa fears that the "bad blood" that has been generated would only fuel a long legal battle. Pippa is not prepared for that result, particularly in light of her plans to have a child.

The dispute is dropped. The construction proceeds to conclusion. John, Pippa and Nancy never become friends. John and Pippa do some extensive landscaping with fast-growing cedar trees that, in about two years, almost make Nancy's house invisible. Unfortunately, the expansive ocean views are also gone, especially after Nancy continued the plantings on her property along the entire horizon. Nancy's landscaping response to John and Pippa's attempt to block Nancy from view led to other actions — on both sides. John and Pippa feel the balance they sought in this property is gone. They sell the property for approximately $200,000 less than they would have got for an identical property with expansive ocean views. John and Pippa's lives are definitely affected forever by their decision to move.

Alternatively, it might have happened that instead of landscaping, Nancy sells her property to a couple. The couple turn out to be great neighbours with many of the same interests (and the same number of children) as John and Pippa. They have many wonderful nights on the neighbour's veranda admiring the expansive ocean views and occasionally retelling this story.

b) Scenario B

John and Pippa see a lawyer. The lawyer advises them that they have a good case to allege breach of contract against Nancy or to plead that Nancy, through her agent, made a misrepresentation that induced John and Pippa to enter into the contract. In either case, one legal remedy is to start a lawsuit and then seek an interim injunction to immediately stop the construction while the lawsuit is heard. Because of court delays, the case would not come up for trial for two to three years. The lawyer also tells John and Pippa that there are possible claims to be made against the real estate agent who made the misrepresentation that Nancy would not build and also against John and Pippa's real estate lawyer who failed to mention the possibility of getting a legal covenant to protect the expansive ocean views from people like Nancy or future purchasers of the property.

The lawyer charges $200 per hour. The lawyer mentions ADR to John and Pippa and although a licensed mediator herself, the lawyer recommends that she first call and attempt to negotiate a resolution. If an acceptable agreement with Nancy is not possible (acceptable means Nancy has to move at the least cost to John and Pippa and provide a binding legal covenant for the future), the lawyer recommends commencing the action against all the possible defendants and then applying to the court for an interim injunction. The interim injunction, if granted, would put a stop to construction until the case comes to trial or is otherwise settled. The presence and potential liability of the other parties with their insurance companies may assist future negotiations, the lawyer says. The lawyer also suggests getting an expert appraiser to quantify the economic losses that John and Pippa have suffered.

4) ADR Analysis and Advice for Scenario B

Consider what the following additional ADR analysis and advice might mean to what happens next.

a) The Analysis

i) Power

The lawyer's advice, both legal and strategic, combined with John and Pippa's decision to take this step despite Pippa's hesitation, creates power. The imbalance of power that initially appeared has been changed dramatically, at least in the eyes of John and Pippa. There are still real economic uncertainties (how long can John and Pippa afford to pay to pursue their goals?); relationship issues (will the clash of conflict styles and behaviours between Pippa and John be too difficult to manage?); intangibles (how will the stresses and uncertainties and the involvement of lawyers affect John and Pippa's balanced lives?); and practice concerns (will the amount of damages be uneconomical to pursue?). These matters demonstrate that the power of a good legal case with competent legal representation is only one factor to be considered. Non-legal factors can be extremely influential. The power to effect change in a conflict setting can alter overnight.

ii) The Methods of Dispute Processing

The lawyer is recommending bargaining in the shadow of the law. If the lawyer is unable to persuade Nancy (or her lawyer) that the site must be moved because of John and Pippa's legal rights, the lawyer suggests commencing a lawsuit. However, given that 90 to 95 percent of all civil cases settle, the lawyer is thinking strategically ahead to these future negotiations.

Assuming that other methods of dispute processing on the dispute resolution continuum are available, deciding on process brings into play a variety of factors. Even though the parties are presently neighbours, this continuing relationship does not seem important enough to John and Pippa to be a critical reason why a consensus process should be used. It is important to John and especially Pippa that the dispute be resolved as quickly and inexpensively as possible. The advantages of resorting to negotiation will be that John and Pippa make any final decision that they have to live with. Given there may be multiple causes to the dispute, a negotiation (or mediation process) could be used to both address and find creative solutions to the issues at stake. How much will it cost for Nancy to move to an equally desirable site on the thirty acres and what else do John and Pippa need to do to make this happen are questions that can be discussed in negotiation or mediation. On the other hand, Nancy may be unwilling to participate meaningfully in such a process if one of her goals is to punish John and Pippa for what she may regard as disrespectful treatment or if her economic desires will be compromised.

iii) The Ideology of ADR

ADR's advice to John and Pippa depends on the shape of ADR. If ADR is the second coming of litigation and mostly about economic efficiencies, this case will proceed, in most respects, just as the lawyer has recommended. Although the preoccupation with an adversarial mindset may be tempered, the filing of the lawsuit and the subsequent negotiations among the parties to the lawsuit will be mostly directed at solving the problem to John and Pippa's satisfaction. Achieving this satisfaction is likely to be resisted by Nancy. The process will be as fast and cheap as possible, and it may be that the presence of one or two lawyers representing insurance monies will be moderating influences on the process otherwise getting out of hand and becoming too polarized, expensive and protracted.

On the other hand ADR may sweep this case into a mediation process because someone suggests harmony between neighbours is a valuable goal and it is normal, natural, and essential that feuding neighbours in most cases need to be able to work out disputes themselves. Resort to mediation might be voluntary if John and Pippa agree with this orientation, or it may be mandatory if this jurisdiction requires mandatory or quasi-mandatory mediation for lawsuits of this nature. If ADR is less prescriptive, and more of an encouragement to disputants to make informed disputing choices, the decision of what to do next will depend on the nature of the decision-making process between John and Pippa and their lawyer and also between Nancy and her soon-to-be-hired lawyer.

b) The Advice

Given the legal advice John and Pippa have received about their rights, the ADR analysis begins to provide helpful information on both the likely alternatives if there is no negotiated agreement and the range of options available and how they might be sequenced to reach a negotiated settlement. Resort to informal methods of dispute resolution while keeping the adjudicative track open may be the best approach for John and Pippa (and Nancy as well) to achieve their goals in a constructive manner.

5) Final Disputing Developments

a) Outcome 1

John and Pippa give instructions to their lawyer to commence an action and proceed to seek an interim injunction if the initial negotiations are not successful. The lawyer contacts Nancy who, almost immediately, states that she will have to contact her lawyer. At the same time, John and Pippa's lawyer contacts the real estate agent and John and Pippa's first lawyer. They both say they will have to contact their lawyer. John and Pippa's lawyer has expected this result.

Later that day John and Pippa's lawyer receives a telephone call from Nancy's lawyer. Nancy's lawyer will not be able to meet with his client for a few days. John and Pippa's lawyer asks if the construction can stop immediately. The other lawyer says that he can't advise his client one way or the other until he has heard her story. With some persistence, John and Pippa's lawyer is able to arrange a meeting with the lawyer for Nancy and the real estate agent and the lawyer's insurance companies in five days' time.

John and Pippa's lawyer takes an adversarial approach to the negotiation. She presents the case as persuasively as possible. She claims John and Pippa are either entitled to have the building site moved or to get damages in lieu. She produces a recent report from a most respected real estate appraiser in the area. This report states that the value of John and Pippa's property will immediately depreciate to $200,000 at best when Nancy's house is completed. The report states the value could be lower. The expansive and uninterrupted ocean views with the privacy afforded by the adjacent thirty-acre lot were the key factors in the original purchase price of $427,000 and the asking price of $435,000. John and Pippa's lawyer also produces a report from a respected architectural firm from the nearby city. This report preliminarily identifies three other building sites on Nancy's property and suggests that the present building site is inferior to the other three. John and Pippa's lawyer suggests that Nancy's misinterpretation of John's actions around the storage appears to explain Nancy's choice to build here. With that John and Pippa's lawyer unfurls a very large map of the two lots in question, which graphically demonstrates exactly how close Nancy chose to build to John and Pippa's home. The only two houses on the thirty-five acre map are marked in red and stand out against the vast expanse of property like two sore thumbs. The lawyers know the visual impact this will make in court. John and Pippa's lawyer announces that who has to pay to correct this situation may depend on negotiations between the other lawyers. However, if the house is not dismantled and moved, John and Pippa will be seeking damages of at least $227,000. This is the figure contained in the real estate appraiser's report. Alternatively, John and Pippa's lawyer suggests that the site can be changed to a better location for $35,000 plus John and Pippa's present legal fees of $5,500. The $40,500 would be the full cost of wasted time and material on the present site and would fully reimburse John and Pippa for all legal costs.

The lawyers for the insurance companies deny there is any liability on their respective client's parts. John and Pippa's lawyer tells them that she will be bringing a motion for an interim injunction on Wednesday (this being late Friday) and leaves.

On Monday, the lawyer for the real estate agent calls John and Pippa's lawyer. Nancy will be moving and has agreed to have a legally binding covenant registered on title. The covenant will legally prohibit anyone from building to block the expansive ocean views.

b) Outcome 2

John and Pippa give instructions to their lawyer to commence an action and proceed to seek an interim injunction if the initial negotiations are not successful. The lawyer contacts Nancy who immediately states that she will have to see her lawyer. Later that day John and Pippa's lawyer receives a telephone call from Nancy's lawyer. Nancy's lawyer has been involved in the ADR movement since the beginning. He suggests mediation.

John and Pippa agree after considering the advantages and disadvantages of the mediation process. Two major factors persuade them to try. First, John and Pippa would like this matter resolved quickly and inexpensively. Mediation might help to accomplish these goals. Second, their lawyer tells them that mediation can serve as a kind of discovery process. Although what happens in the mediation is confidential and privileged, the discussions that take place in the mediation will give John and Pippa's lawyer (and the other lawyers) a chance to assess strengths and weaknesses in their case. John and Pippa have no interest in establishing a friendly neighbour relationship with Nancy although their lawyer tells them that often mediation is seen as advantageous where the parties in dispute are going to have a continuing relationship.

However, John and Pippa's lawyer agrees to the mediation on two conditions. First, the potential parties must attend the mediation. Second, the construction of the house must be suspended while the mediation talks are ongoing. Nancy's lawyer agrees to both conditions. Because the mediation is voluntary, Nancy's lawyer knows that the mediation can be terminated at any time. After some persistence, John and Pippa's and Nancy's lawyers are able to persuade the lawyers for the real estate agent and the real estate lawyer to attend the mediation.

The parties hire a well-known mediator who is also a lawyer. She has a strong reputation and experience in mediating a wide range of cases. The parties agree to share the costs of the mediation equally.

The mediator brings an interest-based approach to the mediation. She helps the parties identify their underlying concerns and interests. After two to three mediation sessions, she gets the parties' agreement to formulate what she calls a neutral goal statement: How can we preserve John and Pippa's interests in privacy and ocean views and their economic investment and, at the same time, respect Nancy's choice of a building site on her property and her economic interests in development while attempting to meet everyone's common interest in having "hassle-free" neighbour relations, given the uncertainties around the legal responsibilities?

The mediation appears to be at an end when Nancy and her lawyer state that the choice of the building site is non-negotiable. The lawyers argue for a time over whether a court would grant an injunction to stop the building or only award damages to John and Pippa if there was any legal liability. The option of Nancy moving to another desirable building site with the costs (estimated to be $35,000 to cover building expenses to date and other removal expenses) shared in some proportion by the parties is rejected by Nancy. None of the parties expresses any willingness in the mediation to share these costs in any event.

A breakthrough occurs when the mediator delves more deeply into the bad blood that exists between Nancy and John. In a caucus, Nancy, who is a strong-willed and competitive person, with little tolerance for people like John, whom she sees as brusque and unsophisticated, tells the mediator that John's treatment of her, in not allowing her property access, was the most disrespectful action she had ever experienced in her life. She tells the mediator she has a legal right to build on the site she chose and she will continue to do that unless a court tells her she cannot. In a caucus with John, the mediator gets a completely different picture of the relationship conflict. John describes Nancy as manipulative and deceitful. His barring her from their property was completely justified. Although this was done firmly, John had no idea that Nancy experienced his response as highly disrespectful.

The mediator suggests that she conduct a mediation within a mediation involving only John and Nancy. The goal would be to see if some kind of resolution could be reached about their relationship. With some strong encouragement from the other parties, John and Nancy meet in mediation. The mediation is a success. Out of the mediation comes a three-page agreement, signed by John and Nancy. The agreement relates only to their relationship. Both John and Nancy are satisfied. They agree that if the costs of moving to another site can be shared fairly, Nancy will move. When the other lawyers hear this, they agree in less than an hour on how to divide up the costs.

The parties agree to sign the final agreement on a sunny afternoon out on the ridge with the expansive ocean views. Nancy and John shake hands.

C. CASE STUDY TWO: THE GOOD-FAITH EVICTION

1) General Facts

Helen is seventy-nine years of age. She had resided at Charles Street, Apartment C, continuously for nine years. She had intended to remain in her apartment as long as her health permitted, unless her tenancy agreement was lawfully ended.

Helen's apartment was one of five spacious suites in a beautifully restored and well-maintained heritage house. The Rattenbury-designed house had been commissioned by Mrs. Robert Dunsmuir in 1904 for her daughter, Elizabeth, and son-in-law, George Kirk, managing director of Turner Beeton and Co. Ltd., a wholesale drygoods firm. The house and surrounding gardens were set back off Charles Street adjacent to the Lieutenant Governor's property.

The main floor of the house was divided into a two-bedroom apartment and a one-bedroom apartment. Two separate one-bedroom apartments were located on the second floor. The top floor has been converted to a two-bedroom apartment. Laundry and storage facilities were housed in the basement.

Helen's bright one-bedroom apartment faced south-west and was located on the second floor. Features of her apartment included immaculate hardwood floors, high ceilings, period fixtures and details, fireplaces in living room *and* bedroom, large deck, water and mountain views, thermal pane windows, electric heat, central vacuum, privacy, a quiet and desirable location and more.

Helen regarded Apartment C as her home. The apartment was affordable. She valued the apartment's features including the spacious and safe grounds where her grandchildren often played. She purchased a number of pieces of furniture to fit the apartment. The location allowed her to walk to activities downtown, to shopping, to the ocean, and to a son and daughter-in-law's house, and this walking was important to Helen's health.

Helen's rent was $700 per month plus utilities.

On August 29, Helen received a notice to end her tenancy agreement. She was given written notice by the landlord pursuant to a section of the *Residential Tenancy Act* that the purchaser of the property, Linda, intended for a family member to occupy Helen's apartment. In fact, Linda requested the landlord to give the same notice to all tenants in the building so that Linda and her two children could occupy the entire building.

Helen heard from a number of sources that Linda intended to do "major renovations" so that Linda's son could occupy the entire second floor, including Helen's apartment. Helen was also advised that Linda's daughter would occupy the top-floor apartment and that Linda herself would occupy the main-floor apartments.

Helen talked over this "surprise" with her son and daughter-in-law, both of whom were lawyers. Helen did not question further Linda's intentions and vacated her apartment on October 31. Helen looked for but was unable to find suitable and similar replacement accommodation to meet her needs at an affordable rent. As a result, she accepted an offer to live with her son and daughter-in-law.

Less than one week after Helen vacated her apartment, a friend called to tell her that Linda was advertising the apartment for rent. On further inquiry, Helen discovered there were rental advertisements for all the apartments at Charles Street in the local newspaper and these advertisements had started running as early as September 30.

Specifically, Linda was offering to rent Apartment C for $900 per month, a rent increase of 29 percent. Linda also advertised to rent the top-floor two-bedroom apartment for $1,100 per month — a rent increase of 57 percent — and part of a main-floor apartment for $800 per month (a rent increase of 25 percent).

The rental advertisements ran unchanged throughout the month of November and into December although the asking rent was reduced from $800–$1,100 to $750–$995 near the end of November. During this period, Linda continued to offer Apartment C for rent and showed this apartment to prospective tenants.

In early December, Helen's son met with Linda. When asked to explain how the apartments could be advertised for rent, Linda stated that the former landlord was responsible for getting the tenants out and that she "just wanted an empty building." Linda also said that her children now would only be occupying the second-floor apartments. After a few minutes, Linda ended the conversation and asked Helen's son to leave.

Helen's son and daughter-in-law reviewed the law. In this jurisdiction, a residential tenancy agreement can only be terminated by a purchaser of the residential premises in specific and limited cases. One of those cases is where the purchaser intends in *good faith* that she or a family member will occupy the residential premises. In such a case, the purchaser must request in writing that the landlord (the seller) give the tenant of the premises two months' notice of the end of the tenancy agreement. The legislation further provides that if the purchaser or family member does not occupy the premises as a residence for at least six months pursuant to the notice of eviction, the purchaser is responsible to pay the tenant's moving expenses and any additional expenses, including any increased rent that the tenant was obliged to pay. However, no expenses are payable if the purchaser establishes that she intended, in good faith, *at the time of giving the notice*, to occupy the premises as specified in the notice.

Helen's son and daughter-in-law discovered that "good faith" had been interpreted by the courts to mean "that the purchaser must truly intend to do what it says, and that it must not be guilty of dishonesty, deception or pretense."

2) ADR Analysis and Advice

Consider what the following ADR analysis and advice might mean to what happens next.

a) The Analysis

i) *The Cause of the Conflict*
Despite Helen's efforts to clear up the confusion, a data dispute is at the heart of this matter. Did Linda truly intend for her and her children to occupy all the apartments at the time she instructed the landlord to give the eviction notice? From Helen's perspective, the facts seem to strongly suggest that there were no bona fides. Neither of Linda's children had yet moved into the apartments. In addition, the new purchaser placed ads to rent out the apartments as early as September 30 and at substantial rent increases that would not have been justified under rent control rules had Helen remained as tenant. On its face, the facts seem to support a conclusion that Linda could not have truly been intending for her family to move in when the notice of eviction was served in August. However, as with all disputes, this is only one side of the story. Clearing up the data dispute will depend on hearing Linda's version of events. Clearly, Linda had made representations

about her intentions because the landlord prepared and delivered the eviction notice on the basis that the purchaser's family would occupy. This suggests that Linda's plans may have unexpectedly changed, which would afford Linda a complete defence.

Determining how any missing data can best be collected could be a challenge, particularly if Linda has anything to hide.

A dispute about Linda's intention, even if objectively determined, is not the only cause of the conflict. A relationship dispute also exists even though the past involvement between Linda and Helen has seemed brief and innocuous. What has happened is that Linda has stepped into the landlord's shoes as owner of the heritage house. The house, tied so closely to Helen and her needs, has created a property relationship between Helen and Linda. Even if Linda were acting in good faith when the notice was given, Helen and the other tenants cannot understand why Linda did not let them know before they had moved out that the apartments were up for rent. Most of the tenants had not finalized their new accommodation plans by September 30 when the first ads appeared. Helen and the other tenants surmise that Linda's motive must have been her own economic interests over any concern for long-term and elderly tenants' needs. This seemingly irrebuttable assumption has fuelled the conflict from a relationship perspective. The dismissive way in which Helen's son (probably now a key party to the dispute) was treated, reinforces the feeling that Linda's actions are disrespectful, even if legal.

Understanding that a relationship dispute, perhaps even a conflict of values, is also at work can point to processes that may be best suited to resolve such matters. This analysis also may help to explain future disputant behaviour.

ii) Methods of Dispute Processing

What happens next in the dispute is ultimately determined by what steps Helen, in consultation with her "lawyers," decides to take next. The accessibility of particular methods of dispute processing can be a significant factor in Helen's decision making.

Had it not been for the involvement of her lawyer-trained family, Helen would likely have avoided any confrontation. The decision might have been understood as mostly reflecting Helen's dispute avoidance style and her wisdom about the value of such an objection, given the change of homes was all for the good. But, in the circumstances, backing away from the conflict would have also been a necessity apart from perhaps calling Linda and asking her for an explanation. Helen could not, alone, have gone further. Her general health and poor eyesight made the complaint process under the residential tenancy legislation, which would have ended up at a hearing, inaccessible.

The legal advice meant that Helen now had some choices about process. The legislation allowed Helen to make a formal complaint to the residential tenancy bureaucracy and in one to two months an adjudicative process before an arbitrator would be held. Linda would bring a lawyer to that hearing. Or, Helen with the other tenants, could negotiate with Linda's lawyer about using another process such as negotiation or mediation. Perhaps Linda's lawyer could clear up the confusion by supplying the missing information. This consensual approach would be fast, cheap, and, perhaps, mutually satisfying. The complaint could be dropped if, through some form of communication, Helen and the other tenants were reasonably satisfied that their legal rights had not been infringed. Once the good faith was straightened out, the relationship would end.

The advantages of negotiating first as opposed to not at all seem obvious. The relationship dispute may be fanning matters on but the fuel for the blaze is Linda's lack of explanation. The negotiation could be opened by filing a formal complaint with the residential tenancy branch and serving a copy of the complaint on Linda. Even if mediation might be an option, complaining to the authorities when informal negotiations have been unsuccessful seems a reliable way to get the discussions going.

iii) The Arbitration Process

The legislation in this jurisdiction provides for mandatory arbitration for this type of landlord-tenant dispute. Few cases now go to court either directly or on the limited grounds of appeal from the arbitration process. The arbitration process, roughly outlined in the statute, is basically fair but of course lacks the procedural safeguards and mechanisms enjoyed in more formal dispute processing systems or applied in more important cases. The arbitrators, both part- and full-time, come from a diverse range of backgrounds and experiences. Some are much better than others.

This process presents advantages and disadvantages for all the disputants. All disputants who have legal advice would know this. The process is mandatory. It will be more expensive to participate if you have a lawyer, unless, of course, the lawyer is acting *pro bono*. The result appears uncertain. Even for Linda, her family, and her lawyer, who have most of the facts, the appearances are poor. A definite victory at the arbitration is not certain. The same is true for the tenants. For them, they must concede that Linda could establish good faith, perhaps without difficulty. More important, all the parties know there is no formal mechanism for discovery of any information prior to the arbitration hearing. In the arbitration hearing, once the case begins, it is sure that a competent arbitrator would allow the parties the opportunities to examine and cross-examine the witnesses within reasonable limits. But the examination-in-chief of Linda by her lawyer would be the first time that Helen and the tenants would be formally permitted to hear Linda's side of the story.

Understanding how the arbitration process works means that consideration must be given to the question of whether it is wise to hear Linda's story for the first time in the midst of the arbitration process. Any responses would have to be immediate. If untangling a good-faith intention is the task, more time may be needed. This concern leads directly back to the negotiation process — the only practical process to obtain information about Linda's intention.

b) The Advice

Without the support of family members, Helen would have little choice except to think about the preventative dispute resolution that might have been. When the eviction notice was served, Helen could have made inquiries from the landlord and purchaser regarding the plans for family occupancy of the heritage house. Those inquiries may have revealed facts that would have confirmed or raised suspicions about Linda's good-faith intentions. Making a complaint to the residential tenancy branch while still in the apartment would have placed Helen in a much stronger position if Linda's bona fides were questionable.

Although there is no right choice for Helen, taking steps to open negotiations seems to make sense from an ADR analysis. The appearance of bad faith may be cleared up by Linda or her lawyer when they receive the formal complaints from the tenants. If the data dispute is not resolved, proceeding to the hearing may be the best alternative to a negotiated agreement depending, of course, on the explanation that Linda gives for the situation.

3) Further Disputing Developments

a) Scenario A

The tenants file their complaints en masse with the residential tenancy branch on December 15. Six days later all the tenants receive a letter from Linda's lawyer. The letter is written "without prejudice," stating that the letter and its contents cannot be revealed in any subsequent arbitration hearing or court proceeding. In the letter, the lawyer says that the tenants' claims are without merit. However, in the interests of ending this matter, the lawyer offers to pay reasonable moving expenses. For Helen, the offer is $460. The lawyer says the offer is open for three days.

After discussions with her family and the other tenants, Helen agrees to accept the offer. Although the letter does nothing to clear up the confusion, the $460 represents more than Helen could reasonably expect to recover even if she were successful at the arbitration hearing. Helen decides that the other tenants are still free to pursue their claims if they wish and her decision to settle will not jeopardize these claims. However, when Helen settles, the other tenants also accept, grudgingly, the cash offers. When Helen's son accepts the offer, on Helen's behalf, he is told by Linda's lawyer that Linda had a change occur in her plans that meant the children had not been able to move in. No more detail is given.

Helen spends the $460 on some upgrades to her stereo system and lived happily with her family for many more years.

b) Scenario B

The tenants file their complaints en masse with the residential tenancy branch on December 15 and shortly thereafter receive settlement offers from Linda's lawyer. Helen's son calls Linda's lawyer and tells the lawyer that the tenants would probably accept the offers if Linda were able to provide a reasonable explanation for her actions. They discuss a meeting with all the tenants, Linda and her two adult children and Linda's lawyer. Possible dates for the meeting are raised.

The next day Linda's lawyer advises that his client and her children are not prepared to meet with the tenants. No explanation is given.

The arbitration hearing begins two months later. Linda is the first witness called. Linda says that she and her family had restored a heritage home in another city and she saw a similar opportunity to do such a project with the house on Charles Street. Linda says that before she made the offer to buy the house, her intention was that her family would move in and share the house and expenses with her. Her son and his wife and three-year-old child agreed to live in the third-floor apartment. Her daughter and husband agreed to take the second floor converting it into one suite.

Linda then described how things changed. A little over a month before she was to take possession, her daughter-in-law raised objections about their three-year-old having to climb stairs to the third floor and safety concerns for playing outside because the house was surrounded by an oval driveway. The son's wife also said she did not want to move out of their neighbourhood, which was close to where she worked and her son's day care. As a result, Linda's son and daughter-in-law decided to stay where they were. Linda also said that in mid to late September her daughter's husband decided that he no longer wished to move. The son and daughter also gave evidence that supported their mother's version of events. There were, however, a few discrepancies. Linda said there had been an agreement, that she, her son and daughter would share the rent equally. The son said that no agreement had been reached on rent. Linda said that the son's wife had viewed the property prior to the notice to evict being served. The son was unsure about this point. Linda said that she had been told of her son and daughter-in-law's change of plans at the end of September. The son said he told his mother of the change in early September.

The arbitration had to be adjourned for three weeks because it was not completed in the scheduled three hours. When the arbitration resumed, the tenants presented their evidence. From the earlier hearing it was obvious that the outcome of the case would depend on whether a good-faith intention not only had to be honest but also reasonable. Clearly, Linda had discussed family occupancy with her children, her real estate agent, and the landlord. The question that had to be answered was how definite and certain did a purchaser's plans for family occupancy have to be to justify terminating a residential tenancy.

At the end of the hearing, Linda's lawyer makes submissions. He says the issue in this case is whether at the time Linda made an offer to purchase the house (then converted to apartments) on Charles Street, she had a genuine intention of occupying it with family members (i.e. herself and her adult children and their family). He argues this was the intention at the time the offer was made. Unfortunately, Linda's children let her down and changed their minds about moving into the house after she was committed to purchase it but before she moved in.

Helen's son makes submissions that the security of tenure protection given to tenants would be seriously eroded if a purchaser could request evictions with only a half-baked plan for family occupancy. Helen's son refers to a legal precedent that says that the good faith on the purchaser's part also applies to the family member who would benefit from the eviction. Helen's son submits that the details of the agreements for Linda's children to move in and become involved in a major restoration project were not good-faith agreements under the legislation because they were merely wishful thinking and not concrete enough.

The arbitrator delivered his decision three weeks after the end of the hearing. He dismissed the tenants' claim but did order in the circumstances that the $30 filing fee paid by the tenants be reimbursed by Linda. In his written reasons, he finds Linda did have a good-faith

intention at the time she gave the eviction notice. The minor discrepancies in Linda and her children's evidence are not substantial enough
to change the arbitrator's mind.

Helen is not disappointed. She is comfortable in her new home and
just glad the case is over.

c)   Scenario C

The tenants file their complaints en masse with the residential tenancy
branch on December 15 and receive settlement offers from Linda's lawyer. Linda's lawyer knows Helen's son and calls him. Both are familiar
with ADR developments. They agree that assisted negotiations would
be helpful in these circumstances given that good faith is not a black
and white issue. Both Linda's lawyer and Helen's son feel that mediating the data dispute and perhaps the relationship issues could work. If
there is no agreement, both Linda's lawyer and Helen's son agree that
the tenants' decision to go to a hearing will depend on the strength of
Linda's good-faith intentions for family occupancy at the time the
notice was given.

The mediation is scheduled to take place in a week. A three-hour
session with a trusted mediator from a local community justice centre
is reserved to keep costs down.

The mediator takes a facilitative approach to the mediation and
plans to follow a six-stage mediation model. The mediation begins with
introductions and a general description of the mediation. Because there
are ten people present, including the mediator, the first stage of the
mediation takes some time. The mediator then invites each of the parties
to tell his or her story and to identify concerns. Linda goes first. She
explains the reasons for the change in her plans in a general way. She
was looking for a heritage home that she and her family could restore as
she had done in the past. She was attracted to the Charles Street property and made arrangement for her son and daughter to see the property.
The children agreed to move in with her daughter and son-in-law living
on the second floor of the house and her son, daughter-in-law, and
three-year-old grandson living on the third floor. A month before Linda
was to take possession, her son and family decided not to move because
the house and surrounding grounds were not suitable for a three-year-
old. At the same time her son-in-law decided that he no longer wished
to move. As a result Linda advertised the apartments for rent to be able
to meet the mortgage payments. Linda's daughter has moved in recently
and is attempting to reconcile with the recalcitrant husband.

In the tenants' stories, including Helen's, it comes clear how attached
the tenants were to their respective homes. There is dismay expressed

at how insensitive Linda has been, and seems to continue to be, to the rights and the feelings of the tenants. At one point in the mediation, one of the tenants stands up, points his finger at Linda, and says: "Why didn't you tell us before we left that the apartments were for rent?" Linda shrugs and suggests she was continuing to hope that her children would change their minds.

The mediator suggests that the issues are (1) identifying fair responsibilities for the decision to evict the tenants, and (2) discussion of the manner in which the parties have interacted. The parties agree to this reframing.

The mediator then helps the parties identify the interests or needs that will be important to them in any mediated agreement and then formulates the following neutral goal statement: What can we do to respond to the tenants' concerns that they want to be treated fairly and respectfully and Linda's concerns that there be no inappropriate interference in her affairs and that her actions be judged fairly and respectfully? The parties begin to talk about solutions. Talk turns to money. The relevant legislation provides that a purchaser without a good-faith intention for family occupancy can be ordered to pay (a) the tenant's actual and reasonable moving expenses to his or her new accommodation, and (b) any additional expenses incurred or to be incurred including any increased rent for a period of up to twelve months. The tenants will settle if their extra rent for twelve months is paid in addition to the payment of the moving expenses already offered. The tenants also say that they want a written apology from Linda for the disrespectful ways in which they have been treated. However, they say if Linda is not prepared to apologize, they will accept the money in full and final settlement but would regard Linda as not having learned from this experience. The dollar difference between the two offers is $7,200. (Linda's first offer totalled $1,300.)

Linda and her lawyer immediately reject the offer. The lawyer states that there is a very good chance that an arbitrator would find good faith on Linda's part and reiterates that the without prejudice offer was an effort to settle the case quickly for its nuisance value and not any admission of legal liability.

The mediator calls a caucus. The tenants do not accept Linda's explanation as an exoneration and argue that some, if not all, monies must be paid for the increased rent. Linda's lawyer expresses the opposition position. The mediator asks all the parties if there are any objective criteria available to narrow the financial gap. Helen's son says that an arbitration hearing would last five to six hours and that Linda would have to pay legal costs in addition to any order for compensation. After a brief break, Linda and her lawyer throw rather contemptuously another $1,000 on the table to be divided by the tenants. The tenants reply that they would be willing to accept the moving expenses offer plus an additional $6,000. The tenants press Linda to explain more fully her plans to have the family move in. In the end, they are not persuaded The mediation terminates.

4) ADR Analysis and Advice for Scenario C

Consider what the following ADR analysis and advice might mean to what happens next.

a) The Analysis

i) Integrative and Distributive Bargaining
The problem has become — perhaps always was — one of distribution. Any consensual solution appears to involve a payment of money from Linda to the tenants. This is not unexpected. Although creative thinking might expand the payment options, the legal norm for solving the problem (a payment or not of certain types of expenses) will make it unlikely that any other alternative will not be a cost to Linda. In distributive bargaining, Linda will usually be attempting to minimize the cost. The tenants will want to get as much as they can to meet their needs.

Some objective criteria do exist that could assist in putting a figure on the expenses that might be acceptable to all the parties. There is the legislation itself that categorizes the possible expenses. There is no "case law" as such although this is a case in which all the parties are fairly confident that the finding or not of good faith will be determinative. If there was a good-faith intention at the time of giving the notice, the tenants get nothing. If the evidence on the balance of probabilities supports a finding that Linda did not have the requisite good faith, the tenants will likely recover all their expenses including extra rent paid. Both lawyers will or should have an opinion as to the strength of the case. This opinion may be translated into a percentage figure (80 percent chance of winning — a very good case; 30 percent chance of winning — a poor case). The parties could use this percentage figure as an objective way to discount the tenants' claim, if they agreed on the percentage.

However, to date, the parties have simply exchanged several offers that both demonstrate typical positional and competitive bargaining. This strategy and behaviour often can result in one party or both being firmly entrenched in a position. Movement from the position ($2,300 and that's it) can be difficult even when such move makes sense. The change must be done in such a way that the negotiator making the move does not lose face. The grudging and minor money concessions granted in the mediation may make more movements impossible. There is a risk with positional bargaining.

ii) Bargaining in the Shadow of the Law

How is the law influencing this negotiation in the mediation? The legal influence may be felt in several ways. The decision to mediate or negotiate itself may be affected by legal process considerations. A lawyer may refuse to negotiate because her BATNA (best alternative to a negotiated agreement) is a speedy and relatively inexpensive arbitration hearing. Any delay to the hearing may simply allow Linda to get her house in order. The tenants may want to negotiate a way of settling quickly and consensually and because the negotiation exchanges can be used as a pre-hearing discovery stage when the arbitration process provides no such luxury. The legal strength of the case also may be a major influence on negotiating behaviour. Considering what the arbitrator might say in any eventual hearing about good faith and allowable claims is a key part of determining a negotiator's best, worst, most likely, least likely, or other assessment of the alternatives to negotiated agreements. The predicted outcome of the case can be used in the actual negotiation to support a position being taken or to challenge an assertion being made by the other side. The shadow of the law in this mediation can be responsible for, or underpin, an important party interest. That interest can be fair treatment — I want to be treated fairly and the only way I will feel fairly treated is if my version of the law is upheld. A response might be persuasive legal arguments to change the way in which the law is understood so that fair treatment does not require payment of $8,500.

iii) Preparation for Negotiation

In a negotiation, there is not always time to fully consider the next move. A statement is made. A document is exchanged. A glance is given. Sometimes the move is the right one — the tactic or behaviour is consistent with the negotiator's strategy and is a help to the negotiator in achieving his or her goals. Sometimes a move can backfire — a comment is too cutting or sarcastic or perceived that way and the negotiation breaks down.

Preparation for negotiation can help. In the dynamic of an actual negotiation or during an adjournment in the negotiations, initial and ongoing preparation can provide information necessary to evaluate the choices to be made in the negotiation.

This analysis applies equally to the negotiations taking place in a mediation. As the distributive problem becomes clearer in this case, good negotiators will be thinking of BATNAs and WATNAs and how what is happening in the negotiation might be useful. This ongoing adjustment in the negotiation will be true even if the mediator or mediation philosophy is trying to take the disputants in a different direction. An interest-based approach to mediation using a six-stage model can lead to consensus. But when the gap between positions seems too yawning, the negotiators in the mediation, without abandoning efforts to reach agreement, can begin to see how the discoveries being or to be made in the negotiations can assist if no agreement is ultimately reached.

b) The Advice

The tenants are claiming $8,500 but would accept $7,300. Linda has offered to pay $2,300. The ADR advice depends on how one views the state of negotiations. The negotiations are at an impasse but that does not mean they are at an end. Either party could attempt to break the impasse with some creative thinking. Linda now seems to be a landlord and one of the tenants might see an opportunity to move back to Charles Street with a rental agreement that helps solve Linda's concerns about paying out cash. This type of solution is probably difficult to implement at this stage of the disputing process without dealing first with the relationship issues. Alternatively, any party could make a further concession but the pattern of offer and counter-offer has not reduced the gap much thus far. The fact that Linda will incur further legal costs might be a factor that warrants another negotiating inquiry.

However, on balance, it would seem that further negotiations will not be fruitful. The parties are fairly entrenched in their positions and an apology from Linda to offset some economic needs does not appear likely. Given the information discovered in the mediation, preparation for the arbitration would appear to be the best alternative.

5) Final Disputing Developments: Outcome

There is no further contact between Linda and the tenants' before the hearing.

Because of the economics and because Linda's lawyer believes Linda has a very good case, Linda's lawyer spends little time preparing for the arbitration hearing. The tenants, as a result of disclosures made in the mediation, realize that the strength of their case is in appealing to the arbitrator's sense of justice. The tenants have to show that a good-faith intention not only requires proof of honesty but also of reasonableness. The tenants prepare to trap Linda on cross-examination at the hearing.

Given time to prepare and the ability to exclude witnesses during the hearing, the tenants are able to show several serious contradictions between Linda's evidence of the agreement to live as a family at Charles Street and the evidence of her children. Because of the information discovered at the mediation, the tenants require Linda in the hearing to give evidence of her agreements with the children in excruciating detail. Linda's version of events and her many instances of "I can't recall" do not mesh with the evidence of her son and daughter.

For example, Linda's evidence at the hearing about her son and daughter-in-law seeing the house varies in several important ways from the evidence of her son. This supports the tenants' argument that the agreement, if any, between Linda and her son was doubtful from the beginning. Linda gives evidence that sharing the mortgage payments equally was agreed upon. The children recall no such agreement.

At the conclusion of the hearing, Linda's lawyer makes an oral submission. The tenants read from a prepared statement and give the arbitrator copies of three court cases that support their arguments.

The arbitrator delivered his decision two weeks after the end of the hearing. He made an order that the full amount of the tenants' claims be paid forthwith by Linda. In his reasons, he found that the letter and the spirit of the residential tenancy legislation had been violated when Linda requested the landlord to serve the eviction notices. The arbitrator held that the good-faith requirement in the statute could only be satisfied if the intention for family occupancy is both honestly and reasonably held. Each discrepancy in the evidence of Linda and her children did not by itself seem significant. However, the arbitrator decides that, taken together, they disclose a lack of required good faith.

Linda appealed the arbitrator's decision to the court. The appeal was heard one year later. The appeal was dismissed. Linda paid her lawyer $8,000 in total and paid $8,500 to the tenants. Helen felt that justice had been done. Helen used her share to help pay for some new hearing aids. She lived happily for many more years.

D. THE USE OF ADR: SIX PRACTICAL PROBLEMS

The following problems are fictionalized accounts of real-life situations. They will provide you with opportunities to do your own ADR analysis, to consider what ADR advice you might offer to the disputants or their representatives, and, as a result of your analysis and advice, to predict what might happen next in these disputes.

1) Problem 9.1: Partners in Law

You are a partner in a two-person law firm. You and your partner are developing an excellent reputation as corporate tax lawyers but have not gotten to "easy street" yet. In fact, your draws from the partnership have been very modest. You are single at this time and the modest draws have not interfered unduly with your lifestyle. You are able to live comfortably on the draws and can see the light at the end of the tunnel.

You recently saw a new oil painting by Robert Bateman entitled "Eagle in Flight" that you would like to buy and put in the office. The price is $25,000. You are certain you can borrow money from the bank. The monthly payments on the loan, taking into account the tax consequences, will reduce your draws. However, you can live with this reduction because you are an art lover and this is a beautiful painting that you will appreciate. You are certain that it will not add any new business to the firm, but it will create the "right" front office ambience. You would like the firm to buy it.

You are worried about your partner's likely reaction. Your partner has a young family. You know your partner is worried about finances and has mentioned having to "scrimp" on some basic items. You suspect that your partner will feel that buying the painting will add further financial restrictions and perhaps create instability at home. However, this particular painting will likely be sold to a foreign investor, and fortunately, you have been able to persuade the dealer to hold it for a few days.

2) Problem 9.2: Fuddle Duddle

Despite its serene setting, a storm is brewing in the Alumni Development Office at the University of Cascadia.

Recent budget cuts have pushed ahead U of C's plans for a major new alumni fundraising project called "Share the Vision." Two senior co-directors were appointed recently to begin coordinating what the university regards as the most important fundraiser in its history. The five-year goal is $100 million. However, in the present uncertain economic climate, with other universities and organizations seeking private funding, it is critical that the fundraising project get off to a fast start. If the first year of the project is not successful, it is very likely that the campaign will not be successful and the economic security of U of C will be seriously threatened.

A serious rift has developed between the co-directors that could spell doom for the project. One director, Pat, is a long-time university manager who was seconded from Personnel Services for this project. The other director, Sandy, is a recent graduate from a top managerial school on the east coast.

The rift developed during the second week of their working together when Sandy sent a letter, under Sandy's signature only, to U of C alumni in senior executive positions at the forty largest companies in Cascadia stating, among other things, "as a director of Share the Vision, I would enjoy meeting with you to discuss opportunities for you to participate in the development of U of C's vision for the twenty-first century."

When Pat discovered the letter had been sent, Pat confronted Sandy and accused Sandy of undermining Pat's position and usurping authority over the project. Pat left Sandy's office and "appeared" to mutter something very disparaging to Sandy.

Both directors have complained about these events to the president of the university, stating they can no longer work with each other. The president has urged them to meet to see if they can resolve their differences for the sake of the fundraising project. However, the president has stated clearly that if there is no resolution, she will take action.

From Pat's perspective, Pat is furious at Sandy for sending the letter without consultation. Although it had been agreed that a letter would be sent to the forty largest companies in Cascadia with U of C alumni in executive positions, Pat cannot believe Sandy sent the letter under one signature without any consultation. Pat believes this action must demonstrate a lack of respect for long-time university experience, poor judgment on Sandy's part generally and probably a selfishness on Sandy's part to further Sandy's reputation ahead of the university.

Pat did mutter "fuddle duddle" to Sandy, but it was inaudible and no one heard this; in any event, Pat was mad.

Pat wants this project to succeed. It would cap off a long and distinguished university career but Pat doesn't want to work with someone who is not a team player and who is not respectful of experience and seniority.

Pat has agreed to meet Sandy at the president's urging. Ideally, Pat would like to clear up matters but if Pat's concerns are not met, Pat is fairly confident of persuading the president to replace Sandy on the project.

From Sandy's perspective, Sandy is also furious at Pat. Sandy took the initiative to prepare and send the letter. Sandy saw the need for a lot of independent work on this project and worrying about Pat's "insecurity" will be a waste of time and energy. The job has to get done. Sandy is also not convinced that Pat is as "industrious" as Sandy would like and seems "too comfortable" and "too easy-going." Sandy knows Pat is up for retirement soon and will qualify for a "generous" U of C pension.

In addition, Sandy was offended by the way in which Pat aggressively confronted Sandy in the office and by what Pat said. Sandy couldn't hear exactly what Pat said but it sounded very insulting.

Sandy wants this project to succeed. A successful campaign will mean a lot to Sandy's career but Sandy doesn't want to be hindered by "petty" complaints and unnecessary bureaucratic delays when there is so much work to do. Nor will Sandy tolerate being treated in such a disrespectful manner.

Sandy has agreed to meet Pat at the president's urging. Ideally, Sandy would like to clear up matters but if Sandy's concerns are not met, Sandy is fairly confident of persuading the president to replace Pat on the project.

3)   Problem 9.3: The Building Is Not Really Suited for You

Alex Nelson has made a complaint to the Council of Human Rights alleging discrimination by a property manager.

The Council has investigated the complaint and found the following facts. Alex has cerebral palsy. Six months ago Alex wanted to rent a one-bedroom apartment very close to the university and a large shopping mall. Alex is attending university and the location of the apartment was ideal because Alex can get disoriented if required to travel long distances. The rent was reasonable, $550 a month. Alex is on income assistance. Alex was refused the apartment and discovered that the manager, representing the property owner, HAL Inc., had rented the apartment to a single university student who applied *after* Alex. Alex thought something was wrong when the manager did not even call back and when Alex called, the manager said, "The building is not really suited for you."

The investigator from the Council of Human Rights has urged Alex's representative to meet with the representative of the property owner. If there is no agreement, the Council will put the matter over for a hearing, scheduled for nine months from now.

It is uncertain what would happen in a hearing. It will depend on how the manager's words are interpreted. Alex does not know that one other complaint was made against the same manager two years ago but was not proceeded with.

Ideally, Alex wants the apartment, a written apology, expenses (Alex was forced to take an apartment ten miles farther away and drive to and from the university five days a week) and compensation for the injuries to Alex's dignity and self-respect. On this latter point, if Alex proved discrimination, Alex could be awarded $2,000 to $5,000 at a hearing. Alex also wants to publicize this discrimination so that this type of discrimination is prevented in the future. In fact, getting some publicity is very important to Alex.

Ideally, HAL Inc. would like the complaint dropped. The company then would probably fire the manager to avoid any future problem. HAL Inc. could agree to give Alex the next available one-bedroom apartment (one is apparently coming up in three months) but any settlement must be confidential. HAL Inc. has other properties and businesses. Publicity would be disastrous, especially given the other complaint made against the same manager.

The meeting is scheduled for tomorrow morning.

4) Problem 9.4: The Holiday Bonus

Gerry is the operator of a licensed family childcare facility (up to 5 children). Fees are $600 a month per child. A written policy, given to all parents, states that the childcare facility will be closed on all statutory holidays and also between Christmas Day and New Year's Day each year.

Chris is a parent of two children who have been attending the childcare since July. Chris wants a refund of fees to be paid for the period between Christmas and New Year's (five working days this year) as it will be necessary to pay extra for childcare since Chris has to work and does not think it is fair to pay for childcare when the facility is closed. Chris read the policy carefully when the children were enrolled and feels that the fee issue should have been made clearer. Chris was also told by a friend that another childcare in the city closes for the month of July and no fees are paid. Chris is completely satisfied with the quality of the childcare but a continuing commitment may depend on what happens here. The refund would be a nice holiday bonus.

Gerry has refused to pay. In four years of operation, no other parent has asked for a refund. Gerry felt the policy was quite clear. Closing during Christmas and New Year's and not reducing fees allows Gerry to give another much-needed paid holiday to the facility's manager, given it is impossible in a childcare facility to pay a salary much more than $2,000 to $2,500 a month (for nine-hour days) with only minimal benefits. Gerry does not want to lose Chris's children but paying a refund (to all the parents?) somehow seems wrong. Gerry has now added a specific clause in the policy stating that the monthly fee is not reduced due to any statutory or holiday closures.

5) Problem 9.5: The Case of Knight and Day

Kellen Day bought an entire living room set of furniture six months ago. The cost was $1,999, with no payments or interest for six months. After six months the total amount became due and payable with interest at 15 percent per annum. Unfortunately, Day's job was eliminated three weeks ago just as debt for the furniture became due and payable. Day was upset and realized the payment for the furniture could not be made. Day had been planning to put the payment on a credit card and then pay the amount back over ten months.

The debt has been due for three weeks. Day did not call the furniture store. Two days ago Day received a nasty call from the Knight Collection Company. The Knight Collection Company had purchased the account from the furniture store for $1,599. When accounts of this type are not paid on time, Knight's policy is to "light a fire" under the debtor. Knight's business reputation and livelihood depends on getting these debts paid in full. Although some small debtors file for bankruptcy, this is a rare risk. Knight does accept terms (payments over time, never more than six months, with full interest).

In the telephone call, the Knight representative called Day "lazy," "irresponsible," and "deceitful," and told Day that unless the money was received by Friday, there would "be hell to pay." A day after the call, Day received a letter from Knight that looked like a legal form and talked about seizing Day's assets and, if required, putting Day in jail.

At the urging of a friend, Day agreed to meet the manager of Knight (not the person who phoned). Day would like to settle this matter. Day has no other debts. Day has assets in the apartment (some jewellery, some cash, family heirlooms, and a grandmother's silver watch) worth about $4,000 in total, but these possessions must be preserved at all costs. Day was a sales clerk, wants to work, but has no immediate job prospects. Ideally, Day would like to return the furniture and get by with some borrowed furniture in the short run. If this is not acceptable, Day could agree to pay $75 a month until a new job is obtained. Day could not afford a penny more. The furniture could be sold privately but would probably raise only $700 to $800.

Day also thinks Knight should apologize for the treatment on the telephone.

6) Problem 9.6: FAT Faculty

There is a new faculty at the University of Cascadia — the Faculty of Advanced Thinking (FAT). FAT has successfully operated for three years without incident — until now.

The creation of this new, multidisciplinary unit at U of C reflects the increasing interest in multidisciplinary approaches to social issues and a recognition that the structured partnerships among faculty members that FAT creates can allow for quantum leaps to the development of new ideas and ways of thinking, whatever the discipline.

The first nine faculty members (hand-picked by the dean of FAT) come from a wide range of disciplines but all take a multidisciplinary approach to their research and writing.

Although most other departments in the university have had new appointments frozen, FAT has been given the green light to hire three new faculty members in the upcoming academic year. This has been made possible through a private donor who feels FAT research can contribute immensely to the advancement of world thinking on many significant issues.

Unfortunately, a serious problem has arisen. The president of the student body at FAT has written the dean of FAT stating:

> It is no longer good enough to hire faculty without student input. We demand full voting membership on the Appointments Committee. Anything less is unacceptable. Failure to agree will result in a lack of confidence by the students in any hiring process and a serious breakdown in future affairs at FAT or other dire consequences.

The dean of FAT wrote back:

> The Tenure Document forbids student participation in hiring decisions. However, you can rest assured that FAT will hire the best candidates available and that student interest in having the best teachers and researchers at FAT will not be forgotten.

This dispute came to the attention of the president of U of C who has advised both the dean of FAT and the student president that if they are unable to agree on appointment procedures, all three appointments could be cancelled permanently because the donor (who also has heard about the squabble) doesn't want such controversy surrounding the donor's gift.

At the urging of the U of C president, the dean of FAT and the student president have agreed to meet.

A fly-on-the-wall has discovered the following information about the dean and the student leader.

The Dean of FAT is S. Pickens (SP for short).

Until SP received the student demand (SP was a bit insulted at the tone), SP was elated at the prospect of hiring three new colleagues. SP is aware of several excellent people who could be recruited for these positions. They are very progressive in their thinking, all are equity candidates, and their addition to FAT would put FAT in a position to lead the world in multidisciplinary research and teaching.

SP does not want to give students full voting membership on any Appointments Committee. SP's biggest concern is that student representatives would probably opt for more conservative candidates than SP has in mind. All the potential candidates SP is aware of are quite "radical." SP also does not believe that students can assess candidates adequately on the criteria used to hire faculty at U of C. Even if students could contribute to the process, decisions about who will be long-term colleagues has to remain with faculty members. Finally, it is SP's assessment that the Tenure Document legally reinforces this position, although it is not absolutely clear. Changing a Tenure Document at U of C would be a big job.

SP also knows that the student president is a grad student at FAT and may be concerned about the impact of this dispute on current grad work and future career opportunities.

SP is very concerned that these new appointments will be cancelled if there is no agreement. This would be a real setback to FAT and also would be personally embarrassing. However, if the student demands are not dropped, SP may have to "pull the plug" on the appointments for the time being.

The president of the study body at FAT is W. Pooh.

Pooh is concerned about the upcoming meeting because Pooh is at FAT doing graduate work. The issue is important to Pooh and the student body but Pooh is concerned about needing (or getting) assurance from the dean that Pooh's graduate work (even Pooh's career) won't be harmed by insisting that students participate in faculty hiring decisions.

There are several reasons that students want full involvement in hiring decisions. Obviously, students are affected in their education by faculty. Many students (like Pooh) think they could assess a candidate's background. In addition, with the increasing cost of university education, it is more important that the students who pay have more say in deciding who will be faculty. Many, but not all, students believe the next few appointments must reflect a "less radical" perspective — how much more ideology, hegemony and post-modernism can they take!

If the Tenure Document is a legal barrier (Pooh doesn't believe it is) Pooh would want a workable interim solution with a firm commitment from the dean to have the document changed to reflect modern conditions.

FURTHER READINGS

GOLDBERG, S.B., F.E.A. SANDER, & N.H. ROGERS, *Dispute Resolution: Negotiation, Mediation and Other Processes* (New York: Aspen Law & Business, 1999) particularly 595–612

THE FUTURE
DEVELOPMENT OF ADR

"And the whole earth was of one language."[1]
— Genesis 11:1, King James Version

A. INTRODUCTION

Taking a broad view of alternative dispute resolution will not likely lead to such a unilingual image but it can lead to the conclusion that all peoples have an interest in the future development of ADR. For anyone who will experience a dispute in the days ahead or come into contact with conflict, the future shape of ADR will likely play a central role in determining how the particular problem is experienced, processed and resolved. Governments, organizations, and individuals — the whole earth can be concerned with the disputing arrangements that the ADR field will inspire.

Apart from such a widespread appeal, the future development of ADR may be of most interest to those readers who see it in a different light. For the ADR practitioners, legal professionals, academics, students, and critics — many of whom are the leaders or future leaders in this modern movement — the importance of ADR can extend well

---

1   H.H. Perritt Jr., "And The Whole Earth Was of One Language — A Broad View of Dispute Resolution" (1983–84) 29 Vill. L. Rev. 1221.

beyond its personal benefits. For this group, ADR is a subject with long-lasting appeal. Their exposure to ADR will have inspired changes in outlooks and attitudes, in career paths and plans, and in practices and beliefs. These individuals will have seen first-hand the positive influences ADR can have on people's lives or the concerns it can cause. For the people and organizations that are already a part of ADR's history, there will be a strong sense that it has something significant to say. For them, its future development may be of ultimate import. Where ADR is heading, what issues addressed, what challenges met, what policies set, what changes made, or what status quo saved are questions that merit close attention.

Of course, any discussion of what lies ahead in ADR must, to a large extent, be general in nature. Whether ADR is narrow or broad, mostly consensus-based or more broadly reframed, its future will surely be more expansive in scope. This prediction appears indisputable even in a field where conflicts flourish. The future seems clearly destined to be filled with more mandatory mediation, anxious on-line negotiations, creative disputing designs, and increasingly complex ADR laws requiring lawyers to advise and conference and research agendas breaking new ground. Indeed, there is current law reform research that now sees all conflict as a relational concept — the relationship between disputing parties having a large bearing on how disputes are handled and a goal for civil and criminal disputes being a transformation of these relationships between parties to the conflict.[2] If relationships are at the core of all disputes in the future, the future scope of ADR, a movement originally heralded as a way of preserving continuing relationships, will surely be complete. There will be more disputes of every imaginable shape and type to come under the ADR purview, a transformed image of civil and criminal justice, and a need for lawyers and others who are trained to work in these new milieus. And, if the context of disputing — the where, who, what, when and why — matters, the study of ADR in the future will bring so much more into play. The diverse disputing details, the multidisciplinarity of views, the broad goals and objectives, the practical skills and best practices — all parts of ADR now — seem only ready to grow. For such a vast domain, general remarks are the only way, in such a short space, to offer observations on future developments.

---

2   See the Discussion Paper "From Restorative Justice to Transformative Justice" of the Law Commission of Canada at <www://lcc.gc.ca>.

A general outlook on ADR's future also fits comfortably with the idea expressed in chapter 1 that ADR can be best appreciated as an ideological expression without missing the practical side. If ADR is ideology, many readers already will have a strong sense of what is natural, normal and essential about the field and about how ADR practice and the preceding pages of this book (or other ADR texts) may fit with that worldview. If its future is also ideologically grounded, general observations on ADR may penetrate closer to the foundations of that ideology rather than comments on more shifting grounds. Thinking generally about ADR's future, foundational ideas, underlying interests, or other central qualities provides opportunities for discussions going to the heart of the matter. Often, in the day-to-day bustle of ADR practice, while uncovering interests or paraphrasing a lot, there is not always enough time for very much more.

Although being general will be helpful, some comments on detail can also be made. The degree of this detail may not be as close as considering whether the co-mediators' surgically implanted Palm Cxs in the future will be a help or a hindrance. The answer to that issue will depend on, among other things, how the environmental and health disputes that emerge around technology implants are resolved by the parties who need these aids most. Technological change is discussed briefly below and preceding chapters have pointed to the fact that the relationship between DRT (dispute resolution technology) and ADR has not yet been fully explored, as it surely will be in the years ahead. Digital technology, virtual reality, discontinuous innovation, and interspatial dodec links will likely be some of the important technical details in ADR's future. However, some specifics around ADR's future do appear to stand out. Those specifics concern the lawyer's role. Although the place of all disciplines in the long-range vision for ADR may not be quite clear, the position of the legal profession seems obviously set. Although ADR may not be the preserve of any one profession, its future development will likely be highly integrated into the practice of law. The leadership of the legal profession in multidisciplinary partnerships with non-lawyer ADR practitioners will surely continue and be strengthened in the future. Some practical detail flowing from this result is addressed below.

B. BACK TO THE FUTURE: TAKING RESPONSIBILITY FOR ADR

A starting point for a reflective journey into the future can be found back at the beginning of the book and its opening query. What is the meaning of ADR? The answer to the question can be an obvious map into ADR's theories and practices for the many people who now regard ADR ideas and skills as part of their work and affairs. But the meaning of ADR also can be the portal into the future. What ADR is today helps clearly see where ADR is going tomorrow.

The preceding pages are, in part, an answer to the question. The answer within suggests that ADR can best be understood and practised by avoiding the assumption that alternative dispute resolution is, by and large, simply about resolving disputes in a better way or by thinking carefully that it is common sense. These can be helpful guides to purpose and policy but a thoughtful inquiry reveals a field of study and an area of practice that are more complex than simple, that make sense to many but certainly not to all. As a result of the importance of ADR to just about everything done in the world and the crucial histories that disputes and dispute resolution make, ADR's ideas about, and approaches to, disputing have become infused with ambiguity, contradiction and politics. It would have been surprising if the topic had avoided these complicated characteristics in light of ADR's omnipresence and potential capability to endorse or reshape the practice of disputing in a worldwide way. Other areas of inquiry such as economics, politics, parenting, law, and religion, to name just a few, are rarely regarded neutrally and, like ADR, can offer up a number of quite different dimensions to their overall view.

ADR's natural multidisciplinary make-up adds to this complexity. Many people of diverse backgrounds and with varying experiences and needs collaborate and even compete in dispute resolution. The convergence of these cross-sectoral and disparate voices, some louder than others, has produced many triumphs. The dramatic growth of ADR in the United States, Canada, New Zealand, Australia, England, and countries and regions in Europe, Asia, and South America is a tribute to the best in interdisciplinary team work and sharing. Although the multiple sources of ADR interest mean that several organizations or professions will desire the responsibility to chart ADR's course, the inclusiveness that is practised in the field often means that everyone pulls together and none are left out. The pressures to standardize and attain professional stature, particularly for mediators, do present challenges for ADR's multidisciplinary followers. There is just so much for one professional to know and the breathtaking diversity, contextual complexity, and enormous uncertainty that usually accompany the emergence of disputes make KSAOs (knowledge, skills, abilities, and other attributes) in disputing difficult to list definitively. Despite the challenges, the multidisciplinarity that is evident in ADR's theories and practices demonstrates most there are opportunities everywhere.

What is the meaning of alternative dispute resolution? Rather than just being intrinsically better or concentrated on consensus, alternative dispute resolution may be best understood as an expression of an ideology that is being used more and more to signal what is or what should be natural, normal and essential about disputing in society. The reframing of ADR as a smaller project in a larger transformative justice undertaking is one obvious representation of its ideological side.[3] By locating ADR within an ideological framework, the professionals and others who work with disputes can make the most sense of what an ADR proposal or initiative means, decide where a program or practice fits on the ideological spectrum and compare how new ideas mesh with existing principles. Understanding the essence of ADR and how this essence influences disputing practices and affects disputing outcomes can result in better-informed decisions about ADR use and acceptance.

However, with many voices collaborating or competing for the final word on ADR's ideology, the question — what is ADR? — may still produce no uniform response. ADR may be mainly viewed as a label for a much-needed overhaul or revitalization of formal systems of justice, both civil and criminal. ADR may encompass disputing innovations and experiments that are better than before, court-connected or not, such as mandatory mediation, interesting negotiation practices, hybrid disputing mechanisms, respect for culture and conflict and statements of standards. ADR may be primarily about

- an economic efficiency exercise on a global scale,
- dispute resolution out of court,
- the preservation or restoration of harmony,
- the transformation of attitudes towards conflict,
- accessibility to justice,
- a recasting of the legal professional as a most nuanced problem solver,
- the making of a new profession of dispute resolutionaries,
- the continued oppression of the disadvantaged,
- a democratic ideal in decision-making,
- a path to world peace,

---

3   *Ibid.*

- a religious revival, or
- an array of approaches to the processing of disputes that are as complicated, unique and uncertain as the contexts that gave rise to the disputes in the first place.

ADR may be the big picture for some or the minute detail for others, the interrelationships among and between formal and informal systems for processing disputes and otherwise structuring society on a global basis, or the understanding of the raised eyebrow in the still of a single negotiation session.

The future development of ADR may continue to mirror a mosaic of images. ADR may go from the heartbeat of a woman in a VOM (victim-offender mediation) forgiving a man for a most violent offence to a lawyer feigning anger for effect in a motor vehicle case; from the theories of equality that underlie the feminist critique of mediation to the legal skills of negotiation; from developing trust to appreciating ethics; from economic efficiency to empowerment. ADR may continue to cover a lot of ground in the future.

What will the future developments in ADR likely be? On the one hand, the factors that gave impetus to ADR's modern emergence and defined the field will probably continue to exert strong influences. For example, economic efficiencies, particularly the desire to make dispute resolution as inexpensive as possible in a world of deficits and global markets, remain a powerful currency for many ADR proponents. Efforts to design and redesign dispute resolution systems both inside and outside the formal justice systems to achieve economic goals may speed up disputing but exacerbate other accessibility problems and raise concerns about second-class or two-tiered justice. A part of the economic drive will come from the new technology. In much the same way that technological change has transformed other areas of endeavour, DRT will revolutionize the way we can process information, communicate and make decisions in conflict settings. The ability, in negotiation, to quickly discover, confidentially and on-line, whether differences can be split or juries hung may save time and money but the face-to-face meetings that have captured so much of ADR's attention may be difficult to maintain, or be sure of, as technology grows. Expert systems may make decision making just speedy and inexpensive. Contrasted with economic imperatives, the terrible human tragedies that often accompany conflict will also move ADR to create more peaceful, less violent interventions. The relationships between ADR, non-governmental organizations, and governance structures such as the United Nations are likely to be strengthened in the future as many ADR proponents see obvious and mutually rewarding common ground.

There may be analogies drawn to the environmental movement and efforts made to make dispute resolution sustainable. The consequences of destructive disputing practices may be seen as jeopardizing everyone's common future. Along similar lines, growing global desires for satisfying and enduring resolutions to disputes of every kind will be another shaping force in ADR's future. These hopes will come not only from needs to stabilize and secure the new world trade routes but also from deeply held human concerns for happiness and prosperity on the planet. The historic rationale behind ADR's modern emergence likely will continue to contribute to future refinements in all the initiatives that the ADR field comprises.

On the other hand, the future development of ADR may lead in an opposite direction. ADR programs, processes, personnel, and products may, as a whole, reflect a much more coherent, contained and uniform description. The emphasis on collaboration and consensus, on interest-basing in mediation, on setting standards and becoming professional may take attention away from other points of pursuit. Economic interests and professional practice may narrow the field, erect barriers, and remove the uncertainties by ignoring or marginalizing critical or alternative perspectives. Much of the complexity and contours that come with the disputing terrain may be evened out.

The modern meaning of ADR may contain both futures. ADR may open up windows to expansive views that invite exploration, or it can be a project that holds little more than efficiencies and self-interests, ignored by the masses who see little of meaning in its endless encouragement to use professional third parties as facilitators in the resolution of their important problems.

The future development of ADR ultimately must depend on what will be said to be true and important about this field. It will depend on what ADR questions are asked and what answers are given. In a general way, the future development of ADR will be determined by what will be taught as good ADR. Just as ADR education has been instrumental in taking the field to where it is today and in defining its meaning, there is every reason to expect that ADR education will be a major force in shaping future developments.

This last statement may be an obvious and non-contentious one, as it is framed. However, details of this future learning may not be conflict-free. What will be taught and learned as being natural, normal, and essential about disputing practices in the future? Will this content be what is known today, mostly to be improved with age? Will there be new disputing innovations or resurrections of ancient ideas at the core of ADR education? And who will have the educational responsibility?

Will it be fragmented or highly integrated into all learning locations with the professional skills acquired in the usual way? Will the uncertainty and complexity be included or not? Will there be consensus or discord on the answers to the educational questions? A brief foray back to the present state of ADR education points to the promise and challenges ahead.

1) ADR Education: Looking Ahead

It was not uncommon in the early days of ADR to believe that the failure of the general public and others to warmly embrace ADR or use mediators was due in large part to a lack of familiarity and understanding. This was particularly true within the legal profession, as discussed in chapter 1, where the lawyer's standard philosophical map at the time did not have much of a place for ADR's emphasis on consensual dispute resolution, disputant empowerment, facilitative problem solving, and being better.[4] As a result, the last two decades of the twentieth century saw an explosion in the publishing of books, articles, manuals and anecdotes about alternative dispute resolution. The literature was intended not only to increase the supply side of ADR services but also to boost disputant demand. Much of this literature has been absolutely critical in shaping the ways in which ADR has come to be understood, accepted, and practised in academic, professional, governmental and public circles. These extraordinary and key writings have been referenced in other chapters. *Getting to Yes* and Moore on mediation became a part of the staples in the educational endeavours.

The need for ADR education was not restricted to adult learners. Helping children be peer mediators, manage their anger, prevent violent outbursts, or be ADR ambassadors was also an important component of the educational mission. There were three reasons for this child-centred focus. First, schools tended to have their fair share of disputes. Whether the conflict was between a teacher and student, a teacher and parent, an administrator and parent or student, a school board chair and taxpayers, a student and student, or any combination thereof, school disputes were common. They could display all the destructive characteristics found in other disputing situations. Much like the best interests of the child in family disputes, there were characteristics of school disputes that could make them hard to resolve. But,

---

4   For an excellent analysis of the tension between mediation and the lawyer's "standard philosophical map", see L. Riskin, "Mediation and Lawyers" (1982) 43 Ohio St. L.J. 29.

unlike family disputes, it was not customary, although there were exceptions, for a teacher, student, or other partner-in-education to take an unresolved conflict to court. Accordingly, it was not surprising that the disputants in schools were eager to learn more about the meaning of alternatives and to incorporate ADR ideas and practices into school curricula and day-to-day activities. ADR education easily flourished in the school setting.

Second, mediation was also not a completely unfamiliar process in the school context. Teachers had been mediating disputes in the schoolyard for years, long before ADR popularized the process. Principals, school administrators, and students had regular experiences in helping other parties in dispute work out satisfactory solutions. The culture of education in many communities had long histories of collaboration and consensual decision-making as part of a larger project on creating a positive learning environment. ADR made sense and school leaders became early ADR proponents fostering peer mediation programs, anger management courses, alternative approaches to discipline, and national associations for mediation in education.

Third, if a lack of ADR education was the problem now, teaching the next generation about ADR was part of the solution. These children as adults would be able to use and pass on the fundamental dispute resolution skills they had learned as kids. Distinguishing interests from positions and therapy from mediation would no longer be necessary for the next generation of ADR users.

To cover the spectrum, ADR education also became linked to continuing education programs. In the 1970s and 1980s, many people had a limited understanding and awareness of ADR and its many components. Mediation could be confused with meditation. Distinctions between interest-based bargaining and distributive bargaining could not easily be made. Active listening wasn't for lawyers. Although conflicts and disputing were pervasive in societies, education in dispute resolution had not been covered completely in the standard curricula, particularly for the people who needed it most. There was clearly a continuing education target population and a tidal wave of courses swept up governments, professionals, organizations, and others who had contacts with disputes and who wanted to become proficient in the better ways. Train-the-trainer programs followed so that other ADR teachers could carry on these educational initiatives that often focused on the mediation process and the skills needed to be a competent mediator.

The mandate to make ADR education an imperative has had an impact. In law, for example, it would have been the unusual student or lawyer who delved deeply, if at all, into ADR twenty years ago. Today, many graduating law students and practising lawyers will have had exposure to alternative dispute resolution and be able to engage in informed conversations on key issues and concepts. The same result will be true for other disciplines such as anthropology, business, social work, psychology, political science and public administration where dispute resolution is an important part of the discipline's work. Children, even pre-schoolers, now will have more opportunities to learn about non-violent responses that can be made when a dispute rears its head in the schoolyard or at home. The enormous developments in the ADR field and ADR's greatest achievements have been grounded in ADR education and training. The recipients of this learning have made ADR's present developments and achievements so profound.

The present state of ADR education points to great promise ahead. National associations for advancing mediation in education already exist.[5] ADR courses and workshops are offered in professional schools, graduate programs and other advanced educational settings. Research and writing in ADR attract attention and support. The future development of ADR appears to have a solid educational foundation.

Yet, despite this impressive educational effort to spread the good word, questions are asked about ADR's future. Goldberg, Sander, and Rogers see "a mixed picture" and despite "encouraging signs that ADR has come of age . . . If we look at the potential, the glass seems not even half full . . . Why is this so?"[6] Why is ADR not more widely used? Is the answer that the users of ADR services are still not knowledgeable enough? Do expectations in disputing still focus on the courts? Do lawyers encourage ADR's use? Are there unresolved problems with ADR's use?

These questions and queries can be answered with further ADR offerings, national gatherings, professionalization activities, and intensifying institutionalization efforts so as "to weave ADR procedures into society's dispute resolution fabric, so that such processes will be automatically considered along the way."[7] Alternatively, the answers may be discovered by looking more closely at two key components in ADR education — content and responsibility — and the challenges these educational elements pose for ADR's future.

---

5   The National Association for Mediation in Education (NAME) in the United States promotes the development, implementation, and institutionalization of school and university-based conflict resolution programs and curricula.

6   S.B. Goldberg, F.E.A. Sander, & N.H. Rogers, *Dispute Resolution: Negotiation, Mediation and Other Processes* (New York: Aspen Law & Business, 1999) at 567–68.

7   *Ibid.* at 570.

The content challenge is surely to keep ADR as an invigorating and demanding subject of multidisciplinary study and practice and to ensure the full potential offered by ADR is realized. The challenge exists because a broad view of alternative dispute resolution can call into question so much. There is a lot to know and be able to do. One language is impossible. Keeping track of the multidisciplinary influences on ADR can be no small task in any higher educational setting, let alone a continuing education venue or office where there is a need to be practical on matters at hand. Keeping current on the burgeoning literature and what are ADR's best practices can be difficult when time is short and educational endeavours have to condense a lot into one- or five-day programs that concentrate mostly on skills. The theories that underlie ADR or that can create controversy may not be able to be incorporated into a five-day course on mediation or a one-day seminar on working together. Let's talk about power in an hour, for example. Accessible and quality graduate programs in dispute resolution and other sophisticated educational courses in conflict resolution can make the necessary links between theory and practice because the degree, diploma or certificate in dispute resolution is usually offered in a university or college setting where such approaches are most often the norm.

However, the content challenge may not be met solely by ensuring ADR education is located in quality venues. In law, for example, there have been recent encouragements that ADR be a mandatory part of the educational requirement for lawyers. The Canadian Bar Association's 1996 report on systems of civil justice[8] recommended reducing the "preoccupation with gaining advantage through an adversarial approach,"[9] "a reduction in the antagonistic nature of litigation," "a reorientation away from fighting the other side to solving a common problem,"[10] "a shift away from the runaway hostility and grandstanding,"[11] and that Canadian law schools "offer mandatory education and training on dispute resolution options and on the means by which they can be integrated into legal practice."[12]

However, the report provides limited guidance to legal educators and law students on what this educational recommendation actually entails. This is perhaps understandable given the rather unprecedented nature of the Task Force's journey into the "who sets law school curric-

8   Canadian Bar Association Task Force on Systems of Civil Justice, *Report of the Task Force on Systems of Civil Justice* (Ottawa: Canadian Bar Association 1996).
9   *Ibid.* at 18.
10   *Ibid.*
11   *Ibid.* at 64.
12   *Ibid.* at 65.

ulum" territory. There are however several winks and nudges in the report about the meaning of dispute resolution options:

> In addition to modifications in the structure of dispute resolution processes, achieving a multi-option civil justice system will require a basic change in orientation on the part of many lawyers, judges, court administrators, educators and clients. As discussed earlier, the traditional approach to litigation has not emphasized problem solving. Rather, the adversarial aspects of the system not only shape but permeate the entire approach to dispute resolution. It is in this regard that the Task Force suggests that a change in orientation is required. This reorientation must focus on early problem solving and dispute resolution, with the prospect of a trial seen not as a matter of immediate focus but as an option of last resort.[13]

And further

> In a multi-option civil justice system, litigation lawyers must move away from a focus on rights-based thinking and adopt a wide problem-solving approach. This involves a fundamental change in approach and the acquisition of new information and skills to assist clients with dispute resolution. The Task Force believes that it will be important, in the civil justice system of the future, to enhance lawyers' skills in dispute resolution. Effective use of these techniques involves sophisticated skills and knowledge that can be analyzed and taught and that should be the subject of in-depth study. The Task Force believes that it is in the public interest as well as the interests of the profession to encourage the development of dispute resolution skills and to support them with institutional processes.
>
> The change in approach urged by the Task Force begins with a new focus on dispute resolution as the goal and a corresponding reduction in the antagonistic nature of the litigation process. For some lawyers this will mean a fundamental re-orientation away from fighting the other side to solving a common problem.[14]

---

13   *Ibid.* at 31.

14   *Ibid.* at 63. See also the MacCrate Report in the United States which also referred to the lawyer's need to be proficient in problem solving and alternative dispute resolution procedures. American Bar Association, *Legal Education and Professional Development — An Educational Continuum: Report of the Task Force on Law Schools and the Profession: Narrowing the Gap* (Chicago: American Bar Association, 1992). The British Columbia Law Society approved a Statement of Pre-Call Requirements in October 1996. The Statement covered the knowledge, skills, attitudes and personal characteristics necessary to enter the profession. ADR was conspicuously present as problem solving, mediating, negotiating, and so on although never mentioned by name.

Whether popular graduate programs and professional educational directions for lawyers or others are able to capture the complex side of ADR, particularly its critical components, depends on the range of factors that would normally accompany the design of any educational venture. Lurking there will be the ideology of ADR. If ADR is understood by educators as having political ambiguity, being contradictory and uncertain and, as a field of study, open to much interpretation, these features would have to be accounted for in any theoretical or practical study of disputing and dispute resolution. The interest-based bargaining approach to problem-solving could not be presented apart from its interesting relationships with economics, culture and gender. Transformative justice would need to be similarly imbued with critical takes on race, power, and the economic rationality embodied in capitalism. If ADR strengthens the state's monopoly on social control utilizing elite professionals, rearranges power structures in informal and private ways, or rationalizes the formality of law to sustain a capitalist economic order, ADR education would need to take these concerns into account and be able to explain their implications, if any, in practical ways on, for example, the six-stage mediation model. On the other hand, if ADR has to be contained, reducible to step-by-step approaches and schematic thinking, and amenable to classical notions of professionalization, it may be that graduate programs and professional education in ADR would need to dispense with or pay scant attention to ADR ideas or theories that were not a part of that thinking. A challenge for ADR education surely will be to resolve its content conflicts without inhibiting its growth.[15]

A second and related challenge for ADR education in the future is directed to responsibility. Who will take on the educational mission?

The usual answer is that ADR is a multidisciplinary field and no one entity should control what is said to be right and wrong about ADR. ADR has been shaped by many disciplines and a host of individuals from diverse backgrounds have been involved in ADR's work making it what the field is today. As ADR evolved from its multidisciplinary roots, it was not feasible or perhaps desirable to stem the flood of those attracted by ADR's allure. Change was rapid; partnerships were formed; different jurisdictions were involved. Organization took some time to occur, and the responsibility for ADR education devolved into many hands.

---

15   For example, Carrie Menkel-Meadow describes the MacCrate view of lawyer as "technocratic problem solver . . . most firmly rooted in a conventional litigation concept." See C. Menkel-Meadow, "Narrowing the Gap by Narrowing the Field: What's Missing from the MacCrate Report — Of Skills, Legal Science and Being a Human (1994) 69 Wash. L. Rev. 593 at 603.

The move to professionalize ADR may, however, change the responsibility picture. The ultimate responsibility for quality and standards in a profession normally lies with a single and independent governing body. Determining just what it is that professional mediators, arbitrators, confidential listeners, and negotiators need to know and be able to do would be established, if ADR were a profession, by this body through some type of internal accrediting structure governing new professionals in dispute resolution.

While ADR might be studied as a useful part of a liberal arts education, the professional side of the equation would need to be learned and practised in the professional way. The various disciplines that now graduate professionals — for example, business, engineering, psychology, law and social work — might contribute to a professional pool for certification or admission. Or, one profession might assume the responsibilities. The legal profession, for example, now repeats that its traditional role has always been "healers of human conflict"[16] or more recently "problem solvers." It is now natural for lawyers to see ADR (or BDR, IDR, or ADRA[17]) and dispute resolution education as within the legal profession's bailiwick. The need for a lawyer to earn ADR or mediation credentials to belong to a new multidisciplinary profession may not be necessary when all lawyers have obtained a sound and satisfactory education in ADR's multidisciplinarity. Unauthorized practice of law in the future might bring into focus for careful review by a judge just what are the distinctions, if any, between problem-solving and lawyering when the problem solver from elsewhere has no legal degree.

A competing image of future responsibility for ADR education is a broader and more inclusive one. Knowledge about disputing, about how best to proceed, about the ins and outs of dispute resolution, could be in everyone's hands and not be seen as a specialized or professionalized field of knowledge. When people are touched by conflict, as they regularly are, there could be a collective responsibility for the individual to view the disputing practices that follow as an integral part of a person's personal and professional life. There would, therefore, need to be capacities in everyone to make the constructive disputing decisions that shape what happens next in any dispute. The individual acquisition or use of this knowledge would not necessitate the need to

---

16   Warren Burger, former chief justice of the United States Supreme Court in "Isn't There a Better Way?" (1982) 68 A.B.A. J. 274.

17   ADRA might be an expression that distinguishes Canadian ADR legal practitioners from ADR lawyers in other jurisdictions. (pronounced ADR eh!)

become part of a profession although a professional working with ADR would be expected to know a great deal more.

This collective responsibility would apply equally to individuals and institutions. Conflicts affect families, business organizations, religious bodies, governments, professional and community groups, and other social structures. Rather than looking under C for conflict resolutionary or M for mediator in the yellow pages when confronted with conflict, these institutions and the people in them could see ADR as an essential presence in their home, office, street, or world affairs. ADR would be the responsibility of all. Dispute resolution would be a way of life and the knowledge that makes up this way could be broadly disseminated. A lawyer asked to mediate a difficult family dispute would need to know how to reframe statements and listen actively — "I can see the break-up was a surprise and a shock. It seems that resolving responsibilities around property and feelings are your most important concerns." But the disputants themselves could also be familiar with the communication skills that can be helpful in conflict. Despite having these skills, they have had to seek help from a mediator who happens this time to be a legal professional. The field of ADR would not be the property of a single or select professional group. There would still be professionals, all of whom knew about and practised ADR at different levels. But for many people, much of ADR would be more akin to reading and writing and communicating, understanding, organizing, or feeling. It would be always present, open to all — some better than others — and be a more collective and constructive response to disputing demands.

Taking collective responsibility for ADR would mean that ADR education in the future would be an integral part of all learning systems. Teaching about the complex nature of disputes, the many ways or processes in which disputes get attended to, and how to practically use the principles, processes, practices, and skills that help disputes move along would be structured in much the same way that other important subjects with differing levels of difficulty are learned. University or professional education in dispute resolution would be able to be much more advanced, theoretical and critical in preparing learners for their role as disputants in the real world or in helping ADR students to become the resolvers for the tougher cases lying ahead. With a progressive system of ADR education, curriculum changes would need to be thought of in fundamental ways, particularly in the professional schools that graduate students to prevent, manage, or resolve conflicts as necessary to their work.

With ADR education spread widely, there would still be no scarcity of difficult disputes although some ADR supporters may conceptualize a garden of Eden or an H.G. Wells future. But emphasizing and educating for a collective responsibility in dispute processing would probably mean that fewer disputes would be suppressed. Many more disputes would be resolved earlier and more satisfactorily by the parties themselves. The overall costs associated with disputing would likely decrease. When resort to professionals, such as lawyers, was required, the professional would have the capacity to provide the fullest range of ADR opportunities. Cases would still go to court but these cases, with technology assisting their management, would be heard in a more timely and cost-efficient way. Most legal cases would still settle but these settlements would be speedier, less expensive, and more just.

Taking collective responsibility for alternative dispute resolution would not mean a new profession but rather renewed professions. The roles of professionals in dispute resolution, wherever their disciplinary homes, would be enhanced. As future educational developments in ADR become more common and widespread, the professionals would be asked to prevent, manage, resolve, or help process mostly those disputes that the parties themselves could not handle alone. The professional's role in dispute resolution would be elevated when disputants are empowered to do so much themselves. Professionals in dispute resolution, whether joined together or associated most with their traditional confines, would be able to show the interest-based lawyers, the partnered executives or the mediators how to resolve their own problems. If the disputants have their own means in a more ADR-educated world, the look of professional practice would take on some changed characteristics. This leads to some details around the future of law practice.

C. THE FUTURE OF LAW PRACTICE: ADR LAWYERING

It would be quite odd in the future for a lawyer in practice to say he had never heard about ADR. "ADR wasn't taught when I attended law school!" would be a shocking statement. "I learned it the hard way — in the trenches!" would make one wonder.

But these experiences were the realities for lawyers today who graduated from law school at a time when adversarial thinking was very much in vogue. Problems were legal and required a careful analysis of the facts, application of the law to the facts, legal advice, and then, in many cases, a lawsuit. The lawsuit might settle early when the service of a writ showed the opposing side you were serious. But often cases settled late, on the courthouse steps or during the first or second day of trial when the sound of the evidence or the lean of the judge pressured the plaintiff or defendant to reassess their positions. Dispute resolution was certainly what lawyers did all the time but its learning was often by doing. With a law degree, articling, and a bar admission course in hand, young lawyers learned, mostly from other lawyers, how the suits were resolved.

The practice of law was tailored, in part, to suit the legal profession's image as "a knight in shining armour whose courtroom lance strikes down all obstacles"[18]and to see the court as central to the experience. Barristers and solicitors did keep their clients out of court but the courtroom specialist had the long-time appeal.

This legal disputing regime was not, of course, static. The history of Western models of formal adjudicatory mechanisms shows the changes that have regularly been made over time to disputing practices. A trial by ordeal, where an accused plunged his arm into boiling water as the key ingredient of a formal justice system, did not stand the test of time. But for a long period the lawyer's standard disputing practices relied heavily on competitiveness, the win-lose ideal, aggressiveness, cleverness or manipulation, and the courts that came naturally with an adversary system. Often the process was still an ordeal.

Today ADR education is taking hold in the law schools and in law students' undergraduate degrees. ADR education is exposing the new generations of lawyers to a field that their legal partners never saw or saw only in pieces. Although the content of this legal education is still being negotiated, legal disclaimers around dispute resolution deficiencies will no longer be available in the future.

But interesting questions surround the long-term impacts ADR will have on the practice of law. As discussed in chapter 2, the move from an adversarial to a non-adversarial mindset has no clear paths. There is also no well-defined intent on the part of the profession that an ethic of care is a state where they necessarily want to go. The combination of advocacy and alternatives can create uncertain results. Yet if the content of ADR education for lawyers is complete, the meaning of ADR can empower lawyers to see ADR as a modern expression of everything they want for an ancient, honourable and learned profession. And, as an added benefit, the ADR jokes about lawyers are a lot less stinging.[19]

---

18   Above note 16.

19   A colleague and I created several mediator jokes as a conscious part of our pedagogy for an early morning mediation training session. We were not sure if these were the first jokes ever made about lawyers as mediators but we think so. One of them goes as follows: Question: How many lawyer-mediators does it take to hang a picture? Answer: Mediators don't hang pictures, they reframe them.

We are already seeing a part of this future today. Frank Sander's image of the multi-doored courthouse in 1976 is here.[20] In law practice, notices to mediate are served, mini-trials are held, settlement conferences are mandatory. There is judicial dispute resolution (JDR). The Canadian Bar Association echoes the Pound conference with a call for "multi-option civil justice," which would sacrifice the autonomies in the system for "access to a more efficient process and choice among more dispute resolution options."[21] Instead of six doors, there are more. The emphasis is on providing a broad array of options for dispute resolution within the court system. While the report on civil justice systems acknowledges that dispute resolution takes place outside the formal system, ADR in all its forms and functions becomes inextricably linked to lawyers and the courts. For example, in the court-based ADR ante-room are openings to mediation, early neutral evaluation, negotiation and other processes with more links back to the court for continuing cases. Through the court door, there are now faster and slower lanes to trial to go along with improved regular routes that caused so much concern before.

For lawyers practising in this justice system, the overarching objective is settlement and particularly early settlement, but multi-option civil justice would also need to extol the following virtues:

1. Justice
2. Fairness
3. Independence
4. Accountability
5. Transparency
6. Responsiveness
7. Understandability
8. Accessibility
9. Affordability
10. Timeliness
11. Proportionality
12. Certainty
13. Efficiency.[22]

---

20   Professor Frank Sander posed the model of not "simply a court house but a Dispute Resolution Centre." The Dispute Resolution Centre has come to be known as the multi-doored courthouse. Sander wanted a "lobby" where disputants could be screened and channelled to a panoply of dispute resolution processes such as mediation, arbitration, fact-finding, malpractice screening panel, superior court, or an ombudsman. See F.E.A. Sander, "Varieties of Dispute Processing," 70 F.R.D. 111 (1976).

21   Above note 8 at 27.

22   *Ibid.* at 28. Most of the definitions are straightforward, (e.g. "The system should be just.") although proportionality means it should provide procedures that are proportional to the matters in issue.

The report also packages new ideas about case management, monetary jurisdictions, discovery procedures, and lawyers' and judges' roles with the dispute resolution options. If this future description of law practice and its goals are realized, it is hard to imagine what improvements could be made. If the ADR-inspired ideals are achieved, what need would there be for an alternative of any kind unless perhaps a private court could do all the above, only faster and cheaper.

However, for the person who is thinking about the future of ADR, this version may seem too lawyer-centred. Does the multi-door courthouse, under whose roof all of ADR can rest, have room for the non-legal groups? Is the courthouse the proper venue? Can ADR exist outside the practice of law?

Given this legal fit between the futures of ADR and law practice, the place of non-lawyers in law practice deserves comment. The professional arrangements that are developed, like any relationship of complexity, will depend on a number of factors.

First, there will be comparisons made to similar partnerships. Lawyers will look closely at other examples to see how a professional might relate to a character that initially challenged its worth. Medicine might be considered. Alternative medicine and traditional medicine could be compared to alternative dispute resolution and law. Medicine may be ahead of law in making its decision but one might expect law would, in a similar way, seek to join with those parts of ADR that can be complementary to law's enterprise and reject those parts of any concern.

Second, how lawyers interact now with other professionals who are engaging in interdependent or mutually-attracted-to activities will be examined. There are, as precedents, the accountant and the immigration consultant. Lawyers will see examples of how legal mergers and partnerships are being formed worldwide and what BATNAs and WATNAs are pushing these high-stake negotiations. The tried and examined professional relationship affairs in the legal profession do not present the same contexts as exist for lawyers and the proliferating non-lawyer ADR professionals. As a result, the negotiations may not go the same way as the others because, as you know, there are distributions to be made and power to be shared. Lawyers may consider how their monopoly on law practice could be strengthened by unauthorized practice of law proceedings. Are parts of dispute resolving preserved for lawyers alone and what will the judges of the future decide? Mediation has become a widely shared task with the costlier cases requiring professional attention. Giving legal advice and drafting legal documents may be all that is left with appearing in court as exclusive to law. As ADR unfolds, court-centred halls or private ADR chambers staffed only by legal professionals proficient in the law may be an obvious response.

Finally, the relationships lawyers develop in practice with other ADR bodies also will depend, like most negotiations, on possible solutions. What would a serious partnership actually entail? While multi-option justice is easy to see and approve, the other sides of the street are not made as clear. Across the road from the multi-level courthouse is the place where lawyers work. These settings vary in grandeur and design. Like the courts, the traditional practice of law, from the office design to the penetrating questions, is a product of a time when ADR did not exist.

Exploring the full advantages and opportunities in ADR will require more changes in law practice. Although many profound alterations already have been made to the lawyering world, part of ADR and the future of law practice could depend on a broad-based professional realization that MDPs (multidisciplinary partnerships) with non-lawyer ADR experts hold a key to unlocking ADR's potential. This solution, as mediators will know, has some details to be worked out, but it is difficult to see how lawyers alone could accomplish as much.

Accordingly, across the street from the impressive Public Justice Centre could be the same image in private practice. There could be multi-doored law offices, Holistic Healing Centres, Dispute Resolution Centres, or ADR Chambers. The lawyer as healer of human conflict, as problem solver, as a master mediator, arbitrator, negotiator, advocate, as a practitioner of ADR would be wired into all the options. The family client or business agent, unable to resolve his affairs, would be seeking disputing help in a variety of ways. There would be sound legal advice about a day (or less) in court, interest-based negotiating discussions so the children are spared, practical decisions about the process to choose and perhaps acupuncture treatment for the underlying cause.

The future practice of law in all its details and the future development of ADR now appear inextricably linked. That future depends on the content ADR is given, the practices that receive support and the questions that are asked and answered.

- What does ADR mean?
- Can acupuncture or music therapy help a young man in conflict?
- What would breath work do for a client when the causes of conflict weren't deep enough?
- What are the limits in dispute resolution?
- Are there insurmountable barriers to a holistic law practice?
- Is there an alternative to ADR and what is its meaning?

FURTHER READINGS

Academy of Family Mediators at<http://www.mediation.org>

ADR Institute of Canada at <http://www.amic.org>

American Arbitration Association at <http://www.adr.org>

BRIN D., "Disputation Arenas: Harnessing Conflict and Competitiveness for Society's Benefit" (2000) 15 Ohio St. J. on Dis. Res. 597

Centre for Dispute Resolution at <http://www.cedr.co.uk>

ConflictNet at <http://www.igc.org >

CPR Institute for Dispute Resolution at <http://www.cpradr.org>

International Alliance of Holistic Lawyers at <http://www.iahl.org>

SANDER, F.E.A., "The Future of ADR" (2000) J. of Dis. Res. 3

Society of Professionals in Dispute Resolution at <http://www.spidr.org>

The Network: Interaction for Conflict Resolution at <http://www.nicr.ca>

UVic Institute for Dispute Resolution at <http://dispute.resolution.uvic.ca>

World Institute for Nonviolence and Reconciliation at <http://www.institute.for.nonviolence.com.au>

SELECTED FEDERAL/ PROVINCIAL STATUTES CONTAINING ADR REFERENCES

The Agri-Food Act, S.S. 1990–91, c. A-15.2

Appeal Committees

22(1) The Lieutenant Governor in Council may, by order:

   (a) establish appeal committees to hear appeals from any person aggrieved by an act or omission of an agency

(3) For the purpose of conducting appeals, an appeal committee:

   (b) may:

   (i) where the committee believes that mediation may resolve the appeal:

   (A) appoint any person to mediate between the agency and the person bringing the appeal; and

   (B) set the terms and conditions pursuant to which the mediation is to be conducted.

The Agricultural Operations Act, S.S. 1995, c. A-12.1

Mediation

16(1) For the purposes of this Act, the board may appoint a person as mediation officer to assist the parties to resolve a dispute.

(7) Evidence arising from anything said, evidence of anything said, or evidence of an admission or communication made in the course of mediation is not admissible in any cause or matter or proceeding before a court, except with the written con-

sent of the mediator and all parties to the cause or matter in which the mediator acted.

Arbitration Act, S.A. 1991, c. A-43.1

Mediation and conciliation

35(1) The members of an arbitral tribunal may, if the parties consent, use mediation, conciliation or similar techniques during the arbitration to encourage settlement of the matters in dispute.

   (2) After the members of an arbitral tribunal use a technique referred to in subsection (1), they may resume their roles as arbitrators without disqualification.

Broadcasting Act, S.C. 1991, c. 11

Regulations generally

10.(1) The Commission may, in furtherance of its objects, make regulations.

   (h) for resolving, by way of mediation or otherwise, any disputes arising between programming undertakings and distribution undertakings concerning the carriage of programming originated by the programming undertakings.

Business Practices Act, R.S.O. 1990, c. B.18

Duties of Director

5. The Director shall,

   (b) receive and act on or mediate complaints respecting unfair practices.

Canada Labour Code, R.S.C. 1985, c. L-2

Promotion of Industrial Peace

Mediators

105. The Minister, on request or on his own initiative, may, where the Minister deems it expedient, at any time appoint a mediator to confer with the parties to a dispute or difference and endeavour to assist them in settling the dispute or difference.

Canadian Environmental Assessment Act, S.C. 1992, c. 37

Definitions

2.(1) In this Act,

   "mediation" means an environmental assessment that is conducted with the assistance of a mediator appointed pursuant to section 30 and that includes a consideration of factors required to be considered under subsections 16(1) and (2).

Mediation report

32.(1) A mediator shall, at the conclusion of the mediation, prepare and submit a report to the Minister and to the responsible authority.

Privilege

(2) No evidence of or relating to a statement made by a mediator or a participant to the mediation during the course of and for the purposes of the mediation is admissible without the consent of the mediator or participant, in any proceeding before a review panel, court, tribunal, body or person with jurisdiction to compel the production of evidence.

Charitable Institutions Act, R.S.O. 1990, c. C.9, as amended

Powers of residents' council

9.21   It is the function of a residents' council of an approved charitable home for the aged, and the council has the power, to

(d) attempt to mediate and resolve a dispute between the approved corporation maintaining and operating the home and a resident of the home.

Chartered Accountants Act, S.A. 1987, c. C-5.1

Mediation

54(1) A person designated by the Council as a mediator may assist in settling a complaint made to the Executive Director if the complainant and the chartered accountant, professional corporation or student about whose conduct the complaint is made agree.

(2) If, within 45 days of the date of receipt of a complaint by the Executive Director, or a longer period agreed to by the persons concerned, a settlement of the complaint does not occur, or in the mediator's opinion is not likely to occur, the mediator shall forward the complaint to the Professional Conduct Chairman forthwith.

Child, Family and Community Service Act, R.S.B.C. 1996, c. 46

Division 2 — Cooperative Planning and Dispute Resolution

Mediation

22. If a director and any person are unable to resolve an issue relating to the child or a plan of care, the director and the person may agree to mediation or other alternative dispute resolution mechanisms as a means of resolving the issue.

Effect of family conference or mediation on court proceeding

23(1) On application the court may adjourn a proceeding under this Part one or more times, for a total period of up to 3 months, so that a family conference or mediation can proceed.

(2) If the proceeding is adjourned, any limit applicable to the proceeding is suspended.

(3) If, as a result of a family conference or mediation, a written agreement is made after a proceeding is commenced to determine if the child needs protection, a director may file the agreement with the court.

Confidentiality of information

24(1) A person must not disclose, or be compelled to disclose, information obtained in a family conference or mediation, except

(a) with the consent of everyone who participated in the family conference or mediation,

(b) to the extent necessary to make or implement an agreement about the child,

(c) if the information is disclosed in an agreement filed under section 23, or

(d) if the disclosure is necessary for a child's safety or is required under section 14.

The Child and Family Services Act, S.S. 1989–90, c. C-7.2

Child protection

Mediation services

15(1) Where an officer has concluded that a child is in need of protection, the officer may offer to the parent to submit the officer's reasons for that conclusion to a mediator for the purpose of obtaining assistance in concluding an agreement with the parent for the provision of family services.

(2) Mediation offered pursuant to subsection (1) shall be carried out by a person who, in the opinion of a director, is:

(a) qualified to provide mediation services; and

(b) representative of community parenting standards.

Non-compellability

73. The minister, members of the board, members of family review panels, mediators, officers and employees of the department, members of boards or directors of agencies, officers and employees of agencies and all other persons who are employed in or assist in the administration of this Act:

(a) are not compellable to give evidence with respect to:

(i) written or oral statements made to them; or

(ii) knowledge or information acquired by them; in the performance of their duties pursuant to this Act; and

(b) shall not be required to produce any written statement mentioned in subclause (a)(i) at a trial, hearing or other proceeding.

The Children's Law Act, S.S. 1990-91, c. C-8.1

Custody and Access

Mediation

10(1) On an application by an applicant or respondent pursuant to this Part or Part III or IV, the court, by order, may appoint a person to mediate a matter that:

(a) is dealt with in the application; and

(b) is at issue between the parties.

Obligation of lawyer

11(1) It is the duty of every lawyer who undertakes to act on behalf of an applicant or respondent in an application pursuant to this Part or Part III or IV to:

(a) discuss with the applicant or respondent the advisability of negotiating the matters that are the subject of the application; and

(b) inform the applicant or respondent of the mediation facilities known to him or her that might be able to assist the parties in negotiating those matters.

(2) Every application presented to the court by a lawyer pursuant to this Part or Part III or IV is to contain a statement signed by the lawyer certifying that he or she has complied with subsection (1).

Children's Law Reform Act, R.S.O. 1990, c. C.12

Custody and Access — Assistance to the Court

Mediation

Duty of mediator
>   (3) It is the duty of a mediator to confer with the parties and endeavour to obtain an agreement in respect of the matter.

Form of report
>   (4) Before entering into mediation on the matter, the parties shall decide whether,
>   (a) the mediator is to file a full report on the mediation, including anything that the mediator considers relevant to the matter in mediation; or
>   (b) the mediator is to file a report that either sets out the agreement reached by the parties or states only that the parties did not reach agreement on the matter.

Admissions made in the course of mediation
>   (7) Where the parties have decided that the mediator's report is to be in the form described in clause (4)(b), evidence of anything said or of any admission or communication made in the course of the mediation is not admissible in any proceeding except with the consent of all parties to the proceeding in which the order was made under subsection (1).

Child, Youth and Family Advocacy Act, R.S.B.C. 1996, c. 47

Powers of advocate
> 4(1) In fulfilling the functions of the office, the advocate may do any of the following:
>   (b) initiate and participate in, or assist children, youths and their families to initiate and participate in, case conferences, administrative reviews, mediations or other processes in which decisions are made about the provision of designated services.
>   (2) In fulfilling the duties of the office, the advocate may try to resolve any matter through the use of negotiation, conciliation, mediation or other dispute resolution processes.

Court of Queen's Bench, S.M. 1988–89, c. 4

Referral to mediator

47(1) Where a judge or master is of the opinion that an effort should be made to resolve an issue otherwise than at a formal trial, the judge or master may, at any stage of the proceeding, refer the issue to a mediator.

Action by mediator

47(2) A mediator to whom an issue is referred under subsection (1) shall attempt to resolve the issue.

Confidentiality

48 Unless the parties otherwise agree,
  (a) a mediator who renders services
    (i) under section 47, or
    (ii) at the request of the parties, or
  (b) a party to a mediation; is not competent to give evidence in respect of
  (c) a written or oral statement made by a party during the mediation, or
  (d) knowledge or information acquired during the mediation by a person under clauses (a) or (b).

Courts of Justice Act, R.S.O. 1990, c. C. 43, as amended

Ontario Judicial Council

Mediation

51.5(1) The Judicial Council may establish a mediation process for complainants and for judges who are the subject of complaints.

Criteria

(2) If the Judicial Council establishes a mediation process, it must also establish criteria to exclude from the process complaints that are inappropriate for mediation.

(3) Without limiting the generality of subsection (2), the criteria must ensure that complaints are excluded from the mediation process in the following circumstances:

1. There is a significant power imbalance between the complainant and the judge, or there is such a significant disparity between the complainant's and the judge's accounts of the event with which the complaint is concerned that mediation would be unworkable.

2. The complaint involves an allegation of sexual misconduct or an allegation of discrimination or harassment because of a prohibited ground of discrimination or harassment referred to in any provision of the Human Rights Code.
3. The public interest requires a hearing of the complaint.

Legal advice

4. A complaint may be referred to a mediator only if the complainant and the judge consent to the referral, are able to obtain independent legal advice and have had an opportunity to do so.

Trained mediator

5. The mediator shall be a person who has been trained in mediation and who is not a judge, and if the mediation is conducted by two or more persons acting together, at least one of them must meet those requirements.

Impartiality

6. The mediator shall be impartial.

The Department of Justice Act, S.S. 1983, c. D-18.2

Mediation services

14.1(1) The minister may appoint a manager of mediation services to:
(a) provide and encourage the provision of mediation services to the public.

Divorce Act, R.S.C. 1985, c. 3

Duty of legal adviser

9.(1) It is the duty of every barrister, solicitor, lawyer or advocate who undertakes to act on behalf of a spouse in a divorce proceeding
(a) to draw to the attention of the spouse the provisions of this Act that have as their object the reconciliation of spouses, and
(b) to discuss with the spouse the possibility of the reconciliation of the spouses and to inform the spouse of the marriage counselling or guidance facilities known to him or her that might be able to assist the spouses to achieve a reconciliation, unless the circumstances of the case are of such a nature that it would clearly not be appropriate to do so.

Idem
   (2) It is the duty of every barrister, solicitor, lawyer or advocate who undertakes to act on behalf of a spouse in a divorce proceeding to discuss with the spouse the advisability of negotiating the matters that may be the subject of a support order or a custody order and to inform the spouse of the mediation facilities known to him or her that might be able to assist the spouses in negotiating those matters.

The Education Act, 1995, S.S. 1995, c. E-0.2

Mediation of conflict involving pupil
   148. Where a difference or conflict arises in the relationship of a pupil to the school, the parent or guardian, on behalf of that pupil, is entitled to immediate access to procedures established by the board of education or the conseil scolaire for the purposes of investigation and mediation of any differences or conflicts.

Electric Utilities Act, S.A. 1995, c. E-5.5

Powers of Board
   66. As part of the rules, practices and procedures referred to in section 65, the Board may
   (a) provide for the appointment of mediators to assist parties in negotiating the settlement of an issue,
   (f) provide that a mediator appointed under this section may issue a bad faith certificate to any party stating
       (i) that, in the mediator's opinion, that party did not participate in the negotiation of a settlement in good faith, and
       (ii) the mediator's reasons for that opinion.

Employment Standards Act, S.N.B., c. E-7.2

   64(1) The Director may, at any point after a complaint has been made, appoint, on such terms and conditions as may be established in the appointment, a mediator to attempt to settle the subject matter of the complaint.
   (2) In the event that the parties reach an agreement with respect to the disposition of the complaint the mediator shall report to the Director the terms and conditions of such agreement.
   (3) The Director may make an order to implement the terms and conditions of such an agreement and an order so made shall have the same force and effect as an order made under section 65.

(4) In the event that mediation is unsuccessful in assisting the parties to reach an agreement within such period as may be established by the Director, the mediator shall report that fact to the Director, but he shall not report to the Director, nor reveal to anyone, any communications that were made during the mediation process, or any information derived from such communication.

(5) A mediator who deals with a complaint made to the Director shall not, upon the completion of his mediation role, participate in any way in any subsequent investigation into the alleged complaint.

Employment Standards Code, S.A. 1996, c. E-10.3

Alternative dispute resolution

73(1) The Director may initiate and encourage the voluntary efforts of employers and employees

(a) to design fair processes in which to resolve complaints or concerns arising under this Act, with or without the assistance of an officer, and

(b) to settle complaints under this Act by appointing or facilitating the appointment of an impartial third party mediator, fact-finder or other person to assist the parties in settling their dispute.

Environmental Assessment Act, R.S.B.C. 1996, c. 119

Mediation may be authorized

66(1) The board or the executive director may make the services of a mediator available to parties interested in the outcome of an application for a project approval certificate.

(2) If satisfied that mediation will be conducive to the settlement of one or more issues related to the review of the application, the board or the executive director may

(a) invite the proponent, and any parties interested in the outcome of the application, to participate in mediation of an issue or issues,

(b) refer the issue or issues to a mediator for mediation, and

(c) require the mediator to report the results of the mediation to the board or the executive director by a time to be specified in the referral.

Environmental Bill of Rights, 1993, S.O. 1993, c. 28

Enhanced public participation for Class II proposals

24(1) A minister required to give notice under section 22 of a Class II proposal for an instrument shall also consider enhancing the right of members of the public to participate in decision-making on the proposal by providing for one or more of the following:

1. Opportunities for oral representations by members of the public to the minister or a person or body designated by the minister.
2. Public meetings.
3. Mediation among persons with different views on issues arising out of the proposal.
4. Any other process that would facilitate more informed public participation in decision-making on the proposal.

96. If the court orders the parties to negotiate a restoration plan, the court may

(b) make any order that the court considers appropriate,

(iv) respecting the negotiation process, including on consent of the parties, an order concerning the use of a mediator, fact finder or arbitrator.

Family Law Act, R.S.O. 1990, c. F.3

Mediation

3.(1) In an application under this Act, the court may, on motion, appoint a person whom the parties have selected to mediate any matter that the court specifies.

Consent to act

(2) The court shall appoint only a person who,

(a) has consented to act as mediator; and
(b) has agreed to file a report with the court within the period of time specified by the court.

Duty of mediator

(3) The mediator shall confer with the parties, and with the children if the mediator considers it appropriate to do so, and shall endeavour to obtain an agreement between the parties.

Full or limited report

(4) Before entering into mediation, the parties shall decide whether,

(a) the mediator is to file a full report on the mediation, including anything that he or she considers relevant; or

(b) the mediator is to file a limited report that sets out only the agreement reached by the parties or states only that the parties did not reach agreement.

Admissions, etc., in the course of mediation

(6) If the parties have decided that the mediator is to file a limited report, no evidence of anything said or of any admission or communication made in the course of the mediation is admissible in any proceeding, except with the consent of all parties to the proceeding in which the mediator was appointed.

The Family Maintenance Act, S.S. 1990–91, c. F-6.1 as amended

Mediation

13(1) On an application by a claimant or respondent pursuant to this Act, the court may appoint a person to mediate any matter that is dealt with in the application and that is at issue between the parties.

(2) No person shall be appointed as a mediator without that person's consent.

(3) Evidence arising from anything said, evidence of anything said or evidence of an admission or communication made in the course of the mediation is not admissible in a proceeding, except with the written consent of all parties to the proceeding in which the mediator was appointed.

Farm Debt Mediation Act, S.C. 1997, c. 21

5.(1) Subject to section 6, a farmer may apply to an administrator for either

(a) a stay of proceedings against the farmer by all the farmer's creditors, a review of the farmer's financial affairs, and mediation between the farmer and all the farmer's creditors for the purpose of assisting them to reach a mutually acceptable arrangement; or

(b) a review of the farmer's financial affairs, and mediation between the farmer and all the farmer's secured creditors for the purpose of assisting them to reach a mutually acceptable arrangement.

Mediation

10.(1) Forthwith after the report mentioned in subsection 9(4) has been prepared, the administrator shall

(a) in accordance with the regulations, appoint as a mediator any person who is unbiased and free from any conflict of interest relative to the application in question;

Fire and Police Services Collective Bargaining Act, R.S.B.C. 1996, c. 142

Settlement of dispute by arbitration

3(1)   If a firefighters' union or a police officers' union and an employer have bargained collectively and have failed to conclude a collective agreement or a renewal or revision of a collective agreement, the trade union or the employer may apply to the minister for a direction that the dispute be resolved by arbitration.

(2) The minister may direct that the dispute be resolved by arbitration if

(a) a mediation officer has been appointed under section 74 of the Code and has conferred with the parties, and

(b) the associate chair of the mediation division of the board has made a report to the minister

(i)   setting out the matters on which the parties have and have not agreed,

(ii) stating whether in the opinion of the associate chair the party seeking arbitration has made every reasonable effort to reach a collective agreement, and

(iii) stating whether in the opinion of the associate chair the dispute or some elements of the dispute should be resolved by applying the dispute resolution method known as final offer selection.

Forest Act, R.S.B.C. 1996, c. 157

Mediation and arbitration under contracts and subcontracts

155.   The Lieutenant Governor in Council may make regulations respecting mediation and arbitration of all or certain disputes that have arisen or may arise between the parties to a contract or subcontract, including, but not limited to, regulations

(a) establishing a system of mediation and arbitration and making the system applicable to

(i)   contracts, or

(ii) subcontracts that do not make any provision or do not make adequate provision for mediation and arbitration.

Register of Timber Harvesting Contract Mediators and Arbitrators

156.   For the purpose of implementing a system of mediation and arbitration established under section 155, the minister may

(a) establish and maintain a Register of Timber Harvesting Contract Mediators and Arbitrators,

(b) enter in the register the names of at least 9 individuals whom the minister considers qualified to mediate or arbitrate disputes under contracts and subcontracts, and

(c) amend the register from time to time by removing names or by adding the names of individuals the minister considers qualified to mediate or arbitrate disputes under contracts and subcontracts.

Freedom of Information and Protection of Privacy Act, S.A. 1994, c. F-18.5

Mediation may be authorized

65. The Commissioner may authorize a mediator to investigate and try to settle any matter that is the subject of a request for a review.

Freedom of Information and Protection of Privacy Act, R.S.O. 1990, c. F.31

Staff

8.(1)   Subject to the approval of the Lieutenant Governor in Council, the Commissioner may employ mediators and any other officers and employees the Commissioner considers necessary for the efficient operations of the office and may determine their salary and remuneration and terms and conditions of employment.

Funeral Directors and Establishments Act, R.S.O. 1990, c. F.36

Principal object

3(2)   The principal object of the Board is to regulate the practices of funeral directors and persons who operate funeral establishments and transfer services in accordance with this Act, the regulations and the by-laws in order that the public interest may be served and protected.

(3)   For the purpose of carrying out its principal object, the Board has the following additional objects:

(6)   To mediate complaints between consumers and licensees.

Homeowner Protection Act, S.B.C. 1998, c. 31

Part 10 — Alternate Dispute Resolution

Dispute resolution processes

29 (1) For the purpose of resolving residential construction disputes before or after an action is commenced rising out of or in connection with the construction of homes, including, without limitation, disputes about home warranty insurance, the Lieutenant Governor in Council may make regulations respecting the mediation or arbitration of residential construction disputes.

(2) For the purposes of the mediation of residential construction disputes referred to in subsection (1), the Lieutenant Governor in Council may make regulations including, without limitation, regulations

(a) providing to a party to a residential construction dispute the ability to require the parties to engage in mediation and setting out when and how that ability may be exercised and prescribing any other results that flow from the exercise of that ability, and

(b) respecting

(i) the forms or procedures that must or may be used or followed before, during and after the mediation process,

(ii) requiring and maintaining confidentiality of information disclosed for the purposes of mediation,

(iii) the circumstances and manner in which a party to a residential construction dispute may opt out of or be exempted from mediation,

(iv) the costs and other sanctions that may be imposed in relation to mediation, including, without limitation, in relation to any failure to participate in mediation when and as required or otherwise to comply with the regulations,

(v) the mediators' fees and disbursements, and

(vi) the qualifications required for, and the selection and identification of, individuals who may act as mediators in the mediation process contemplated by the regulations.

Homeowner Protection Act Regulations, B.C. Reg. 152/99

Notice to Mediate

(Residential Construction) Regulation

Definitions
1. In this regulation:

"mediation" means a collaborative process in which 2 or more parties meet and attempt, with the assistance of a mediator, to resolve issues in dispute between them;

"mediator" means a neutral and impartial facilitator with no decision making power who assists parties in negotiating a mutually acceptable settlement of issues in dispute between them;

"roster organization" means any body designated by the Attorney General to select mediators for the purposes of this regulation.

Delivery of Notice to Mediate
2.(1) Any party to a residential construction action may initiate mediation in that action by delivering a Notice to Mediate in Form 1 to
 (a) every other party to the action, and
 (b) the Dispute Resolution Office in the Ministry of the Attorney General.
 (2) A Notice to Mediate may be delivered under subsection (1) at any time after the action has been commenced and, unless the court otherwise orders or the parties otherwise consent, no later than 180 days before the date set for the commencement of the trial.
 (3) Unless the court otherwise orders, not more than one mediation may be initiated under this regulation in relation to any residential construction action.

Conduct of a mediation
12. The mediator may conduct the mediation in any manner he or she considers appropriate to assist the participants to reach a resolution that is timely, fair and cost-effective.

Confidentiality and compellability
15.(1) A person must not disclose, or be compelled to disclose, in any civil, criminal, quasi-criminal, administrative or regulatory action or proceeding, oral or written information acquired or an opinion formed, including without limitation,
 (a) any document made for the mediation, or

(b) any offer or admission made in anticipation of, during or in connection with a mediation session.

(2) Nothing in this section precludes a party from introducing into evidence in any civil, criminal, quasi-criminal, administrative or regulatory action or proceeding any information or records produced in the course of the mediation that are otherwise producible or compellable in those proceedings.

Homes for the Aged and Rest Homes Act, R.S.O. 1990, c. H.13

Powers of residents' council

30.8 It is the function of a residents' council of a home or joint home, and the council has the power, to,

(d) attempt to mediate and resolve a dispute between a resident of the home or joint home, as the case may be, and the municipality maintaining and operating the home, the municipalities maintaining and operating the joint home or the board of management of the home, as the case may be.

Hospitals Act, R.S.A. 1980, c. H-11

Investigation or mediation committee

43(1) When he is requested to do so by the board of an approved hospital, the Minister may authorize

(a) an investigation into the administration or operation of the hospital or any particular matter or problem that has arisen in connection with the administration or operation of the hospital, or

(b) the mediation of any dispute that has arisen in the course of the administration or operation of the hospital.

Human Rights Code, R.S.B.C. 1996, c. 210

Definitions

1. In this Code

"commissioner of investigations and mediation" means the commissioner of investigation and mediation appointed under section 15.

Mediation and settlement

29(1) The commissioner of investigation and mediation, a human rights officer or any person appointed, engaged or retained under section 17 may assist the parties to a complaint, through mediation and other means, to achieve a settlement.

(2) The terms of each settlement agreement entered into in respect of a complaint must be provided to the commission.

(3) Subject to section 40, a member of the commission, a human rights officer or any person appointed, engaged or retained under section 17 must not disclose any information concerning the terms of a settlement agreement provided to the commission under subsection (2) that would identify a party to the agreement unless that party consents to the release.

Industrial Relations Act, R.S.N.B. 1973, c. I-4

71(1) Notwithstanding any provision of this Act, the Minister may at any time appoint a person as a mediation officer when he is satisfied that the appointment of a mediation officer may bring about settlement of a dispute or prevent a dispute.

(2) It shall be the function of a mediation officer appointed under this section to investigate the causes of an existing or potential dispute, to attempt to bring about a settlement of the dispute or to prevent the dispute, and to assist a trade union and employer in the development of effective labour-management relations.

Insurance Act, R.S.O. 1990, c.I.8, as amended

Mediators

9 The Commissioner may appoint employees of the Commission or other persons to act as mediators.

Mediators

11(5) A mediator shall not be required to testify in a civil proceeding or in a proceeding before any tribunal respecting any mediation conducted under this Act or respecting information obtained in the discharge of the mediator's duties under this Act.

Neutral evaluation

(6) A person who performs an evaluation under section 280.1 shall not be required to testify in a civil proceeding or in a proceeding before any tribunal respecting the evaluation or respecting information obtained in the discharge of the person's duties under this Act.

Mediation

258.6(1) A person making a claim for loss or damage from bodily injury or death arising directly or indirectly from the use or operation of an automobile and an insurer that is defending an action in respect of the claim on behalf of an insured or that receives a notice under clause 258.3(1)(b) in respect of the claim shall, on the request of either of them, participate in a mediation of the claim in accordance with the procedures prescribed by the regulations.

Neutral evaluation
280.1(1) If mediation fails, the parties jointly or the mediator who conducted the mediation may, for the purpose of assisting in the resolution of the issues in dispute, refer the issues in dispute to a person appointed by the Director for an evaluation of the probable outcome of a proceeding in court or an arbitration under section 282.

Litigation or arbitration
281(1) Subject to subsection (2),
    (a) the insured person may bring a proceeding in a court of competent jurisdiction;
    (b) the insured person may refer the issues in dispute to an arbitrator under sections 282; or
    (c) the insurer and the insured person may agree to submit any issue in dispute to any person for arbitration in accordance with the Arbitration Act, 1991.

Limitation
    (2) No person may bring a proceeding in any court, refer the issues in dispute to an arbitrator under sections 282 or agree to submit an issue for arbitration in accordance with the Arbitration Act, 1991 unless mediation was sought, mediation failed and, if the issues in dispute were referred for an evaluation under section 280.1, the report of the person who performed the evaluation has been given to the parties.

International Commercial Arbitration Act, R.S.B.C. 1996, c. 233

Settlement
30(1) It is not incompatible with an arbitration agreement for an arbitral tribunal to encourage settlement of the dispute and, with the agreement of the parties, the arbitral tribunal may use mediation, conciliation or other procedures at any time during the arbitral proceedings to encourage settlement.

International Commercial Arbitration Act, R.S.O. 1990, c. I-9

Conciliation and other proceedings

3. For the purpose of encouraging settlement of a dispute, an arbitral tribunal may, with the agreement of the parties, use mediation, conciliation or other procedures at any time during the arbitration proceedings and, with the agreement of the parties, the members of the arbitral tribunal are not disqualified from resuming their roles as arbitrators by reason of the mediation, conciliation or other procedure.

Job Protection Act, R.S.B.C. 1996, c. 240

Objects

2. The objects of this Act are
    (a) to minimize job loss and the consequent destabilization of regional or local economies, particularly those mainly dependent on one industry, and
    (b) to preserve, restore and enhance the competitiveness of business enterprises in British Columbia and in the global marketplace

    by introducing temporary measures designed

    (c) to encourage business enterprises to obtain management consulting and counselling services,
    (d) to provide mediation services to business enterprises and interested parties in order to encourage cooperation conducive to the effective operation of the business enterprises, and
    (e) to enable business enterprises and interested parties to establish, subject to this Act, economic plans.

Labour Relations Act, 1995, S.O. 1995, c. 1

Disputes Advisory Committee

39.(1) The Minster may appoint a Disputes Advisory Committee composed of one or more representatives of employers and one or more representatives of employees.

Purpose of Committee

(2) At any time during the course of bargaining, either before or after the commencement of a strike or lock-out, where it appears to the Minister that the normal conciliation and mediation procedures have been exhausted, the Minister may request that the Disputes Advisory Committee be convened to confer with, advise and assist the bargaining parties.

Consensual mediation-arbitration

50.(1) Despite any grievance or arbitration provision in a collective agreement or deemed to be included in the collective agreement under section 48, the parties to the collective agreement may, at any time, agree to refer one or more grievances under the collective agreement to a single mediator-arbitrator for the purpose of resolving the grievances in an expeditious and informal manner.

Labour Relations Code, S.A. 1988, c. L-1.2

Informal mediation

62. Any time after a notice to commence collective bargaining is served, either or both parities to the collective bargaining may request the Director to provide the services of a mediator to informally assist in the negotiation process.

Labour Relations Code, R.S.B.C. 1996, c. 244

2(1) The following are the purposes of this Code:

(f) to encourage the use of mediation as a dispute resolution mechanism.

Landlord and Tenant Act, R.S.Y. 1986, c. 98

Mediation and arbitration

80.(1) Subject to subsection (2), a rentals officer may mediate or arbitrate any dispute between a landlord and a tenant in respect of the tenancy.

(2) A rentals officer may refuse to mediate or arbitrate a dispute where he is of the opinion that

(a) the dispute is of such a serious nature that it should be dealt with only by a court,

(b) the complaint is frivolous, vexatious, or concerns a trivial matter,

(c) the complaint primarily affects some person other than the complainant and the complainant does not have a sufficient personal interest in it.

(3) A rentals officer shall not mediate or arbitrate a dispute where

(a) the landlord or the tenant has commenced proceedings in a court for the resolution of the dispute, and

(b) the dispute has been previously resolved by the court or it remains before the court.

Legal Profession Act, S.B.C. 1998, c. 9

Specialization and restricted practice

    29. The benchers may make rules to do any of the following:

        (d) establish qualifications for and conditions under which practising lawyers may practise as mediators.

Metis Settlement Act, S.A. 1990, c. M-14.3

Alternative methods of dispute resolution

    188(1) The Appeal Tribunal may establish or provide for the establishment of any means of dispute resolution that it considers appropriate, including mediation, conciliation and arbitration processes.

      (2) A dispute in respect of which a person has a right of appeal to the Appeal Tribunal under this or any other enactment, a regulation, General Council Policy or a by-law may not be diverted to another dispute resolution process without the consent of the appellant or the parties concerned.

      (3) The Appeal Tribunal may agree to act as an arbitrator under the Arbitration Act or to appoint an arbitrator.

Municipal Government Act, S.A. 1994, c. M-26.1

    570. If a disagreement between municipalities is referred to the Minister by a council of a municipality or if the Minister is satisfied that it is desirable for the Minister to become involved in a disagreement between municipalities, the Minister may do one or more of the following:

      (b) appoint a mediator to assist the municipalities in resolving the disagreement.

The Ombudsman and Children's Advocate Act, R.S.S. 1998, c. O-4, as amended

    12. (5) The Ombudsman may try to resolve any problem raised in a complaint through the use of negotiation, conciliation, mediation or other non-adversarial approaches.

    12.6(1) The Children's Advocate has the power to do all things necessary to carry out the responsibilities given to the Children's Advocate pursuant to this Act.

      (2) The Children's Advocate shall:

        (c) where appropriate, try to resolve those matters mentioned in clause (b) that come to his or her attention through the use of negotiation, conciliation, mediation or other non-adversarial approaches.

Planning Act, R.S.O. 1990, c. P.13, as amended

Discretionary dispute resolution techniques

65. The Minister, the council of a municipality, a local board, a planning board or the Municipal Board or their agents shall, if they consider it appropriate, at any time before a decision is made under this Act, use mediation, conciliation or other dispute resolution techniques to attempt to resolve concerns or disputes in respect of any planning application or matter.

The Private Vocational Schools Regulation Act, 1995, S.S. 1995, c. P-26.2

14(1) In the event of a dispute between a student and an operator and with the consent of the student and the operator, the minister may appoint and pay for a mediator to assist the student and the operator in resolving the dispute.

Professional Engineers Act, R.S.O. 1990, c. P.28

32.(1) No person who is a member of the Complaints Committee or the Discipline Committee shall be a member of the Fees Mediation Committee.

Duties of Fees Mediation Committee

(2) The Fees Mediation Committee

(a) shall, unless the Committee considers it inappropriate to do so, mediate any written complaint by a client of a member of the Association or of a holder of a certificate of authorization, a temporary licence or limited licence in respect of a fee charged for professional engineering services provided to the client; and

(b) shall perform such other duties as are assigned to it by the Council.

Arbitration by Fees Mediation Committee

(3) The Fees Mediation Committee with the written consent of all parties to the dispute, may arbitrate a dispute in respect of a fee between a client and a member of the Association or a holder of a certificate of authorization, temporary licence or limited licence and in that case the decision of the Fees Mediation Committee is final and binding on all parties to the dispute.

Public Service Labour Relations Act, R.S.B.C. 1996, c. 388

Settlement of disputes

14(1) On the written request of either party, the associate chair of the Mediation Division of the board must appoint a mediator to confer with the parties and assist them in reaching a collective agreement if the parties are unable to agree.

The Queen's Bench (Family Law Division) Amendment Act, S.S. 1994, c. 27

23.4(1) A judge, on application or on the judge's own motion, may adjourn a family law proceeding where he or she considers that any party to the proceeding or any child affected by the proceeding would benefit from counselling or mediation or professional services.

The Queen's Bench (Mediation) Amendment Act, S.S. 1994, c. 20

Mediation re family law proceedings

54.1(1) Where a family law proceeding is commenced, the local registrar shall arrange for, and the parties shall attend, a mediation screening and orientation session prior to taking any further step in the proceedings.

(2) After the mediation screening and orientation session:

(a) the parties may continue with the mediation; or

(b) any party may discontinue the mediation and continue with the proceeding.

Mediation re non-family law proceedings

54.2(1) After the close of pleadings in a contested cause or matter that is not a family law proceeding, the local registrar shall arrange for, and the parties shall attend, a mediation session prior to taking any further step in the cause or matter.

(2) After the mediation session:

(a) the parties may continue with the mediation; or

(b) any party may discontinue the mediation and continue with the cause or matter.

Evidence not admissible

54.3 Evidence arising from anything said, evidence of anything said or evidence of an admission or communication made in the course of mediation or in a mediation screening and orientation session is not admissible in any cause or matter or proceeding before a court, except with the written consent of the mediator and all parties to the cause or matter in which the mediator acted.

Mediator not liable

54.4   No action lies or shall be instituted against a mediator for any loss or damage suffered by a person by reason of anything in good faith done, caused, permitted or authorized to be done, attempted to be done or omitted to be done by the mediator in:

(a) the carrying out or supposed carrying out of any duty or power conferred by this Act; or

(b) the carrying out or supposed carrying out of any order made pursuant to this Act.

Residential Tenancies Act, S.N.B. 1975, c. R-10.2

26(2) A rentalsman

(b) may receive complaints and mediate disputes between landlords and tenants.

Residential Tenancy Act, R.S.B.C. 1996, c. 406

Application for dispute resolution

69(1) A tenant or landlord of a manufactured home pad may apply for mediation of a dispute between them by filing an application for mediation with the dispute resolution committee in the form and manner required by the committee, and by paying the prescribed fee, if any.

71(3) If within 30 days after the application for mediation is filed under section 69(1) the dispute resolution subcommittee is satisfied that the parties have failed to enter into a written agreement resolving the dispute, the dispute resolution subcommittee must promptly give the parties a written notice

(a) containing a recommendation for ending the dispute, or

(b) ending the mediation without a recommendation.

Conflict of interest

76.   A person must not act as a member of a dispute resolution subcommittee if the person has or appears to have an interest in the matter being mediated.

The Saskatchewan Farm Security Act, S.S. 1988-89, c. S-17.1

Mediators

8(1) The minister may appoint persons as mediators for the purpose of this Act.

(2) The minister may appoint a person as the manager of mediation services.

12(9) For the purposes of subsection (7), "not participating in mediation in good faith" includes:

(a) failure on a regular or continuing basis to attend and participate in mediation sessions without cause;

(b) failure to provide full information regarding the financial affairs of the parties in relation to the matter before the mediator;

(c) failure of the mortgagee to designate a representative to participate in the mediation with the authority to make binding commitments within:

(i) 10 business days of a mediation session; or

(ii) any further time that the mediator permits;

to fully settle, compromise or otherwise mediate the matter;

(d) failure to provide debt restructuring alternatives or reasons why alternatives are unacceptable;

(e) other similar behaviour which evidences lack of good faith.

Court supervised mandatory mediation

15(1) Where:

(a) an application for an order is made pursuant to section 11; and

(b) a mediator's certificate is filed pursuant to subsection 12(7) with respect to the application mentioned in clause (a) indicating that the mortgagee has not participated in mediation in good faith; the farmer may request that the court order supervised mandatory mediation.

Voluntary mediation

42.1(1) A farmer or a recognized financial institution may make a request for voluntary mediation to the manager of mediation services.

The Saskatchewan Insurance Amendment Act, S.S. 1984–85–86, c. 82

Regulations

466.1(4) Without limiting the generality of subsection (3), the Lieutenant Governor in Council may make regulations granting to a council, on any terms and conditions that he considers appropriate, the power to:

(d) investigate complaints and adjudicate or mediate disputes regarding services provided by any member of an occupational group in the insurance industry.

The Saskatchewan Medical Care Insurance Act, R.S.S. 1978, c. S-29, as amended

Insured services

41. The Lieutenant Governor in Council may make regulations providing for the settling of any differences that may arise:
   (a) with respect to; or
   (b) out of a proposed alternation in; the general rates of payments being made pursuant to this Act in respect of insured services provided to beneficiaries by persons other than physicians, by negotiation or, where negotiations do not result in settlement, to be dealt with by mediation.

48.2 Notwithstanding section 48.3, at any time after a notice is served pursuant to subsection 48.1(2) the board and the minister may agree to refer any or all matters under consideration by the committee to an independent person acceptable to both parties, and the board and the minister shall specify whether that person is to act as a mediator or a conciliator.

School Boards and Teachers Collective Negotiations Act, R.S.O. 1990, c. S.2

60.(1) It is the duty of the Commission,
   (b) to maintain an awareness of negotiations between teachers and boards.
   (e) to select and, where necessary, to train persons who may act as mediators, fact finders, arbitrators or selectors.

The Surface Rights Acquisition and Compensation Act, R.S.S. 1978, c. S-65

65(1) An owner or occupant may lodge a complaint in writing with the board concerning the operations of the operator on or adjoining the surface rights, well site, battery site, roadway or power line, or any one or more of them, acquired by the operator and request that the complaint be referred to a mediation officer; or

(2) Where a matter in dispute under this Act is pending a determination by the board, the board may, of its own volition or upon the written request of an owner, occupant or operator, refer the matter to a mediation officer.

(3) Where the board has referred a matter to a mediation officer, further proceedings pending before the board with respect to that matter shall be stayed until the mediation officer to whom the matter is referred has made his report to the board pursuant to section 68.

66   The mediation officer shall, immediately after the receipt by him of a complaint or request, investigate the matter complained of or that is in dispute and for that purpose the mediation officer may interview such persons as he deems necessary or desirable, inspect any land or other property of the owner or occupant, if any, that is involved, examine the operations of the operator relevant to the complaint or matter of dispute and, if possible, arrange for the parties or their representatives to meet with him and endeavour to negotiate a settlement between the parties.

Tenant Protection Act, S.O. 1997, c. 24

181.(1)   The Tribunal may attempt to mediate a settlement of any matter that is the subject of an application if the parties consent to the mediation.

(2)   Despite subsection 2(1) and subject to subsection (3), a settlement mediated under this section may contain provisions that contravene any provision under this Act.

Trade Practice Act, R.S.B.C. 1996, c. 457

5.(2)   The director may attempt to resolve complaints under subsection (1)(b) by mediation or by other methods acceptable to the parties.

The Trade Union Act, R.S.S. 1978, c. T-17, as amended

23.1(1)   On the request of either party to a labour-management dispute or on the minister's own initiative, the minister may:

(a)   appoint a special mediator to investigate, mediate and report to the minister on any labour-management dispute.

The Water Corporation Act, S.S. 1983-84, c. W-4.1

72.   The corporation has no power to determine liability or award damages or other compensation in respect of a complaint, but the corporation may act as mediator between the parties to a complaint in an attempt to bring about a settlement of claims for damages or compensation.

West Coast Ports Operation Act, 1995, S.C. 1995, c. 2

Appointment of mediator-arbitrator

8.(1)   The Minister shall, after the coming into force of this Act, appoint a mediator-arbitrator and refer to the mediator-arbitrator all matters relating to the amendment or revision of the collective agreement that, at the time of the appointment, remain in dispute between the parties to the collective agreement.

TABLE OF CASES

INDEX

ABOUT THE AUTHOR

Andrew Pirie is a professor of law at the University of Victoria, British Columbia, Canada. Professor Pirie has a long-time relationship with the ADR movement. He was a founding director of the Mediation Development Association of British Columbia, Co-Chair of the Conflict Resolution Council of British Columbia, a member of the Fund for Dispute Resolution in Ontario, a Visiting Professor at the University of Ottawa in 1985 teaching ADR, a litigation associate with the law firm of Osler, Hoskin and Harcourt, and the Executive Director of the UVic Institute for Dispute Resolution from 1989 to 1996.

Professor Pirie teaches courses in Dispute Resolution: Theories and Skills, Mediation and Lawyers, Negotiation, and Civil Procedure, and he has conducted ADR training workshops in Canada and the United States and in other countries such as Cambodia, England, Fiji, and Thailand. Andrew has acted as a mediator in various dispute settings. He is co-editor of *Qualifications for Dispute Resolution: Perspectives on the Debate* and the author of several shorter works on ADR.

AGMV Marquis

MEMBRE DU GROUPE SCABRINI

Québec, Canada
2000